Lecture Notes of the Institute for Computer Sciences, Social Informatics and Telecommunications Engineering 128

T0212653

For further volumes:
http://www.springer.com/series/8197

Phan Cong Vinh · Vangalur Alagar
Emil Vassev · Ashish Khare (Eds.)

Context-Aware Systems and Applications

Second International Conference,
ICCASA 2013
Phu Quoc Island, Vietnam,
November 25–26, 2013
Revised Selected Papers

 Springer

Editors
Phan Cong Vinh
Faculty of Information Technology
Nguyen Tat Thanh University
Ho Chi Minh City
Vietnam

Vangalur Alagar
Concordia University
Montreal
Canada

Emil Vassev
University of Limerick
Limerick
Ireland

Ashish Khare
University of Allahabad
Allahabad
India

ISSN 1867-8211
ISBN 978-3-319-05938-9
DOI 10.1007/978-3-319-05939-6
Springer Cham Heidelberg New York Dordrecht London

ISSN 1867-822X (electronic)
ISBN 978-3-319-05939-6 (eBook)

Library of Congress Control Number: 2014936289

Printed on acid-free paper

Springer is part of Springer Science+Business Media (www.springer.com)

Preface

ICCASA 2013, an international scientific conference for research in the field of context-aware computing and communication, was held during November 25–26, 2013, in Phu Quoc Island, Vietnam. The aim of the conference is to provide an internationally respected forum for scientific research in the technologies and applications of context-aware computing and communication. This conference gave researchers an excellent opportunity to discuss modern approaches and techniques for context-aware systems and their applications. The proceedings of ICCASA 2013 are published by Springer in the series *Lecture Notes of the Institute for Computer Sciences, Social Informatics and Telecommunications Engineering* (LNICST; indexed by DBLP, EI, Google Scholar, Scopus, Thomson ISI).

For this second edition, repeating the success of the previous year, the Program Committee received over 100 submissions from 22 countries and each paper was reviewed by at least three expert reviewers. We chose 36 papers after intensive discussions held among the Program Committee members. We really appreciate the excellent reviews and lively discussions of the Program Committee members and external reviewers in the review process. This year we chose three prominent invited speakers, Dr. Emil Vassev, a research fellow at Lero (the Irish Software Engineering Research Centre) at the University of Limerick in Ireland, Prof. Vangalur Alagar from Concordia University in Canada, and Prof. Ashish Khare from the University of Allahabad in India. Their excellent talks focus on hot topics of context-awareness.

ICCASA 2013 was jointly organized by The European Alliance for Innovation (EAI) and Nguyen Tat Thanh University (NTTU). This conference could not have been held without the strong support from the staff members of both organizations. We would especially like to thank Prof. Imrich Chlamtac (University of Trento and Create-NET), Elisa Mendini (EAI), and Volha Shaparava (EAI) for their great help in organizing the conference. We also appreciate the gentle guidance and help from Dr. Nguyen Manh Hung, Chairman and Rector of NTTU, and Prof. Thai Thanh Luom, Director of Kien Giang Department of Information and Communications.

November 2013

Phan Cong Vinh
Vangalur Alagar
Emil Vassev
Ashish Khare

Organization

Steering Committee

Imrich Chlamtac   Create-Net and University of Trento, Italy
Thanos Vasilakos   University of Western Macedonia, Greece
Phan Cong Vinh   NTTU, Vietnam

Organizing Committee

General Chair

Phan Cong Vinh   NTTU, Vietnam

TPC Chairs

M.H. Williams   Heriot-Watt University, UK
Ondrej Krejcar   University of Hradec Kralove, Czech Republic
Junichi Suzuki   UMass, USA
Phan Cong Vinh   NTTU, Vietnam
Nguyen Thanh Tung   Hanoi Vietnam National University, Vietnam

Organizing Chairs

Nguyen Manh Hung   Chairman and Rector of NTTU, Vietnam
Le Huy Ba   NTTU, Vietnam
Thai Thanh Luom   KGDIC, Vietnam
Nguyen Van Sanh   Mahidol University, Thailand
Nguyen Van Luong   NTTU, Vietnam
Nguyen Tuan Anh   NTTU, Vietnam

Publicity Chair

Le Tuan Anh   PTIT, Vietnam

Publication Chairs

Nguyen Thanh Tung   Hanoi Vietnam National University, Vietnam
Vu Ngoc Hai   NTTU, Vietnam

Web Chair

Thai Thi Thanh Thao   NTTU, Vietnam

Technical Program Committee

Antonio Loureiro	Universidade Federal de Minas Gerais, Brazil
Antonio Manzalini	Telecom Italia Future Center, Italy
Ashiq Anjum	Bristol Institute of Technology, UK
Chien-Chih Yu	National ChengChi University, Taiwan
Corrado Moiso	Telecom Italia Future Center, Italy
Cem Safak Sahin	BAE Systems, USA
Costin Badica	University of Craiova, Romania
Cristian-Gyozo Haba	"Gheorghe Asachi" Technical University of Iasi, Romania
Dongkyun Kim	KISTI, South Korea
Emil Vassev	Lero at University of Limerick, Ireland
Eugenio Almeida	National Institute for Space Research (INPE), Brazil
Fatos Xhafa	Technical University of Catalonia, Spain
Gabrielle Peko	University of Auckland, New Zealand
George C. Alexandropoulos	Athens Information Technology, Greece
Giovanna Di Marzo Serugendo	University of Geneva, Switzerland
Hiroshi Wada	NICTA, Australia
Huynh Thi Thanh Binh	Hanoi University of Technology, Vietnam
Jason Jung	Yeungnam University, South Korea
Jonathan Bowen	London South Bank University, UK
Juan Li	North Dakota State University, USA
Kaiyu Wan	Xi'an Jiaotong-Liverpool University, China
Kuan-Ching Li	Providence University, Taiwan
Kurt Geihs	University of Kessel, Germany
Le Tuan Anh	PTIT, Vietnam
Marco Aldinucci	University of Torino, Italy
Massimiliano Rak	Second University of Naples, Italy
Massimo Villari	University of Messina, Italy
Mubarak Mohammad	Concordia University, Canada
Myungchul Kim	KAIST, South Korea
Nedal Ababneh	Letterkenny Institute of Technology, Ireland
Ngo Thanh Long	Le Quy Don Technical University, Vietnam
Nguyen Thanh Binh	University of Technology—HCMVNU, Vietnam
Nguyen Van Phuc	NTTU, Vietnam
Paolo Bellavista	DEIS - University of Bologna, Italy
Pham Ngoc Hung	University of Engineering and Technology— HNVNU, Vietnam
Phan Trung Huy	Hanoi University of Technology, Vietnam
Quan Thanh Tho	University of Technology—HCMVNU, Vietnam
Radu Calinescu	Aston University, UK
Sherif Abdelwahed	Mississippi State University, USA
Tiziana Calamoneri	"Sapienza" University of Rome, Italy

Tran Ngoc Bao	HCMC University of Pedagogy, Vietnam
Tran Viet	Institute of Informatics, SAS, Slovakia
Vladimir Vlassov	KTH Royal Institute of Technology, Sweden
Vo Bay	Ton Duc Thang University, Vietnam
Wei Wei	Xi'an University of Technology, China
Yaser Jararweh	Jordan University of Science and Technology, Jordan

Additional Reviewers

Huynh Trung Hieu	Ho Chi Minh City University of Industry, Vietnam
Nong Thi Hoa	Thai Nguyen University of Information Technology and Communications, Vietnam
Nguyen Thi Thanh Tu	Hanoi University of Technology, Vietnam
Nguyen Kim Quoc	NTTU, Vietnam

Sponsors

Create-NET
Vietnam National Foundation for Science and Technology Development (NAFOSTED)

Contents

Context-Aware Systems and Applications

A Temporal Description Logic for Resource-Bounded Rule-Based
Context-Aware Agents 3
   Abdur Rakib, Hafiz Mahfooz Ul Haque, and Rokan Uddin Faruqui

A Trust Propagation Model for New-Coming in Multi-agent System 15
   Manh Hung Nguyen and Dinh Que Tran

Modelling Circulation Behaviour of Vietnamese: Applying for Simulation
of Hanoi Traffic Network 24
   Manh Hung Nguyen and Tuong Vinh Ho

Storing and Managing Context and Context History 35
   Alaa Alsaig, Ammar Alsaig, Mubarak Mohammad, and Vangalur Alagar

Drought Monitoring: A Performance Investigation of Three Machine
Learning Techniques... 47
   Pheeha Machaka

Inbooki: Context-Aware Adaptive E-Books 57
   Daniele Grassi, Anas Bouhtouch, and Giacomo Cabri

Resistance of Trust Management Systems Against Malicious Collectives ... 67
   Miroslav Novotný and Filip Zavoral

A Context-Aware Model for the Management of Agent Platforms
in Dynamic Networks 77
   Phuong T. Nguyen, Volkmar Schau, and Wilhelm R. Rossak

Building Consensus in Context-Aware Systems Using Ben-Or's Algorithm:
Some Proposals for Improving the Convergence Speed............... 87
   Phuong T. Nguyen

Power-Aware Routing for Underwater Wireless Sensor Network 97
   Nguyen Thanh Tung and Nguyen Sy Minh

Fuzzy Logic Control for SFB Active Queue Management Mechanism 102
   Nguyen Kim Quoc, Vo Thanh Tu, and Nguyen Thuc Hai

Ultrasound Images Denoising Based Context Awareness in Bandelet Domain ... 115
   Nguyen Thanh Binh, Vo Thi Hong Tuyet, and Phan Cong Vinh

Human Object Classification in Daubechies Complex Wavelet Domain   125
  Manish Khare, Rajneesh Kumar Srivastava, Ashish Khare,
  Nguyen Thanh Binh, and Tran Anh Dien

An Efficient Method for Automated Control Flow Testing of Programs   133
  Quang-Trung Nguyen and Pham Ngoc-Hung

Awareness of Entities, Activities and Contexts in Ambient Systems   144
  Bent Bruun Kristensen

A Method and Tool Support for Automated Data Flow Testing
of Java Programs   157
  Van-Cuong Pham and Pham Ngoc-Hung

Rule-Based Techniques Using Abstract Syntax Tree for Code Optimization
and Secure Programming in Java   168
  Nguyen Hung-Cuong, Huynh Quyet-Thang, and Tru Ba-Vuong

Overall Security Solutions for OPC UA Based Monitoring and Control
Application   178
  Nguyen Thi Thanh Tu and Huynh Quyet Thang

The Evolutionary Approach of General Systems Theory Applied
to World Wide Web   188
  Aneta Bartuskova and Ondrej Krejcar

Impact of Mobility on the Performance of Context-Aware Applications
Using Floating Content   198
  Shahzad Ali, Gianluca Rizzo, Marco Ajmone Marsan, and Vincenzo Mancuso

Towards Classification Based Human Activity Recognition
in Video Sequences.   209
  Nguyen Thanh Binh, Swati Nigam, and Ashish Khare

A New Fuzzy Associative Memory.   219
  Pham Viet Binh, Nong Thi Hoa, Vu Duc Thai, and Quach Xuan Truong

Content-Based Image Retrieval Using Moments.   228
  Prashant Srivastava, Nguyen Thanh Binh, and Ashish Khare

Coinductively Combinational Context-Awareness.   238
  Phan Cong Vinh and Nguyen Kim Quoc

Formal Modeling and Verification of Context-Aware Systems
Using Event-B   250
  Hong Anh Le and Ninh Thuan Truong

A Method of Context-Based Services Discovery in Ubiquitous Environment   260
  Pallapa Venkataram and M. Bharath

Towards an Adaptive Visualization System in Context-Aware Environments   271
  Xiaoyan Bai, David White, and David Sundaram

Human Sensing for Tabletop Entertainment System   283
  Hafizuddin Yusof, Eugene Ch'ng, and Christopher Baber

Adaptive Sustainable Enterprises: A Framework, Architecture
and Implementation.   293
  Gabrielle Peko, Ching-Shen Dong, and David Sundaram

A Stability-Aware Approach to Continuous Self-adaptation of Data-Intensive
Systems.   304
  Marco Mori, Anthony Cleve, and Paola Inverardi

A Comprehensive View of Ubiquitous Learning Context Usage
in Context-Aware Learning System.   316
  Raoudha Souabni, Ines Bayoudh Saadi, Kinshuk, and Henda Ben Ghezala

Context-Based Recommendation Systems

Data Mining Assisted Resource Management in Wide WLANs   329
  Thuy Van T. Duong, Dinh Que Tran, and Cong Hung Tran

Social Context-Based Movie Recommendation: A Case Study
on MyMovieHistory   339
  *Yong Seung Lee, Xuan Hau Pham, Duc Nguyen Trung, Jason J. Jung,
  and Hien T. Nguyen*

Understanding Effect of Sentiment Content Toward Information Diffusion
Pattern in Online Social Networks: A Case Study on TweetScope   349
  Duc Nguyen Trung, Tri Tuong Nguyen, Jason J. Jung, and Dongjin Choi

A Method for Normalizing Non-standard Words in Online Social Network
Services: A Case Study on Twitter   359
  Dongjin Choi, Jeongin Kim, and Pankoo Kim

Combining Heuristics and Learning for Entity Linking   369
  Hien T. Nguyen

Author Index   379

Context-Aware Systems
and Applications

A Temporal Description Logic
for Resource-Bounded Rule-Based
Context-Aware Agents

Abdur Rakib[1][✉], Hafiz Mahfooz Ul Haque[1], and Rokan Uddin Faruqui[2]

[1] School of Computer Science,
The University of Nottingham Malaysia Campus, Semenyih, Malaysia
{Abdur.Rakib,khyx2hma}@nottingham.edu.my
[2] Department of Computing and Software, McMaster University, Hamilton, Canada
faruqumr@mcmaster.ca

Abstract. We propose a logical framework for modelling and verifying context-aware multi-agent systems. We extend CTL^* with belief and communication modalities, and the resulting logic $\mathcal{L}_{OCRS}$ allows us to describe a set of rule-based reasoning agents with bound on time, memory and communication. The set of rules which are used to model the systems is derived from OWL 2 RL ontologies. We provide an axiomatization of the logic and prove it is sound and complete. We show how Maude rewriting system can be used to encode and verify interesting properties of $\mathcal{L}_{OCRS}$ models using existing model checking techniques.

Keywords: Modal logic · Context-aware · Multi-agent systems · Ontology · Model checking

1 Introduction

The vision of pervasive computing technology intends to provide invisible computing environments so that a user can utilize services at any time and everywhere [1]. Context-awareness is a key concept in pervasive computing. In context-aware pervasive computing every user may have several computing devices, where information can be collected by using tiny resource-bounded devices, such as, e.g., PDAs, smart phones, and wireless sensor nodes [2]. These systems interact with human users, they often exhibit complex adaptive behaviours, they are highly decentralised and can naturally be implemented as multi-agent systems. An agent is a piece of software that requires to be reactive, pro-active, and that is capable of autonomous action in its environment to meet its design objectives.

In the literature, various logical frameworks have been developed for modelling and verification of multi-agent systems [3]. However, such frameworks may not be very suitable to model context-aware applications. This is because, most of those existing frameworks consider propositional logic as a simple knowledge

P.C. Vinh et al. (Eds.): ICCASA 2013, LNICST 128, pp. 3–14, 2014.
DOI: 10.1007/978-3-319-05939-6_1, © Springer International Publishing Switzerland 2014

representation language which is often not suitable for modelling real life complex systems. For example, propositional logic cannot directly talk about properties of individuals or relations between individuals. Much research in pervasive computing has been focused on incorporation of context-awareness features into pervasive applications by adapting the semantic web technology (see e.g., [4–6]), where description logic (*DL*)-based ontology languages are often used for context representation and reasoning. *DL* is a decidable fragment of first order logic (*FOL*). In [6], it has been shown how context-aware systems can be modelled as resource-bounded rule-based systems using ontologies. In that paper, the resources required by the agents to solve a given problem were considered the time and communication bandwidth. But not the space requirements for reasoning. Since context-aware systems often run on resource limited devices, memory requirement is an important factor for their reasoning. In this paper, we propose a logical framework based on the earlier work of Alechina and colleagues [7–9], and the resulting logic $\mathcal{L}_{\mathcal{OCRS}}$ allows us to describe a set of ontology-driven rule-based reasoning agents with bound on time, memory, and communication. In addition to the incorporation of space (memory) requirements for reasoning in [7], $\mathcal{L}_{\mathcal{OCRS}}$ also uses first order Horn clause rules derived from OWL 2 RL ontologies. While the frameworks presented in [7,8] provide a useful basis for experimentation with both the logical representation and verification of heterogeneous agents, it has become clear that a more expressive logical language is required if these frameworks are to be used for real world context-aware agents. Though the logic developed by [9] is based on *FOL*, memory bounds have not been imposed in that framework. The proposed framework allows us to determine how much time (measured as rule-firing cycles) are required to generate certain contexts, how many messages must be exchanged among agents, and how much space (memory) is required for an agent for the reasoning. For verification, we show how we can encode a $\mathcal{L}_{\mathcal{OCRS}}$ model using the Maude LTL model checker [10] and verify interesting resource-bounded properties.

The remainder of the paper is organized as follows. In Sect. 2, we discuss how contexts are represented using OWL 2 RL and SWRL. In Sect. 3, we describe our model of communicating multi-agent context-aware systems. In Sect. 4, we develop logic $\mathcal{L}_{\mathcal{OCRS}}$, in Sect. 5 we present an example system and experimental results, and conclude in Sect. 6.

2   Context Modelling

We view context is any information that can be used to identify the status of an entity. An entity can be a person, a place, a physical or a computing object. This context is relevant to a user and application, and reflects the relationship among themselves [11]. A context can be formally defined as a *(subject, predicate, object)* triple that states a fact about the subject where — the subject is an entity in the environment, the object is a value or another entity, and the predicate is a relationship between the subject and object. According to [11], *"if a piece of information can be used to characterize the situation of a participant in an* *interaction, then that information is context".* For example, we can represent a context "Fiona is the caregiver of Tracy" as *(Fiona, isCareGiverOf, Tracy)*. Here, the caregiver of a patient is dynamically identified based on the care status of the caregiver. For context modelling we use OWL 2 RL, a profile of the new standardization OWL 2, and based on pD^* [12] and the description logic program (DLP) [13]. We choose OWL 2 RL because it is more expressive than the RDFS and suitable for the design and development of rule-based systems. An OWL 2 RL ontology can be translated into a set of Horn clause rules based on [13]. Furthermore, we express more complex rule-based concepts using SWRL [14] which allow us to write rules using OWL concepts. In our framework, a context-aware system composed of a set of rule-based agents, and firing of rules that infer new facts may determine context changes and representing overall behaviour of the system.

For illustration, we construct an ontology-based context-aware model for a healthcare epilepsy scenario adapted from [15]. The scenario is based on the monitoring of epileptic patients to detect epileptic seizures. An epileptic alarm may activate several actions such as warning the patient about potential danger, informing patient's caregivers to take appropriate actions, and sending SMS messages to patient's relatives who are currently near to the patient.

"The goal of the epileptic patients' monitoring context-aware system is to detect the seizures, and to react in the following ways: (i) notify the epileptic patient of an upcoming seizure; and (ii) notify his/her nearby caregivers of an upcoming seizure of the patient by showing a map with the location of the patient. The caregivers who receive the notification for help should be (i) assigned as one of the caregivers of that particular patient; (ii) available for helping; and (iii) physically close to the patient. Upon a notification for help, caregivers may either accept or reject the request for helping the epileptic patient. When a particular caregiver accepts to help, the other caregivers who had received the notification for help are informed that a certain caregiver has already accepted to help that

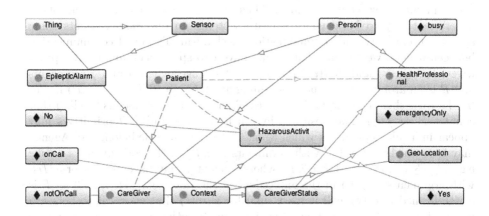

Fig. 1. A fragment of the epileptic patients' monitoring ontology

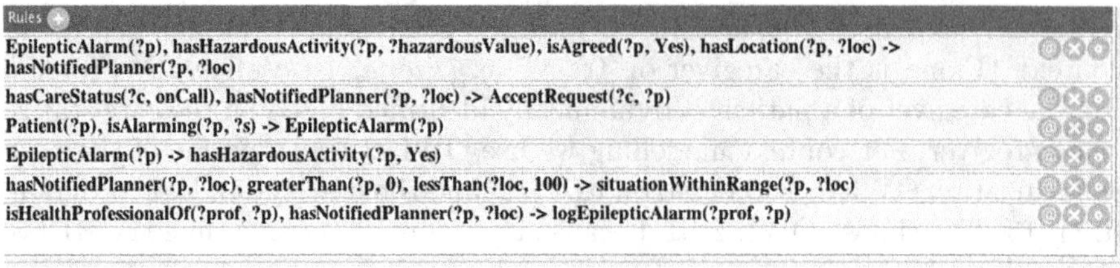

Rules ⊕	
EpilepticAlarm(?p), hasHazardousActivity(?p, ?hazardousValue), isAgreed(?p, Yes), hasLocation(?p, ?loc) -> hasNotifiedPlanner(?p, ?loc)	⊙⊗⊙
hasCareStatus(?c, onCall), hasNotifiedPlanner(?p, ?loc) -> AcceptRequest(?c, ?p)	⊙⊗⊙
Patient(?p), isAlarming(?p, ?s) -> EpilepticAlarm(?p)	⊙⊗⊙
EpilepticAlarm(?p) -> hasHazardousActivity(?p, Yes)	⊙⊗⊙
hasNotifiedPlanner(?p, ?loc), greaterThan(?p, 0), lessThan(?loc, 100) -> situationWithinRange(?p, ?loc)	⊙⊗⊙
isHealthProfessionalOf(?prof, ?p), hasNotifiedPlanner(?p, ?loc) -> logEpilepticAlarm(?prof, ?p)	⊙⊗⊙

Fig. 2. Example SWRL rules

patient" [15]. Using Protégé [16], we build an OWL 2 RL ontology to capture the static behaviour of the system. A fragment of this ontology is depicted in Fig. 1. The dynamic aspect of the system is captured using SWRL rules. A snapshot of some SWRL rules is given in Fig. 2. In order to design a context-aware rule-based system from the above ontology, we extract Horn clause rules using the technique described in [6]. We show an example system encoding in Maude in Sect. 5 based on the logic developed in Sect. 4.

3 Context-Aware Agents

In our model a multi-agent context-aware system consists of n_{Ag} (≥ 1) individual *agents* $A_g = \{1, 2, \ldots, n_{Ag}\}$. Each agent $i \in A_g$ has a program, consisting of Horn clause rules of the form $P_1, P_2, \ldots, P_n \rightarrow P$ (derived from OWL 2 RL and SWRL), and a working memory, which contains ground atomic facts (contexts) taken from ABox representing the initial state of the system. In the rule, the antecedents $P_1, P_2, \ldots, P_n$ and the consequent P are context information. The antecedents of the rule form a complex context which is a conjunction of n contexts. In a resource-bounded system, it is quite unrealistic to presume that a single agent can acquire and understand available contextual information and infer new contexts alone. Thus sharing knowledge among agents is an efficient way to build context-aware systems. In our model, agents share a common ontology and communication mechanism. To model communication between agents, we assume that agents have two special communication primitives $Ask(i, j, P)$ and $Tell(i, j, P)$ in their language, where i and j are agents and P is an atomic context not containing an Ask or a $Tell$. $Ask(i, j, P)$ means 'i asks j whether the context P is the case' and $Tell(i, j, P)$ means 'i tells j that context P' ($i \neq j$). The positions in which the Ask and $Tell$ primitives may appear in a rule depends on which agent's program the rule belongs to. Agent i may have an Ask or a $Tell$ with arguments (i, j, P) in the consequent of a rule; e.g., $P_1, P_2, \ldots, P_n \rightarrow Ask(i, j, P)$ whereas agent j may have an Ask or a $Tell$ with arguments (i, j, P) in the antecedent of the rule; e.g., $Tell(i, j, P) \rightarrow P$ is a well-formed rule (we call it trust rule) for agent j that causes it to believe i when i informs it that context P is the case. No other occurrences of Ask or $Tell$ are allowed. When a rule has either an Ask or a $Tell$ as its consequent, we call it a communication rule. All other rules are known as deduction rules. These include rules with *Asks* and *Tells* in the antecedent as well as rules containing neither an *Ask* nor a *Tell*. Note that OWL 2 is limited to unary and binary predicates and it is function-free. Therefore, in the Protégé editor all the arguments of *Ask* and *Tell* are represented using constant symbols and these annotated symbols are translated appropriately when designing the target system using the Maude specification.

4 Logic $\mathcal{L}_{\mathcal{OCRS}}$

A *DL* knowledge base *(KB)* has two components: the Terminology Box *(TBox)* $\mathcal{T}$ and the Assertion Box *(ABox)* $\mathcal{A}$. The *TBox* introduces the terminology of a domain, while the *ABox* contains assertions about individuals in terms of this vocabulary. The *TBox* is a finite set of general concept inclusions *(GCI)* and role inclusions. A *GCI* is of the form $C \sqsubseteq D$ where C, D are *DL*-concepts and a role inclusion is of the form $R \sqsubseteq S$ where R, S are *DL*-roles. We may use $C \equiv D$ (concept equivalence) as an abbreviation for the two *GCIs* $C \sqsubseteq D$ and $D \sqsubseteq C$ and $R \equiv S$ (role equivalence) as an abbreviation for $R \sqsubseteq S$ and $S \sqsubseteq R$. The *ABox* is a finite set of concept assertions in the form of $C(a)$ and role assertions in the form of $R(a, b)$.

Definition 1 (Interpretation of DL-knowledge bases). *An Interpretation of a DL knowledge base is a pair $\mathcal{I} =< \Delta^{\mathcal{I}}, .^{\mathcal{I}} >$ where $\Delta^{\mathcal{I}}$ is a non-empty set (the domain of interpretation) and $.^{\mathcal{I}}$ is a function that maps every concept to a subset of $\Delta^{\mathcal{I}}$, every role to a subset of $\Delta^{\mathcal{I}} \times \Delta^{\mathcal{I}}$, and each individual name to an element of the domain $\Delta^{\mathcal{I}}$.*

An interpretation $\mathcal{I}$ satisfies the concept assertion $C(a)$, denoted by $\mathcal{I} \models C(a)$, iff $a^{\mathcal{I}} \in C^{\mathcal{I}}$ and it satisfies the role assertion $R(a, b)$, denoted by $\mathcal{I} \models R(a, b)$, iff $(a^{\mathcal{I}}, b^{\mathcal{I}}) \in R^{\mathcal{I}}$, where a and b are individuals.

We now introduce the logic $\mathcal{L}_{\mathcal{OCRS}}$ which is an extension of the logic developed by [7]. Let us define the internal language of each agent in the system. Let the set of agents be $A_g = \{1, 2, ..., n_{Ag}\}$, $\mathcal{C} = \{C_1, C_2, ... C_n\}$ be a finite set of concepts, $\mathcal{R} = \{R_1, R_2, ..., R_n\}$ be a finite set of roles, and $\mathcal{A}$ be a finite set of assertions. We also define a set $\mathcal{Q} = \{Ask(i, j, P), Tell(i, j, P)\}$, where $i, j \in A_g$ and $P \in \mathcal{C} \cup \mathcal{R}$. Note that $\mathcal{C}$ and $\mathcal{R}$ are the sets of concepts and roles that appear in $\mathcal{A}$. Let $\Re = \{r_1, r_2, ..., r_n\}$ be a finite set of rules of the form $P_1, P_2, ..., P_n \rightarrow P$, where $n \geq 0$, $P_i, P \in \mathcal{C} \cup \mathcal{R} \cup \mathcal{Q}$ for all $i \in \{1, 2, ..., n\}$ and $P_i \neq P_j$ for all $i \neq j$. For convenience, we use the notation $ant(r)$ for the set of antecedents of r and $cons(r)$ for the consequent of r, where $r \in \Re$. Let $g : \wp(\mathcal{A}) \rightarrow \Re$ be a substitution function that uses a forward-chaining strategy to instantiate the rule-base. We denote by $\mathcal{G}(\Re)$ the set of all the ground instances of the rules occurring in $\Re$, which is obtained using g. Thus $\mathcal{G}(\Re)$ is finite. Let $\bar{r} \in \mathcal{G}(\Re)$ be one of the possible instances of a rule $r \in \Re$. Note that $C(a)$, $R(a, b)$, $Ask(i, j, C(a))$, $Ask(i, j, R(a, b))$, $Tell(i, j, C(a))$, and $Tell(i, j, R(a, b))$ are ground facts, for all $C \in \mathcal{C}, R \in \mathcal{R}$. The internal language $\mathcal{L}$ includes all the ground facts and rules. Let us denote the set of all formulas by Ω which is finite.

In the modal language of $\mathcal{L}$ we have belief operator B_i for all $i \in A_g$. We assume that there is a bound on communication for each agent i which limits agent i to at most $n_C(i) \in \mathbb{Z}^*$ messages. Each agent has a communication counter, $cp_i^{=n}$, which starts at 0 $(cp_i^{=0})$ and is not allowed to exceed the value $n_C(i)$. We divide agent's memory into two parts as rule memory (knowledge base) and working memory. Rule memory holds set of rules, whereas the facts are stored in the agent's working memory. Working memory is divided into static memory $(S_M(i))$ and dynamic memory $(D_M(i))$. The $D_M(i)$ of each agent $i \in A_g$ is bounded in size by $n_M(i) \in \mathbb{Z}^*$, where one unit of memory corresponds to the ability to store an arbitrary formula. The static part contains initial information to start up the systems, e.g., initial working memory facts, thus its size is determined by the number of initial facts. The dynamic part contains newly derive facts as the system moves. Only formulas stored in $D_M(i)$ may get overwritten if it is full. Note that unless otherwise stated, in the rest of the paper we shall assume that memory means $D_M(i)$. For convenience, we define the following sets: $CP_i = \{cp_i^{=n} \mid n = \{0, \ldots, n_C(i)\}\}$, $CP = \bigcup_{i \in A_g} CP_i$.

The syntax of $\mathcal{L}_{OCRS}$ includes the temporal operators of CTL^* and is defined inductively as follows:

- $\top$ (tautology) and *start* (a propositional variable which is only true at the initial moment of time) are well-formed formulas (wff) of $\mathcal{L}_{OCRS}$;
- $cp_i^{=n}$ (which states that the value of agent i's communication counter is n) is a wff of $\mathcal{L}_{OCRS}$ for all $n \in \{0, \ldots, n_C(i)\}$ and $i \in A_g$;
- $B_i C(a)$ (agent i believes $C(a)$), $B_i R(a, b)$ (agent i believes $R(a, b)$), and $B_i r$ (agent i believes r) are wffs of $\mathcal{L}_{OCRS}$ for any $C \in \mathcal{C}, R \in \mathcal{R}, r \in \mathfrak{R}$ and $i \in A_g$;
- $B_k Ask(i, j, C(a))$, $B_k Ask(i, j, R(a, b))$, $B_k Tell(i, j, C(a))$, and $B_k Tell(i, j, R(a, b))$ are wffs of $\mathcal{L}_{OCRS}$ for any $C \in \mathcal{C}, R \in \mathcal{R}, i, j \in A_g, k \in \{i, j\}$, and $i \neq j$;
- If φ and ψ are wffs of $\mathcal{L}_{OCRS}$, then so are $\neg \varphi$ and $\varphi \wedge \psi$;
- If φ and ψ are wffs of $\mathcal{L}_{OCRS}$, then so are $X\varphi$ (in the next state φ), $\varphi U \psi$ (φ holds until ψ), $A\varphi$ (on all paths φ).

Other classical abbreviations for $\bot, \vee, \rightarrow$ and $\leftrightarrow$, and temporal operations: $F\varphi \equiv \top U \varphi$ (at some point in the future φ) and $G\varphi \equiv \neg F \neg \varphi$ (at all points in the future φ), and $E\varphi \equiv \neg A \neg \varphi$ (on some path φ) are defined as usual.

The semantics of $\mathcal{L}_{OCRS}$ is defined by $\mathcal{L}_{OCRS}$ transition systems which are based on ω-tree structures. Let (S, T) be a pair where S is a set and T is a binary relation on S that is total, i.e., $\forall s \in S \cdot \exists s' \in S \cdot sTs'$. A branch of (S, T) is an ω-sequence $(s_0, s_1, \ldots)$ such that s_0 is the root and $s_i T s_{i+1}$ for all $i \geq 0$. We denote $B(S, T)$ to be the set of all branches of (S, T). For a branch $\pi \in B(S, T)$, π_i denotes the element s_i of π and $\pi_{\leq i}$ is the prefix $(s_0, s_1, \ldots, s_i)$ of π. A $\mathcal{L}_{OCRS}$ transition system $\mathbb{M}$ is defined as $\mathbb{M} = (S, T, V)$ where

- (S, T) is a ω-tree frame
- $V : S \times A_g \rightarrow \wp(\Omega \cup CP)$; we define the belief part of the assignment $V^B(s, i) = V(s, i) \setminus CP$ and the communication counter part $V^C(s, i) = V(s, i) \cap CP$. We further define $V^M(s, i) = \{\alpha \mid \alpha \in D_M(i)\}$. V satisfies the following conditions:

1. $|V^C(s,i)| = 1$ for all $s \in S$ and $i \in A_g$.
2. If $(s,t) \in T$ and $cp_i^{=n} \in V(s,i)$ and $cp_i^{=m} \in V(t,i)$ then $n \leq m$.

- we say that a rule $r : P_1, P_2, \ldots, P_n \to P$ is applicable in a state s of an agent i if $ant(\bar{r}) \in V(s,i)$ and $cons(\bar{r}) \notin V(s,i)$. The following conditions on the assignments $V(s,i)$, for all $i \in A_g$, and transition relation T hold in all models:
  1. for all $i \in A_g$, $s, s' \in S$, and $r \in \Re$, $r \in V(s,i)$ iff $r \in V(s',i)$. This describes that agent's program does not change.
  2. for all $s, s' \in S$, sTs' holds iff for all $i \in A_g$, $V(s',i) = V(s,i) \cup \{cons(\bar{r})\} \cup \{Ask(j,i,C(a))\} \cup \{Tell(j,i,C(a))\} \cup \{Ask(j,i,R(a,b))\} \cup \{Tell(j,i,R(a,b))\}$. This describes that each agent i fires a single applicable rule instance of a rule r, or updates its state by interacting with other agents, otherwise its state does not change.

The truth of a $\mathcal{L}_{\mathcal{OCRS}}$ formula at a point n of a path $\pi \in B(S,T)$ is defined inductively as follows:

- $\mathbb{M}, \pi, n \models \top$,
- $\mathbb{M}, \pi, n \models start$ iff $n = 0$,
- $\mathbb{M}, \pi, n \models B_i \alpha$ iff $\alpha \in V(s,i)$,
- $\mathbb{M}, \pi, n \models cp_i^{=m}$ iff $cp_i^{=m} \in V(s,i)$,
- $\mathbb{M}, \pi, n \models \neg\varphi$ iff $\mathbb{M}, \pi, n \not\models \varphi$,
- $\mathbb{M}, \pi, n \models \varphi \sqcap \psi$ iff $\mathbb{M}, \pi, n \models \varphi$ and $\mathbb{M}, \pi, n \models \psi$,
- $\mathbb{M}, \pi, n \models X\varphi$ iff $\mathbb{M}, \pi, n+1 \models \varphi$,
- $\mathbb{M}, \pi, n \models \varphi U \psi$ iff $\exists m \geq n$ such that $\forall k \in [n,m)$ $\mathbb{M}, \pi, k \models \varphi$ and $\mathbb{M}, \pi, m \models \psi$,
- $\mathbb{M}, \pi, n \models A\varphi$ iff $\forall \pi' \in B(S,T)$ such that $\pi'_{\leq n} = \pi_{\leq n}$, $\mathbb{M}, \pi', n \models \varphi$.

We now describe conditions on the models. The transition relation T corresponds to the agent's executing actions $\langle act_i, act_2, \ldots, act_{n_{Ag}} \rangle$ where act_i is a possible action of an agent i in a given state s. The set of actions that each agent i can perform are: $Rule_{i,\bar{r},\beta}$ (agent i firing a rule instance $\bar{r}$ and adding $cons(\bar{r})$ to its working memory and removing β), $Copy_{i,\alpha,\beta}$ (agent i copying α from other agent's memory and removing β, where α is of the form $Ask(j,i,P)$ or $Tell(j,i,P)$, and $Idle_i$ (agent i does nothing but moves to the next state). Intuitively, β is an arbitrary facts which gets overwritten if it is in the agent's dynamic memory $D_M(i)$. If agent's memory is full $|V^M(s,i)| = n_M(i)$ then we require that β has to be in $V^M(s,i)$. Not all actions are possible in a given state. For example, there may not be any matching rule instances. When the counter value reaches to $n_C(i)$, i cannot perform copy action any more. Let us denote the set of all possible actions by agent i in a given state s by $T_i(s)$ and its definition is given below:

Definition 2 (Available actions). *For every state s and agent i,*

1. *$Rule_{i,r,\beta} \in T_i(s)$ iff $r \in V(s,i)$, $ant(\bar{r}) \subseteq V(s,i)$, $cons(\bar{r}) \notin V(s,i)$, $\beta \in \Omega$ or if $|V^M(s,i)| = n_M(i)$ then $\beta \in V^M(s,i)$;*
2. *$Copy_{i,\alpha,\beta} \in T_i(s)$ iff there exists $j \neq i$ such that $\alpha \in V(s,j)$, $\alpha \notin V(s,i)$, $cp_i^{=n} \in V(s,i)$ for some $n < n_C(i)$, α is of the form $Ask(j,i,P)$ or $Tell(j,i,P)$, and β as before;*
3. *$Idle_i$ is always in $T_i(s)$.*

Definition 3 (Effect of actions). *For each $i \in A_g$, the result of performing an action act_i in state s is defined if $act_i \in T_i(s)$ and has the following effect on the assignment of formulas to i in the successor state s':*

1. *if act_i is $Rule_{i,r,\beta}$: $V(s', i) = V(s, i) \setminus \{\beta\} \cup \{cons(\bar{r})\}$;*
2. *if act_i is $Copy_{i,\alpha,\beta}$, $cp_i^{=n} \in V(s, i)$ for some $n \leq n_C(i)$: $V(s', i) = V(s, i) \setminus \{\beta, cp_i^{=n}\} \cup \{\alpha, cp_i^{=n+1}\}$;*
3. *if act_i is $Idle_i$: $V(s', i) = V(s, i)$.*

Now, the definition of the set of models corresponding to a system of rule-based reasoners is given below:

Definition 4. $\mathbb{M}(n_M, n_C)$ *is the set of models (S, T, V) which satisfies the following conditions:*

1. *$cp_i^{=0} \in V(s_0, i)$ where $s_0 \in S$ is the root of (S, T), $\forall i \in A_g$;*
2. *$\forall s, s' \in S$, sTs' iff for some tuple of actions $\langle act_i, act_2, \ldots, act_{n_{Ag}} \rangle$, $act_i \in T_i(s)$ and the assignment in s' satisfies the effects of act_i, $\forall i \in A_g$;*
3. *$\forall s \in S$ and a tuple of actions $\langle act_i, act_2, \ldots, act_{n_{Ag}} \rangle$, if $act_i \in T_i(s), \forall i \in A_g$, then $\exists s' \in S$ s.t. sTs' and s' satisfies the effects of act_i, $\forall i \in A_g$;*
4. *The bound on each agent's memory is set by the following constraint on the mapping V: $|V^M(s, i)| \leq n_M(i), \forall s \in S, i \in A_g$.*

Note that the bound $n_C(i)$ on each agent i's communication ability (no branch contains more than $n_C(i)$ Copy actions by agent i) follows from the fact that $Copy_i$ is only enabled if i has performed fewer than $n_C(i)$ copy actions in the past. Below are some abbreviations which will be used in the axiomatization:

- $ByRule_i(P, n) = \neg B_i P \wedge cp_i^{=n} \wedge \bigvee_{r \in \mathcal{R} \wedge cons(\bar{r})) = P}(B_i r \wedge \bigwedge_{Q \in ant(\bar{r})} B_i Q)$. This formula describes the state before the agent comes to believe formula P by the $Rule$ transition, n is the value of i's communication counter, P and Q are ground atomic formulas.
- $ByCopy_i(\alpha, n) = \neg B_i \alpha \wedge B_j \alpha \wedge cp_i^{=n-1}$, where α is of the form $Ask(j, i, P)$ or $Tell(j, i, P)$, $i, j \in A_g$ and $i \neq j$.

Now we introduce the axiomatization system.

A1 All axioms and inference rules of CTL^* [17].
A2 $\bigwedge_{\alpha \in D_M(i)} B_i \alpha \rightarrow \neg B_i \beta$ for all $D_M(i) \subseteq \Omega$ such that $|D_M(i)| = n_M(i)$ and $\beta \notin D_M(i)$. This axiom describes that, in a given state, each agent can store maximally at most $n_M(i)$ formulas in its memory,
A3 $\bigvee_{n=0,\ldots,n_C(i)} cp_i^{=n}$,
A4 $cp_i^{=n} \rightarrow \neg cp_i^{=m}$ for any $m \neq n$,
A5 $B_i r \wedge \bigwedge_{P \in ant(\bar{r})} B_i P \wedge cp_i^{=n} \wedge \neg B_i cons(\bar{r}) \rightarrow EX(B_i cons(\bar{r}) \wedge cp_i^{=n})$, $i \in A_g$. This axiom describes that if a rule matches, its consequent belongs to some successor state.

A6 $cp_i^{=n} \wedge \neg B_i\alpha \wedge B_j\alpha \rightarrow EX(B_i\alpha \wedge cp_i^{=n+1})$ where α is of the form $Ask(j,i,P)$ or $Tell(j,i,P)$, $i,j \in A_g$, $j \neq i$, $n < n_C(i)$. This axiom describes transitions made by *Copy* with communication counter increased.

A7 $EX(B_i\alpha \wedge B_i\beta) \rightarrow B_i\alpha \vee B_i\beta$, where α and β are not of the form $Ask(j,i,P)$ and $Tell(j,i,P)$. This axiom says that at most one new belief is added in the next state.

A8 $EX(B_i\alpha \wedge cp_i^{=n}) \rightarrow B_i\alpha \vee ByRule_i(\alpha,n) \vee ByCopy_i(\alpha,n)$ for any $\alpha \in \cup\Omega$. This axiom says that a new belief can only be added by one of the valid reasoning actions.

A9a $start \rightarrow cp_i^{=0}$ for all $i \in A_g$. At the start state, the agent has not performed any *Copy* actions.

A9b $\neg EX\ start$. $start$ holds only at the root of the tree.

A10 $B_i r$ where $r \in \Re$ and $i \in A_g$. This axiom tells agent i believes its rules.

A11 $\neg B_i r$ where $r \notin \Re$ and $i \in A_g$. This axiom tells agent i only believes its rules.

A12 $\varphi \rightarrow EX\varphi$, where φ does not contain $start$. This axiom describes an *Idle* transition by all the agents.

A13 $\bigwedge_{i\in A_g} EX(\bigwedge_{\alpha\in\Gamma_i} B_i\alpha \wedge cp_i^{=n_i}) \rightarrow EX \bigwedge_{i\in A_g}(\bigwedge_{\alpha\in\Gamma_i} B_i\alpha \wedge cp_i^{=n_i})$ for any $\Gamma_i \subseteq \Omega$. This axiom describes that if each agent i can separately reach a state where it believes formulas in Γ_i, then all agents together can reach a state where for each i, agent i believes formulas in Γ_i.

Let us now define the logic obtained from the above axiomatisation system.

Definition 5. $\mathbb{L}(n_M, n_C)$ *is the logic defined by the axiomatisation* **A1 - A13**.

Theorem 1. $\mathbb{L}(n_M, n_C)$ *is sound and complete with respect to* $\mathbb{M}(n_M, n_C)$.

Sketch of Proof. The proof of soundness is standard. The proofs for axioms and rules included in **A1** are given in [17]. Axiom **A2** assures that at a state, each agent can store maximally at most $n_M(i)$ formulas in its memory. Axioms **A3** and **A4** force the presence of a unique counter for each agent to record the number of copies it has performed so far. In particular, **A3** makes sure that at least a counter is available for any agent and **A4** guaranties that only one of them is present. In the following, we provide the proof for **A5**. The proofs for other axioms are similar.

Let $\mathbb{M} = (S, T, V) \in \mathbb{M}(n_M, n_C)$, $\pi \in B(S,T)$ and $n \geq 0$. We assume that $\mathbb{M}, \pi, n \models B_i r \wedge \bigwedge_{P\in ant(\bar{r})} B_i P \wedge cp_i^{=m} \wedge \neg B_i cons(\bar{r})$, for some $r \in \Re$, and $|V^M(s,i)| \leq n_M(i)$. Then $P \in V(\pi_n, i)$ for all $P \in ant(\bar{r})$, and $cons(\bar{r}) \notin V(\pi_n, i)$. This means that the action performed by i is $Rule_{i,r,\beta}$. According to the definition of $\mathbb{M}(n_M, n_C)$, $\exists s' \in S \cdot \pi_n T s'$ and $V(s',i) = V(\pi_n,i)\backslash\{\beta\}\cup\{cons(\bar{r})\}$. Let π' be a branch in $B(S,T)$ such that $\pi'_{\leq n} = \pi_{\leq n}$ and $\pi'_{n+1} = s'$. Then we have $\mathbb{M}, \pi', n+1 \models B_i cons(\bar{r}) \wedge cp_i^{=m}$. Therefore, it is obvious that $\mathbb{M}, \pi, n \models EX(B_i cons(\bar{r}) \wedge cp_i^{=m})$.

Completeness can be shown by constructing a tree model for a consistent formula φ. This is constructed as in the completeness proof introduced in [17]. Then we use the axioms to show that this model is in $\mathbb{M}(n_M, n_C)$. Due to space limitations we omit the proof of this result. □

5 Maude Encoding

We build a multi-agent rule-based system whose rules are derived from the ontology of the healthcare epilepsy scenario described in Sect. 2. The system consists of four agents: Patient (1), Planner (2), CareGiver (3), and HealthProfessional (4). The set of rules and initial working memory facts that are distributed to the agents are shown in Table 1. For the specification and verification of the system we use Maude LTL model checker. The choice of LTL is not essential, it is straightforward to encode a $\mathcal{L}_{OCRS}$ model for a standard model checker. We use LTL because it is the logic supported by the Maude system used in our case study. We chose the Maude LTL model checker because it can model check systems whose states involve arbitrary algebraic data types. The only assumption is that the set of states reachable from a given initial state is finite. Rule variables can be represented directly in the Maude encoding, without having to generate all ground instances resulting from possible variable substitutions.

Due to space limitation we omit the encoding here, however, it is similar to [6], apart from the implementation of agents memory bounds. We verified a number of interesting resource-bounded properties of the system including the following:

Table 1. Horn-Clause rules for the epileptic patients' monitoring context-aware system

Patient's rule
Initial facts: Patient('Tracy), isAlarming('Tracy, 'Beep), hasGeolocation('Tracy, 'DownTown)
Patient(?p),isAlarming(?p,?s) → EpilepticAlarm(?p)
EpilepticAlarm(?p) → hasHazardousActivity(?p, 'Yes)
hasHazardousActivity(?p, 'Yes) → isAgreed(?p,'Yes)
hasHazardousActivity(?p, 'Yes) → isAgreed(?p,'No)
EpilepticAlarm(?p), hasHazardousActivity(?p, 'Yes), hasGeoLocation(?p, ?location) → hasNotifiedPatient(?p, ?location)
EpilepticAlarm(?p), hasHazardousActivity(?p, 'Yes), hasGeoLocation(?p, ?location), isAgreed(?p, 'Yes) →Tell(1, 2, has-NotifiedPlanner(?p,?location))
Planner's rules
Initial facts: isCareGiverOf('Fiona,'Tracy), isCareGiverOnCall('Fiona, 'OnCall)
Tell(1, 2, hasNotifiedPlanner(?p,?location)) → hasNotifiedPlanner(?p,?location)
hasNotifiedPlanner(?p,?location),lessThan(?location,'30), greaterThan(?location,0)→ situationWithinRange(?p,?location)
situationWithinRange(?p,?location),isCareGiverOf(?c,?p),isCareGiverOnCall(?c,?stat) → Ask(2,3, hasCareStatus(?c, 'stat)
Tell(3,2,hasCarStatus(?c,'onCall))→ hasCarStatus(?c,'onCall) hasCarStatus(?c,'onCall), hasNotifiedPlanner(?p,?location) → AcceptRequest(?c, ?p)
Tell(3,2,hasCarStatus(?c, 'Busy))→ hasCareStatus(?c, 'Busy)
hasNotifiedPlanner(?p,?location) → Tell(2, 5, hasNotifiedPlanner(?p,?location))
CareGiver's rules
Initial facts:
Ask(2,3, hasCareStatus(?c, ?stat)) → hasCareStatus(?c, ?stat)
hasCareStatus(?c, ?stat) → Tell(3,2,hasCarStatus(?c, 'OnCall))
hasCareStatus(?c, ?stat) → Tell(3,2,hasCarStatus(?c, 'Busy))
hasCareStatus(?c, ?stat) → Tell(3,2,hasCarStatus(?c, 'NotOnCall))
hasCareStatus(?c, ?stat) → Tell(3,2,hasCarStatus(?c, 'EmergencyOnly))
HealthProfessional's rules
Initial facts: isHealthProfesional('John, 'Tracy)
Tell(2, 5, hasNotifiedPlanner(?p,?location)) → hasNotifiedPlanner(?p,?location)
hasNotifiedPlanner(?p,?location), isHealthProfesional(?prof, ?p) → logEpilepticAlarm(?prof,?p)

$$G(B_1 \, EpilepticAlarm('Tracy)$$
$$\rightarrow X^n B_1 \, Tell(1, 2, hasNotifiedPlanner('Tracy,' DownTown))$$
$$\wedge (msg_1 = m) \wedge (n_M(1) \geq l))$$

the above property specifies that whenever there is an epileptic alarm for Tracy, agent 1 notifying agent 2 that "Tracy" has hazardous activity and she is located in "DownTown" within n time steps, while exchanging m messages and space requirement for agent 1 is at least l units, and

$$G(B_2 \, Tell(1, 2, hasNotifiedPlanner('Tracy,' DownTown))$$
$$\rightarrow X^n B_2 \, AcceptRequest('Fiona,' Tracy) \wedge (msg_2 = m) \wedge (n_M(2) \geq l))$$

which specifies that whenever agent 2 gets notified that "Tracy" has hazardous activity and she is located in "DownTown" it believes that care giver Fiona accepts the request within n time steps, while exchanging m messages and space requirement for agent 2 is at least l units.

The above properties are verified as true when the values of n, m, and l are 3, 1, and 3 in the first property, and the values of n, m, and l are 9, 3, and 2 in the second property. However, the properties are verified as false and the model checker returns counterexamples when we assign a values to n, m, and l which are less than 3, 1, and 3 in the first property, and values to n, m, and l which are less than 9, 3 and 2 in the second property.

6   Conclusions and Future Work

In this paper, we presented a formal logical framework for modelling and verifying context-aware multi-agent systems. Where agents reason using ontology-driven first order Horn clause rules. We considered space requirement for reasoning in addition to the time and communication resources. We modelled an ontology-based context-aware system to show how we can encode a $\mathcal{L}_{OCRS}$ model using Maude LTL model checker and formally verify its resource-bounded properties. In future work, we would like to develop a framework that will allow us to design context-aware system automatically from a given scenario described in natural languages. This requires extracting specification to build its corresponding ontology for the desired system.

References

1. Weiser, M.: The computer for the 21st century. ACM SIGMOBILE Mob. Comput. Commun. Rev. (Special Issue Dedicated to Mark Weiser) **3**(3), 3–11 (1999)
2. Viterbo Filho, J., da Gama Malcher, M., Endler, M.: Supporting the development of context-aware agent-based systems for mobile networks. In: Proceedings of the 2008 ACM Symposium on Applied Computing, pp. 1872–1873. ACM (2008)
3. Rakib, A.: Formal approaches to modelling and verifying resource-bounded agents-state of the art and future prospects. Inform. Tech. Softw. Eng. **2**(4) (2012)
4. Wang, X.H., Zhang, D.Q., Gu, T., Pung, H.K.: Ontology based context modeling and reasoning using OWL. In: PerCom Workshops 2004, pp. 18–22 (2004)

5. Esposito, A., Tarricone, L., Zappatore, M., Catarinucci, L., Colella, R., DiBari, A.: A framework for context-aware home-health monitoring. In: Sandnes, F.E., Zhang, Y., Rong, C., Yang, L.T., Ma, J. (eds.) UIC 2008. LNCS, vol. 5061, pp. 119–130. Springer, Heidelberg (2008)
6. Rakib, A., Faruqui, R.U.: A formal approach to modelling and verifying resource-bounded context-aware agents. In: Vinh, P.C., Hung, N.M., Tung, N.T., Suzuki, J. (eds.) ICCASA 2012. LNICST, vol. 109, pp. 86–96. Springer, Heidelberg (2013)
7. Alechina, N., Logan, B., Nga, N.H., Rakib, A.: Verifying time and communication costs of rule-based reasoners. In: Peled, D.A., Wooldridge, M.J. (eds.) MoChArt 2008. LNCS, vol. 5348, pp. 1–14. Springer, Heidelberg (2009)
8. Alechina, N., Logan, B., Nga, N.H., Rakib, A.: Verifying time, memory and communication bounds in systems of reasoning agents. Synthese **169**(2), 385–403 (2009)
9. Alechina, N., Jago, M., Logan, B.: Modal logics for communicating rule-based agents. In: Proceedings of the 17th European Conference on Artificial Intelligence, pp. 322–326 (2006)
10. Eker, S., Meseguer, J., Sridharanarayanan, A.: The Maude LTL model checker and its implementation. In: Ball, T., Rajamani, S.K. (eds.) SPIN 2003. LNCS, vol. 2648, pp. 230–234. Springer, Heidelberg (2003)
11. Dey, A., Abwowd, G.: Towards a better understanding of context and context-awareness. Technical report GIT-GVU-99-22, Georgia Institute of Technology
12. ter Horst, H.J.: Completeness, decidability and complexity of entailment for RDF Schema and a semantic extension involving the OWL vocabulary. Web Semant. Sci. Serv. Agents World Wide Web **3**(2–3), 79–115 (2005)
13. Grosof, B.N., Horrocks, I., Volz, R., Decker, S.: Description logic programs: combining logic programs with description logic. In: WWW 2003, pp. 48–57. ACM Press (2003)
14. Horrocks, I., Patel-Schneider, P.F., Boley, H., Tabet, S., Grosof, B., Dean, M.: SWRL: a Semantic Web Rule Language combining OWL and RuleML. Acknowledged W3C submission, standards proposal research report: Version 0.6 (April 2004)
15. Costa, P.D.: Architectural support for context-aware applications: from context models to services platforms. Ph.D. thesis, Centre for Telematics and Information Technology, University of Twente, AE Enschede, The Netherlands (2007)
16. Protégé: The Protégé ontology editor and knowledge-base framework (Version 4.1). http://protege.stanford.edu/ (July 2011)
17. Reynolds, M.: An axiomatization of full computation tree logic. J. Symb. Log. **66**(3), 1011–1057 (2001)

A Trust Propagation Model for New-Coming in Multi-agent System

Manh Hung Nguyen[1,2]($\boxtimes$) and Dinh Que Tran[1]

[1] Posts and Telecommunication Institute of Technology (PTIT), Hanoi, Vietnam
[2] IRD, UMI 209 UMMISCO, IFI/MSI, Vietnam National University of Hanoi,
Hanoi, Vietnam
{nmhufng,tdque}@yahoo.com

Abstract. In order to cooperate in the open distributed environment, truster agents need to be aware trustworthiness of trustee agents for selecting suitable interaction partners. Most of the current computational trust models make use of the truster itself experience or reputation from community on trustees to compute the trust values. However, in some circumstances, a truster agent may have no experience with a new trustee or may not obtain the information about the reputation of the new trustee agent. And then the truster agent could not utilize the traditional mechanisms based on experience or reputation to infer some trust value for the new trustee. In this paper, we introduce a novel mechanism for estimating trustworthiness in such a situation. Our proposed mechanism is based on the similarity in profiles of the new trustee and ones of well known agents. A weighted combination model is used for integrating experience trust, reputation and similar trust.

Keywords: Trust · Reputation · Trust propagation · Trust similarity · Multi-agents system

1 Introduction

Trust is a directional relationship between two parties in which one side called truster assesses trustworthiness on another side called trustee. This concept has been investigated and utilized in various application areas. Josang et al. [9] consider trust as the extent to which a given party is willing to depend on something or somebody in a given situation with a feeling of relative security, even though negative consequences are possible.

From the computational point of view, Grandison and Sloman [3] define trust as a quantified belief by a truster with respect to the competence, honesty, security and dependability of a trustee within a specified context. This understanding of trust has been accepted and applied to constructing open distributed multiagent systems. The model given by Nefti et al. [12] considers some kind of information on a merchant website that is shown to increase customer trust. Yu and Singh [22–24] propose a model to store values of the quality of

P.C. Vinh et al. (Eds.): ICCASA 2013, LNICST 128, pp. 15–23, 2014.
DOI: 10.1007/978-3-319-05939-6_2, © Springer International Publishing Switzerland 2014

direct interactions among agents and only consider the most recent experiences with each partner for the calculations. Sen and Sajja's [19] reputation model considers both types of direct experiences: direct interaction and observed interaction. While the main idea behind the reputation model presented by Carter et al. [2] is that the reputation of an agent is based on the degree of fulfillment of roles ascribed to it by the society. Sabater and Sierra [17,18] introduced ReGreT - a modular trust and reputation system oriented to complex small/mid-size e-commerce environments, where social relations among individuals play an important role. Ramchurn et al. [16] developed a trust model based on confidence and reputation. It makes use of fuzzy techniques to guide agents in evaluating past interactions and in establishing new contracts with one another. Huynh et al. [7,8] described FIRE, which is a trust and reputation model. It integrates a number of information sources to produce a comprehensive assessment of an agent's likely performance in open systems. Victor et al. [20] advocate the use of a trust model in which trust scores are (trust, distrust)-couples. These scores are drawn from a bilattice that preserves valuable trust provenance information including gradual trust, distrust, ignorance, and inconsistency. Nguyen and Tran [13–15] introduced a computational model of trust, which is also combination of experience and reference trust by using fuzzy computational techniques and weighted aggregation operators. Katz and Golbeck [10] introduces a definition of trust suitable for use in Web-based social networks with a discussion of the properties that will influence its use in computation. Hang et al. [5] describes a new algebraic approach, shows some theoretical properties of it, and empirically evaluates it on two social network datasets. Guha et al. [4] develop a framework of trust propagation schemes, each of which may be appropriate in certain circumstances, and evaluate the schemes on a large trust network. Vogiatzis et al. [21] propose a probabilistic framework that models agent interactions as a Hidden Markov Model. Burnett et al. [1] describes a new approach, inspired by theories of human organisational behaviour, whereby agents generalise their experiences with known partners as stereotypes and apply these when evaluating new and unknown partners. Hermoso et al. [6] present a coordination artifact which can be used by agents in an open multi-agent system to take more informed decisions regarding partner selection, and thus to improve their individual utilities.

However, the current models fail to deal with the situation of a new entrant trustee, in which there is neither the experience trust nor the reputation of the trustee to refer. A question is how does a truster agent estimate some trust value about the given trustee in the situation? Intuitively, a simple solution for initiation of trust in this situation is assigning a random value for the trust of the new coming trustee. This will be fine if the model is applied to the application which has many contacts/transactions between trusters and trustees. Because this initial value of trust will be rapidly updated by the experience trust from contacts/transactions. Conversely, in the applications where the number of transactions are small, the initial value of trust will strongly affect on the lifetime of the overall trust of a trustee. Therefore, it is better to avoid the random initial value. In order to overcome this limitation, we could use other information resource such as profile, and/or other personal data about new coming trustee to compare with a well known other trustee by solving the following issues:

First, if an agent A has a well known trust on agent B with a value of x, and that the similarity level on profile between agent B and a new coming agent C is y. How much should the initial trust of agent A on agent C be assigned?

Second, in the case an agent A has the well known trusts on a set of agents $\{B_1, B_2, ...B_n\}$, with respective values $\{x_1, x_2, ...x_n\}$, and that the similarity level on profile between each agent B_i and a new coming agent C is y_i. How much should the initial trust of agent A on agent C be assigned?

In this paper, we first propose a new mechanism for trust propagation which is based on the similarity of a new trustee profile and the other well known ones. Then we describe a weighted combination model for integrating types of experience trust, reputation and similar trust. The remainder of the paper is structured as follows. Section 2 presents the similarity based mechanism for trust propagation. Conclusion is presented in Sect. 3.

2 Similarity-Based Mechanism for Trust Propagation

In this model, we distinguish three types of trust among agents in multiagent systems:

- *Experience trust*: the trust that a truster obtained based on the history of interaction with a trustee. An interaction is called a *transaction*, and trust from the interaction is called *transaction trust*.
- *Similar trust*: the trust that a truster obtained by reasoning itself on the similarity of a trustee with other well known trustees. A trustee is considered as *well known* with a truster if there is an interaction between the truster and the trustee and the truster has its own experience trust about this trustee.
- *Reputation*: the trust about a trustee that a truster refers from other agents in the system. We assume that agents are willing and trustworthy to share their experience trust about some trustee to other agents.

Let $A = \{1, 2, ...n\}$ be a set of agents in the system and denote E_{ij}, S_{ij}, R_{ij} and T_{ij} to be the experience trust, the similar trust, the reputation and the overall trust that agent i obtains on agent j, respectively. The following subsections will describe a computational model to estimate the values of E_{ij}, S_{ij}, R_{ij} and T_{ij}. Subsection 2.1 presents the experience trust. Subsection 2.2 presents the similar trust. Section 2.3 presents reputation. Section 2.4 presents the overall trust of a truster about a trustee.

2.1 Experience Trust

Intuitively, experience trust of agent i on agent j is the trustworthiness about j that agent i collects from all transactions between i and j in the past. Let U_{ij} be a set of transactions having been performed between agent i and agent j until the current time.

Experience trust of agent i in agent j, denoted as E_{ij}, is defined by the formula:

$$E_{ij}(t_{ij}, w) = \sum_{k=1}^{|U_{ij}|} t_{ij}^k * w_k \tag{1}$$

where:

- t_{ij} is the vector of transaction trust of agent i in its partner j: $t_{ij} = (t_{ij}^k)$, $k = 1, ..., |U_{ij}|$ and $i, j = 1, ..., n$. $t_{ij}^k \in [0, 1]$ is the trustworthiness of agent i about agent j from the kth latest transaction between i and j.
- $w = (w_1, w_2, ...w_{|U_{ij}|})^T$ is called the transaction weight vector if $w_k \in [0, 1]$, $k = 1, ..., |U_{ij}|$, is the weight of the kth latest transaction based on agent i evaluation such that:

$$\begin{cases} w_{k_1} \geqslant w_{k_2} \text{ if } k_1 < k_2 \\ \sum_{k=1}^{|U_{ij}|} w_k = 1 \end{cases} \tag{2}$$

The weight vector is decreasing from the head to the tail of the sequence since the aggregation focuses more on the later transactions and less on the older transactions. It means that the later the transaction is, the more its trust is important to estimate the experience trust of the correspondent partner. This vector may be computed by means of Regular Decreasing Monotone (RDM) linguistic quantifier Q (Zadeh [25]) as a function $Q : [0, 1] \rightarrow [0, 1]$ which satisfies the following conditions:

(i) $Q(0) = 1$;
(ii) $Q(1) = 0$;
(iii) $Q(i_1) \geqslant Q(i_2)$ if $i_1 < i_2$.

For example, the following functions are RDM functions:

(i) $Q(x) = (1 - x)^m$ with $m \geq 1$
(ii) $Q(x) = 1 - \sqrt{1 - (1 - x)^2}$

And then, the vector w_i, which is defined by the following formula, is the transaction weight vector:

$$w_i = Q\left(\frac{i - 1}{|U_{ij}|}\right) - Q\left(\frac{i}{|U_{ij}|}\right) \text{ for } i = 1, ..., |U_{ij}|$$

2.2 Similar Trust

Similar trust is the trust that a truster obtained by reasoning itself on the similarity of a trustee with other well known trustees. Without loss of generality, we assume that there are n concerned characteristics $\{a^1, a^2, ...a^n\}$, which are objects or attributes of some object, to measure the similarity between two agents. There are several methods to measure the similarity between two objects (cf. D. Lin [11]). In order to keep our model as simple as possible, we use *distance* between two agents based on a weighted average operator over the differences on the evaluation of characteristics given by these agents. For the sake of computation, results in evaluation are usually normalized into values of the unit interval $[0, 1]$. And then from now on, we only consider normalized values which given by agents in the system.

Definition 1. *Suppose that a_i^k a_j^k are two normalized values on the characteristics a^k, which have been evaluated by agent i and agent j, respectively. The difference between agent i and agent j $(i, j \in A)$ on characteristics a^k is defined by the formula:*

$$d_{ij}^k = \mid a_i^k - a_j^k \mid \tag{3}$$

The difference between two agents is then estimated by averaging the difference between them on all considered characteristics:

Definition 2. *The difference between agent i and agent j $(i, j \in A)$ is defined by the function $f_d : [0, 1]^n \to [0, 1]$, which is a mapping from the differences on all considered characteristics into the overall difference between them:*

$$d_{ij} = \frac{\sum\limits_{k=1}^{n} w^k * d_{ij}^k}{\sum\limits_{k=1}^{n} w^k} \tag{4}$$

where w^k, d_{ij}^k are respectively the weight of the characteristics a^k and the difference on the attribute a^k between agent i and agent j.

The estimation of similar trust of truster i about trustee j via another trustee l is based on the combination of the experience trust of i about l, and the difference between l and j. Intuitively, this combination must satisfy the following conditions:

- The more the experience trust of i about l is high, the more the similar trust is high;
- The more the difference between l and j is low, the more the similar trust is close to the experience trust of the well known trustee.

These constraints may be represented by the following *Similar Trust Function - STF*:

Definition 3. *A function $t_s : [0, 1]^2 \to [0, 1]$ is called the similar trust function, denote STF, if and only if it satisfies the following conditions:*

$$(i).\ t(e_1, d) \leqslant t(e_2, d)\ if\ e_1 \leqslant e_2;$$
$$(ii).\ \mid e - t(e, d_1) \mid \leqslant \mid e - t(e, d_2) \mid\ if\ d_1 \leqslant d_2;$$

It is easy to prove the following proposition.

Proposition 1. *The following functions are STF functions:*

(i). $s(e,d) = \begin{cases} e + d * (1-e) & \text{if } e < 0.5 \\ e - d * e & \text{if } e \geq 0.5 \end{cases}$

(ii). $s(e,d) = \begin{cases} e - d * e & \text{if } e < 0.5 \\ e + d * (1-e) & \text{if } e \geq 0.5 \end{cases}$

Now we can define the individual similar trust of a truster i about a trustee j via the similarity between the trustee j and another trustee l as follows.

Definition 4. *The individual similar trust of a truster i about a trustee j via the similarity between the trustee j and another trustee l is a function f_s : $[0,1] \times [0,1] \rightarrow [0,1]$ from the experience trust of truster i about trustee l and the difference between trustee l and trustee j defined as follows:*

$$s^l_{ij} = f_s(E_{il}, d_{lj}) \tag{5}$$

where f_s is a STF function, E_{il} is the experience trust of truster i on trustee l, d_{lj} is the difference between agent j and agent l.

Based on the concept of the individual similar trust, we can now define the similarity trust via a set of trustee agents. Let $O \subseteq A$ be the set of all agents who have already executed at least one transaction with agent i. The similar trust of truster i about trustee j via all well known trustee $k \in O$ of the truster i is then defined as follows:

Definition 5. *The similar trust of truster i about trustee j in general is a function: $[0,1]^{|O|} \rightarrow [0,1]$ from all individual similar trust of truster i about trustee j via trustee $k \in O$:*

$$S_{ij} = \frac{\sum_{k=1}^{|O|} n_k * s^k_{ij}}{\sum_{k=1}^{|O|} n_k} \tag{6}$$

where s^k_{ij} is the individual similar trust of truster i on trustee j via trustee k, n_k is the number of transactions made between agent i and agent k.

2.3   Reputation

Reputation of agent j is the trustworthiness on agent j given by other agents in the system. We share the point of view given by Huynh et al. [8] who suppose that any agent in the system is willing and trustworthy to share its experience trust a bout a particular trustee to other agents.

Suppose that j is an agent which the agent i has not yet interacted with but needs to evaluate to cooperate with. Let $V_{ij} \subseteq A$ be a set of agents that an agent i knows and have had transactions with j in the past.

Reference trust of agent i on agent j:

$$R_{ij} = \begin{cases} \dfrac{\sum\limits_{l \in V_{ij}} r_{ij}^l}{|V_{ij}|} & \text{if } V_{ij} \neq \varnothing \\ 0 & \text{otherwise} \end{cases} \qquad (7)$$

where r_{ij}^l the individual reference trust of agent i on agent j via agents l ($l \in V_{ij}$), $r_{ij}^k = E_{kj}$, E_{kj} is the current experience trust of k on j.

2.4 Overall Trust

Resulting from these partial trust measures, we may construct a definition of combination of these types of trust.

Combination trust T_{ij} of agent i on agent j is defined by the formula:

$$T_{ij} = w_{ie} * E_{ij} + w_{is} * S_{ij} + w_{ir} * R_{ij} \qquad (8)$$

where E_{ij}, S_{ij}, R_{ij} are experience trust, similar trust and reputation about trustee j in the point of view of truster i, respectively and $w_{ie} + w_{is} + w_{ir} = 1$ are weights of these trusts.

3 Conclusion

In this paper, we have introduced a new mechanism for trust propagation which is based on the similarity of a new trustee profile and the other well known agent ones. The trust inferred from similar computation mechanism has been combined in the weighted computation with the experience trust and reputation to achieve an overall trust. In our work, all agents are supposed to be faithful. It means that they always provide reliable information for computing reputation and similarity. However, in the reality, there may be some lying agents who intend to provide unreliable information for the sake of their own utility. Dealing with the situation when considering similar trust and reputation with such unreliable information of liars will be our future research topics. The research results will be presented in the other work.

References

1. Burnett, C., Norman, T.J., Sycara, K.: Bootstrapping trust evaluations through stereotypes. In: Proceedings of the 9th International Conference on Autonomous Agents and Multiagent Systems: AAMAS '10, vol. 1, pp. 241–248. International Foundation for Autonomous Agents and Multiagent Systems, Richland (2010)
2. Carter, J., Bitting, E., Ghorbani, A.: Reputation formalization for an information-sharing multi-agent system. Comput. Intell. 18(2), 515–534 (2002)

3. Grandison, T., Sloman, M.: Specifying and analysing trust for internet applications. In: Monteiro, J.L., Swatman, P.M.C., Tavares, L.V. (eds.) Towards the Knowledge Society. IFIP, vol. 105, pp. 145–157. Springer, Heidelberg (2003)

4. Guha, R., Kumar, R., Raghavan, P., Tomkins, A.: Propagation of trust and distrust. In: Proceedings of the 13th International Conference on World Wide Web, WWW '04, pp. 403–412. ACM, New York (2004)

5. Hang, C.-W., Wang, Y., Singh, M.P.: Operators for propagating trust and their evaluation in social networks. In: Proceedings of The 8th International Conference on Autonomous Agents and Multiagent Systems, AAMAS '09, vol. 2, pp. 1025–1032. International Foundation for Autonomous Agents and Multiagent Systems, Richland (2009)

6. Hermoso, R., Billhardt, H., Ossowski, S.: Role evolution in open multi-agent systems as an information source for trust. In: Proceedings of the 9th International Conference on Autonomous Agents and Multiagent Systems: AAMAS '10, vol. 1, pp. 217–224. International Foundation for Autonomous Agents and Multiagent Systems, Richland (2010)

7. Huynh, D., Jennings, N.R., Shadbolt, N.R.: Developing an integrated trust and reputation model for open multi-agent systems. In: Proceedings of the 7th International Workshop on Trust in Agent Societies, New York, USA, pp. 65–74 (2004)

8. Huynh, T.D., Jennings, N.R., Shadbolt, N.R.: An integrated trust and reputation model for open multi-agent systems. Auton. Agents Multi-Agent Syst. 13(2), 119–154 (2006)

9. Josang, A., Keser, C., Dimitrakos, T.: Can we manage trust? In: Herrmann, P., Issarny, V., Shiu, ChSK (eds.) iTrust 2005. LNCS, vol. 3477, pp. 93–107. Springer, Heidelberg (2005)

10. Katz, Y., Golbeck, J.: Social network-based trust in prioritized default logic. In: Proceedings of the 21st National Conference on Artificial Intelligence (AAAI-06), vol. 21, pp. 1345–1350. AAAI Press, Boston (2006)

11. Lin, D.: An information-theoretic definition of similarity. In: Proceedings of 15th International Conference on Machine Learning, pp. 296–304. Morgan Kaufmann, San Francisco (1998)

12. Nefti, S., Meziane, F., Kasiran, K.: A fuzzy trust model for e-commerce. In: Proceedings of the Seventh IEEE International Conference on E-Commerce Technology (CEC05), pp. 401–404 (2005)

13. Nguyen, M.H., Tran, D.Q.: A computational trust model with trustworthiness against liars in multiagent systems. In: Nguyen, N.-T., Hoang, K., Jędrzejowicz, P. (eds.) ICCCI 2012, Part I. LNCS, vol. 7653, pp. 446–455. Springer, Heidelberg (2012)

14. Nguyen, M.H., Tran, D.Q.: A multi-issue trust model in multiagent systems: a mathematical approach. South-East Asian J. Sci. 1(1), 46–56 (2012)

15. Nguyen, M.H., Tran, D.Q.: A combination trust model for multi-agent systems. Int. J. Innovative Comput. Inf. Control 9(6), 2405–2420 (2013)

16. Ramchurn, S.D., Sierra, C., Godo, L., Jennings, N.R.: Devising a trust model for multi-agent interactions using confidence and reputation. Int. J. Appl. Artif. Intell. 18(9–10), 833–852 (2004)

17. Sabater, J., Sierra, C.: Regret: a reputation model for gregarious societies. In: Proceedings of the Fourth Workshop on Deception Fraud and Trust in Agent Societies, Montreal, Canada, pp. 61–69 (2001)

18. Sabater, J., Sierra, C.: Reputation and social network analysis in multi-agent systems. In: Proceedings of the First International Joint Conference on Autonomous

Agents and Multiagent Systems (AAMAS-02), Bologna, Italy, 15–19 July 2002, pp. 475–482 (2002)

19. Sen, S., Sajja, N.: Robustness of reputation-based trust: Boolean case. In: Proceedings of the First International Joint Conference on Autonomous Agents and Multiagent Systems (AAMAS-02), Bologna, Italy, pp. 288–293 (2002)

20. Victor, P., Cornelis, C., De Cock, M., da Silva, P.P.: Gradual trust and distrust in recommender systems. Fuzzy Sets Syst. **160**(10), 1367–1382 (2009). (Special Issue: Fuzzy Sets in Interdisciplinary Perception and Intelligence)

21. Vogiatzis, G., Macgillivray, I., Chli, M.: A probabilistic model for trust and reputation. In: AAMAS, pp. 225–232 (2010)

22. Yu, B., Singh, M.P.: Towards a probabilistic model of distributed reputation management. In: Proceedings of the Fourth Workshop on Deception Fraud and Trust in Agent Societies, Montreal, Canada, pp. 125–137 (2001)

23. Yu, B., Singh, M.P.: Distributed reputation management for electronic commerce. Comput. Intell. **18**(4), 535–549 (2002)

24. Yu, B., Singh, M.P.: An evidential model of distributed reputation management. In: Proceedings of the First International Joint Conference on Autonomous Agents and Multiagent Systems (AAMAS-02), Bologna, Italy, pp. 294–301 (2002)

25. Zadeh, L.A.: A computational approach to fuzzy quantifiers in natural languages. Comput. Math. Appl. **9**, 149–184 (1983)

Modelling Circulation Behaviour of Vietnamese: Applying for Simulation of Hanoi Traffic Network

Manh Hung Nguyen[1,2(✉)] and Tuong Vinh Ho[1]

[1] IRD, UMI 209 UMMISCO; IFI/MSI,
Vietnam National University of Hanoi, Hanoi, Vietnam
[2] Posts and Telecommunications Institute of Technology (PTIT), Hanoi, Vietnam
nmhufng@yahoo.com, ho.tuong.vinh@ifi.edu.vn

Abstract. Recently, there are many simulation models proposed for traffic simulation. Although there are some models which are able to simulate with a big number of transports, they are not easy to apply to the traffic situation and the circulation culture of Vietnamese. In Vietnam, most of transports are motorbikes. Their drivers do not always respect the circulation laws: they could go to anywhere as long as there is enough place in ahead to go. Moreover, most of streets in Vietnam have no lanes and no one respect the rule of following only one lane on a street. This paper introduces a simulation model and tool typically for the traffic situation and the circulation culture of Vietnamese. The model is also based on multi-agent system and then, it is applied to the traffic network of Hanoi city.

Keywords: Traffic status aware · Traffic network · Intelligent transportation network · Multi-agents system · Simulation model

1 Introduction

Recently, there have been many researches interested in the field of transportation network simulation. Therefore, there have been many models and tools proposed. Most of them are agent-based models. In which, intelligent agent and multiagent system seem to be suitable for simulate transportation network at the micro level. Each transport is thus modelled as an intelligent agent. It could observe other transports and obstacles to change its own speed as well as direction to go to its destination as fast as possible. The transportation network therefore could be modelled as a multiagent system whose each agent has a personnel goal (its destination to go) and they have to coordinate and/or interact together in order to prevent accidents from happening.

There are many models proposed in this tendency. For instance, MATSim development team [3] is developing a framework and platform for a transportation network simulation, called MATSim. MATSim provides a toolbox to implement large-scale agent-based transport simulations. The toolbox consists of

P.C. Vinh et al. (Eds.): ICCASA 2013, LNICST 128, pp. 24–34, 2014.
DOI: 10.1007/978-3-319-05939-6_3, © Springer International Publishing Switzerland 2014

several modules which can be combined or used stand-alone: toolbox for demand-modeling, agent-based mobility-simulation (traffic flow simulation), re-planning, a controller to iteratively run simulations as well as methods to analyze the output generated by the modules. SUMO (Simulation of Urban MObility) [2,6] is a highly portable, microscopic road traffic simulation package designed to handle large road networks. It is mainly developed by employees of the Institute of Transportation Systems at the German Aerospace Center. SUMO allows to simulate how a given traffic demand which consists of single vehicles moves through a given road network. The simulation allows to address a large set of traffic management topics. It is purely microscopic: each vehicle is modelled explicitly, has an own route, and moves individually through the network. Al-Dmour [1] developed TarffSim, a Multiagent Traffic Simulation for micro-simulation and macro-simulation of traffic. Gokulan and Srinivasan [5] have been implemented two different types of multi-agent architectures on a simulated complex urban traffic network in Singapore for adaptive intelligent signal control. Piórkowski et al. [9] are developing TraNS, an open-source simulation environment, as a necessary tool for proper evaluation of newly developed protocols for Vehicular Ad Hoc Networks (VANETs). Mengistu et al. [8] provided a framework for development and execution of parallel applications such as multi-agent based simulation (MABS) in large scale. Lotzmann [7] presented an agent-based traffic simulation approach which sees agents as individual traffic participants moving in an artificial environment.

In spite of many advantages in modelling of individual's behaviors in circulation of agent-based models, they have a limitation in the number of agents in a simulation, especially in a large scale as a transportation network. Although there are some models which are able to simulate with a big number of transports, they are not easy to apply to the traffic situation and the circulation culture of Vietnamese. In Vietnam, most of transports are motorbikes. Their drivers do not always respect the circulation laws: they could go to anywhere as long as there is enough place in ahead to go. Moreover, most of streets in Vietnam have no lanes and no one respect the rule of following only one lane on a street.

Our objective thus is to develop a simulation model and tool typically for the traffic situation and the circulation culture of Vietnamese. The model is also based on multi-agent system. However, in order to get over the limitation of scale in agent-based models, we do not visualise all the agents in their instant circulations. We show only the instant status of streets to see the level of congestion in streets as well as the global status of the traffic network. All calculation of activities and attributes such as speed, travel path, time, plans of individual agent and the level of congestion on streets, etc. are done in background processes of the model.

This paper is organised as follows: Sect. 2 presents our agent-based model for simulation of traffic network status. Section 3 presents the modelling of the agents in the proposed agent-based model. Section 4 presents a case study in which we apply the proposed model to simulate the traffic network status of Hanoi. Finally, Sect. 5 discusses the presented work and draws some perspectives for future work.

2   Propose Model

Our model is depicted in the Fig. 1. The main idea is to separate the visual level (presentation level) and the calculation level (Modeling and simulation level). This makes our model more flexible: it is easy to change the input data to display. The input data thus could be either that from simulation, or the realistic data captured from on site cameras. Moreover, this separation also limits the effects of processing speed on the visualisation: we could simulate the traffic network with a huge number of transports with a bit slow speed, but the results are then displayed as those of fast speed because the display is now independent from the calculation in simulation. This section presents the mains steps in our model. The module of *Agent Modeling* will be presented in Sec. 3.

– *Step 1: Load GIS files.* This step loads the GIS (Geographic Information System) files to create the roads network. The use of GIS files enables us to work with the realistic data from the real transportation network.
– *Step 2: Initiate agent position.* The second step initiates the agent's position. The position of agents is determined by a zone.
– *Step 3: Generate agent plans.* This step generate plans for each individual agent. The plans are generated based on the population distribution, the structure of jobs in society, and the distribution of offices, commercial centres, schools, hospitals, etc... in the city.
– *Step 4: Simulation.* Each individual is represented by an agent with its daily plans. At any moment, we can detect the position of agent on the road by considering two factors:

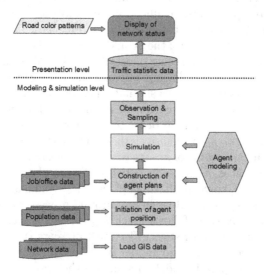

Fig. 1. Steps and processing data in the propose model

- Its circulation path: this is either statically determined by the Dijkstra's algorithm (Dijkstra [4]), or dynamically optimum algorithm (modelled in Sect. 3.1).
- Its speed: the real speed of agent.
- *Step 5: Observation and sampling.* The actual status of road is determined by the observation of the current through put of road a pre-planned time, this through put could be represented by the average speed of circulation on the road.
- *Step 6: Display road/network status.* The displayed color of road (intersection) depends on the circulation status of the road (intersection resp.):
  - Red: the road (intersection) is blocked
  - Orange: the road almost full, the vehicles movement is very slow
  - Yellow: the road contains many transports, the movement is slow
  - Gray: the road has a normal traffic, the movement is normal

3   Agent Modelling

In this section, we model all types of agent in the system. Section 3.1 will model the transport agent. Section 3.2 will model the traffic light agent.

3.1   Transport Agent

A transport could be a trunk, a bus, a car (including taxi), a motor. It has some attributes, behaviors and ability to move. So we need to model it as an agent in the system. Because a driver is assigned to his transport so we consider the whole of a driver and his transport as an unique transport agent.

Attributes. A transport has these attributes:

- *name*: name of a transport.
- *length (denoted as l)*: real length of a transport.
- *width (denoted as d)*: real width of the transport.
- *max speed (denoted as v_{max})*: the maximal allowed speed, for the transport, by law.
- *current speed (denoted as v)*: the current speed of the transport.
- *max technical speed (denoted as v_{tech})*: the maximal technical speed of a transport, limited by the engine of the transport.
- *safe front distance (denoted as d_f)*: the minimum distance to the nearest transport in front that keep safe for circulation. This distance is estimated by following formula:

$$d_f = \frac{l * v}{v_{max}} + \theta \tag{1}$$

where θ is the minimum distance allowed among transports when stopping.

– *safe beside distance (denoted as d_b)*: the minimum distance to the nearest beside transport that keep safe for circulation. This distance is estimated by following formula:

$$d_b = \frac{d * v}{v_{max}} + \theta \tag{2}$$

– *accelerate factor (denoted as α)*: the ability to speed up in an unit of time.
– *decelerate factor (denoted as β)*: the ability to slow down in an unit of time.
– A set of *circulation plans* as depicted in Sect. 2.

Behavior. Behavior of obedient transport agents:

– *find a path*: this will find a path to go. A transport agent finds a path when: either it starts a new plan; or it want to change the path when it is blocked somewhere on the way.
– *observation*: this is an action of the driver of a transport, including of observation of the traffic light, observation of obstacles.
– *stop*: a transport agent stops at an intersection when the traffic light is in red.
– *accelerate*: a transport agent will accelerate when: (1) there is no obstacles in *safe front distance* and *safe beside distance* of it; and (2) its speed does not reach the *max speed* yet. The new speed will accelerate to:

$$v_{t+1} = min\{v_t + \alpha, v_{max}\} \tag{3}$$

where v_t, v_{t+1} are the speed of the transport agent at the simulation step $t, t + 1$, respectively.
– *decelerate*: a transport agent has to decelerate when: (1) there is some obstacles in *safe front distance* or *safe beside distance* of it; or (2) it intends to stop. The new speed will decelerate to:

$$v_{t+1} = max\{v_t - \beta, 0\} \tag{4}$$

Behavior of disobedient transport agents who break the law has some differences in these actions:

– *accelerate*: a disobedient transport agent will accelerate when there is no obstacles in *safe front distance* and *safe beside distance* of it. The new speed will accelerate to:

$$v_{t+1} = min\{v_t + \alpha, v_{tech}\} \tag{5}$$

where v_t, v_{t+1} are the speed of the transport at the simulation step $t, t + 1$, respectively.
– *decelerate*: a disobedient transport agent has to decelerate when: (1) there is some obstacles in *safe front distance* or *safe beside distance* of it; or (2) it intends to stop. The new speed will decelerate to:

$$v_{t+1} = max\{v_t - \beta, 0\} \tag{6}$$

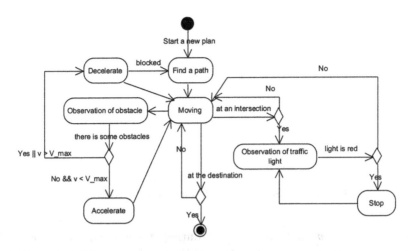

Fig. 2. Behaviors of transport agent

The transition among behaviors of a transport agent is depicted in the Fig. 2: A transport agent starts his movement by starting a plan on time. Firstly, it finds a path to go. During moving, it observes three kinds of objects: the traffic light, the destination, and the obstacle. In observing the traffic light at an intersection: if the light is red, it will *stop*; otherwise, it will continue to move. In observing the obstacle, it will *accelerate* if there is no obstacle and its current speed v is still lower than the allowed speed v_{max}. It will *decelerate* if there are some obstacles or its speed v is already higher than the allowed speed v_{max} (for the case of obey transport). It could re-find the path if it is blocked somewhere. Otherwise, it continues to move with the current speed. In observing the destination, if it is at the destination, it finishes the circulation. Otherwise, it continues to move.

3.2 Traffic Light

A traffic light plays the role of a traffic controller at an intersection. Although a traffic light can not move, it still has some attributes and behaviors as an agent. We thus need to model a traffic light as an agent in the system.

Attributes. A traffic light has attributes:

- A set of *control directions*: the directions that is controlled by a traffic light agent. An intersection could have several control directions (e.g. in the Fig. 3, there are four control direction for the intersection).
- Each control direction has:
  - *duration for green light (denoted d_g)*: during this interval (in seconds), the light is green for a control direction, and the transports could pass the intersection via the control direction of the traffic light agent.

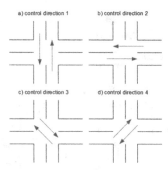

Fig. 3. An intersection with four control directions

- *duration for red light (denoted d_r)*: during this interval (in seconds), the light is red for a control direction, and the transports have no right to pass the intersection via the control direction of the traffic light agent.
- *minimum time for green light (denoted MIN_TIME)*: the minimum green light duration to avoid the case that the light color changes too fast.
- *maximum time for green light (denoted MAX_TIME)*: the maximum green light duration to avoid the case that the other control directions are blocked too long.
- *timer counting (denoted counter)*: the time counting variable to change the color of the light.

Behavior. A traffic light has three behaviors:

- *change to green*: when the light is in red and the *counter* value equals to d_r, the light will change to green, and the *counter* value is re-initiated by zero.
- *change to red*: when the light is in green and the *counter* value equals to d_g, the light will change to red, and the *counter* value is re-initiated by zero.
- *optimisation of green/red time*: the traffic light is able to dynamically update the d_g and d_r to optimise the traffic routing at the intersection. The algorithm will be presented in the next section.

The transition among behaviors of a traffic light agent is depicted in the Fig. 4: Firstly, it initiates the green/red time for each control direction. Then there is a loop of transition between *change to red* and *change to green*. This transition is controlled by the value of *counter*, in comparing with that of d_r and d_g. This loop works in parallel with the function of *Optimisation of green/red time*.

4   A Case Study: Simulation of Hanoi Traffic Network Status

This section applies the proposed model to simulate the circulation in the traffic network of Hanoi (the capital of Vietnam). Section 4.1 presents the modelling

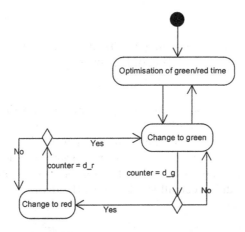

Fig. 4. Behaviors of traffic light agent

and simulation of the traffic network status. Section 4.2 presents the results in several points of view.

4.1 Simulation Setup

This section presents the applying of mains steps in the proposed model to model and simulate the traffic network of Hanoi.

Initiation of agents population.
The initial position of agents is created with the same rate of realistic population distribution of Hanoi, by districts. The destination of agents is determined based on its jobs and family situation. For instance, a student will go to his university. An officer may go directly to his office or pass over his or her son's school. The data about the distribution of offices, hospitals, schools, universities, tourist sites, commercial centres, manufactures, etc. is stocked in a GIS file. This enables us to capture the realistic position of an individual's destination, and then the real travel distance for each agent on its plans.

Construction of agent plans.
An agent's plan is created based on many information about the agent: its home position, its jobs will determine an office or a school. This will then determine the time and destination to move.

Once all agents' plans are planned for each day, we launch the simulation for the day and calculate the intensity of transportation on each street as the proposed model.

4.2   Results

This section presents some beginning results of the simulation at several levels: displaying, analysing, and validation of the dynamic optimum path finding.

Displaying level
The results of traffic network status are presented in the Fig. 5. These visual representations of traffic network status enable us to track and to compare the overall status of traffic network at many daily moments. These also show whether a moment is a rush hour or not. In order to represent more detail on the traffic network, our tool also enables to see in detail on any point on the network by clicking on it, there will be a small window with the detail information appears.

Fig. 5. Traffic network status and detail view on a point

Dynamic path finding.
The results are presented in Fig. 6. We compare the results from two different traffic conditions: low traffic condition and that in rush hour.

In the case of low traffic condition (all roads are in green status - normal speed, Fig. 6a), the found fastest path is very similar to the physical shortest path (Fig. 6b). This is reasonable: in a low traffic condition, drivers could drive with normal speed, this is the case to estimate the *static fastest path* which is identical with the physical shortest path.

In the case of high traffic condition (many roads are in red, orange, yellow - Fig. 6c), the found fastest path is different from that from the low traffic condition (Fig. 6d vs Fig. 6b). This difference indicates the dynamic in optimisation as well as the effects of taking into account the user preferences: If we choose the preference k different, the found fastest path will be different.

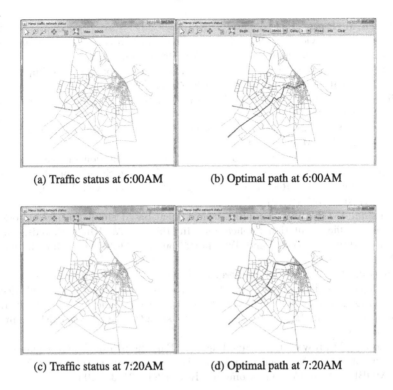

(a) Traffic status at 6:00AM   (b) Optimal path at 6:00AM

(c) Traffic status at 7:20AM   (d) Optimal path at 7:20AM

Fig. 6. The variations of optimal path depending on the traffic status

5   Conclusion

This paper proposed an agent-based model for simulation the traffic network status. The model is then applied to simulate the traffic network status of Hanoi. This model enables to show the instant traffic network status at any daily moment. This also helps us to analyse the statistic on some particular street as well as those of all streets in the network. Another advantage of this model is that it could simulate the traffic network status for any city as long as we have data about the real traffic network, the population distribution, and the jobs/age distribution of the city.

Testing some real scenarios in the traffic network to find out the best scenario, simulating to optimise some routing strategies, or evaluate some new propose policies on the urban circulation are our works in the near future.

References

1. Al-Dmour, N.A.A.-H.: TarffSim: multiagent traffic simulation. Eur. J. Sci. Res. **53**(4), 570–575 (2011)

2. Behrisch, M., Bieker, L., Erdmann, J., Krajzewicz, D.: SUMO - simulation of urban mobility: an overview. In: SIMUL 2011, The Third International Conference on Advances in System Simulation, pp. 63–68, Barcelona, Spain, October 2011
3. MATSim Development Team (ed.): MATSIM-T: aims, approach and implementation. Technical report, IVT, ETH Zürich, Zürich (2007)
4. Dijkstra, E.W.: A note on two problems in connexion with graphs. Numer. Math. 1, 269–271 (1959)
5. Gokulan, B.P., Srinivasan, D.: Multi-agent system in urban traffic signal control. IEEE Comp. Int. Mag. 5(4), 43–51 (2010)
6. Krajzewicz, D.: Traffic simulation with SUMO – simulation of urban mobility, Chap. 7. In: Barceló, J. (ed.) Fundamentals of Traffic Simulation. International Series in Operations Research & Management Science, vol. 145, pp. 269–293. Springer, New York (2010)
7. Lotzmann, U.: TRASS: a multi-purpose agent-based simulation framework for complex traffic simulation applications. In: Bazzan, A., Klügl, F. (eds.) Multi-Agent Systems for Traffic and Transportation, pp. 79–107. IGI Global, Hershey (2009)
8. Mengistu, D., Tröger, P., Lundberg, L., Davidsson, P.: Scalability in distributed multi-agent based simulations: the JADE case. In: Proceedings of the 2008 Second International Conference on Future Generation Communication and Networking Symposia, FGCNS '08, vol. 05, pp. 93–99, Washington, DC, USA. IEEE Computer Society (2008)
9. Piórkowski, M., Raya, M., Lezama Lugo, A., Papadimitratos, P., Grossglauser, M., Hubaux, J.-P.: TraNS: realistic joint traffic and network simulator for VANETs. SIGMOBILE Mob. Comput. Commun. Rev. 12(1), 31–33 (2008)

Storing and Managing Context
and Context History

Alaa Alsaig, Ammar Alsaig, Mubarak Mohammad$^{(\boxtimes)}$, and Vangalur Alagar

Concordia University, Montreal, Canada
ms_moham@cse.concordia.ca

Abstract. Bringing context into systems design has added a new dimension to modern technology. In service-centric and social-centric systems, the personalization of services to accommodate the preferences of each individual is essentially based on context information. Due to this importance, a significant amount of research work is being done on structuring and modeling contexts. However, no work has been done on storing these models using recent database technologies and techniques. Also, there is no reported work that considers a structure for context history, which is essential to maximize accessibility and scalability of context information in dynamic settings. Motivated by these issues, we have developed a general structure for storing context using three different database models. Additionally, we have compared the three models in terms of their performance and modeling ability. In this paper we present the data models for context, context history, and provide a summary of the experimental analysis conducted on them.

1 Introduction

As the technology evolves, the dependency of society on the technology becomes more intense. This increases the need for smarter systems that can provide specific services rather than general ones. Services in the Health Care sector is an example. As a result many service-oriented systems have become pervasive, requiring context for service provision. Context can be either a location of a subject or any environmental surrounding such as temperature or weather affecting the subject. There has been many studies on defining and modeling context [1]. However, there is no work yet in designing context databases. A context database is essential to manage a heterogeneous collection of contexts and their history in order that context information, both past and current, are made available in a time-critical manner for providing critical services. This is the motivation for us to provide a general implementation structure for context that could be

Alaa and Ammar are sincerely thankful to Saudi Arabia Government and the Saudi Cultural Bureau for their financial support.

Vangalur Alagar—The work reported in this paper is supported by a grant received by this author from Natural Sciences and Engineering Research Council (NSERC), Canada.

P.C. Vinh et al. (Eds.): ICCASA 2013, LNICST 128, pp. 35–46, 2014.
DOI: 10.1007/978-3-319-05939-6_4, © Springer International Publishing Switzerland 2014

embedded in a Service-oriented Application (SOA) or any other ubiquitous computing system. Additionally, we propose a design for storing context history that maximizes data management and enhances accessibility.

1.1 Contributions and Organization of Paper

Our contributions include (1) a general model for storing and managing contexts, (2) an implementation for the proposed context model in three different database models, (3) a comparison of the three implementations based on experimental studies, and (4) a general database structure for storing and managing context history. These contributions are organized as follows. In Sect. 2, we introduce a definition of context, types of context, and a generic context model. In Sect. 3, we provide the three database structures for the generic context model and compare them. In Sect. 4, we provide a solution for handling the context history. In Sect. 5, we provide a brief literature survey of context modeling and implementation. In Sect. 6 we summarize our ongoing research work.

2 Context

There exists a large body of literature in context, as understood in different fields such as linguistics, AI, philosophy, and Human Computer Interface. In ubiquitous computing, *context* is a meta-information that qualifies either data or information or an entity of interest in the system. Within SOA we can regard context as any element that could affect the service provision and execution operations. In general, [11] mentions that context is any environment element of an entity that gives rise to meaningful interpretation of a function computation. As an example, location of a subject is the context which will decide whether or not mobile service could be provided to that subject. In [15], context is formalized and defined as a set of dimensions and tags. The set of dimensions "Who, Where, When, What, and why" are introduced to construct any general context. This definition has been considered in [10] for configuring a service. In the definition of "configured service", context is split into *ContextInfo* and *ContextRule*, where *ContextInfo* is the context representation introduced by [15] and *ContextRule* is the service qualifier rule that has to be met for getting the service. Below, we first provide an extension to the work done by [15] and introduce a detailed study on the context structure from an empirical point of view. Next, we introduce types of contexts, and provide a design for the context considering all contexts' types.

2.1 Context Types

The three important entities in any SOA are *service*, *service requester* (SR), and *service provider* (SP). Each entity will be influenced by their own set of contexts. Thus, we define the three categories *Service Context* (SC) *Service Requester Context* (SRC), and *Service provider Context* (SPC). A context of type SC is to describe the service status. For example, a service may be "temporarily unavail-able" in some contexts or is available only in "certain contexts". A context of SRC qualifies the status while requesting or receiving the service. For exam-ple, the location and time parameters characterize the context of a client while requesting or receiving a service. A context of type SPC is to qualify service availability and service quality for a service provided by a SP. As an example, a SP may have license to provide service within 10 km of the location where SP is registered. So, his location and the authorized zonal information for his service contribute to constructing SPC contexts. Contexts from these categories regu-late and restrict service provisioning in SOA. Contexts of SC and SPC types must be pre-defined in the system, although contexts of type SRC may vary dynamically due to the mobility of SRs. In general, a context type can be put into one of the three subtypes *permanent*, *temporal*, and *transient*. A permanent context needs to be saved. Contexts that arise in Health Care service domain are examples of this type. A temporal context may undergo changes. Many contexts that arise in business applications are of this type. As an example, a business rule of a multinational corporation might change depending upon the govern-ment imposed legalities. A transient context arises dynamically, and after its use it may never arise again. Contexts that arise in many game playing systems are of this type.

2.2 Generic Context Model

The generic context model has the three main parts *ContextInfo*, *ContextRule* and *ContextValue*. Based on the context representation introduced in [15] we have structured *ContextInfo* and *ContextRule* as shown in Fig. 1. However, *ContextValue* requires a more sophisticated structure in order to capture the change of values. We decided to include information such as the identifier of the context's collector and a date and time of collection.

The information included in the *ContextValue* is included in two different nodes. A dimension node information is specific to each dimension separately. This information includes source ID which is the context collector's identifier. Since information for each dimension can be collected by several collectors, it is

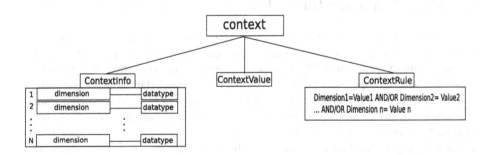

Fig. 1. The main structure of the context

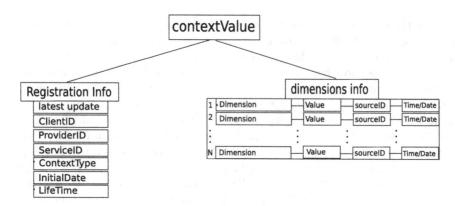

Fig. 2. The structure of *contextValue*

important to know which collector has collected the information to track it in case of a failure. Also, date and time of collection are made part of *Context Value* in order to record the history of change. The second node of *Context Value* is the registration node. This node includes information that is general for all dimensions such as context's type, requester ID, provider ID, service ID and date/time of the last update. This information except date/time of last update, is not updated frequently. Rather, they are set when the service is executed and will remain the same for other updates (Fig. 2). The fields in this node are defined below.

- lastupdate: includes the date and time of last update of the *Context Value*
- requesterID: includes the ID of the requester to whom the service is provided
- providerID: includes the ID of the service provider
- serviceID: includes the ID of the service
- ContextType: can be permanent, temporal or transient
- intialdate: includes the date and time when the context was initialized
- lifetime: includes the time window for the life of the context

3   NoSql Implementation for Generic Context Structure

NoSql technology is selected to implement the generic context structure for the following reasons: (1) it supports semi or free schema [14] which makes it suitable for managing dynamic data, (2) it supports hierarchical structures, (3) it is highly scalable which makes it suitable for distributed databases, (4) it manages attributes with multiple values, and (5) it provides efficient query processing mechanisms [3]. There are three main categories of NoSql database, classified based on their storing techniques: *Document-Oriented*, *Key-Value*, and *Column-Oriented*. Each of these NoSql technologies has many tools to support its operations. Thus, we decided to use these three database technologies for managing contexts. We choose one implementation from each class: *MongoDB* for Document-Oriented, *Redis* for

Key-Value, and *Hbase* for Column-oriented. The following describes how each of these technologies can be used to implement context.

3.1 Service Context Model in MongoDB

MongoDB is an open source *document-oriented database*. Each record in this style is called a *document*. A document is made up of a group of *fields* and their associated values. It can contain *embedded documents* with an overall size that does not exceed 16 MB. The number of fields need not be the same in all documents. That is, each record can have different structure. Each document has a unique key by default. A secondary key can be assigned. A *collection* is a pool of documents, which is equivalent to a table in SQL. The database supports all primitive types (Integer, String, Float), and arrays.

Figure 3 shows our proposed MongoDB model for the generic context structure. In this figure, the *ContextInfo* node is modeled as an embedded document that contains all dimensions as fields with their types as values. The *ContextRule* is modeled as an embedded document with one field of string type. The *ContextValue* is modeled as an embedded document that contains fields and arrays as follows. The *datetime, clientID, providerID,* and *serviceID* are modeled as regular fields. Each dimension of the context is modeled as an array structure, which wraps the information specific to each dimension in one memory block. Thus, all information regarding one dimension including *sourceID, date/time of collection,* and *value* of the dimension can be retrieved by the name of the dimension. The rational for representing dimensions as arrays instead of embedded documents is to reduce the levels of document embedding. Increasing the levels of document embedding makes MongoDB's operations resource intensive and causes complex query processing and retrieval. Thus, with the current structure, when an update operation is performed, only *lastupdate* field and dimensions' values are updated with a single query.

3.2 Service Context Model in Redis

Redis is an open source advanced *key-value* database. A record in the key-value database consists of a key mapped to its corresponding value. Redis is considered

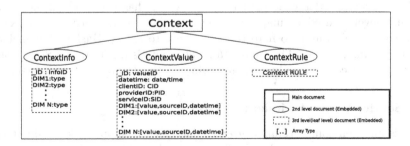

Fig. 3. Service context model in MongoDB

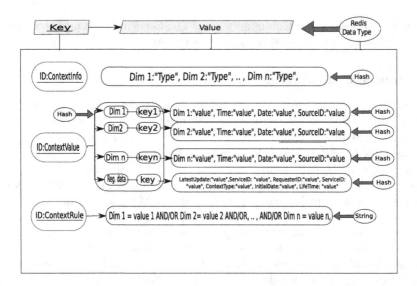

Fig. 4. Service context model in Redis

advanced because it provides five possible data structures for the value type. These data structures are *String, Hash, Set, List,* and *Sorted Set.* A String is a single value with a maximum size of 512 MB. A Hashes is a set of pairs where each pair consists of a name field and its corresponding value. A single Hashes record could have up to $2^{32} - 1$ pairs. A Set is an unsorted and not duplicated group of elements connected to a single key. In a Set, the maximum number of elements is $2^{32} - 1$. A List is simply a list of string values that are ordered as they are entered. A List could have a maximum size of $2^{32} - 1$ values. A Sorted Set is similar to Set, but each value is attached with a score. A score is an integer number attached to each value of a Sorted set. The values of a Sorted set are sorted in ascending order based on their score. The maximum number of values in a Sorted Set is similar to a Set.

Figure 4 depicts our Redis, key-value model, for context structure. The model uses strings and Hashes to model elements. Because *ContextInfo* consists of many pairs of dimension names and their types, Hash is a good data type to use. Similarly, *ContextValue* contains pairs. However, it has two levels of hierarchy. The first level is used to map the names of dimensions to their value keys. The second level is used to map the value keys to nested Hashes that include dimensions' information. The *ContextRule* attribute is modeled as a String data type because it contains only one value which is the *ContextRule* statement.

3.3   Service Context Model in Hbase

Hbase is an open source *column-oriented* database. It supports key-value techniques, and it is based on the *BigTable* technology [7], which is designed by Google. It provides flexible table structure. An Hbase table contains a bunch

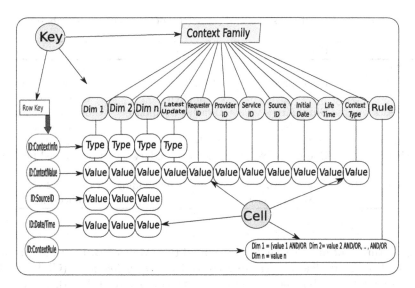

Fig. 5. Service context model in Hbase

of Key-Values wrapped together under one name. This name is called *Column Family* (CF). *Column Qualifier* (CQ) is a field of data. *Row Key* is a unique key that differentiates a row from another. *Cell* stores an atomic value. To store this value or retrieve it, three keys are needed. These keys are row key, column family, and column qualifier. The size of a cell could be from 10 to 50 MB [6]. *Version* is characterized by a time stamp. Every time data is inserted/updated in a cell, the system stores a time stamp for this action. If time stamp is not specified when retrieving data, the system automatically returns the latest one.

Hbase does not have a fixed pre-defined schema which makes it very flexible to structure Context Model. Figure 5 shows the Service Context Model in Hbase, in which we have named the column family as Context Family. The Context Family is mapped to the set of dimension names. It is also mapped to some columns that provide information to the *ContextValue*. Actually, columns are the data that are related to one or more rows. Rows are the data that are related to the dimensions. As illustrated by Fig. 5, only the *ContextValue* needs all the fields represented by columns. This results in rows with different length. The third row key is *ContextRule* which does not need any data of column defined in the structure. Thus, a new column qualifier is added and named Rule.

3.4   A Comparison of the Three Models

We compare the three models in terms of the features afforded by the underlying database models and in terms of their performances. Table 1 compares their structural features and Table 2 compares their performance.

The *CAP Theorem* [2], which studied *consistency*, *availability*, and *partition tolerance* of NoSql databases, states that any NoSql database should have two

Table 1. A comparison of the structural properties of three context database models

	Redis	MongoDB	Hbase
CAP theorem	CPT	CPT	CPT
Strengths	High speed	Flexibility, simplicity	Versions support, compressions
Weaknesses	Durability problem	Difficult to update	Can't work alone, or scale down
Maximum size	Section 3.2	16 MB	Cell 10-50 MB
Indexing	One index	Allows secondary index	Cell queried by (row key, CF, CQ)
Modeling ability	One structure, No hierarchy	Supports embedding	Tables and embedding

strong features out of three. In [9], it is stated that MongoDB, Redis, and Hbase have the two strong features *consistency* and *partition tolerance* (CPT). Redis is a flexible database but has some limitations, compared to the other two. The constraints on data type, indexing system, and key value structure make it more difficult to use with complex rich data. On the other hand, both MongoDB and Hbase can handle complex data. MongoDB supports hierarchical structures by permitting nested documents and allowing secondary indexing [4]. In Hbase, hierarchical structures are supported by nested columns with multiple indexing [7]. These features help developers to structure rich context data. MongoDB is easier than Hbase in configuring and coding Table 1.

We tested the performance of the three databases using YCSB benchmarking tool [5]. We used different workloads, defined by YCSB, where each workload differs from the other by the number and types of operations performed. The numbers shown in Table 2 represent the average result of each workload examined on different number of records that range from 10,000 to 1,000,000 records. We tested the performance based on two factors: runtime and throughput[1]. In our results, Redis occupies the first place in terms of runtime and throughput followed by MongoDB and, finally, Hbase. However, YCSB does not consider complexity of structure. Therefore, the results could change dramatically with more complex structures. Specifically, because Redis does not have pre-defined data structures, it consumes more operations to perform a single query. As a result, Redis performance decreases, whereas MongoDB and Hbase seem to perform better with complex structures.

4   Database for Managing Context History

An analysis of historical information of contexts will provide valuable lessons to service providers in modifying their business practices in future. Historical data regarding clients is very valuable for improving businesses and capturing

---

[1] Throughput is the number of operations performed per millisecond.

Table 2. A comparison of the performances of three context database models

Workloads	Redis		MongoDB		HBase	
-	Runtime (ms)	Throughput	Runtime (ms)	Throughput	Runtime (ms)	Throughput
Workload (a)	459.25	2279.725	759	1322.43	11477	8682.03
Workload (b)	391.75	2589.860	737.25	1363.452	12508.5	425.7
Workload (c)	356.00	2899.95	660.25	1514.95	8136.74	443.93
Workload (d)	368.50	2785.15	700	1431.6	5331.75	485.44
Workload (e)	5196.25	192.65	3922.25	424.91	7351.5	299.07
Workload (f)	471.50	2132.19	1124.5	933.87	4295	506.41

the market needs and business trends. Through the accumulated contexts, service providers can observe and evaluate the services provided in the past and re-evaluate their business policies. In particular, service providers can perform some data mining and discover the contexts in which the frequency of service requests peaked. When some of these contexts occur in future, providers can be better prepared to serve the clients. Also, historical information can be critical in health-related applications where there is an essential need to access the history of patients. For example, in providing health care for mental illness, it is very useful to investigate a patient's reactions in different situations for understanding and identifying the problem. The volume of data involved in historical evolution of contexts is rather immense. Consequently, we need a structure in which information is allowed to grow in an orderly manner, data access time is optimized, and insertion and deletion of information are done efficiently.

We propose a hierarchical structure that categorizes the historical contexts based on services associated with providers of the services. Figure 6 shows the hierarchy, where the subtree rooted at a service provider contains the services and the contexts of providing these services. Thus, with the help of information included in the data registration node, reaching the contexts of a specific service for a specific client can be an easy process. Also, the hierarchical classification helps in keeping the growth manageable by narrowing it down to a specific provider, and service. Thus, the data related to one provider to one service is clustered together. Therefore, when providers are to access services' contexts they only need to surf their own contexts between their own clients. This classification can also be furthered by clustering the contexts for providers based on contexts' types. Thus, permanent contexts are clustered together and remain untouched, whereas temporal contexts are visited periodically for cleaning.

Additionally, to keep the history manageable we introduced *lifetime, intialdate* and *contextType* fields in Sect. 2.2. Based on *contextType* a context is either to be deleted or retained. In case the type of context is *permanent*, context is persisted. If the context type is *transient*, it is not saved at all. If the type is *temporal*, the lifetime field is added to the field *intialdate* which will define the expiry date of the context. This expiry date is calculated whenever the clean-up process is activated and the record is deleted if either the current date information in it is equal or past the expiry date information.

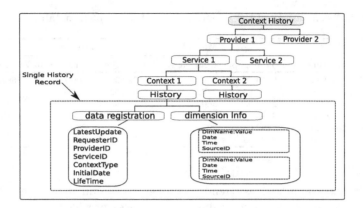

Fig. 6. Context history hierarchical structure

5   Related Work

There exists a large body of literature in the study of context. In this section we have chosen some recent published work on context modeling to compare our work. In general, to our knowledge there is no work done yet on database models for managing context and context history.

The UML context model proposed in [12] considers atomic and complex contexts. An atomic context is modeled as a class in which the two attributes are the name of the context and the source name of context. The only attribute of the complex context is the aggregation of its different contexts, with some logical operations. The two context models are independent of service. However, there is a class, called context-awareness, which is a component of the service. The proposed context model is both abstract and incomplete. It is abstract in the sense that the authors did not provide any language or database support that are necessary for implementing the model. It is incomplete in the sense that the type information necessary to capture the heterogeneity of information, the nature of context (permanent or temporal), and rules for using it in services are not modeled. Although the authors [8] claim to have put forth a context-aware service application, the work does not provide any view of the context structure and how it is defined. Actually, the work is an extension to [12] that they considered as state and event based context. On one hand, a state-based context includes data of attributes that could be entity, device or user related. On the other hand, the event-based context encompasses a bunch of entity events. These events could be related to an application or a user with consideration to events' history. However, there is no elaboration for how the context is structured and where the data is stored. Also, there is no specific structure for the history and what data could be included. In [13], the authors have introduced a context structure mainly for *Mashup* application requirements. They have considered the dimensions *when*, *where*, *what* and *who* to construct contexts. However, the structure assigns several entities for each dimension. This makes context structure complex. In general, not all applications require the same context information. Consequently, their model could result in aggregating useless information. The model does not provide any mechanism to add another dimension. In addition, although the context change history was mentioned in the paper, there was not any information regarding history structure, model or attributes and data of the history.

6 Conclusion

The significant virtue of the context structure that we have proposed in this paper is its ability to handle the richness of context information. It can fit the needs of service definition, service provider characterization, and service requester preferences. The context model is independent from service models of service providers, yet the context structure can be adapted to fit in service models. The three database structures that we have investigated seem to adequately handle the management requirements of a large collection of contexts and their histories. We have compared the three database organization from both structural and performance characteristics. We are currently embedding the context databases in service registries, the central publishing house in a service-oriented architecture.

References

1. Bettini, C., Brdiczka, O., Henricksen, K., Indulska, J., Nicklas, D., Ranganathan, A., Riboni, D.: A survey of context modelling and reasoning techniques. Pervasive Mob. Comput. **6**(2), 161–180 (2010)
2. Brewer, E.A.: Towards robust distributed systems. In: PODC, p. 7 (2000)
3. Chakraborty, S., Sarkar, M., Mukherjee, N.: Implementation of execution history in non-relational databases for feedback-guided job modeling. In: Proceedings of the CUBE International Information Technology Conference, pp. 476–482. ACM (2012)
4. Chodorow, K.: MongoDB: The Definitive Guide. O'Reilly, Sebastopol (2013)
5. Cooper, B.F., Silberstein, A., Tam, E., Ramakrishnan, R., Sears, R.: Benchmarking cloud serving systems with YCSB. In: Proceedings of the 1st ACM Symposium on Cloud Computing, pp. 143–154. ACM (2010)
6. Dimiduk, N., Khurana, A., Ryan, M.H.: HBase in Action. Manning, Shelter Island (2013)
7. George, L.: HBase: The Definitive Guide. O'Reilly Media Inc., Sebastopol (2011)
8. Grassi, V., Sindico, A.: Towards model driven design of service-based context-aware applications. In: International Workshop on Engineering of Software Services for Pervasive Environments: in Conjunction with the 6th ESEC/FSE Joint Meeting, pp. 69–74. ACM (2007)
9. Han, J., Haihong, E., Le, G., Du, J.: Survey on NoSQL database. In: 2011 6th International Conference on Pervasive Computing and Applications (ICPCA), pp. 363–366. IEEE (2011)
10. Ibrahim, N.: Specification, composition and provision of trustworthy context-dependent services. Technical report, Concordia University (2012)

11. Keith, J.: Building a contextaware service architecture. http://www.ibm.com/developerworks/architecture/library/ar-conawserv/index.html
12. Sheng, Q.Z., Benatallah, B.: ContextUML: a UML-based modeling language for model-driven development of context-aware web services. In: International Conference on Mobile Business, 2005, ICMB 2005, pp. 206–212. IEEE (2005)
13. Treiber, M., Kritikos, K., Schall, D., Dustdar, S., Plexousakis, D.: Modeling context-aware and socially-enriched mashups. In: Proceedings of the 3rd and 4th International Workshop on Web APIs and Services Mashups, p. 2. ACM (2010)
14. Tweed, R., James, G.: A universal NoSQL engine, using a tried and tested technology (2010)
15. Wan, K.: Lucx: lucid enriched with context. Ph.D. thesis, Concordia University (2006)

Drought Monitoring: A Performance Investigation of Three Machine Learning Techniques

Pheeha Machaka[(⊠)]

School of Computing, University of South Africa, Science Campus,
Florida Park, Johannesburg 1709, South Africa
machap@unisa.ac.za

Abstract. This paper investigates the use of Soft Computing techniques on a drought monitoring case study. This is in effort to create an intelligent middleware for Ubiquitous Sensor Networks (USN) using machine learning techniques. Algorithms in Artificial Immune System, Neural Networks and Bayesian Networks were used. The paper reveals the results from an experiment on data collected over 95 years in the Trompsburg region of the Free State Province, South Africa.

Keywords: Machine learning · Algorithms · Neural networks · Artificial immune systems · NaiveBayes · Standard precipitation index

1 Introduction

Drought is a natural, environmental disaster that can be classified together with earthquakes, epidemics and floods. It has substantial impact on humans and its impact can persist for several years. A current example of an extreme drought case is that of East Africa. East Africa has experienced its worst drought in 60 years, affecting more than 11 million people. It was declared as a famine-stricken region, with overcrowded refugee camps in Kenya and Ethiopia. Livestock is dying at a rapid rate, with one farmer reporting have lost 17 goats in one day. Officials also warn that over 800 000 children could die from malnutrition across East Africa nations of Somalia, Ethiopia, Eritrea and Kenya.

Given the impacts of drought, there is a need for developing strategies for drought monitoring and early warning systems that are able to determine drought severity. These systems can help in planning and managing water resources, and can help reduce and avoid impacts of drought.

As part of our drought monitoring research study in our research group, Masinde and Bagula in [14] proposed a drought prediction framework that combines mobile phones and wireless sensor networks to be able to capture and relay micro drought parameters. The framework is an enhancement of ITU's Ubiquitous Sensor Network (USN) Layers. Ubiquitous Sensor Networks are described in [9] as networks of intelligent sensor nodes that could be deployed anywhere, anytime, by anyone and anything. The framework is further described as composing 5 layers: **Sensor**

P.C. Vinh et al. (Eds.): ICCASA 2013, LNICST 128, pp. 47–56, 2014.
DOI: 10.1007/978-3-319-05939-6_5, © Springer International Publishing Switzerland 2014

Networking, USN Access Network, Network Infrastructure, USN Middleware, and USN Applications Platform.

Our focus in this research study is on the 4th layer, the USN Middleware. This is composed of intelligent software that will help with drought monitoring and prediction. In this study we investigate available drought monitoring tools, and look into the use of learning algorithms in drought forecasting. Three learning algorithms, viz. Artificial Immune Systems, Bayesian Networks and Artificial Neural Networks, are studied and their performance on a South African precipitation dataset is compared.

2 Background and Related Work

2.1 Drought Indices

Research in previous years has developed indices that measure drought. These indices can be used in early warning and drought monitoring systems. These indices are very important in measuring the drought severity, intensity, duration, coverage and magnitude. Mishra and Singh in [18] made great attempts to make comparisons and find out which of the drought indices are most suitable for drought monitoring. In their research they listed the relevant indices and evaluated them according to regions were the indices are used; the type of drought being monitored; how indices are used; advantages and disadvantages; and the overall general usefulness.

The comparison between SPI (Standard Precipitation Index) and PDSI (Palmer Drought Severity Index) came out with the following results:

1. "SPI is more representative of short-term precipitation than PDSI and thus is a better indicator for soil moisture variation and soil wetness" [20].
2. "SPI provides a better spatial standardization than does PDSI with respect to extreme drought events" [12].
3. It was found that the SPI was a valuable estimator for drought severity [18].
4. SPI detects the onset of a drought earlier than PDSI [7].

Based on this, it can be inferred that the SPI is a better monitoring tool to use. We will therefore focus on the SPI for the remainder of this case study.

2.2 Algorithms

There are various algorithms that exist with different variations for the three chosen methods. The algorithms that were used for this paper's experiments, were those found in the WEKA libraries [21].

- **Artificial Neural Networks.** ANN's are mathematical or computational models that get their inspiration from biological neural systems. In this paper the neural network model, Multilayer Perceptron (MLP) was used to conduct experiments. The MLP is a feed forward neural network model in which vertices are arranged in layers. MLP have one or more layer(s) of hidden nodes, which are not directly connected to the input and output nodes [5]. For the purpose of this experiment we employed Weka's Multilayer Perceptron implementation.

- **Bayesian Networks.** Bayesian Networks can be described briefly as Acyclic Directed Graph (DAG) which defines a factorisation of a joint probability distribution over the variables that are represented by the nodes of the DAG, where the factorisation is given by the direct links of the DAG [11]. The NaiveBayes algorithm was used for the experiments. It makes a strong assumption that all attributes of the examples are independent of each other given the context of the class. The Weka's NaiveBayes implements this probabilistic Naïve Bayes classifier [23].
- **Artificial Immune Systems.** The AIS takes inspiration from the robust and powerful capabilities of the Human Immune System's (HIS) capabilities to distinguish between self and non-self [13]. The Algorithm employed in this paper's experiments is the Weka's Artificial Immune Recognition System (AIRS) learning algorithm [22]. The AIRS is a supervised AIS learning algorithm that has shown significant success on a broad range of classification problems [3, 6, 13].

2.3   Related Work

There has been creditable work done to predict weather condition using Bayesian Networks, and in [10] they were applied to the problem of predicting sea breeze. Bayesian Networks were then compared with existing rule-based system and it was found out that the Bayesian network outperformed the traditional rule-based system in prediction accuracy.

Authors in [2] introduce a Bayesian Network framework that deals with multivariate spatiality distributed time series. They used it to predict precipitation for 100 stations in the North basin of the Iberian Peninsula during winter of 1999. In [4], Bayesian networks are used to estimate forecasts of peak and average temperatures. In this case study, data derived from a power utility system is used to forecast electric load with imperfect information.

Considerable weather forecast work has focused on the use of Artificial Neural Networks (ANN) and Bayesian Networks, but only a few use artificial immune systems for weather forecasting. Authors in [23] implemented an immune-based algorithm that was applied on weather data for forecasting. The immune algorithm was compared to an artificial neural network algorithm and the results reveal that the implemented immune algorithm had a higher forecast accuracy rate than that of the neural network.

There has also been great work done in the field of using artificial neural networks in drought monitoring. Antonic et al. [1] used feed-forward ANN with Multilayer Perceptron (MLP) for empirical model development using seven climatic variables (monthly mean air temperature, monthly mean daily minimum and maximum air temperature, monthly mean relative humidity, monthly precipitation, monthly mean global solar irradiation and monthly potential evapotranspiration).

Authors in [17] used a record of SPI time series data and linear stochastic models, recursive multistep neural networks (RMSNN) for drought forecasting in the Kangsabati river basin, which lies in the Purulia district of West Bengal, India. In their comparison they found neural networks to be more suitable for drought forecasting. Sajikumar [19] used a Temporal Back-Propagation Neural Network (TBP-NN) for monthly rainfall-runoff modeling in scarce data conditions.

In this study, we would like to investigate the performance of the three learning algorithms in the aim to answer the following questions:

- Which method performs better?
- How do the methods perform across different SPI time scales?
- What kind of mined data is extracted using the methods?

3   Research Design

The section that follows will describe the methods and techniques used to carry out the research presented in this paper.

3.1   Drought Monitoring Region and Data Collection

The region of monitoring is Trompsburg, Free State, South Africa. Trompsburg is a small town located in the southern Free State. It is in the ecotone between Nama-Karoo and the grassland biome. The main land use in the region is livestock farming, especially sheep and cattle farming. Monthly precipitation data was collected from this region by the South African Weather Services for the period January 1913 to May 2009; making a total of 96 years of observations.

3.2   Algorithms Performance Evaluation

To measure performance of the algorithms, the following accuracy measures were used:

- **True Positive Rate.** This refers to the function of true positives out of the positives.
- **False Positive Rate.** This refers to the function of false positives out of the positives.
- **Kappa Statistic.** This is used to measure the success of a predictor, the agreement between predicted and observed categorisation of a dataset, while correcting for agreement that occurs by chance [23].
- **F-Measure.** There is a trade-off between Precision and Recall measures. When one tries to improve the first measure, there is often deterioration in the second measure. The F-measure provides a harmonic mean precision and recall.

3.3   Test Cases

In the literature reviewed above, it was found out that there are four different types of drought: meteorological, hydrological, agricultural, and socio-economic droughts.

Using Standard Precipitation Index (SPI) allows for monitoring the different types of drought, by using different time scales [8, 15–18].

This case study will focus on the following time scales: SPI 3 months, SPI 6 months, SPI 12 months and SPI 24 months for the Trompsburg region.

3.4   Experiment Design

Precipitation data was used for the Trompsburg region. We had to transform and calculate the data into precipitation data in such a way that we can create training and testing dataset. The steps taken for completing the experiments in this study are shown below by Fig. 1.

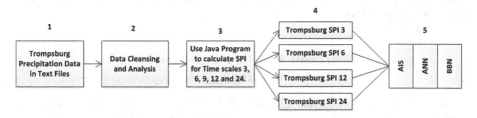

Fig. 1. Trompsburg experiment

1. The data is prepared into text files for further processing.
2. Data cleansing and Analysis: Data is checked for any missing data. If there is missing data, the average precipitation is used.
3. A Java program is designed for calculating the monthly SPI when given time-scale inputs and monthly precipitation data. This program can be found and downloaded from (http://greenleaf.unl.edu/downloads/).
4. The files are output produced by the Java Program for time scales 3, 6, 12 and 24.
5. The data is then used by the Weka program to test performance measures using the AIS, ANN and BNN algorithms. A 10-fold cross validation technique was used, and for each of the four test cases, the experiments were iterated 10 times. The mean algorithm performance measures of each experiment's iteration were recorded and used for statistical comparisons.

The results for the Trompsburg drought experiment follows in the section below. In the evaluation the t-test statistics are used.

4   Results and Discussion

The results of the research are discussed below and algorithms are assessed based on the following algorithm performance measures: Kappa Statistic, True Positive Rate, False Positive Rate and F-measure.

4.1　True Positive Rate Performance

The MLP had an average true positive rate of 68.58 %, while the NaiveBayes' was slightly lower at 68.75 %. The AIRS2 had an even lower average true positive rate performance of 55.47 %.

For the test:

$$\text{True Positive Rate: } H_0: \mu_{MLP} - \mu_{NaiveBayes} = 0$$
$$\text{True Positive Rate: } H_1: \mu_{MLP} - \mu_{NaiveBayes} \neq 0$$
$$(1)$$

In Table 1, the value of the t-Statistic is -2.5572 and its two-tailed p-value is 0.0109. At the 5 % confidence level, the test is significant and there is strong evidence to infer that the alternative hypothesis is true. Therefore we reject the null hypothesis and conclude that there is a difference in the mean true positive rate for the MLP and NaiveBayes algorithms.

For the test:

$$\text{True Positive Rate: } H_0: \mu_{MLP} - \mu_{AIRS2} = 0$$
$$\text{True Positive Rate: } H_1: \mu_{MLP} - \mu_{AIRS2} \neq 0$$
$$(2)$$

In Table 1, the value of the t-Statistic is 60.5019 and its two-tailed p-value is 0.0000. At the 5 % confidence level, the test is significant and there is overwhelming evidence to infer that the alternative hypothesis is true. Therefore we reject the null hypothesis and conclude that there is a difference in mean true positive rate for the MLP and AIRS2 algorithms.

4.2　False Positive Performance

The average false positive rate for the MLP was 68.21 % across all SPI test cases, while that of the NaiveBayes was slightly lower at 68.61 %. The AIRS2 had an impressive lower average false positive rate performance of 54.82 %.

For the test:

$$\text{False Positive Rate: } H_0: \mu_{MLP} - \mu_{NaiveBayes} = 0$$
$$\text{False Positive Rate: } H_1: \mu_{MLP} - \mu_{NaiveBayes} \neq 0$$
$$(3)$$

Table 1. Results for true positive rate t-test for paired two samples for means

t-Test: Paired Two Sample for Means					
	Multilayer Perceptron	NaiveBayes		Multilayer Perceptron	AIRS2
Mean	0.6859	0.6878	Mean	0.6859	0.5548
Variance	0.0003	0.0002	Variance	0.0003	0.0015
Observations	400	400	Observations	400	400
Hypothesized Mean Difference	0		Hypothesized Mean Difference	0	
t Stat	-2.5572		t Stat	60.5019	
P(T<=t) two-tail	0.0109		P(T<=t) two-tail	0.0000	

Table 2. Results for false positive rate t-test for paired two samples for means

t-Test: Paired Two Sample for Means	Multilayer Perceptron	NaiveBayes		Multilayer Perceptron	AIRS2
Mean	0.6821	0.6862	Mean	0.6821	0.5482
Variance	0.0006	0.0004	Variance	0.0006	0.0026
Observations	400	400	Observations	400	400
Hypothesized Mean Difference	0		Hypothesized Mean Difference	0	
t Stat	-4.0369		t Stat	50.5275	
P(T<=t) two-tail	0.0001		P(T<=t) two-tail	0.0000	

In Table 2, the value of the t-Statistic is -4.0369 and its two-tailed p-value is 0.0001. At the 5 % confidence level, the test is significant and there is overwhelming evidence to infer that the alternative hypothesis is true. Therefore we reject the null hypothesis and conclude that there is a difference in the mean false positive rate for the MLP and NaiveBayes algorithms.

For the test:

$$\text{False Positive Rate: } H_0: \mu_{MLP} - \mu_{AIRS2} = 0$$
$$\text{False Positive Rate: } H_1: \mu_{MLP} - \mu_{AIRS2} \neq 0 \tag{4}$$

In Table 2, the value of the t-Statistic is 50.5275 and its two-tailed p-value is 0.0000. At the 5 % confidence level, the test is significant and there is overwhelming evidence to infer that the alternative hypothesis is true. Therefore we reject the null hypothesis and conclude that there is a difference in mean false positive rate for the MLP and AIRS2 algorithms.

4.3 Kappa Statistic Performance

Across all SPI test cases, the MLP had an average Kappa statistic of 0.51 %, while that of the NaiveBayes was 0.27 %. The AIRS2 had an average kappa statistic of 0.67 %.

For the test:

$$\text{Kappa Statistic: } H_0: \mu_{MLP} - \mu_{NaiveBayes} = 0$$
$$\text{Kappa Statistic: } H_1: \mu_{MLP} - \mu_{NaiveBayes} \neq 0 \tag{5}$$

In Table 3, the value of the t-Statistic is 1.865 and its two-tailed p-value is 0.0628. At the 5 % confidence level, the test is not statistically significant and there is weak evidence to infer that the alternative hypothesis is true. Therefore we do not reject the null hypothesis and conclude that the difference in the mean Kappa statistic for the MLP and NaiveBayes algorithms equals zero, the hypothesised mean.

Table 3. Results for Kappa statistic t-test for paired two samples for means

t-Test: Paired Two Sample for Means	Multilayer Perceptron	NaiveBayes		Multilayer Perceptron	AIRS2
Mean	0.0052	0.0028	Mean	0.0052	0.0068
Variance	0.0006	0.0004	Variance	0.0006	0.0033
Observations	400	400	Observations	400	400
Hypothesized Mean Difference	0		Hypothesized Mean Difference	0	
t Stat	1.8658		t Stat	-0.5169	
P(T<=t) two-tail	0.0628		P(T<=t) two-tail	0.6055	

For the test:

$$\text{Kappa Statistic: } H_0: \mu_{MLP} - \mu_{AIRS2} = 0$$
$$\text{Kappa Statistic: } H_1: \mu_{MLP} - \mu_{AIRS2} \neq 0 \tag{6}$$

In Table 3, the value of the t-Statistic is -0.5169 and its two-tailed p-value is 0.6055. At the 5 % confidence level, the test is not statistically significant and there is little to no evidence to infer that the alternative hypothesis is true. Therefore we do not reject the null hypothesis and conclude that the difference in mean Kappa statistic for the MLP and AIRS2 algorithms equals zero, the hypothesised mean.

4.4 F-Measure Performance

The MLP had an average SPI F-measure performance of 56.86 %, and that of the NaiveBayes was slightly lower at 56.79 %. The AIRS2 algorithm had a lower average SPI F-measure performance of 52.53 %.

For the test:

$$\text{F-Measure: } H_0: \mu_{MLP} - \mu_{NaiveBayes} = 0$$
$$\text{F-Measure: } H_1: \mu_{MLP} - \mu_{NaiveBayes} \neq 0 \tag{7}$$

In Table 4, the value of the t-Statistic is 1.4567 and its two-tailed p-value is 0.1467. At the 5 % confidence level, the test is not statistically significant and there is

Table 4. Results for F-measure t-test for paired two samples for means

t-Test: Paired Two Sample for Means	Multilayer Perceptron	NaiveBayes		Multilayer Perceptron	AIRS2
Mean	0.5686	0.5679	Mean	0.5686	0.5254
Variance	0.0003	0.0002	Variance	0.0003	0.0009
Observations	400	400	Observations	400	400
Hypothesized Mean Difference	0		Hypothesized Mean Difference	0	
t Stat	1.4567		t Stat	28.6235	
P(T<=t) two-tail	0.1460		P(T<=t) two-tail	0.0000	

little or no evidence to infer that the alternative hypothesis is true. Therefore we do not reject the null hypothesis and conclude that the difference in the mean recall for the MLP and NaiveBayes algorithms equals zero, the hypothesised mean.

For the test:

$$\text{F-Measure: } H_0: \mu_{MLP} - \mu_{AIRS2} = 0$$
$$\text{F-Measure: } H_1: \mu_{MLP} - \mu_{AIRS2} \neq 0$$

(8)

In Table 4, the value of the t-Statistic is 28.6235 and its two-tailed p-value is 0.0000. At the 5 % confidence level, the test is significant and there is overwhelming evidence to infer that the alternative hypothesis is true. Therefore we reject the null hypothesis and conclude that there is a difference in mean recall for the MLP and AIRS2 algorithms.

5 Conclusions

The statistical experiments conducted above for algorithm performance measures indicate that the mean Kappa statistic for the MLP, NaiveBayes and AIRS2 algorithms were statistically similar. The mean F-measure for the MLP and NaiveBayes were also statistically similar.

Overall, across all performance measures, one can then safely conclude that there was a significant difference in mean algorithm performance measures for the MLP, NaiveBayes and AIRS2 algorithms. The MLP had a better performance than the NaiveBayes and the AIRS2 algorithms. If applied to the drought case study, the MLP will produce better results. The average rate for most performance measures was below 65 % and in some cases, 15 %. But when one carefully examines the results, one finds out that the three algorithms had a mediocre to poor classification performance.

References

1. Antonic, O., Krizan, J., Marki, A., Bukovec, D.: Spatio-temporal interpolation of climatic variables over large region of complex terrain using neural networks. Ecol. Modelling **138**, 255–263 (2001)
2. Antonio, S.C., Rafael, C., Carmen, S., Jose, M.G.: Bayesian networks for probabilistic weather prediction. In: Anonymous, pp. 695–700 (2002)
3. Dasgupta, D., Gonzales, F.: An immunity-based technique to characterize intrusions in computer networks. IEEE Trans. Evol. Comput. **6**, 281–291 (2002)
4. Douglas, A.P., Breilphol, A.M., Lee, F.N., Adapa, R.: The impacts of temperature forecast uncertainty on Bayesian load forecasting. IEEE Trans. Power Syst. **13**, 1507–1513 (1998)
5. Dunne, R.A.: A Statistical Approach to Neural Network for Pattern Recognition. Wiley-Interscience, New York (2007)
6. Forrest, S., Hofmeyer, S.A., Somayaji, A., Longstaff, T.A.: A sense of self for Unix processes. In: Proceedings of the 1996 IEEE Symposium on Security and Privacy, pp. 120–128. Anonymous (1996)

7. Hayes, M.J.: Monitoring the 1996 drought using the standardized precipitation index. Bull. Am. Meteorol. Soc. **80**, 429 (1999)
8. Hughes, B.L., Saunders, M.A.: A drought climatology for Europe. Int. J. Climatol **22**, 1571–1592 (2002)
9. Jin, H., Jiang, W. (eds.): Handbook of Research on Developments and Trends in Wireless Sensor Networks: From Principle to Practice. Information Science Reference (IGI Global), Hershey (2010)
10. Kennett, R.J., Korb, K.B., Nicholson, A.E.: Seabreeze prediction using Bayesian networks. In: Cheung, D., Williams, G.J., Li, Q. (eds.) PAKDD 2001. LNCS (LNAI), vol. 2035, pp. 148–153. Springer, Heidelberg (2001)
11. Kjaerulff, U.B., Madsen, A.L.: Bayesian Networks and Influence Diagrams: A Guide to Construction and Analysis, 1st edn. Springer, New York (2007)
12. Lloyd-hughes, B., Saunders, M.A.: A drought climatology for Europe. Int. J. Climatol. **22**, 1571–1592 (2002)
13. Luther, K., Bye, R., Alpcan, T., Muller, A., Albayrak, S.: A Cooperative AIS framework for intrusion detection. In: IEEE International Conference on Communications. ICC '07, pp. 1409–1416. Anonymous (2007)
14. Masinde, M., Bagula, A.: A framework for predicting droughts in developing countries using sensor networks and mobile phones. In: Anonymous, pp. 390–393 (2010)
15. McKee, T.B., Doesken, N.J., Kleist, J.: The relationship of drought frequency and duration to time scales. In Proceedings of the 8th Conference of Applied Climatology, 17–22 January 1993
16. McKee, T.B., Doesken, N.J., Kleist, J.: Drought monitoring with multiple time scales. In: 9th AMS Conference on Applied Climatology, pp. 233–236 (1995)
17. Mishra, A.K., Desai, V.R.: Drought forecasting using feed-forward recursive neural network. Ecol. Modelling **198**, 127–138 (2006)
18. Mishra, A.K., Singh, V.P.: A review of drought concepts. J. Hydrol. **391**, 202–216 (2010)
19. Sajikumar, N.: A non-linear rainfall-runoff model using an artificial neural network. J. Hydrol. **216**, 32–35 (1999)
20. Sims, A.P.: Adopting drought indices for estimating soil moisture: a North Carolina case study. Geophys. Res. Lett. **29**, 1183 (2002)
21. Watkins, A., Timmis, J., Boggess, L.: Artificial immune recognition system (AIRS): an immune-inspired supervised learning algorithm. Genet. Program. Evol. Mach. **5**, 291–317 (2004)
22. Witten, I.H., Frank, E.: Data Mining: Practical Machine Learning Tools and Techniques. Morgan Kaufmann Series in Data Management Systems, 2nd edn. Morgan Kaufmann, San Francisco (2005)
23. Xu, C., Li, T., Huang, X., Jiang, Y.: A weather forecast system based on artificial immune system. In: Wang, L., Chen, K., Ong, Y.S. (eds.) ICNC 2005. LNCS, vol. 3611, pp. 800–803. Springer, Heidelberg (2005)

Inbooki: Context-Aware Adaptive E-Books

Daniele Grassi[1], Anas Bouhtouch[1], and Giacomo Cabri[2(✉)]

[1] DM Digital, Modena, Italy
{grassi,anas}@dmdigital.it
[2] Università di Modena e Reggio Emilia, Modena, Italy
giacomo.cabri@unimore.it

Abstract. Traditional e-books are more and more exploited by readers, thanks to the chance of reading them on different devices and to the capability of storing a whole library of books in a light and portable device. However, they are still very rigid and do not adapt to the context of the readers. In this paper we propose a system for writing and reading enhanced e-books that are able to *adapt* to the context where they are read and to the user's choices during the reading. Our approach take advantage of the possibilities offered by today's devices, like context-awareness and user interaction. Past proposals are limited to a specific field or did not consider a wide range of external conditions and interactions, providing a very limited adaptation.

Keywords: Context-dependency · E-book

1 Introduction

E-books can be considered as both an evolution of classic paper books and a revolution in the way contents are delivered and read [6]; they are becoming part of our life. Although e-books cannot completely replace conventional books [7] in a very near future, and their spread must face some challenges [9,13], the trend seems to be unfolding in this direction [5,12].

Today's e-books have several *advantages* over conventional books; for example: they can be read using different devices and technologies, letting people choose the preferred one; their visualization can be adapted to the devices' features or to readers' necessities; a single device can store a great number of books, relieving people from the need of carrying heavy books (or a heavy set of books).

Nevertheless, available e-books mainly consist of an electronic version of their paper edition. In our opinion, this leads to a main drawback: they do not take advantage of the possibilities offered by today's devices, such as the information received from *sensors* (light, temperature, orientation, position, etc.), from external *services* (weather, near places, news of the day, etc.), or from the *user's profile and history* (age, sex, previous readings, etc.). As a consequence, today's e-books cannot adapt their content to the context in which they are read, or to the specific user who is reading them.

P.C. Vinh et al. (Eds.): ICCASA 2013, LNICST 128, pp. 57–66, 2014.
DOI: 10.1007/978-3-319-05939-6_6, © Springer International Publishing Switzerland 2014

The contribution of this paper lies in proposing a system to develop and read *adaptive* e-books. Our concept of adaptive e-book is realized by means of *context-awareness* that is provided to the e-book. Differently from previous approaches, the proposed one aims at being more general and at considering many sources of information. The proposed system, Inbooki, enables writers to structure their book taking into consideration different aspects of the context where readers will actually read the e-book. The produced e-books are called *immersive*-books (shortly *in-books*), suggesting that the readers are "immersed" *in* the context where they read the e-books.

2   Related Work

According to [2], existing systems related to our work can be classified as:

- Location-aware systems, which exploit only a part of the context;
- Context-aware systems, which fully exploit all the context information;
- Context-aware frameworks, which provide an abstract framework for specific context-aware applications.

As said, there are some systems that exploit information about the location (location-awareness) to display customized information to users [3,8,11]. Examples of location-aware systems are e-guides for tourists, as the Cyberguide project [1], which aims at building a mobile context-aware tour guide. The implemented system considered several context parameters to adapt the tour to the reader in a form similar to an e-book. However, this project is mostly focused on geographic information related to the tour, and it cannot be exploited for a general-purpose context-dependent book content.

A few examples of context-aware system are reported in the literature. For instance, Muñoz et al. [10] propose a context-aware system for hospitals that take into consideration several context parameters (not only the user's location) such as patient turnaround time, the location of other users, devices or artifacts, and the user's role. This is an interesting approach but strictly oriented to a specific field.

To summarize, the approaches we can find in the literature suffer of being very bound to a specific field or of exploiting little context information. Our aim is to propose a more general approach that considers a wider range of information available.

3   In-Books

3.1   Context Model

The context of the reading is modeled around three sets of parameters: *environment* parameters, *profile* parameters, *reading* parameters.

Environment parameters are the set of external conditions surrounding the user while reading an in-book. Currently, the in-book structure supports GPS

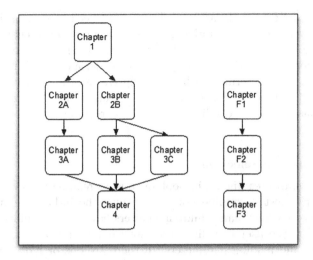

Fig. 1. Example of in-book graphs

localization, weather, air temperature, season and time of the day. Weather and air temperature are determined using third-party web services and GPS location. *Profile* parameters contain the essential data about the user's profile: gender and age. The user sets these parameters during the registration process, and they can be modified in the reader apps. *Reading* parameters contain the "history" of the user's reading process for a given in-book: chapters read, reading conditions' status while reading each chapter, progress.

All these context parameters are used by the Inbooki mobile app[1] to determine which content to show the reader, as explained in the following.

3.2 In-Book's Structure

An *in-book* is an e-book composed of one or more graphs of chapters. Figure 1 reports examples of an in-book graph. Each chapter can have one or more parents and one or more children, and it is composed of an ordered series of blocks. Each block has a specific type ("title", "text", "image") and it can count on one or more variations, depending on the reading conditions. Variations can be grouped in 2 sets: *narrative* and *descriptive*.

Since an in-book is a graph, each chapter can have more than one child: narrative variations occur when the user completes the reading of a chapter and the Inbooki mobile app determines (using the user's reading conditions) which child chapter to show next among the possibilities. If the reading conditions meet the requirements of more than one chapter, a choice is presented to the user (a *fork*). If there is only one child chapter and its display conditions are not met, the user is forced to wait (or to take action) until they are met (e.g. the user can be

---

[1] This is the app to read in-books, see 4.4.

required to go to a specific location, or he can be forced to wait until a specific time of the day comes). Descriptive variations occur inside a chapter's block. Each block can have one or more variations, each one of them having different display conditions. When the reader app has to render a chapter's text, it parses its whole content and determines which descriptive variations have their display conditions satisfied by the current user's reading conditions; if, for a given block, no variation has its display conditions met by the reading conditions, the whole block is not rendered.

3.3 Next Chapter Selection

When the user starts reading an in-book or finishes reading a previous chapter, the reader apps must determine how to continue the in-book rendering. The first step is to count how many children chapters have their visibility conditions fully satisfied by the user's reading conditions (environment parameters, profile parameters and reading parameters): if there are one or more results, they will be added to the possible following chapters set; if there are no results, the reader app tries to find the children chapters that have their profile and reading parameters satisfied: if there are one or more results, they are added to the possible following chapters set; if not, a virtual "book-end" chapter is added to the possible following chapters set. At this point the possible following chapters set consists of one or more chapters. A query is made to obtain free chapters that have their reading conditions satisfied, and the results are added to the possible following chapters set. The possible following chapters set is then analysed: if it consists of two or more chapters, a fork is displayed to the user, who can choose which path to follow. At this point, only one chapter is chosen for rendering. If it is a virtual "book-end" chapter, the book ends. If it is a real chapter, this is further analysed to determine whether its reading conditions are fully satisfied or not: if one or more parameters are not met yet, a "waiting screen" is shown to the user, who will have to wait in order to continue until the reading conditions are met; if the reading conditions are met, the chapter is rendered.

4   Inbooki's Architecture

The architecture powering Inbooki is composed of four subsystems, sketched in the following subsections but not detailed due to space limitation.

4.1 The Inbooki Platform

The platform is the *core* subsystem of Inbooki, providing a substrate which is used by the other subsystems to interact using a private API framework. There are two main API components: *AccountAPI*, which provides access to account utilities such as user registration, login, purchased books listing, account management, etc.; and *MarketAPI*, which provides an interface to the marketplace, including functions like in-book download, in-books information retrieval, marketplace search, etc. API security is ensured by a proprietary OAuth 2.0 implementation, written in PHP.

4.2   The Web Interface

This subsystem comprises a web interface to the marketplace and to account registration and management utilities. The main endpoint for the web interface is the Inbooki website (http://www.inbooki.com), which was developed using HTML, PHP and Javascript using a Bootstrap template.

4.3   The Inbooki Editor

The Inbooki Editor plays an important role in the Inbooki architecture: it provides the authors with a user-friendly web application that allows them to write in-books in an easy-to-use yet complete environment. Using the editor, the authors can add *immersive* and *interactive* features to their in-books using a graphic interface. A built-in compiler gives the authors the possibility of creating deployable in-books that can be read on mobile devices running the Inbooki app for iOS or Android.

Using the editor authors can submit their in-books to the marketplace. The editor is written in PHP, HTML and Javascript, using additional libraries as jQuery to enhance the user experience.

Snapshots of the web interface will be shown in Sect. 5.

4.4   Mobile Apps for iOS and Android Devices

An in-book contains several immersive and interactive features that are not supported by current e-books standards like ePub, mobi, etc. This is the reason why conventional e-book readers cannot display an in-book. iOS and Android Inbooki apps fill this gap, providing a reading experience that is extremely similar to the one provided by classic e-book readers (e.g. the user swipes to go to the next page), while introducing immersive and interactive features that allow the readers to fully enjoy the possibilities offered by the in-books.

The Inbooki apps give the reader the possibility of downloading the available in-books and automatically syncing the reading progress on all their devices (e.g. a given reader can use the same Inbooki account on an iPhone and on an Android device).

The immersive variations to the in-book's text–such as variations determined by weather conditions, time of the day, day of the year, user profile, etc.–are automatically processed during the reading, and each chapter is compiled on the fly using the conditions set by the author and determined by the reader's environment: the story itself, or single paragraphs, can thus change according to these conditions.

The Inbooki apps rely mainly on GPS localization to detect the reader's environment and to define the context: the data received is used to interact with external services to retrieve weather conditions and temperature, as well as to determine the "visibility" of geolocation-conditioned chapters (chapters that can be read only if the reader is within a certain distance from a specific geographical point).

The user's reading "history" is recorded and can be used by the authors while writing the in-book to determine story variations according to the path followed by each reader: for example, the story can change according to the path the reader chose in earlier chapters.

In-books also present interactive features: the author can design *forks* along the story where the reader is actually asked to make a decision. When the reader encounters a fork, the mobile app shows them the list of possible decisions and then calculates the following chapter according to this choice.

5 Example of Use and Impact

In this section we show how the Inbooki system can be exploited to write and to read in-books. We provide also an overview of possible applications.

5.1 Developing an In-Book

To develop an in-book, the writer must first fill in the text of the chapters (see Fig. 2) as in a traditional editor.

The chapters have a customizable display order in the editor (see Fig. 3 left) which doesn't necessarily correspond to the narrative order that is seen by the readers. For instance, the chapter "Scegli di confidarti" is a sibling of "Rispondi che non te lo ricordi": they both follow "Colazione in famiglia" (the reader is shown one of them depending on his context), but they continue in different narrative threads.

This leads to a non-linear chapters graph (see Fig. 3 right); using the editor the writer can keep under control the structure of the in-book.

Fig. 2. Inbooki chapter text

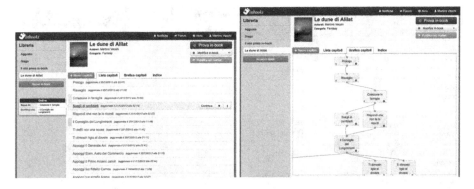

Fig. 3. Inbooki chapters (left) and graph (right)

Fig. 4. Inbooki chapter conditions

Furthermore, different conditions can be associated to each chapter. Figure 4 shows a dialog in which the following conditions can be defined: time of the day; weather conditions; age of the reader; external temperature; season; gender of the reader; location. Advanced conditions can be specified as well.

Inbooki has the capability of setting geolocalization conditions for a chapter: the writer can decide where in the world a given chapter can be read or, form the point of view of chapters, which ones will be triggered by a reader's given location.

5.2 Enjoying an In-Book on Devices

We are aware that it is impossible to provide readers with the true experience of an in-book, since it is very dynamic, anyway in this section we sketch how the readers can enjoy the in-book using a mobile device (in this case, an Apple iPhone). As it can be seen from Fig. 5 left, the reading of in-books is very similar to the reading of standard e-books.

One of the specific enhancements offered by in-books is the possibility to set some parameters before starting the reading; Fig. 5 center reports the reader's choice of gender, age, weather conditions, hour of the day, season, and temperature. The values of all these parameters can be defined in an automatic way: they can be retrieved from sensors, from (web) services, or from the user's profile.

Fig. 5. App interface: reading interface with menu (left), user's profile (center), Reader's choice (right)

In Fig. 5 right we show a distinctive feature of in-books: facing a fork, the reader can choose which path to follow, which will lead to two different chapters, according to the structure of the in-book as defined by the writer.

5.3   Possible Applications

From a literary point of view, Inbooki introduces a new kind of e-book, in which stories can unfold in different directions depending on the user's choices and environment. An in-book could be seen as an enhanced version of the old game-books, quite popular in the '80s. Using the Inbooki Editor, the creation of an interactive and immersive e-book does not require any technical skills, and this represents an opportunity for authors to express their creativity without resorting to software developers to create their interactive e-books.

A practical example of use of Inbooki is found in the *guidebooks* field: currently, the creation of an interactive guidebook, able to use the reader's location to provide enhanced information, is restricted to who is willing and able to contract a software house and develop a dedicated mobile app. This means having to cope with the difficulties of deploying and distributing an app among different platforms (iOS, Android), and to depend on the software development team to provide the users with the updated content. Inbooki allows guidebook authors and editors to create their in-books using the Inbooki Editor and distribute them automatically to iOS and Android mobile devices, without needing any technical knowledge. The updating of the in-book content can be done using the Editor, and the release of new versions of the in-book is notified automatically to users, who can download it to their devices. In the guidebooks' field, an in-book can provide immersive and interactive e-books that can suggest to the user different tours and paths depending on the environment (e.g. the weather), on their personal interests (using forks) or their profile (gender and age). Using free chapters, specific content can be displayed depending on the location of the user and the environment conditions.

The concept of in-book can have a big impact on the e-book market, creating a niche for interactive and immersive stories and guidebooks. The supported features of the in-book can be easily further extended, thanks to its open structure which allows different types of blocks to compose a single chapter, and thanks to the flexible format of chapters' conditions. In the future, for example, video support could be introduced, or web-enhanced blocks could be defined to integrate web pages inside chapters.

Outside the literary field, Inbooki can be a useful tool to create simple context-aware applications without the need of any specific technical knowledge. A typical application could be the creation of business scenario tests, where MBA students have to make business decisions based on the information provided in the text. These business scenario tests could be easily developed by teachers using the Inbooki interface, making use of the "fork" features of in-books, or provided directly by authors or publishers.

6   Conclusion and Future Work

In this paper we have presented Inbooki, a system to develop adaptive e-books that take into consideration the context where they are read and which allow user interaction. We have sketched some of their uses, but we believe that many others could be possible.

An important aspect for the spread of e-books in general and *immersive* e-books in particular is the fact that people should be aware not only of the capabilities of this format, but also of the availability of these kinds of books [4]. Currently there are some in-books available, but a lot of advertisement is needed to have a good spread of this kind of formats.

Regarding future work, the system can be further extended to widen the set of sensors and context information that authors can use to define the in-books' behavior. In this direction, we are defining new reading conditions which will be available in the web editor in the next months. Interactivity can be enhanced enabling the readers to directly add content to the in-books, and encouraging the author-reader relationship adding specific communication tools to the Inbooki apps. User experience and usability will be improved by the implementation of specific user testing sessions. Non-alphabetic language support must be enhanced to make in-books available worldwide.

References

1. Abowd, G.D., Atkeson, C.G., Hong, J., Long, S., Kooper, R., Pinkerton, M.: Cyberguide: a mobile context-aware tour guide. Wirel. Netw. **3**, 421–433 (1997)
2. Baldauf, M., Dustdar, S., Rosenberg, F.: A survey on context-aware systems. Int. J. Ad Hoc Ubiquitous Comput. **2**, 263–277 (2007)

3. Burrell, J., Gay, G.K.: E-graffiti: evaluating real-world use of a context-aware system. Interact. Comput. **14**(4), 301–312 (2002)
4. Croft, R., Davis, C.: E-books revisited: surveying student e-book usage in a distributed learning academic library 6 years later. J. Libr. Adm. **50**(5–6), 543–569 (2010)
5. Duncan, R.: Ebooks and beyond: the challenge for public libraries. Australas. Public Libr. Inform. Serv. **23**(2), 44 (2010)
6. Živković, D.: The electronic book: evolution or revolution? Bilgi dünyasi **9**(1), 1–19 (2008)
7. Kang, Y.Y., Wang, M.J.J., Lin, R.: Usability evaluation of e-books. Displays **30**(2), 49–52 (2009)
8. Kerer, C., Dustdar, S., Jazayeri, M., Gomes, D., Szego, A., Burgos Caja, J.A.: Presence-aware infrastructure using web services and rfid technologies. In: Malenfant, J., Bjarte, M. (eds.) Object-Oriented Technology. ECOOP 2004 Workshop Reader (2004)
9. Lam, P., Lam, S.L., Lam, J., McNaught, C.: Usability and usefulness of ebooks on ppcs: how students' opinions vary over time. Australas. J. Educ. Technol. **25**(1), 30–44 (2009)
10. Munoz, M.A., Rodriguez, M., Favela, J., Martinez-Garcia, A.I., Gonzalez, V.M.: Context-aware mobile communication in hospitals. Computer **36**(9), 38–46 (2003)
11. Priyantha, N.B., Chakraborty, A., Balakrishnan, H.: The cricket location-support system. In: Proceedings of the 6th Annual International Conference on Mobile Computing and Networking, MobiCom '00, pp. 32–43. ACM, New York (2000)
12. Soules, A.: The shifting landscape of e-books. New Library World **110**(1/2), 7–21 (2009)
13. Woody, W.D., Daniel, D.B., Baker, C.A.: E-books or textbooks: students prefer textbooks. Comput. Educ. **55**(3), 945–948 (2010)

Resistance of Trust Management Systems Against Malicious Collectives

Miroslav Novotný and Filip Zavoral[⊠]

Faculty of Mathematics and Physics, Charles University in Prague,
118 00 Prague, Czech Republic
{novotny,zavoral}@ksi.mff.cuni.cz

Abstract. Malicious peers in Peer-to-peer networks can develop sophisticated strategies to bypass existing security mechanisms. The effectiveness of contemporary trust management systems is usually tested only against simple malicious strategies. In this paper, we propose a simulation framework for evaluation of resistance of trust management systems against different malicious strategies. We present results of five TMS that represent main contemporary approaches; the results indicate that most of the traditional trust managements are vulnerable to sophisticated malicious strategies.

Keywords: Trust management · Peer to peer networks

1 Introduction

One of the promising architectures of large-scale distributed systems is based on peer to peer architecture (P2P). However, providing proper protection to such systems is tricky. The P2P applications have to deal with treacherous peers that try to deliberately subvert their operation. The peers have to trust the remote party to work correctly. The process of getting this trust is, however, far from trivial.

Many trust management systems (TMS) have been developed to deal with treacherous peers in P2P networks. The main idea of these systems is sharing experience between honest peers and building reputations. Nevertheless, the group of cooperating malicious peers is often able to bypass their security mechanisms and cause a great deal of harm. The malicious collectives represent the main reasons why managing trust represents the biggest challenge in the current P2P networks.

In this paper, we investigate several TMSs and use the simple taxonomy to organize their major approaches. Using the simulation framework called P2PTrustSim we investigate different strategies used by malicious peers. Beside traditional strategies, we propose new, more sophisticated strategies and test them against five trust management systems. These systems have been chosen as the representatives of major approaches. Our goal was to verify the effectiveness of various TMSs under sophisticated malicious strategies. We have chosen five contemporary TMS: EigenTrust [1], PeerTrust [2], H-Trust [3], WTR [4], and BubbleTrust [5]. These TMS represent main contemporary approaches in Trust Management.

P.C. Vinh et al. (Eds.): ICCASA 2013, LNICST 128, pp. 67–76, 2014.
DOI: 10.1007/978-3-319-05939-6_7, © Springer International Publishing Switzerland 2014

2 Malicious Strategies and Evaluation Criteria

In order to facilitate comparison of different TMSs and their behaviour under different malicious strategies we created a simulation framework [6] called P2PTrustSim. We used FreePastry, a modular, open-source implementation of the Pastry [12], P2P structured overlay network. Above the FreePastry, we created the peer simulation layer which implements various peers' behaviour.

2.1 Malicious Strategies

Most of the TMSs work well against straightforward malicious activities. However, the malicious peers can develop strategies to maintain their malicious business. Each peer can operate individually but the biggest threat is the collusion of malicious peers working together.

2.1.1 Individual Malicious Strategies

These strategies do not involve the cooperation between malicious peers.

False Meta-data - Malicious peers can insert false, attractive information into the meta-data describing their bogus resources to increase the demands for them.

Camouflage - The malicious peers that are aware of the presence of the TMS can provide a few honest resources. There can be many variants of this strategy, differing in the ratio of honest and bogus services or the period between changing behaviour. In some literature, the variant of this strategy is called Traitors [7, 8–10].

2.1.2 Collective Malicious Strategies

Malicious peers have a significantly higher chance to succeed if they work in a cooperative manner; this is considered as the biggest treat for P2P applications [11].

Full Collusion - All members of a malicious collective provide bogus resources and create false positive recommendations to all other members of the collective.

Spies - The malicious collective is divided into two groups: spies and malicious. The spies provide honest services to earn a high reputation and simultaneously provide false positive recommendations to the malicious part of the collective.

2.1.3 Newly Proposed Malicious Strategies

We analyzed published TMSs and known malicious tactics carefully and we suggest three new collective malicious strategies. Each strategy is designed for a particular type of TMS and tries to exploit its specific weakness.

Evaluator Collusion - If the TMS assesses credibility of the feedback source according to the truthfulness of its previous feedback, malicious peers can try to trick the TMS by using the services from peers outside the collective and evaluating them correctly. This feedback increases the credibility of malicious peers as recommenders and gives more weight to their feedback towards other members of collective.

Evaluator Spies - This strategy is a combination of Evaluator Collusion and Spies. The spies implement three techniques to maintain a credibility as a feedback source: they provide honest service, they use resources outside the collective and evaluate them correctly, and they create positive recommendations towards other spies.

Malicious Spies - This slight modification of the previous strategy is based on the idea that spies do not require a high reputation as resource providers. They can provide bogus resources and generate negative recommendations between each other. These recommendations are still truthful and should increase their credibility.

2.2 Evaluation Criteria

Each transaction within the framework is categorized on both sides (provider and consumer). The categories distinguish the type of the peer (honest or malicious), on which side of the transaction the peer was (provider or consumer), and the result of the transaction. The ulterior transactions represent honest transactions which malicious peers have to perform to fix their reputation. If no provider is sufficiently trustful, the transaction is refused and counted as ConsumeRefused. The originated peer typically tries to pick different service and repeat the transaction.

Let us suppose that all the malicious peers cooperate within a malicious collective in the network and all transactions from honest peers are honest. Our primary goal is to evaluate the success of each malicious strategy in different TMSs. Therefore, we defined four criteria:

MaliciousSuccessRatio (MSR) is a ratio between bogus transactions provided by malicious peers in the network with TMS and in the network without TMS (DummyTrust). It reflects the contribution of the given TMS and it is defined by the following formula:

$$MaliciousSuccessRatio = \frac{TotalBogus_{withTMS}}{TotalBogus_{withoutTMS}}$$

BogusRatio (BR) is a ratio between bogus and all services consumed by the honest peers. It is defined by the following formula:

$$BogusRatio = \frac{100 * TotalBogus}{\sum ConsumeHonest + TotalBogus}$$

MaliciousCost (MC) monitors the load associated with a malicious strategy. It is a ratio between extra transactions performed by the malicious peers to trick the TMS and the bogus transactions in the network. These extra transactions include faked and ulterior transactions and represent additional overhead for malicious peers which they try to minimize. We defined it by the following formula:

$$MaliciousCost = \frac{TotalUlterior + TotalFaked/2}{TotalBogus}$$

This metric gives us an idea of how much computational power and network utilization is required for a given malicious strategy.

The last criterion is a **MaliciousBenefit (MB)**. It represents how much beneficial transactions the malicious peers have to perform to pass one malicious service. It is defined by the following formula:

$$MaliciousBenefit = \frac{TotalUlterior}{TotalBogus}$$

The value above 1 means that there is benefit from the malicious collective which is bigger than the damage caused by the collective.

3   Simulation Results

We focused on two problems: the effectiveness of the strategies and the reaction of the TMSs to changes in peers' behaviours. The first problem was studied in a network that contains 200 peers and 80 peers are malicious; 40 % of nodes in the network are malicious, which represents a very dangerous environment. The honest peers wake up every 10 min and use one service from the network. The malicious peers also wake up every 10 min and perform a given number of faked or ulterior transactions. We ran 56 different simulations (7 TMSs each with 8 strategies). Each of the simulations represents 24 h. The data is counted in the last hour of the simulations when the TMSs are stabilized. Each simulation was repeated 20 times and average values are taken. The variation of results is expressed in the form of a relative standard deviation (RSD). The size of the network was designed with regards to simulation possibilities of the FreePastry and the load produced by our simulation. The results of other series of tests with the different settings were almost identical.

We set similar parameters for all TMSs. The most important parameter is the history period which determines how long the peers remember the information about previous transactions. We set this parameter to 30 cycles (5 h, in order to have a history period appropriate to the total simulation time) in all TMSs. The EigenTrust is not able to work correctly without pre-trusted peers, so we had to set 10 % honest peers as pre-trusted. Therefore, the EigenTrust has an advantage over other TMSs. Also, the numbers of ulterior and faked transactions are the same for all malicious strategies which use them.

3.1   Representative TMSs

The first simulations were performed in the network without TMS (DummyTrust) and in the network with the simplest version of TMS (SimpleTrust). We focused on the number of bogus transactions; these values will be used as a base for calculation of MaliciousSuccessRatio for other TMSs. The results are shown in Table 1.

As expected, the False Meta-data is the only useful strategy in DummyTrust. Other malicious mechanisms are useless or even counterproductive. The strategies Malicious Individual, Full Collusion, Evaluator Collusion and Malicious Spies have

Table 1. Number of bogus transactions in DummyTrust and SimpleTrust.

Strategy	DummyTrust		SimpleTrust		
	TotalBogus	RSD (%)	TotalBogus	RSD	Diff.
Simple Malicious Individual	262.20	8.95	247.15	6.25	6
Malicious Individual	435.65	3.05	387.70	4.12	11
Camouflage	310.85	4.02	281.20	3.54	10
Full Collusion	430.75	2.84	391.45	2.83	9
Evaluator Collusion	436.90	2.62	388.10	4.40	11
Spies	297.25	4.00	249.20	5.17	16
Evaluator Spies	301.30	4.31	244.80	7.00	19
Malicious Spies	433.65	2.54	386.65	3.17	11

almost the same results. All these strategies use False Meta-data, unlike The Simple Malicious Individual, which reaches fewer bogus transactions. The rest of the malicious strategies sacrifice a part of bogus transactions to circumvent TMSs, however these transactions have no effect in DummyTrust. The biggest variation in results has been measured in Simple Malicious Individual. In this strategy, honest peers completely rely on a random choice of communication partner.

The SimpleTrust has only slightly better results. The biggest improvement was measured in Evaluator Spies and Spies. These strategies are not suitable for simple TMSs. In fact, we have expected a bigger improvement. The limited factor is the size of the history period which was set to 30 cycles in all TMSs. Without cooperation with other peers, the information about peer's maliciousness is lost after 30 cycles and the delay between two transactions towards the same peer can be longer.

3.2 Efficiency Criterion

We measured the criteria described in Sect. 3. The most important of them is the MaliciousSuccessRatio (MSR); the measured values are in Tables 2 and 3 along with average numbers of bogus transactions and standard deviations. The MSR values above the threshold 0.5 are displayed in a bold font. We can see that only the BubbleTrust is resistant against all malicious strategies. There is at least one effective malicious strategy against all other TMSs. The EigenTrust, despite its advantage, is completely vulnerable to Spies and Evaluator Spies. These strategies are even able to perform more bogus transactions than it would be possible in a network without TMS. PeerTrust is resistant against only the simplest malicious strategies, on the other hand, malicious strategies like Evaluator Collusion and Evaluator Spies are 100 % effective. Also H-Trust does not work well, it is completely vulnerable to Evaluator Collusion and Evaluator Spies and the resistance against other strategies is not convincing either. WTR copes very well with individual strategies; especially the Camouflage is ineffective due to the risk factor. But the collective strategies can easily circumvent it. There are noticeable deviations in some malicious strategies. However, none of these deviations influence the MSR value that much that cross the limit 0.5. The next criterion is BogusRatio. Table 4 shows BogusRatio of each malicious strategy in all TMSs. In the worst case scenario, only 29 % of all transactions in the P2P network

Table 2. Malicious Success Ratio in BubbleTrust, EigenTrust and PeerTrust.

Strategy	BubbleTrust			EigenTrust			PeerTrust		
	Total Bogus	RSD (%)	MSR	Total Bogus	RSD (%)	MSR	Total Bogus	RSD (%)	MSR
Simple M Individual	6.2	66.2	0.0	64.2	21.6	0.2	17.5	20.3	0.1
Malicious Individual	1.5	89.9	0.0	137.9	15.2	0.3	0.0	0.0	0.0
Camouflage	1.55	84.96	0.00	87.85	24.82	0.28	200.60	6.84	0.65
Full Collusion	58.25	13.13	0.14	0.00	0.00	0.00	426.90	3.55	0.99
Evaluator Collusion	109.2	10.17	0.25	0.00	0.00	0.00	440.05	2.70	1.01
Spies	21.5	23.93	0.07	323.45	3.83	1.09	282.25	4.53	0.95
Evaluator Spies	48.3	11.44	0.16	295.50	28.08	0.98	300.00	4.65	1.00
Malicious Spies	53.5	11.21	0.12	0.55	–	0.00	297.95	4.87	0.69

Table 3. Malicious Success Ratio in HTrust and WTR.

Strategy	HTrust			WTR		
	Total Bogus	RSD (%)	MSR	Total Bogus	RSD (%)	MSR
Simple Malicious Individual	54.00	20.70	0.21	0.00	0.00	0.00
Malicious Individual	142.15	8.69	0.33	0.00	0.00	0.00
Camouflage	56.30	15.94	0.18	0.00	0.00	0.00
Full Collusion	138.05	8.23	0.32	435.45	2.26	1.01
Evaluator Collusion	411.00	4.30	0.94	436.70	3.73	1.00
Spies	108.10	8.74	0.36	293.30	5.57	0.99
Evaluator Spies	296.60	3.84	0.98	302.65	4.39	1.00
Malicious Spies	299.55	4.04	0.69	304.40	3.86	0.70

Table 4. BogusRatio for different malicious strategies and TMSs.

Strategy	EigenTrust (%)	H-Trust (%)	PeerTrust (%)	WTR (%)	BubbleTrust (%)
Simple M Individual	13	11	4	0	2
Malicious Individual	34	35	0	0	1
Camouflage	21	13	38	0	0
Full Collusion	0	34	72	73	18
Evaluator Collusion	0	70	73	73	29
Spies	55	22	48	49	5
Evaluator Spies	63	50	50	50	11
Malicious Spies	1	56	57	57	16

with the BubbleTrust can be bogus. Other TMS tolerate 63 % (EigenTrust), 70 % (H-Trust), 73 % (PeerTrust and WTR) bogus transactions.

Table 5 shows MaliciousCost of malicious strategies which use ulterior or faked transactions. Other strategies (Simple Malicious Individual and Malicious Individual) have no additional cost. MaliciousCost of the strategies with no measurable MSR is infinite and the cells contain 'N/A'.

Table 5. MaliciousCost for different malicious strategies and TMSs.

Strategy	EigenTrust	H-Trust	PeerTrust	WTR	BubbleTrust
Camouflage	0.17	0.19	0.09	N/A	0.16
Full Collusion	N/A	8.58	2.78	2.72	20.31
Evaluator Collusion	N/A	9.67	9.06	9.12	36.47
Spies	1.95	5.79	2.23	2.13	29.87
Evaluator Spies	5.87	5.74	5.72	5.69	36.23
Malicious Spies	N/A	5.65	5.68	5.56	31.63

Table 6. MaliciousBenefit for different malicious strategies and TMSs.

Strategy	EigenTrust	H-Trust	PeerTrust	WTR	BubbleTrust
Camouflage	0.17	0.19	0.09	N/A	0.16
Evaluator Collusion	N/A	6.79	6.36	6.41	25.64
Spies	0.10	0.24	0.11	0.09	1.96
Evaluator Spies	2.85	2.73	2.75	2.74	17.73
Malicious Spies	N/A	2.67	2.68	2.63	14.95

The attacker most likely uses a strategy which has the best price/performance ratio. For instance, in the PeerTrust the most successful strategy is Evaluator Collusion but it is very expensive (above 9), better choice is Full Collusion with success ratio 0.99 and cost only 2.78. The Camouflage strategy is relatively efficient; although it has low a success ratio in the most TMSs, it is compensated by its very low price. In the BubbleTrust, all strategies have cost above 20 (except Camouflage) and the most expensive strategy (Evaluator Collusion) has almost 37. This is significantly higher value than the other TMSs have.

Table 6 shows MaliciousBenefit of malicious strategies which have some beneficial transactions. Again, MaliciousBenefit of the strategies with no measurable MSR is infinite and the cells contain 'N/A'.

The strategies like Evaluator Collusion, Evaluator Spies and Malicious Spies have always more beneficial transactions than bogus ones. Strictly speaking, the designation of the collective as malicious is no longer suitable. The attackers, whose primary goal is to destroy the network functionality for other peers, probably would not choose malicious strategy with a high MaliciousBenefit. But attackers desired to spread their malicious services at any cost do not bother with MaliciousBenefit.

3.3 Influence of Simulation Settings

We have tried different simulation settings. We have adjusted the number of nodes in the network while preserving the ratio of malicious nodes. We have made the following observation: increasing the number of nodes does not affect the MaliciousSuccess-Ratio. The reason is that each TMS can handle only a limited number of nodes in the calculation of ratings. A similar limitation can be found in all TMSs. The information from nodes which are very distant in a trust chain is negligible. On the other hand, the results change if we decrease the number of nodes. This change can be in both

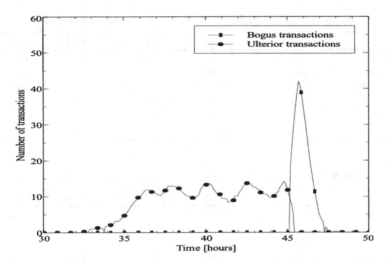

Fig. 1. Rehabilitation after treason in BubbleTrust.

directions dependent on the TMS and the malicious strategy. In this case the TMS has to rely on information from a smaller number of nodes than it expects (Fig. 1).

Next, we have altered the ratio of malicious nodes. Figure 2 shows the results for BubbleTrust. As we can see, the malicious success increases with the ratio of malicious nodes in the network. BubbleTrust resists relatively well even in the network with more than 50 % of malicious nodes. In our tests we stayed at 40 % because it is very unlikely that the overlay network beneath the P2P application can handle the situation in which half of the peers are malicious. The defence techniques described in

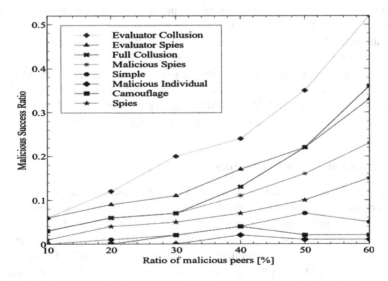

Fig. 2. Ratio of malicious peers on Malicious Success Ratio in BubbleTrust.

2.1 assume that only a small fraction of nodes is malicious. In fact, 40 % already causes big problems.

3.4   Result Summary

H-index calculation used in H-Trust proved to be vulnerable to traitors. It takes too long to detect traitors and malicious peers are rehabilitated too quickly. The system WTR permits the highest number of bogus transactions from all tested TMSs, but it is followed closely by PeerTrust and HTrust. EigenTrust has better results than H-Trust, WTR and PeerTrust but it has advantage in the form of pre-trusted peers.

Our tests proved that it is very difficult to resist against the sophisticated malicious techniques. Especially the calculation of the evaluator rating is susceptible to rigging. The previously published TMSs do not pay as much attention to the evaluator rating as they pay to the provider rating. This must be changed if the TMS should be resistant against the Evaluator Collusion or the Evaluator Spies.

The best TMS in our comparison is BubbleTrust. It has the shortest treason detection time, the longest rehabilitation time and allows only 28 % of bogus transaction under the most successful malicious strategy. As far as we know, it is the only one TMS using global experience as feedback verification.

4   Conclusion

In this paper, using simulation framework called P2PTrustSim we compared trust management systems against different malicious strategies. We also proposed several efficiency criteria which can be evaluated using this framework. We analysed known malicious tactics and suggested three new collective malicious strategies against the most representative systems for each type of TMS. We can expect that malicious peers working in a collective will try to use the most effective strategy against TMS currently used in the network. Therefore, the quality of TMSs has to be assessed according to the most successful malicious strategy. Nevertheless, other properties have to be taken into account too; e.g. the cost connected with the malicious strategy can exceed the potential benefit for malicious peers. The results indicate that only the BubbleTrust is resistant against all considered malicious strategies; it is, therefore, the best choice for deployment in the secured P2P networks.

Acknowledgment. This work was supported in part by grants 204/13/08195 and SVV-2013-267312.

References

1. Kamvar, S.D., Schlosser, M.T., Garcia-Molina, H.: The Eigentrust algorithm for reputation management in P2P networks. In: WWW'03: Proceedings of the 12th International Conference on World Wide Web, pp. 640–651. ACM Press (2003)
2. Xiong, L., Ling, L.: PeerTrust: supporting reputation-based trust for peer-to-peer electronic communities. IEEE Trans. Knowl. Data Eng. **16**, 843–857 (2004)

3. Huanyu, Z., Xiaolin, L.: H-Trust: a group trust management system for peer-to-peer desktop grid. J. Comput. Sci. Technol. **24**, 447–462 (2009)
4. Bonnaire, X., Rosas, E.: WTR: a reputation metric for distributed hash tables based on a risk and credibility factor. J. Comput. Sci. Technol. **24**, 844–854 (2009)
5. Novotny, M., Zavoral, F.: BubbleTrust: a reliable trust management for large P2P networks. In: Meghanathan, N., Boumerdassi, S., Chaki, N., Nagamalai, D. (eds.) CNSA 2010. CCIS, vol. 89, pp. 359–373. Springer, Heidelberg (2010)
6. Novotny, M., Zavoral, F.: Resistance against malicious collectives in BubbleTrust. In: The 12th International Conference on Parallel and Distributed Computing, Gwangju, Korea (2011)
7. Hoffman, K., Zage, D., Nita-Rotaru, C.: A survey of attack and defense techniques for reputation systems. ACM Comput. Surv. **42**(1), 1–31 (2009)
8. Marti, S., Garcia-Molina, H.: Taxonomy of trust: categorizing P2P reputation systems. Comput. Netw. **50**, 472–484 (2006)
9. Selvaraj, C., Anand, S.: Peer profile based trust model for P2P systems using genetic algorithm. Peer-to-Peer Netw. Appl. **4**, 1–12 (2011)
10. Suryanarayana, G., Taylor, R.N.: A survey of trust management and resource discovery technologies in peer-to-peer applications. Technical report, UC Irvine (2004)
11. Bonnaire, X., Rosas, E.: A critical analysis of latest advances in building trusted P2P networks using reputation systems. In: Weske, M., Hacid, M.-S., Godart, C. (eds.) WISE Workshops 2007. LNCS, vol. 4832, pp. 130–141. Springer, Heidelberg (2007)
12. Druschel, P., Rowstron, A.: PAST: a large-scale, persistent peer-to-peer storage utility. In: Proceedings of the Eighth Workshop Hot Topics in Operating Systems (2001)

A Context-Aware Model for the Management of Agent Platforms in Dynamic Networks

Phuong T. Nguyen[1(✉)], Volkmar Schau[2], and Wilhelm R. Rossak[2]

[1] Research and Development Center, Duy Tan University, 182 Nguyen Van Linh, Danang, Vietnam
phuong.nguyen@duytan.edu.vn

[2] Department of Computer Science, Friedrich Schiller University Jena, Ernst-Abbe-Platz 2-4, 07743 Jena, Germany
{volkmar.schau,wilhelm.rossak}@uni-jena.de

Abstract. A network infrastructure in a mass casualty incident rescue scenario is normally characterized by multiple of working domains scattered over a wide area. For mobile agent systems working in these networks, the management of agent platforms contributes to achieving fault tolerance and reliability. We employ a honey bee inspired approach for imposing a self-organizing mechanism on the colony of mobile agent platforms. This paper presents our approach as well as introduces some preliminary evaluations of the proposed mechanism.

Keywords: Context-aware systems · Mobile agents · Bio-inspired computing

1 Introduction

For the support of mass casualty incident (MCI) rescue, at the University of Jena a project named SpeedUp[1] has been in development since April 2009. The project aims to develop a technological framework for providing support of rescue forces in MCI situations so that in disaster events, rescue tasks can be performed in a more effective way [1].

In SpeedUp's communication infrastructure the mobile agent concept [2] has been chosen as one of the key technologies. In MCI rescue scenario of the SpeedUp-Type, rescue forces may be distributed widely. Each geographical location forms most likely a technological region in which different forces work together to do rescue tasks (Fig. 1). It is expected that agent platforms are able to adapt to changes that happen at execution time. In this paper, we present an overview to our model, a honey bee inspired mechanism for the management of dynamic mobile agent platforms [6,7]. Afterwards, we introduce some preliminary evaluation results on the key functionalities of the model.

---

[1] The project was funded by the German Federal Ministry of Education and Research (BMBF), http://www.speedup-projekt.de.

P.C. Vinh et al. (Eds.): ICCASA 2013, LNICST 128, pp. 77–86, 2014.
DOI: 10.1007/978-3-319-05939-6_8, © Springer International Publishing Switzerland 2014

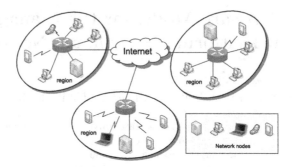

Fig. 1. Network infrastructure in an MCI rescue scenario

2 An Approach for the Management of Dynamic Agent Platforms in MCI Rescue Scenarios

2.1 Network Model

The SpeedUp solution is a communication and data platform for coordination and integration of all rescue teams in catastrophic situations [6]. Because of its characteristics, such as autonomous, reactive, opportunistic, and goal-oriented, the mobile agent technology has been selected for the SpeedUp-Type's MCI communication infrastructure [11]. The main components are as follows:

- Agent Platform: A software platform that provides executing environment for agents.
- Region: A region is made up of agent platforms that have the same authority.
- RegionMaster: An agent platform in a region that undertakes the context-aware tasks for the whole region.

One crucial issue in the SpeedUp context is to manage the dynamics of agent platforms efficiently as they join and quit in an unforeseeable manner. To achieve industrial strength, we propose a context-aware model for the management of agent platforms.

2.2 Biological Background

The main idea of bio-inspired computing in computer systems is to emulate activities in nature so that these systems can have alike features. As a result, they can react to environmental changes. So far, there have been several computational models inspired by colonies in nature [4,5,10]. Regarding the SpeedUp network model, we found some coincidental similarities between the model and the honey bee colony. In addition, honey bees already have good mechanisms to deal with their organizational issues.

In a bee colony, foraging takes place in summer, forager bees spread out to search for food sources. The forager bees may find different food sources, but as

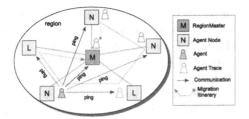

Fig. 2. A scout agent observes nodes and their mutual connectivity

the time goes by, honey bees tend to head for rich food source where they can get more nectar and pollen. A bee, after finding a new food source, returns to the hive and performs a *waggle dance* to notify other honey bees about the food source. As a result, other honey bees are able to know where and how far they must fly in order to get to the food sources [3,9].

Swarming in a bee colony occurs when the bee population increases. Before swarming the queen bee raises a new queen bee. The old queen takes a number of workers with her and they fly to a new temporary location, e.g. a tree branch. The most experienced foragers in the swarm, called scout bees, are then deployed to find new suitable locations. When one round of exploration is finished, each scout bee returns to the bee cluster to inform the whole colony about the place she has found. The scout bee then flies to the site and evaluates it again and then backs to the swarm to dance for it. Other bees either perform their own dance or watch or follow other dances. If the number of scout bees gathered in a site constitutes a quorum then the scouts make a decision, they choose the site as the new hive [3,9].

2.3 A Self-organizing Model for the Management of Dynamic Agent Platforms

We proposed an adaptive mechanism for the management of working regions in the SpeedUp context based on honey bees' activities. In the algorithm, two mappings from the honey bee colony to the SpeedUp's network model are employed.

Mapping 1: RegionMaster plays the role of a beehive, at regular intervals, it deploys scout agents to all platforms of the region to collect information related to connectivity between a platform and others, and platform's performance. When a scout agent arrives at a platform, it sends messages to all platforms to measure the latency between the current platform and other platforms. The process is illustrated in Fig. 2. Once all ping messages have returned, the platform calculates the average latency τ_{avg} as specified below:

$$\tau_{avg} = \frac{1}{n} \sum_{i=1}^{n-1} t(i) \tag{1}$$

In which n is the number of nodes in the region; $t(i)$ is the transfer time between the current platform and the ith neighbour platform. The average latency represents the level of closeness between the platform and its neighbourhood. A low average latency means the platform has a good connection quality to the remaining platforms. In contrast, a high latency relates to a degraded connection quality between the platform and the others.

A platform holds a boolean value *split* to indicate whether it expects its region to segregate or not. After τ_{avg} has been calculated, it will then be compared to the latency to RegionMaster τ_{RM}. If $\tau_{RM} \gg \tau_{avg}$ then the node expects the region to be splitted; it sets the value *split* to *true*. The platform hands out the two values τ_{avg} and *split* to the scout agent.

After performing its routine at a platform, the agent migrates to the next platform. The process repeats until all nodes of the itinerary have been visited. En route, the scout agent also nominates a candidate node as possible new region master based on platform's performance and connection quality. Once all platforms in its itinerary have been visited, the scout migrates back to RegionMaster to submit all information it has collected. A scout provides the knowledge of each node in its path it has visited by submitting information to RegionMaster like a scout bee dances to notify other bees of a food source. RegionMaster can then build a map of connection quality of the region.

Mapping 2 is inspired by bee swarming. In a region RegionMaster is considered as the queen bee and all others are worker bees. After visiting all nodes, scout agents go back to RegionMaster and submit the information they have collected. RegionMaster counts the number of values that satisfy *split* = *true*. If the number constitutes a quorum, the region is about to be splitted. RegionMaster promotes a new RegionMaster. The new RegionMaster forms a new region from the nodes it inherits. The two regions are independent from each other, but logically connected.

3   Implementation

The implementation is based on the open source multi-agent system Ellipsis which is developed by our workgroup at the Chair of Software Engineering of the University of Jena.

3.1   Network Monitoring

In the course of time, the performance of an agent platform as well as its connectivity to the neighbourhood can change. The monitoring process takes place at every platform at regular intervals to ensure that environmental stimuli occurring during execution are to be observed and processed adequately.

3.2   Network Organizing

After all nodes of a region have been vesicated, the information gathered by a scout needs to be processed and served as a base for decision making. Self-organizing activities are conducted to maintain an equilibrium between the internal organization of the platforms and the external perturbations. These activities allow agent platforms to recover to a stable state if changes or failures occurred.

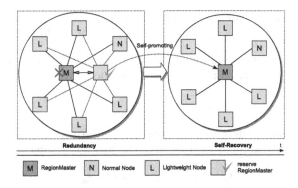

Fig. 3. Fault tolerance by using redundancy

3.3 Fault Tolerance

In the proposed approach, RegionMaster plays a decisive role, which may generate a single point of failure. Given that RegionMaster breaks down or disconnects suddenly, the node community has no information about the network and, therefore, cannot re-organize wherever necessary. To eliminate the effects of network failure, a reserve for RegionMaster is voted based on information fetched by the scouts. En route each scout agent compares information it has collected from the visited platforms, and connection quality of each platform, it nominates a reserve RegionMaster. The reserve RegionMaster senses the presence of RegionMaster by periodically sending pings to it. If RegionMaster is no longer available, the reserve RegionMaster replaces this node (Fig. 3).

4 Evaluation Parameters

For the software prototype, there are many important functionalities that need to be evaluated. However, due to space limitations, in this paper we concentrate on validating the feasibility and the ability of being context-aware. Interested readers are referred to [7] for more evaluation results.

4.1 The Feasibility

In a dynamic network environment the cost for monitoring network might be considerably high. The proposed mechanism is beneficial only if network monitoring gains a good performance whilst keeping a reasonable running cost. The feasibility of the proposed mechanism means that it maintains a reasonable cost for monitoring while providing necessary information for the self-organizing tasks. To validate the feasibility, scouts are deployed to monitor network, the parameters regarding processing time and exploration time are measured. One round of exploration happens when a scout is created, travels through all nodes of the region, performs its routine and migrates back to RegionMaster. The following information is going to be acquired:

– The time a scout needs for accomplishing its tasks at a platform: $t_{processing}$.
– The time a scout needs for performing one round of exploration: $t_{exploration}$.

The processing time at a platform is the duration from when an agent arrives until it completes its tasks and leaves for the next node. It is calculated as follows:

$$t_{processing} = t_l - t_a \tag{2}$$

where t_a is the time when a scout arrives at a platform and t_l is the time when it leaves for the next node of its itinerary. The processing time is:

$$t_{processing} = t_{RTT} + t_s + t_d \tag{3}$$

in which: t_{RTT} is the period from the first ping message sent until the last response received; t_d is the time to deserialize a scout agent from an incoming stream of byte; t_s is the time to serialize a scout agent into a byte stream. The average exploration time is computed:

$$t_{exploration} = t_{end} - t_{begin} \tag{4}$$

where t_{begin} and t_{end} are the time when a scout starts and completes one round of exploration, respectively. This parameter indicates how often a scout agent supplies a RegionMaster with up-to-dated information.

4.2   Context Awareness

For agent systems working in highly dynamic networks, being context aware is an important feature. Agent platforms should be able to take appropriate measures to counteract adverse effects happening to them. In the scope of this paper, we investigate the ability of the framework to detect and provide the system with adequate measures to deal with perturbations happening to RegionMaster.

5   Evaluation

5.1   Experiment Setup

To evaluate the software prototype, we build a laboratory scale test system where conditions of a real network are imitated, without a real scenario being present. Characteristics of a dynamic network are simulated using other softwares. The test network consists of eight computers connected through a local Gigabit Ethernet LAN 1000 Mbps (Table 1).

5.2   The Feasibility

Figure 4 shows the logical connection for the first test. In this scenario, one scout is created at RegionMaster. RegionMaster assigns the list of agent platforms $\{D1, D2, D3, D4, FJ, PT, T1, T2\}$ to the scout. Figure 5 depicts the processing

Table 1. Hardware configuration for the experiments

Computer	Alias	OS	Kernel	RAM	Processor
Desktop	D1	Fedora 12	2.6.31	2.0 GB	AMD 2.2 GHz
Desktop	D2	Debian 6.0.4	2.6.32	4.0 GB	Intel 2*2.0 GHz
Desktop	D3	Debian 6.0.4	2.6.32	4.0 GB	Intel 2*2.0 GHz
Desktop	D4	Debian 6.0.4	2.6.32	4.0 GB	Intel 2*2.0 GHz
Fujitsu	FJ	Fedora 12	2.6.31	3.0 GB	Intel 2*2.8 GHz
Portégé	PT	Windows 7	N/A	4.0 GB	Intel 2*2.4 GHz
Thinkpad	T1	Fedora 12	2.6.31	2.4 GB	Intel 2*2.4 GHz
Thinkpad	T2	Windows XP	N/A	1.0 GB	Intel 1.7 GHz

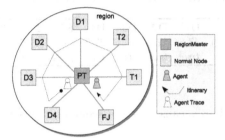

Fig. 4. Logical representation of the experiments

time of the platforms. This parameter represents the time that the agent needs to perform its tasks at a platform. It is dependent on the processing power of agent platforms and the latencies to the other platforms, which are in turn dependent on the network speed. It can be seen that, except $T2$ that has a higher processing time because of its limited processing power (Table 1), the processing time for the other platforms is considerably low. It guarantees that the processing activities place comparatively little burden on the system performance.

To measure $t_{exploration}$, the agent is sent around the network for different number of rounds r. In the second experiment r is set to different values, i.e. $r = \{100; 200; 300; 500; 1000; 2000; 3000; 5000\}$. The average exploration time is:

$$t_{exploration} = \frac{t_{end} - t_{begin}}{r} \qquad (5)$$

This parameter demonstrates how fast the scout supplies RegionMaster with up-to-date information of the network. If the agent needs a long time to perform its tasks at the platforms, the information submitted to RegionMaster might be out-of-date. As a consequence, the reactions produced by RegionMaster would not be adequate. However, the measurement results show that this is not the case. In Fig. 6, the curve represents the accumulated exploration time. The straight line which depicts the average time for finishing one round of surveillance provides evidence that the parameter is stable, no matter how many rounds the

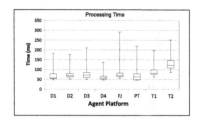

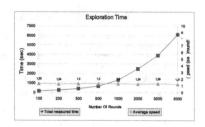

Fig. 5. Processing time for every platform

Fig. 6. Average time for a scout agent to explore the region

Table 2. Metrics measured at the time of self-organizing

Platform	D1	**D2**	D3	D4	FJ	PT	T1	T2
τ_{avg}/τ_{RM} (%)	47,8	47,6	37,5	27,5	—	37,5	44,4	29,7
Split	true	true	true	true	false	true	true	true

agent has migrated. This means that the scout produces no overhead when it works in the long run.

5.3   Context Awareness

FJ is RegionMaster, a scout is deployed to survey the region. In this scenario, the connectivity between RegionMaster and the remaining platforms is degraded using software. This aims to investigate the countermeasures of the system given that the quality of the connection to RegionMaster has declined. Given the circumstances, it is expected that the software helps the platforms recover from the degradation.

In this experiment, a certain network traffic between RegionMaster and the other platforms is created, resulting in a smaller bandwidth left to the remaining platforms. To produce network traffic, we utilize the open source software Iperf [8]. This tool is used to produce both TCP and UDP data streams over networks; data sent by the client will be received and eventually discarded by the server. Since Iperf consumes a certain bandwidth on the connection between RegionMaster and the rest of the region, there is smaller bandwidth left for other applications. As a result, each platform experiences effects from the traffic generator. The latencies between the platforms and RegionMaster grow sharply. These changes are sensed by the scout. Every platform sets the value *split* based on the ratio $\Theta = \tau_{avg}/\tau_{RM}$; where τ_{avg} is the average latency and τ_{RM} is the latency to RegionMaster, respectively. The splitting threshold is set to $\Theta < 50\%$. Table 2 shows the ratio and the corresponding value *split* for every platform.

Since most of the platforms set the value *split* to *true* the region is splitted. There is only RegionMaster staying at the old region. The remaining nodes join the new region with *D2* promoted to be the new RegionMaster. In this case, an

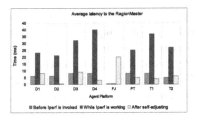
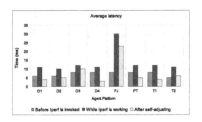

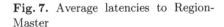

Fig. 7. Average latencies to Region-Master

Fig. 8. Average latencies of all platforms

adaptation has been made, the old RegionMaster relinquishes its leadership in the only-one platform region and becomes an inferior node of the new region. A new region emerges from the original region.

Figure 7 displays the latency to RegionMaster τ_{RM} of every platform in three phases. For a platform, the left column is the latency before Iperf is activated; the middle column represents the time while Iperf is operating and the right column is the latency of the platform after the self-adapting process has occurred. In the beginning and while Iperf was working FJ was RegionMaster so $\tau_{RM}(FJ) = 0$. Similarly, after $D2$ has taken its job as RegionMaster $\tau_{RM}(D2) = 0$. As usual expected, while Iperf is working, the latencies to RegionMaster for every platform increase significantly. However, once $D2$ takes over as RegionMaster, the latencies decrease proportionally. Figure 8 shows the average latencies τ_{avg} of every platform in the corresponding phases. These latencies also shift in the same pattern as by τ_{RM}. Before additional bandwidth was produced, the average latencies had been at a normal level. While Iperf was operating the latencies rose markedly. After the region has been restructured, these values resume to a normal level. The network monitoring activities supply the framework with up-to-date information about network situation, thereby facilitating the decision making process. The measurement results suggest that the swap in role of RegionMaster from FJ to $D2$ brings a more stable connectivity to every platform compared to that of the old arrangement, right after Iperf started producing bandwidth.

6 Conclusion

In this paper we have introduced a mechanism for the management of agent platforms in highly dynamic networks based on the organizational model of honey bees.

Experimental results show that the software framework has an acceptable operating overhead as well as a practical processing speed. The test scenarios demonstrated that the framework is able to detect degradations in connectivity once they occurred. Based on the information gathered by scout agents, the framework provides the system with a measure to adequately overcome the problem that adversely affects the platform colony. The countermeasures appear to be effective since they help the colony to promote a new equilibrium in connectivity between the platforms. The connection qualities from a platform to RegionMaster as well as from a platform to the others have been improved. From our perspective, the evaluation validates that the software framework principally fulfils the requirements regarding the feasibility and being self-adaptive.

References

1. FSU Jena, The SpeedUp Project (2011)
2. Braun, P.: The migration process of mobile agents. Ph.D. dissertation, Friedrich Schiller University, Jena (2003)
3. Seeley, T.D., Kirk Visscher, P.: Group decision making in nest-site selection by honey bees. J. Apidologie **35**, 101–116 (2004)
4. Karaboga, D., Bahriye, A.: A survey: algorithms simulating bee swarm intelligence. J. Artif. Intell. Rev. **31**, 61–85 (2009)
5. Pham, T., Afify, A., Koc, E.: Manufacturing cell information using the bees algorithm. In: Proceedings Innovative Production Machines and Systems Virtual Conference (2007)
6. Nguyen, P.T., Schau, V., Rossak, W.R.: Towards an adaptive communication model for mobile agents in highly dynamic networks based on swarming behaviour. In: The 9th European Workshop on Multi-agent Systems (EUMAS) (2011)
7. Nguyen, P.T., Schau, V., Rossak, W.R.: An adaptive communication model for mobile agents inspired by the honey bee colony: theory and evaluation. In: The 10th European Workshop on Multi-agent Systems (EUMAS) (2012)
8. Network Performance Measurement. http://sourceforge.net/projects/iperf/
9. Seeley, T.D., Buhrman, S.C.: Nest-site selection in honey bees: how well do swarms implement the best-of-N decision rule? J. Behav. Ecol. Sociobiol. **49**, 416–427 (2001)
10. Brocco, A.: Exploiting self-organization for the autonomic management of distributed system. Ph.D. thesis, University of Fribourg, Switzerland (2010)
11. Buford, J.F., Jakobson, G., Lewis, L.: Multi-agent situation management for supporting large-scale disaster relief operations. Int. J. Intell. Control Syst. **11**, 284–295 (2006)

Building Consensus in Context-Aware Systems Using Ben-Or's Algorithm: Some Proposals for Improving the Convergence Speed

Phuong T. Nguyen[⊠]

Research and Development Center, Duy Tan University, 182 Nguyen Van Linh,
Danang, Vietnam
phuong.nguyen@duytan.edu.vn

Abstract. For context-aware systems, it is essential for the constituent components to react flexibly to changes happening in the surrounding environment. In distributed networks, a failure of some nodes might disrupt the whole system. Given the circumstances, it is necessary for the remaining nodes to find consensus on a new organizational structure. In this paper, we propose an approach for improving the convergence speed of a prominent algorithm for finding consensus: Ben-Or's algorithm.

Keywords: Context-aware systems · Ben-Or's algorithm

1 Introduction

Our problem involves searching for consensus in a group of network nodes where the nodes have to self-organize to deal with environmental stimuli occurring at execution time [4]. Fault tolerance, when being confronted with, means that in the event of network crashes network nodes are able to organize themselves to recover to a stable state. This leads to the problem of searching for an eventual agreement among distributed nodes.

Building consensus among distributed network nodes in presence of failure has been identified as a thorny issue in distributed computing. When at least one node fails, it has been shown that there exists no deterministic algorithm for solving consensus using asynchronous message passing [2,3]. In this paper, we present an approach of building consensus in distributed systems as an amendment for an existing randomized consensus algorithm, Ben-Or's algorithm [1]. The experimental results have shown that our proposed algorithm considerably improves the convergence speed of the original approach.

The paper is organized as follows. Section 2 introduces consensus in distributed systems. Section 3 presents a biological background. Section 4 brings in our approach, a honey bee inspired algorithm for attaining consensus. An implementation as well as simulation and the experimental results for the two algorithms are highlighted in Sect. 5. Section 6 draws future work and finally concludes the paper.

P.C. Vinh et al. (Eds.): ICCASA 2013, LNICST 128, pp. 87–96, 2014.
DOI: 10.1007/978-3-319-05939-6_9, © Springer International Publishing Switzerland 2014

2 Literature Review

2.1 The Problem of Finding Consensus

The problem of building consensus in distributed systems is described in detail as follows: A set of $n \geq 2$ nodes $P = \{p_1, p_2, .., p_n\}$ has to negotiate using asynchronous message passing and decide on the same value from a common set of inputs. In the scope of this paper, we discuss binary consensus, i.e. the input values $v \in \{0, 1\}$ [1,3,9,12]. The properties of consensus [9]:

- At most f nodes may fail. The nodes that fail are called faulty nodes; the nodes that still work are called non-faulty nodes.
- Each node p broadcasts its proposal as a message to all other nodes.
- A node makes a decision based on the set of messages it received.
- A message never fails once it has been sent.
- A node p can send its report or proposal value v to some nodes, and it may crash before sending the message to the remaining non-faulty nodes. As a result, some nodes have v and some don't.

Three key requirements need to be met by every consensus algorithm [3]:

- Termination: Every node must ultimately decide.
- Agreement: All correct nodes decide on the same value.
- Validity: The chosen value must be the input of at least one of the nodes.

2.2 The FLP Theorem

No matter how simple the definition is, the solution for the problem remains a challenge in distributed computing. In [2] Fischer, Lynch and Paterson prove that with an asynchronous message passing system, there exists no deterministic algorithm for solving the problem described in Sect. 2.1 in presence of failures. The theorem has been named after the authors - the FLP theorem [2].

2.3 Randomized Consensus: Ben-Or's Algorithm

Ben-Or's randomized consensus algorithm is considered as the first one for solving consensus. In his approach, it is assumed that at most $f < n/2$ nodes may fail during execution. The algorithm is described in the pseudo code Algorithm 1 [1]. A proof for the correctness of the algorithm is available in [8].

- Procedure $Report(k, x)$ broadcasts a message containing information about the current round k and the proposed value to all other non-faulty nodes.
- Procedure $WaitFor(k, *)$ waits for all incoming messages containing k and a report/proposal value.
- Procedure $Propose(k, v)$ broadcasts a proposal value v in round k to all non-faulty nodes.
- Procedure $Decide(v)$ makes a decision on the value v.
- Procedure $ChooseRandom(0, 1)$ returns either 0 or 1 with equal probability.

Algorithm 1. Ben-Or's Consensus Algorithm

1: **procedure** BENORCONSENSUS(v_p)
2:     $x \leftarrow v_p$
3:     $k \leftarrow 0$
4:     **while** *true* **do**
5:         $k \leftarrow k + 1$
6:         **Report**(k,x)
7:         **WaitFor**($k,*$) from n-f nodes   ▷ * is either 0 or 1
8:         **if** there are more than n/2 messages containing v **then**
9:             **Propose**(k,v)
10:        **else**
11:            **Propose**($k,abstention$)
12:        **end if**
13:        **WaitFor**($k,*$) from n-f nodes
14:        **if** there are at least f+1 messages containing v **then**
15:            **Decide**(v)
16:        **else if** there is at least 1 message containing v **then**
17:            $x \leftarrow v$
18:        **else**
19:            $x \leftarrow$ **ChooseRandom**(0,1)
20:        **end if**
21:    **end while**
22: **end procedure**

Remarks. In Algorithm 1, the *abstention* value in Line 11 indicates that a node p prefers neither 0 nor 1, it abstains. The value is something like a "nuisance" since it does not contribute to a convergence of consensus.

In [8], it has been proven that in a round k if every two nodes propose then they propose the same value. Once a node p decides in Line 15 in round k then all nodes will decide in the next round $k+1$ [8]. But a node decides on a value v only if it receives more than f propose messages containing v in Line 14. In Line 9, a node proposes a value only if it has received more than $n/2$ report messages with the same value v. That means, when the number of messages containing the same value does not exceed $n/2$ then the node cannot propose any value. If so, then a quorum cannot be reached in Line 14. Given the circumstances Ben-Or's algorithm gains a consensus very slowly.

3   Biological Background

3.1   Bio-inspired Computing

The main idea of bio-inspired computing is to emulate activities from natural communities in computer systems to infuse alike features. As a result, they can react to environmental changes and be resilient to perturbations and errors. So far, there have been several computational solutions inspired by colonies in nature, e.g. ant and honey bee optimization algorithms. By looking into the honey bee colony, we found that honey bees have a mechanism to reach an agreement on choosing a new beehive given that various candidate sites may have been nominated during the decision making process. To our knowledge, the mechanism is notable and can be applied to the problem of consensus among distributed network nodes.

3.2   Bee Communication

Foraging takes place in summer, worker bees spread out to collect and accumulate food for the whole year. Each individual bee may find different food sources, but as the time goes by, the colony tends to head for rich food source where they can get more nectar and pollen. A scout bee, after finding a new food source, returns to the hive and performs a *waggle dance* to notify other honey bees about the food source. With this information, other honey bees are able to know where and how far they must fly in order to get to the food sources.

3.3   Consensus

Swarming occurs when the bee population increases thus causing congestion and difficulties in maintaining good hygiene in the beehive. Before swarming, the queen lays eggs to raise a new queen bee. When the new queen bee arrives, the old queen bee takes a number of workers with her and they fly to a new temporary location, e.g. a tree branch, that is near to their beehive. The swarm stays on the temporary residence for a short time while waiting for a new residence. Although many sites may have been nominated during swarming, eventually all scouts make a unanimous decision, they reach a final agreement for a site, normally the best one. The honey bee colony has a mechanism to build consensus among all scout bees. Scout bees dance for good sites vigorously and lastingly than for sites with inferior quality [5]. It has been shown that the strength of a dance is decreased linearly over the time [6]. When the dance expires, scout bee stops dancing for the site and chooses randomly a new site to follow and dance for. The rate of recruitment for a site is proportionate to the number of waggle dances by bees. Since dances for good sites prolong, a good site attracts more bees. As a result, a good site gains a quorum much easier than sites with inferior quality [7]. The consensus mechanism is summarized as follows:

- Phase 1: Each scout explores a site, evaluates and assigns a quality to the site.
- Phase 2: The scout flies back to the swarm and dances to advertise for the site it has found. The better the site quality, the stronger and livelier the bee dances for it.
- Phase 3: After dancing, the bee returns and explores the site and then backs to the cluster. It dances for the site again, but less stronger. This step is repeated and the strength of the dance is decreased until it reaches 0.
- Phase 4: When the dance expires, the scout selects randomly a dance to follow. It then flies to the site that is being promoted by the dance it follows. The process repeats from Step 1 to Step 4.

– Phase 5: If the number of bees gathering around a site exceeds a certain threshold then a quorum is reached. The scouts fly back to the swarm and signal the whole colony to depart for the chosen site. The search ends.

4   A Honey Bee Inspired Algorithm for Building Consensus in Distributed Systems

4.1   Similarities

We see that Ben-Or's algorithm may reach a pretty slow convergence given that nodes do not choose the same value in the randomization phase. Regarding the problem of reaching an eventual agreement among nodes in distributed computing, we witness a substantial coincidence between consensus in distributed systems and consensus in the honey bee colony as shown in Table 1.

The fact that the two phenomena have a lot in common and honey bees possess a good mechanism to deal with consensus encourages us to employ the honey bee's consensus mechanism in building consensus in distributed computing.

4.2   Proposed Amendments

We call $M_p(k)$ is the set of messages received by node p at round k; $C_p(k,0)$ and $C_p(k,1)$ are the cardinality of the set of messages that contain 0 and 1, respectively. When $C_p(k,0) = C_p(k,1)$ we say it is a tie for the two sets. As we have seen in Algorithm 1, it is expected that the majority of nodes report the same value in Line 6 and then a quorum is reached in Line 14. However, a node proposes a value only if it receives more than $n/2$ messages containing the same value, otherwise it proposes the value *abstention*. We may "waste" the chance that nodes report the same value in round $k + 1$ given that almost $n/2$ messages containing the same value v are sent in Line 13.

It should be noted that from rounds $k > 1$, the value x reported in Line 6 is the result from either Line 15 or 17 or 19 in round $k - 1$. We propose a

Table 1. Analogies

Honey bee consensus	Distributed system consensus
Scout bees	Nodes
Sites	Values
Each scout bees dances for a site	Each node reports a value
Scouts nominate a site by dancing	Nodes propose a value by broadcasting messages
Scouts select a site if the number of bees gathering around it exceeds a threshold	Nodes decide on a value v if they receive more than f report messages containing v
All bees reach eventual agreement for a site	All nodes eventually decide on the same value

way to *guide* the nodes to opt for the most sensible value v instead of choosing a random value. We consider the case that the majority requirement is not satisfied: $C_p(k,v) < n/2$; but there is a *plurality* of nodes that report v, that means: $C_p(k, 1 - v) < C_p(k, v) < n/2$. The honey bee inspired algorithm for building a consensus is illustrated in the pseudo code Algorithm 2. The main functions are explained as follows:

Algorithm 2. Honey Bee Consensus Algorithm

```
 1: procedure HONEYBEECONSENSUS(v_p)
 2:     x ← v_p
 3:     k ← 0
 4:     strength ← 0
 5:     while true do
 6:         k ← k + 1
 7:         Report(k,x)
 8:         WaitFor(k,*) from n-f nodes
 9:         if there are more than n/2 messages containing v then
10:             Propose(k,v)
11:         else
12:             if strength ≤0 and C_p(k,0) ≠ C_p(k,1) then        ▷ start to follow v
13:                 v ← Plurality(0,1)
14:                 Follow(v)
15:                 strength ← Evaluate(0,1)
16:             end if
17:             Propose(k,abstention)
18:         end if
19:         WaitFor(k,*) from n-f nodes
20:         if there are more than f messages containing v then
21:             Decide(v)
22:         else if there is at least 1 message containing v then
23:             x ← v
24:         else
25:             if strength >0 and Follow(v) then        ▷ currently follow a value
26:                 x ← v
27:                 Decrease(strength)
28:             else
29:                 x ← ChooseRandom(0,1)
30:                 strength ← 0
31:             end if
32:         end if
33:     end while
34: end procedure
```

- Function $Plurality(0,1)$ returns 0 if $C_p(k,0) > C_p(k,1)$ and returns 1 if $C_p(k,0) < C_p(k,1)$.
- Procedure $Follow(v)$ indicates that a node prefers a value v.

- Function $Evaluate(0,1)$ calculates a correlative value between $C_p(k,0)$ and $C_p(k,1)$; a proposal is $Evaluate(0,1) = abs(C_p(k,0) - C_p(k,1))$.
- Procedure $Decrease(strength)$ subtracts a specified number from $strength$.

By a node, the internal variable $strength$ is added and it is decreased linearly at every round. This aims to make sure that a node does not insist on a fixed value and as a result, a deadlock can be averted. The variable $strength$ is calculated in the sense that the bigger the difference between the two cardinalities, the larger the value. The value that is being favoured by the plurality of the nodes will be more likely to be followed by others.

The value that is being reported by plurality of nodes can be expressed as a site with a better quality in the metaphor of bee swarming. A node prefers a value v so long as $strength > 0$. If $strength \leq 0$ the node chooses randomly a new value (Line 29). Randomization is also invoked in the worst case when there is no plausible argument of choosing 0 or 1, i.e. $C_p(k,0) = C_p(k,1)$. In the given case, deliberate choosing a fixed value, either 0 or 1, would not make sense.

With this approach, the chance that the majority of nodes report the same v in Line 7 should be higher than that in Ben-Or's algorithm. In the best case, if all nodes receive the same set of report messages in round k (Line 8), they all will follow the same value and as a result will report it in Line 7 in round $k+1$. Afterwards, they all propose the same value in the next step. That leads to a consensus which is impossible in the original Ben-Or's algorithm.

It should be noted that the while loop from Line 5 to Line 33 does not have a stop statement. In a real implementation, it is necessary to specify a point where the loop halts. In [8] the authors propose a solution for the problem. In their approach, after a node decides on a value v it sends a message with the content $(decide, v)$ to all nodes and then stops. Every node that receives the message also decides on the value and sends the message to other nodes and halts.

We acknowledge that the changes made by the honey bee inspired approach might possibly have a side effect on the stability of the original algorithm. The issue needs to be thoroughly studied and should be considered as an open research topic. It is unfortunately beyond the scope of this paper.

5   Evaluation

5.1   A Test Program: Multicast Delivering of Messages

To evaluate the performance of the algorithm inspired by honey bees, we implement a test program in the Java programming language. The program consists of two modules, sending and receiving multicast messages. A group of connected computers equipped with this program can exchange multicast messages to negotiate a common solution.

5.2   Simulation Tools: NS2 and AgentJ

Since a more precise evaluation result can be obtained if performance tests are performed with presence of several nodes, we decided to export the test program to run on a simulation environment. Network Simulator NS2 is a discrete

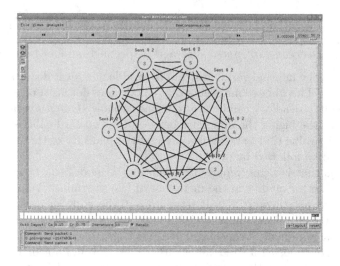

Fig. 1. NAM screenshot for NS2 simulation with 9 network nodes

event simulation framework. It was written in the programming languages C++ and Python and has been used widely for simulating applications running in wired and wireless networks. NS2 supports various routing protocols, e.g. TCP, UDP, multicast. Tcl (Tool Command Language) is used for scripting simulation scenarios in NS2 [11].

AgentJ is a software tool for embedding real applications written in Java in the NS2 simulation environment. AgentJ allows Java source code to execute on NS-2 with minor modification [10]. The use of AgentJ is practical given that there is a need for simulating applications written in Java with a large number of nodes. The combination NS2 and AgentJ provides us with a convenient way to simulate evaluation tests without needing to setup a real network.

Figure 1 depicts an example of multicast network nodes in Network Animator, a circle represents a node and a line between one pair of nodes corresponds to the link between them. In a multicast scenario, each node is connected to all other nodes. For a clear representation, in the figure we depict only a handful of nodes, however, we can increase the number of network nodes to meet our requirement.

5.3 Experimental Results

For deploying some test scenarios, we setup NS2 and AgentJ in Linux Fedora 12. Network crash is simulated by shutting down some nodes randomly during execution given that at most $f < n/2$ nodes may fail. A node fails with a probability of a randomized value ranging from 0 to 1. In the evaluation, the number of nodes is set to the following values $n = 5, 10, 15, 20, 25, 30$, $f \in \{0, \lfloor n/2 \rfloor\}$. We ran the tests with different sets of input values and with

Table 2. Performance comparison

$n = 5, 10, 15$												
n	5				10				15			
f	—	0	1	2	—	0	3	4	0	4	6	7
r_{BenOr}	—	1	1	12	—	1	10	20	1	4	23	60
$r_{HoneyBee}$	—	1	1	2	—	1	2	2	1	2	2	2
$n = 20, 25, 30$												
n	20				25				30			
f	0	6	8	9	0	8	10	12	8	10	12	14
r_{BenOr}	1	17	32	189	1	32	291	1319	29	112	1531	7554
$r_{HoneyBee}$	1	2	2	2	1	2	3	2	2	2	4	2

repetition. For the implementation, Function $Evaluate(0,1)$ in Line 15 is determined as $Evaluate(0,1) = abs(C_p(k,0) - C_p(k,1))$. Once a node starts to follow a value v, it assigns the difference to the strength value $strength = Evaluate(0,1)$. Every time it is called, Procedure $Decrease(strength)$ subtracts 1 from $strength$ until it is smaller than 0.

The outcomes of the execution are shown in Table 2. For each category, the first row represents the number of nodes taking part in building consensus n. The second row is the number of nodes that fail during execution f. The third and fourth rows are the corresponding numbers of rounds r that Ben-Or's algorithm and the honey bee inspired version reach a consensus, respectively.

It can be seen that, the larger the number of nodes is, the more difficult a consensus can be reached. If no node fails, that means $f = 0$ then both approaches can gain a swift consensus. When failure is present, there are differences in performance. By the original Ben-Or's algorithm, if the number of failed nodes increases, the number of rounds that it gains a consensus increases correspondingly. Especially, when f is nearly approaching $n/2$ a large number of rounds can be seen. Both tables show that the honey bee inspired algorithm has a considerably better computational performance, especially when network nodes fail en masse. Compared to Ben-Or's algorithm, it can gain a consensus after a small number of rounds of exchanging messages. In addition, its performance is stable towards the number of failed nodes. We witness an improvement in performance when applying the honey inspired mechanism.

6   Conclusion and Future Work

In this paper, we have introduced our approach for solving consensus in distributed systems. In the algorithm we proposed some changes to the original Ben-Or's randomized consensus algorithm based on the organizing model inspired by the honey bee colony. The experimental results showed that the approach gains an improvement in computational performance in comparison to the original Ben-Or's algorithm.

For future work, we expect to perform further investigations on the proposed algorithm. We anticipate that the amendments might have side effects on specific circumstances that have not been perceived yet in the scope of this paper. This issue needs to be scrutinized and remains and open topic. In addition, the performance of the algorithm needs to be thoroughly analysed as well as compared with that of other existing algorithms.

References

1. Ben-Or, M.: Another advantage of free choice (extended abstract): completely asynchronous agreement protocols. In: Proceedings of the Second Annual ACM Symposium on Principles of Distributed Computing (1983)
2. Fischer, M.J., Lynch, N.A., Paterson, M.S.: Impossibility of distributed consensus with one faulty process. In: Proceedings of the 2nd ACM SIGACT-SIGMOD Symposium on Principles of Database Systems, pp. 1–7 (1983)
3. Vavala, B., Neves, N., Moniz, H., Veríssimo, P.: Randomized consensus in wireless environments: a case where more is better. In: Proceedings of the 2010 Third International Conference on Dependability, pp. 7–12 (2010)
4. Nguyen, P.T., Schau, V., Rossak, W.R.: Towards an adaptive communication model for mobile agents in highly dynamic networks based on swarming behaviour. In: EUMAS 2011 European Workshop on Multi-agent Systems (2011)
5. Seeley, T.D., Kirk Visscher, P.: Choosing a home: how the scouts in a honey bee swarm perceive the completion of their group decision making. J. Behav. Ecol. Sociobiol. **54**, 511–520 (2003)
6. Seeley, T.D., Kirk Visscher, P.: Group decision making in nest-site selection by honey bees. J. Apidologie **35**, 101–116 (2004)
7. Seeley, T.D., Buhrman, S.C.: Nest-site selection in honey bees: how well do swarms implement the best-of-N decision rule? J. Behav. Ecol. Sociobiol. **49**, 101–116 (2001)
8. Aguilera, M.K., Toueg, S.: The correctness proof of Ben-Or's randomised consensus algorithm. Distrib. Comput. **25**, 371–381 (2012)
9. Aspnes, J.: Randomized protocols for asynchronous consensus. J. Distrib. Comput. **16**, 165–175 (2003)
10. Taylor, I., Downard, I., Adamson, B., Macker, J.: AgentJ: enabling java NS-2 simulations for large scale distributed multimedia applications. In: Second International Conference on Distributed Frameworks for Multimedia DFMA 2006, Penang, Malaysia, pp. 1–7 (2006)
11. The Network Simulator NS2. http://www.cs.virginia.edu/~cs757/slidespdf/cs757-ns2-tutorial1.pdf
12. Aspnes, J.: Fast deterministic consensus in a noisy environment. J. Algorithms **45**(1), 16–39 (2002)

Power-Aware Routing for Underwater Wireless Sensor Network

Nguyen Thanh Tung[1,2(✉)] and Nguyen Sy Minh[3]

[1] International School, Ho Chi Minh, Vietnam
[2] Vietnam National University, Hanoi, Vietnam
tungnt@isvnu.vn
[3] The Social and Political Science Department,
The Armed Police College, Hanoi, Vietnam
nguyensyminh84@gmail.com

Abstract. Water covers more than 70 % of the entire planet, contains much of its natural resources. With the increasing use of underwater sensors for the exploitation and monitoring of vast underwater resources, underwater wireless sensor network (UWSN), mostly based on acoustic transmission technologies, have been developing steadily in terms of operation range and data throughput. In an energy-constrained underwater system environment it is very important to find ways to improve the life expectancy of the sensors. Compared to the sensors of a terrestrial Ad Hoc Wireless Sensor Network (WSN), underwater sensors cannot use solar energy to recharge the batteries, and it is difficult to replace the batteries in the sensors. This paper reviews the research progress made to date in the area of energy consumption in underwater sensor networks (UWSN) and concentrates on developing routing algorithms that support energy efficiency. These algorithms are designed to carry out data communication while prolonging the operation time of WSNs.

Keywords: Sensor · Under water · Routing · Linear programming

1 Introduction

Nowadays few underwater sensor networks exist because commercially available underwater acoustic modems are too costly and energy inefficient to be practical for this applications. The commercially available acoustic modems provide data rates ranging from 100 bps to about 40 Kbps, and they have an operating range of up to a few km and an operating depth in the range of thousands of meters. The cost of a single commercial underwater acoustic modem is at least a few thousand US dollars. It can be concluded that Micro-modem is much more advanced for physical layer research. However, the modem of J. Willis et al. consumes less power and has a much simpler design; although this modem is designed only for short range communication (50–500 m).

Underwater acoustic transmission has been heavily studied during the last decade. Recently, significant advances in routing protocols for underwater sensor networks have been achieved. Good surveys reviewing the recent advances and challenges in underwater sensor networks can be found in the Section below.

P.C. Vinh et al. (Eds.): ICCASA 2013, LNICST 128, pp. 97–101, 2014.
DOI: 10.1007/978-3-319-05939-6_10, © Springer International Publishing Switzerland 2014

2 Routing Protocols in UWSNs

DBR (Depth Based routing) [7] routes the messages from the bottom of the ocean to the surface using only depth information. The depth of the source node and the depth of the forwarder are attached to the packet, that way, an intermediate node forwards a packet only if its depth difference with the forwarder is higher than a certain predefined threshold. In addition, an intermediate node has to wait to forward a packet for a certain amount of time called the holding time during which, if a copy of the packet is received, the transmission is cancelled. This way, the protocol avoids flooding and the routing can be made without exact location information.

A similar algorithm to DBR is DSR (Direction-Sensitive Routing) [8]. This algorithm utilizes a fuzzy logic inference system to decide which nodes should forward a packet based on the distance and angle between two neighbouring sensor nodes, and the remaining energy left in the sensor node. In addition, in order to save energy, the protocol restricts the forwarding of the packet when the broadcast tree grows larger than a specified tree level. According to the authors, DSR can achieve the same packet delivery ratio as DBR but with lower end-to-end delay and less energy consumption.

In [9] a centralized routing protocol based on geographic information is proposed. The master node computes the topology and the routing paths. The main drawback of this protocol lies in the complexity of the algorithm that computes the topology and the routing paths, since it is NP-complete.

Minimum Cost Clustering Protocol (MCCP) is a distributed clustering protocol proposed in [10]. The authors propose a cluster-centric cost-based optimization problem for the cluster formation. Although cluster-heads have the ability to send the data in a multi-hop manner to reach the sink, all nodes are supposed to be able to reach the sink. The cluster-head selection algorithm does not assure that the cluster-heads far away from the sink are able to relay their data to other cluster-heads.

EDETA (Energy-efficient aDaptive hiErarchical and robusT Architecture) is a routing protocol originally proposed for WSN [11, 12] and recently adapted to UWSN. It is a hierarchical protocol and nodes arrange themselves in clusters with one of them acting as a cluster-head (CH). The CHs form a tree structure between themselves in order to send the collected and aggregated data from the other nodes to the sink in a multi-hop manner. The protocol supports more than one sink in order to provide more scalability and some fault tolerant mechanisms.

Operation of the EDETA protocol is divided into two phases (i) the initialization phase and (ii) the normal operation phase. During the initialization phase, clustering is done and cluster-heads are elected.

During the normal operation phase, the nodes send their data periodically, at their scheduled times, to their CHs. Finally, cluster-heads send their data to their parents until the data reaches the sink.

In this protocol, similarly to the LEACH election mechanism [13], the CH election mechanism is distributed among the nodes in the network. Moreover, in order to distribute the energy consumption, the network structure is broken up after a certain amount of time and the initialization phase starts again. An enhanced version of

EDETA, called EDETA-e (EDETA-enhanced), also allows the designers of the network to accurately plan and choose nodes acting as CHs. In this variant of the protocol the initialization phase is done only once.

3 Mathematical Model for the Routing Problem in UWSNs

A sensor network is modeled as $G(V, L)$, where V be the set of nodes and L be the set of links between the nodes. Each node i has the initial battery energy of E_i, and the amount of energy consumed in transmitting a packet across link $L_{(i,j)}$ is $el_{i,j}$. Let Q_i be the amount of traffic generated or sink at Node i. Let T be the time until the first sensor node run out of energy. Let $q_{i,j}$ be traffic on the link $L_{(i,j)}$ during the time T. The problem is formulated to maximize the lifetime of the sensor networks.

$$\underline{\text{Maximize:}} \quad T$$
$$\underline{\text{Subject to:}}$$

$$\sum_{j=1}^{N} q_{j,i} + QT = \sum_{j=0}^{N} q_{i,j} : \forall i \in [1\ldots N] \tag{1}$$

$$\sum_{i=1}^{n} q_{i,j} el_{i,j} < = E_i : \forall i \in [1\ldots n]$$

$$\sum_{i=1}^{n} q_{i,0} = Qn$$

$$q_{i,j} > = 0 : \forall i,j \in [1\ldots n]$$

4 Heuristic Method for the Routing Problem

The heuristic algorithm (RE_heuristic) is given as below:

RE_heuristic:

In every round of data transmission to the base station, select a path in order to minimize the total of the reverse of residual energy of all sensor nodes in the path.

Let us define a weight for a link on any path as:

$$W(i) = \frac{1}{e(j)}$$

where e(j) is the remaining energy of source Node j on the link. Given a source node s and a destination node d, find a simple path Π from s to d that minimizes the total weight by all links participating in the data transmission.

$$\sum_{i \in \Pi - d} W(i) \ is \ minimized$$

(End of algorithm).

5   Simulation Results

In the first set of simulations, the performance of RE_heuristic is compared to the solution given by Formulation (1). In the simulations, 100 random 50-node sensor networks are generated. Each node begins with 1 J of energy. The network settings for the simulations in this section are given below. The energy model was used in [1, 2, 6].

Network size $(100m \times 100m)$

Base station $(50m, 200m)$

Number of sensor nodes   100 nodes

Position of sensor nodes: Uniform placed in the area

Energy   model: $E_{elec} = 50*10^{-9}$ J, $\varepsilon_{fs} = 10*10^{-12}$ J/bit/m^2 and

$\varepsilon_{mp} = 0.0013*10^{-12}$ J/bit/m^4

Figure 1 shows the ratio of the number of rounds of RE_chain and the Linear Programming solution of Formulation (1). From the simulation result, it can be said that RE_chain performs within 1 % of the Linear Programming solution.

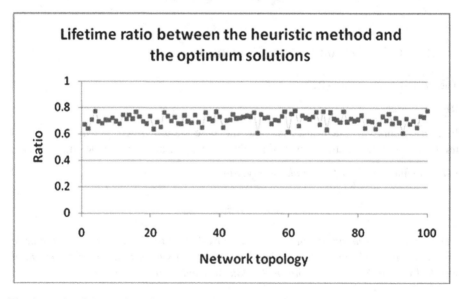

Fig. 1.   Ratio of the number of rounds between the heuristic method and the optimum solution

References

1. Tung, N.T., Van Duc, N.: Optimizing the operating time of wireless sensor network. EURASIP J. Wirel. Commun. Netw. (2013). doi:10.1186/1687-1499-2012-348. ISSN: 1687-1499 (SCIE)
2. Tung, N.T., Vinh, P.C.: The energy-aware operational time of wireless ad-hoc sensor networks. ACM/Springer Mob. Netw. Appl. (MONET) J. **17**, 629–632 (2012). doi:10.1007/s11036-012-0403-1. (SCIE)
3. Dung, N.T., Van Duc, N., Tung, N.T., Hieu, P.T., Tuan, N.N., Koichiro, W.: Routing dual criterion protocol. In: ICUIMC 2013: The 7th International Conference on Ubiquitous Information Management and Communication (2013)
4. Tung, N.T., Van Duc, N., Thanh, N.H., Vinh, P.C., Tho, N.D.: Power save protocol using chain based routing. In: Vinh, P.C., Hung, N.M., Tung, N.T., Suzuki, J. (eds.) ICCASA 2012. LNICST, vol. 109, pp. 183–191. Springer, Heidelberg (2013). ISBN: 978-1-936968-65-7
5. Dung, N.T., Van Duc, N., Tung, N.T., Van Tien, P., Hieu, P.T., Koichiro, W.: An energy-efficient ring search routing protocol using energy parameters in path selection. In: Vinh, P.C., Hung, N.M., Tung, N.T., Suzuki, J. (eds.) ICCASA 2012. LNICST, vol. 109, pp. 72–85. Springer, Heidelberg (2013). ISBN: 978-1-936968-65-7
6. Tung, N.T.: Heuristic energy-efficient routing solutions to extend the lifetime of wireless ad-hoc sensor networks. In: Pan, J.-S., Chen, S.-M., Nguyen, N.T. (eds.) ACIIDS 2012, Part II. LNCS, vol. 7197, pp. 487–497. Springer, Heidelberg (2012)
7. Yan, H., Shi, Z.J., Cui, J.-H.: DBR: depth-based routing for underwater sensor networks. In: Das, A., Pung, H.K., Lee, F.B.S., Wong, L.W.C. (eds.) Networking 2008. LNCS, vol. 4982, pp. 72–86. Springer, Heidelberg (2008)
8. Huang, C.J., Wang, Y.W., Shen, H.Y., Hu, K.W.: A direction-sensitive routing protocol for underwater. J. Internet Technol. **11**, 721–729 (2010)
9. Pompili, D., Melodia, T., Akyildiz, I.: A resilient routing algorithm for long-term applications in underwater sensor networks. In: Proceedings of the Mediterranean Ad Hoc Networking Workshop (Med-Hoc-Net), Sicily, Italy, 14–17 June 2006
10. Wang, P., Li, C., Zheng, J.: Distributed minimum-cost clustering protocol for underwater sensor networks (UWSNs). In: Proceedings of the IEEE International Conference on Communications (ICC '07), Glasgow, UK, 24–28 June 2007, pp. 3510–3515
11. Capella, J.V., Bonastre, A., Ors, R., Climent, S.: A new energy-efficient, scalable and robust architecture for wireless sensor networks. In: Proceedings of the 3rd International Conference on New Technologies, Mobility and Security, Cairo, Egypt, 20–23 December 2009, pp. 1–6
12. Capella, J.V.: Wireless sensor networks: a new efficient and robust architecture based on dynamic hierarchy of clusters. Ph.D. thesis, Universitat Politècnica de València, València, Spain (2010)
13. Heinzelman, W., Chandrakasan, A., Balakrishnan, H.: Energy-efficient communication protocol for wireless microsensor networks. In: Proceedings of the 33rd Annual Hawaii International Conference on System Sciences, Maui, HI, USA, 4–7 January 2000, pp. 10–16

Fuzzy Logic Control for SFB Active Queue Management Mechanism

Nguyen Kim Quoc[1(✉)], Vo Thanh Tu[2], and Nguyen Thuc Hai[3]

[1] Faculty of IT, Nguyen Tat Thanh University, Ho Chi Minh, Vietnam
nkquoc@ntt.edu.vn
[2] Faculty of IT, Hue University of Science, Hue, Vietnam
vothanhtu_hue@yahoo.com
[3] Institute of IT, Ha Noi University of Technology, Hanoi, Vietnam
haint.fit@gmail.com

Abstract. Internet is growing not only in the number of connected devices but also the diversity of the application layers. Therefore, the bottleneck problem in the router is a pressing issue in congestion control. So using the mechanisms of active queue management for congestion control at routers is playing an important role for the reliable and effective Internet network operation for users. Mechanism of active queue management SFB works well in the router, but not highly effective. Therefore, we propose to incorporate intelligent computation through fuzzy logic control system into the mechanism SFB which can operate more efficiently to improve service quality and network performance.

Keywords: Congestion control · Active queue management · Fuzzy logic controller

1 Introduction

Engineering active queue management (AQM: Active Queue Management) is mechanism controlling queue and loading operations at the routers. AQM controls the number of packets in the router queues by scheduling, removing proactively a coming packet or notifying blockage to regulate traffic on the network [2, 4, 5, 12]. In recent years, researchers have proposed a number of queue management mechanisms in routers based on the size of the queue (such as RED...) [19], packet loss factor and performance airtime usage (such as BLUE...)[7–9]. However, these mechanisms do not ensure good fairness for flows [6, 11, 22]. The mechanism SFB (Stochastic Fair BLUE) activities based on BLUE mechanisms ensure fairness for the flows, but do not achieve high throughput, haven't got low packet loss rate and small queue used space yet, so latency is still high [24]. Therefore, in this paper we propose to make active queue management mechanism FSFB (Fuzzy SFB) by using fuzzy logic controller (FLC) integrated active queue management mechanism SFB to proactively detect and control congestion better [10].

The results of the analysis and evaluation of simulation experiments based on NS2 software [13, 18] installed show that: queue management mechanism FSFB actively works well at each router, reduces packet drop and the latency and increases

P.C. Vinh et al. (Eds.): ICCASA 2013, LNICST 128, pp. 102–114, 2014.
DOI: 10.1007/978-3-319-05939-6_11, © Springer International Publishing Switzerland 2014

throughput of the flows. Therefore, the new queue management mechanism FSFB has improved network performance and responded quickly to the changes of network traffic of packets on the transmission line, so the quality of network services enhanced.

This article consists of five parts. The first part points out the necessity of queue management and proposed idea of new queue management mechanism FSFB. The second part discuses new queue management mechanism FSFB and relating issues. The third part focuses on the new queue management FSFB of the authors. The fourth part shows the process of simulation installation, test of experimental results with the process of theoretical study. The last part compares the performance of proposed queue management mechanism with the current queue management mechanism to make judgments and conclusions.

2   Related Works

2.1   Operation of SFB Mechanism

SFB divided queue into calculation bins, each bucket maintains a packet marking probability p_m. This probability increased /decreased linearly depending on the packet drop rate or extent of use of the transmission line. If at queue, there is a continuousness of packet cancellation because large transduction overflows queue, it will increase p_m, increases severity of obstructive message that it will sends back to the source. Conversely, if the queue becomes empty due to weak transduce or idle transmission line, then packet marking probability p_m reduces. Packet marking probability of each bin is determined as follows [23, 24]:

Based on the packet loss: if ((now-last_update) > freeze_time) then

$$p_m = p_m + \delta_1 \text{ and } Last\_update = now \tag{1}$$

Based on the idle connection: if ((now-last_update) > freeze_time) then

$$p_m = p_m - \delta_2 \text{ and } Last\_update = now \tag{2}$$

Where, p_m packet marking probability, δ_1 the increasing amount of p_m, δ_2 the reducing amount of p_m, *now* current time, *last_update* last time when p_m changed, *freeze_time* amount of time between successful changes.

The bins are organized in L levels, each level has N bins. In addition, SFB uses L independent hash functions, each function corresponding to a level. Each hash function maps a flow into one of the coming bins at this level. The bins are used to track and capture the statistics of queue occupation of the packet in that bin. When a packet comes to queue, it is hashed into L bins, each level is a bin. If the number of packets mapped in a bin exceeds a certain threshold (e.g., the size of the bin), the probability p_m in that bin increases. If the number of packets in the bin is reduced until the end, p_m reduces. Figure 1 below shows the operation model of the active queue management mechanism SFB:

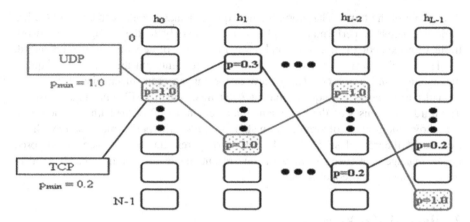

Fig. 1. The operation model of the mechanism SFB

Observation shows that with an unresponsive flow hashed into L bins, probability p_m at the bins rapidly rises to 1. The responsive flows can share one or two bins with unresponsive flows. However, if the number of unresponsive flows is not too large as compared to the number of bins, the responsive flow is able to be hashed at least into one bin without unresponsive flow, thus there is normal value p_m. The marking decision of a package based on p_{min} that is the minimum value of p_m of the mapped bins. If p_{min} is 1, the packet is defined as unresponsive flow and limited transmission speed of flow.

Here, the flows are defined as limited and unresponsive flows to save bandwidth. This strategy is done by limiting the speed of packet flowing in queue for flows with p_{min} value of 1. Picture above is an example that shows how SFB works. An unresponsive flow mapped into the bins, marking probability in these bins is 1. While TCP flows can be mapped into the same bin with the unresponsive flows at a particular level, it can also be mapped into the bins at other levels. Thus, the lowest marking probability of TCP flows is less than 1, so it is not defined as unresponsive flows. On the other hand, when the marking probability of unresponsive flows is 1, it will be limited transmission speed.

2.2   Effect of Boxtime Parameter

In SFB, all unresponsive flows are processed as a whole. How many the bandwidth used for the unresponsive flows has? It depends on the key parameter Boxtime. Boxtime is the interval without packet of such unresponsive flow coming into the queue. When a packet of UDP flow comes, if it is detected as packet of unresponsive flow, SFB will compare the current time with the nearest time when a packet of any unresponsive flow comes to the queue. If the period of these two events is greater than Boxtime, the packet will be in the queue, otherwise it will fall. If it is in the queue, the current time is updated for the next comparison. By this way, Boxtime indirectly controls how bandwidth is used for unresponsive flows. The large parameter Boxtime means that unresponsive flows can only achieve a low throughput, average queue length of the UDP flows is small. Conversely, if the value of Boxtime is small, the average queue size of the UDP flow is large. It is reasonable when the value of small Boxtime results throughput for large unresponsive flows. From the Boxtime is a static parameter, it can only be set by hand and hard to configure automatic adaptation, Boxtime value in a case cannot be applied to other case. This is a main drawback of SFB that should be addressed.

To improve fairness among UDP flows, we propose a method to create Boxtime as a random bit. By this way, the fairness among UDP flows is improved. However, this method only improves the fairness of unresponsive flows when they are limited the speed to create stability of bandwidth through the bottleneck transmission line. The high bandwidth streams will have higher mark probability as compared to the low bandwidth streams.

2.3 SFB Algorithm

Step 1: Calculate the hash functions (h_0, h_1,.., h_{L-1}).

Step 2: Check at each level. If the bin size is larger than allowed limit, then goes through Step 3. Conversely, if the bin is empty, goes through Step 4, if not goes through Step 5.

Step 3: Check if the interval from last update of the bin to the present time is greater than the allowed threshold, the increase of packet dropping probability (p) appears, goes through Step 5.

Step 4: Check if the interval from last update of the bin to the present time is less than the allowed threshold, the reduction of packet dropping probability (p) appears, goes through Step 5.

Step 5: Check if the smallest probability at the bins of packets mapped is of 1, the transmission speed of the flows is limited, in contrast coming packet is marked with probability p. Figure 2 shows the SFB algorithm.

3   Proposed Fuzzy Approach

3.1   Fuzzy Logic Controller

Fuzzy logic controllers, such as expert systems, can be used to model human experiences and decision making human behavior. FLC in the input-output relationship is expressed by using a set of linguistic rules or relational expressions. A FLC basically consists of four important parts including a fuzzifier, a defuzzifier, an inference engine and a rule base. In many fuzzy control applications, the input data are often clear, therefore, a fuzzification is necessary to convert the input crisp data into an appropriate value set with linguistic that is needed in inference engine. Singleton fuzzifier is the general fuzzification method used to map the crisp input to a singleton fuzzy set. In the rule base of a FLC, a set of fuzzy control rules, which characterizes the dynamic behavior of system, is defined. The inference engine is used to form inferences and draw conclusions from the fuzzy control rules. Figure 3 shows the fuzzy logic

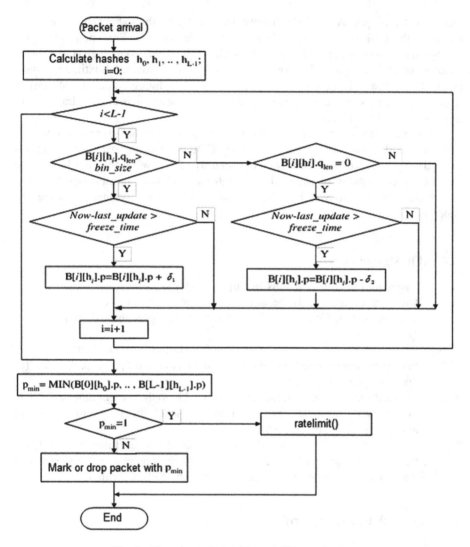

Fig. 2. Flowchart of algorithm of SFB mechanism

controller architecture. The output of inference engine is sent to defuzzification unit. Defuzzification is a mapping from a space of fuzzy control actions into a space of crisp control actions [26].

Suppose the FLC has n input variables $x_1, x_2,.., x_n$. Furthermore, suppose the rule base consists of K rules with the following general form: IF $(x_1$ is $A_1) \wedge...\wedge (x_i$ is $A_i) \wedge...\wedge(x_n$ is $A_n)$ THEN y is B. Where in the A_i and B are fuzzy sets of linguistic variables $x_1, x_2,.., x_n$ and y respectively. The output function $f(X)$ of this fuzzy controller with singleton fuzzifier, inference engine of result and center-average defuzzification method can be calculated as follows:

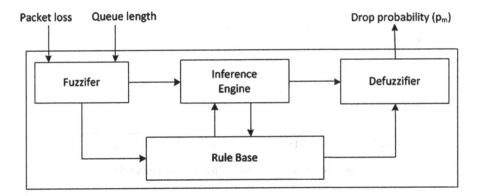

Fig. 3. Architecture of fuzzy inference system

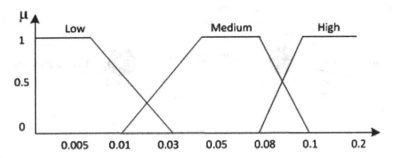

Fig. 4. Membership function of packet loss rate

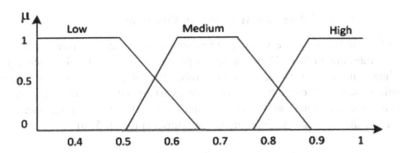

Fig. 5. Member function of level of using the size of the queue

$$f(x) = \frac{\sum_{j=1}^{k} y_0^j \cdot \prod_{i=1}^{n} \mu_i^j(x_i)}{\sum_{j=1}^{k} \prod_{i=1}^{n} \mu_i^j(x_i)} \qquad (3)$$

Where y_0 is the center value of the output fuzzy set b, $\mu(x)$ is the membership function for fuzzy sets. In our proposed model, we use two input variables for fuzzy controller which shows the current congestion including the packet loss rate and current queue length and the output will be the packet making probability value.

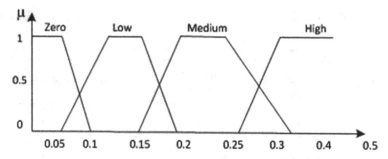

Fig. 6. Membership function of packet loss probability

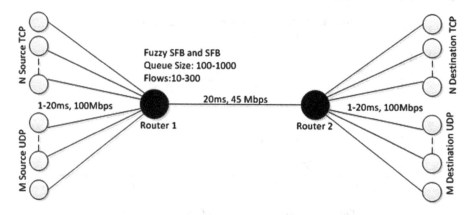

Fig. 7. Network simulation model

3.2   Linguistic Variables and Membership Functions

Input linguistic variables are variables representing the main affecting factors on the operation mechanism SFB. Here, we select packet loss factor, level of queue use to make input linguistic variables and the probability of packet loss used as output linguistic variables. Because the method of fuzzy triangular /trapezoidal is simple and effective noise reduction, so we choose this method to construct the membership function for the linguistic variable input and output (Figs. 4, 5, 6).

3.3   Construction of Fuzzy Rules

The fuzzy IF-THEN rules are built on experience from the experimental results and the value of the membership functions of the linguistic variables. There are two approaching methods: trial and error approaching method based on the knowledge gained from the experiment, a set of rule base based on IF-THEN rules and then system is tested. If the experimental results are deduced from the unsatisfactory laws, the laws will be amended. This process is continued until the function of the controller is satisfied. Based on functions of experiment and theory, we build rules in the rule base as follows:

Rule 1: **if** packet loss is low **and** queue length is low **then** p_m is zero;
Rule 2: **if** packet loss is low **and** queue length is medium **then** p_m is zero;
Rule 3: **if** packet loss is low **and** queue length is high **then** p_m is zero;
Rule 4: **if** packet loss is medium **and** queue length is low **then** p_m is zero;
Rule 5: **if** packet loss is medium **and** queue length is medium **then** p_m is zero;
Rule 6: **if** packet loss is medium **and** queue length is high **then** p_m is medium;
Rule 7: **if** packet loss is high **and** queue length is low **then** p_m is zero;
Rule 8: **if** packet loss is high **and** queue length is medium **then** p_m is low;
Rule 9: **if** packet loss is high **and** queue length is high **then** p_m is high;

4 Simulation and Results

4.1 Simulation Settings

During experimental process, network model is described according by following model: in simulation, we use N flows TCP and M unresponsive flows UDP responses flows. The transmission lines from source TCP and UDP to bottleneck and from bottleneck to destinations has a 100 Mbps bandwidth, latency is changed from 1 to 20 ms. Transmission line in the script is the link between two routers. We put the transmission bandwidth is 45 Mbps and the latency is 20 ms. Router at bottleneck is installed algorithms to evaluate and queue size at bottleneck changes in each circumstance [14, 21, 22] (Fig. 7).

In addition, parameters such as packet size of all TCP and UDP flows are set to 1000 bytes, TCP window size is 2000 packets, transmission speed of UDP flows changes in the simulation as an evaluation basis. Selected simulation time is 60 s.

Parameters for the mechanisms: δ_1, δ_2, freeze_time, N, L, bin_size, Boxtime. In particular, δ_1 is set large enough as compared to δ_2. We have chosen the following values: δ_1 is 0.0025, δ_2 is 0.00025 and freeze_time is 10 ms. N, L depends on the amount of flows to the bottleneck, if the number of unresponsive flows is large while N and L are small, the TCP flows are easy to be classified error layer as unresponsive flows. In our simulations, set as its default value is N = 6 and L = 2. Bin_size is set to equal of (1.5 / N)* queue size. We set the value for Boxtime as its default is 50 ms. However, this parameter must be calculated for each specific network model. So maybe it is ideal for a case but cannot be good for other case.

4.2 Evaluation Metrics

The performance evaluation of congestion control mechanisms is usually through criteria such as packet loss probability at place where congestion occurs, achieved network throughput, transmission line utilization level, the level of fairness of transmission line when the together connection to the transmission bottleneck and the queue utilization level at bottleneck [1, 3, 15–17, 20, 25].

Packet loss rate: The ratio of the number of loss packet and the total sending package. For stability network, the rate is low, whereas this rate is very high. Packet loss rate is determined by the formula:

$$packet\ loss\ percentage = \frac{\sum_{i=1}^{N} packet\ loss}{\sum_{1}^{N} packet\ sent} \tag{4}$$

Transmission line utilization level: As the ability to take advantage of network traffic that said the index's ability to communicate through the network connection is strong or weak and is calculated by the following formula:

$$utilization = \frac{byte\_departures_t}{bandwidth \times t} \tag{5}$$

Where utilization is the level of using transmission lines, byte_departurest is the number of bytes transmitted in t seconds, the bandwidth is the bandwidth of the transmission line and t is time of transmission.

Fairness level: is level of flows in network with ensuring fairness of connections when network has many other throughput types. Level of fairness is 1 when throughput of flows is equal, unless when throughput of flows is unequal, this value is less than 1. This value demonstrates greater, assurance of the congestion control algorithms is well. Fairness level is calculated as following formula:

$$fairness = \frac{\left(\sum_{i=1}^{N} x_i\right)^2}{N \times \sum_{i=1}^{N} x_i^2} \tag{6}$$

In particular, Fairness is fair level of flows, Fairness $\in$ [0, 1], x_i: is the throughput of flow i and N is the number of flows.

Average Queue Size: The index indicates directly the level of resource use at router. This index is defined as the ratio of the average queue size to the actual size of the queue. Mechanism with this small ratio will have small latency at the queue and risk of overflew queue is low. In contrast, the mechanism will make large latency and high risk of overflew queue. We use the quadratic average of control deviation to be index of queue utilization level and it is defined as:

$$S_e = \sqrt{\frac{1}{M+1} \sum_{i=0}^{M} e_i^2} = \sqrt{\frac{1}{M+1} \sum_{i=0}^{M} \left(Q_i - Q_{ref}\right)^2} \tag{7}$$

In particular, Q_{ref} is the queue size, Q_i is the queue size at the ith sampling time and M is the number of samples.

4.3   Evaluation of Packet Loss Rate

From the graph Fig. 8, we see that the queue size in the router increases, the packet loss rate of mechanisms reduces and when the number of connections to the router increases, the packet loss rate increases. In all cases, SFB always has the highest packet loss rate and the FSFB always have the lowest packet loss, when the queue size of 400 or more and the number of connections is less than 100, the packet loss rate of FSFB less than 2.5 %.

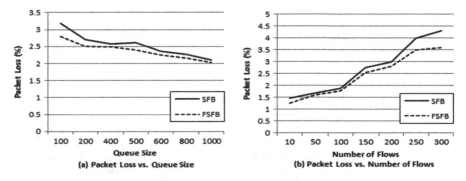

Fig. 8. Packet loss rate of the mechanisms of active queue management

4.4   Evaluation of Transmission Utilization Level

The graph in Fig. 9 shows the level of transmission line utilization of the mechanisms. The ability to take advantage of the transmission line utilization of the mechanisms increases, when the queue size and loading (number of connection flows) increases. When the queue size from 400 and over or the number of connections into router from 100 and over, mechanism FSFB uses better of transmission line, transmission rate used is over 90 %, and is always higher than the mechanism SFB.

4.5   Evaluation of Fairness

Based on the graph of Fig. 10 shows the fairness of the algorithm, we found that the fairness level of the algorithm by SFB and FSFB is very high at over 80 % for all cases. Particularly, mechanism FSFB always balance over 90 % in the cases which there are the changed number of connection flows.

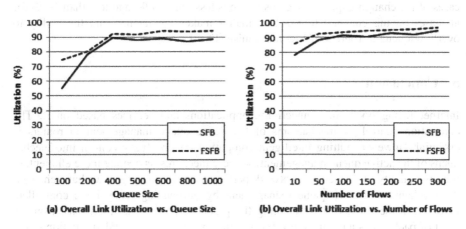

Fig. 9. The usage level of the transmission line of mechanisms of active queue management

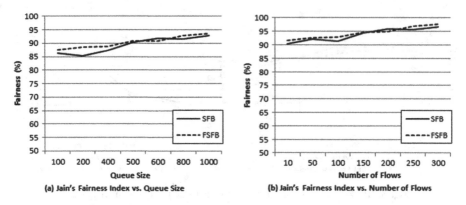

Fig. 10. The balance of the mechanism of active queue management

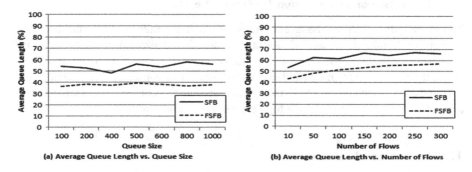

Fig. 11. The usage of the active queue management mechanisms

4.6 Evaluation of medium queue size

Based on the simulation results and graph demonstrating usage rate of the queue size of algorithm in Fig. 11, we found that FSFB usage level is always lower than SFB, in cases of the changing queue size, this figure is less than 40 %, and less than 60 % for all cases having changed flows. This matter makes the latency and the ability to overflow queue at routers of low mechanism FSFB.

5 Conclusion

Internet facing boom in connectivity, applications and services based on it. The congestion control by mechanisms of the active queue management in routers is essential. However, putting intelligent computing factors, fuzzy control into mechanisms of the active queue management, so these mechanisms operate more efficient, to improve quality of service and network performance. In this paper, we have changed the mechanism SFB of queue management by introducing fuzzy logic controllers involved in the process of calculating the probability of packet mark based on the level of packet loss and queue use level at the router. Experimental simulation based on software NS2 to the traditional mechanisms SFB and SFB with fuzzy controller (FSFB) in the same network model, showed FSFB has low packet loss rate, the use of high transmission and small latency at router queue. So FSFB controls and conducts congestion control better than the FSB. Results of the study group would contribute to the study of the world to improve network performance, enhance network quality of service.

References

1. Kapadia, A., Feng, W., Campbell, R.H.: GREEN: a TCP equation-based approach to active queue management. U.S Department of Energy through Los Alamos National Laboratory contract W-7045-ENG-36 (2011)
2. Dana, A., Malekloo, A.: Performance comparison between active and passive queue management. Int. J. Comput. Sci. Issues (IJCSI) **7**(3) No 5, 13–17 (2010)
3. Bitorika, A., Robin, M., Huggard, M., Goldrick, M.: A Comparative Study of Active Queue Management Schemes. Department of Computer Science Trinity College, Dublin (2011)
4. Wydrowski, B.P.: Techniques in Internet Congestion Control. Electrical and Electronic Engineering Department, The University of Melbourne (2003)
5. Wydrowski, B., Zukerman, M.: GREEN: an active queue management algorithm for a self. ARC Special Research Centre for Ultra-Broadband Information Networks, EEE Department, The University of Melbourne, Parkville, Vic. 3010, Australia (2010)
6. Ali Ahammed, G.F., Banu, R.: Analyzing the performance of active queue management algorithms. Int. J. Comput. Netw. Commun. (IJCNC) **2**(2), 1–19 (2010)
7. Thiruchelvi, G., Raja, J.: A survey on active queue management mechanisms. Int. J. Comput. Sci. Netw. Secur. (IJCSNS) **8**(12), 130–145 (2008)
8. Hasegawa, G., Murata, M.: Analysis of dynamic behaviors of many TCP connections sharing tail-drop – RED. CybermediaCenter, Osaka University, Japan (2003)
9. Chandra, H., Agarwal, A., Velmurugan, T.: Analysis of active queue management algorithms & their implementation for TCP/IP networks using OPNET simulation tool. Int. J. Computer Appl. (0975 – 8887) **6**(11), 12–15 (2010)
10. Tabash, I.K., Mamun, M.A.A., Negi, A.: A fuzzy logic based network congestion control using active queue management techniques. J. Sci. Res. **2**(2), 273–284 (2010)
11. Chung, J., Claypool, M.: Analysis of active queue management. Computer Science Department Worcester Polytechnic Institute Worcester, MA 01609, USA (2008)
12. Chitra, K., Padamavathi, G.: Classification and performance of AQM-based schemes for congestion avoidance. Int. J. Comput. Sci. Inform. Secur. (IJCSIS) **8**(1), 331–340 (2010)
13. Fall, K., Varadhan, K.: The ns Manual, A Collaboration between researchers at UC Berkeley, LBL, USC/ISI, and Xerox PARC (2010)
14. Le, L., Jeffay, K., Donelson Smith, F.: A loss and queuing-delay controller for router buffer management. In: Proceedings of the 26th IEEE International Conference on Distributed Computing Systems (ICDCS'06) (2006)
15. Le, L., Aikat, J., Jeffay, K., Donelson Smith, F.: The effects of active queue management and explicit congestion notification on web performance. IEEE/ACM Trans. Netw. **15**(6), 1217–1230 (2007)
16. Kwon, M., Fahmy, S.: A comparison of load-based and queue-based active queue management algorithms. Department Of computer Science, Purdue University, West Lafayette, IN 47906-1398, USA (2010)

17. Soyturk, M., Design and Analysis of TCP/IP Networks. G.Y.T.E., Spring (2011)
18. Ns-2.: Network Simulator. http://www.isi.edu/nsnam/ns
19. Floyd, S., Jacobson, V.: Random early detection gateways for congestion avoidance. Lawrence Berkeley Laboratory, University of California (1993)
20. Athuraliya, S., Low, S.H., Li, V.H., Yin, Q.: REM active queue management. IEEE Netw. **15**(3), 48–53 (2001)
21. Ahmad, S., Mustafa, A., Ahmad, B., Bano, A., Hosam, A.A.: Comparative study of congestion control techniques in high speed networks. IJCSIS **6**(2), 222–231 (2009)
22. Bhaskar Reddy, T., Ahammed, A., Banu, R.: Performance comparison of active queue management techniques. IJCSNS Int. J. Comput. Sci. Netw. Secur. 9(2), 405–408 (2009)
23. Feng, W., Kandlurz, D.D., Sahaz, D., Shin, K.G.: BLUE-a new class of active queue management algorithms. Department of EECS Network Systems, University of Michigan (2009)
24. Feng, W., et al.: Stochastic fair blue: a queue management algorithm for enforcing fairness. In: Proceedings of IEEE, April 2001
25. Stallings, W.: High-Speed Network: TCP/IP and ATM Design Principles. Prentice Hall, Upper Saddle River (1998). ISBN 0-13-525965
26. Zadeh, L.A.: Fuzzy sets. Inf. Control **8**, 333–353 (1965)

Ultrasound Images Denoising Based Context Awareness in Bandelet Domain

Nguyen Thanh Binh[1(✉)], Vo Thi Hong Tuyet[1], and Phan Cong Vinh[2]

[1] Faculty of Computer Science and Engineering,
Ho Chi Minh City University of Technology, Ho Chi Minh City, Vietnam
[2] Faculty of Information Technology,
Nguyen Tat Thanh University, Ho Chi Minh City, Vietnam
ntbinh@cse.hcmut.edu.vn, tuyetlaml508@gmail.com,
pcvinh@ntt.edu.vn

Abstract. Ultrasound is widely used modalities in medical imaging. Ultrasound imaging is used in cardiology, obstetrics, gynecology, abdominal imaging, etc. Almost ultrasound image contains some noise, poor contrast. This paper describes a method to denoise ultrasound image based context awareness in bandelet domain. Our proposed method uses bandelet filters to remove noise in ultrasound images. For demonstrating the superiority of the proposed method, we have compared the results with the other recent methods available in literature.

Keywords: Bandelet · Denoising · Multilevel thresholding · Context-aware

1 Introduction

Almost every kind of ultrasound image data contains some noise. The noise has variability from one condition to other such as machine specification, detector specifications, surroundings, etc. The goal of denoising is to remove noise details from a given possibly corrupted ultrasound image while maintaining edges features. Many algorithms have been proposed for noise removal, but the recent trend to noise removal is use of wavelet transform [6–11] and some paper remove noise using curvelet, contourlet transform [12, 19, 22].

The discrete wavelet transform have serious disadvantages, such as shift-sensitivity [14] and poor directionality [15]. Several researchers have provided solutions for minimizing these disadvantages. Some of them have suggested stationary [16], cycle-spinning [13], shiftable [17], steerable [18] wavelet transforms, etc. By using a translation invariant wavelet as the first stage of the curvelet transform, Starck [12] used the curvelet transform for image denoising. A double filter banks structure, which be developed the contourlet transform, has used for denoising experiments by Do and Vetterli [13, 20]. The ridgelet transform is proposed by Donoho and Candes [21] to remove noise. However, the area of image denoising is hard work and still a great challenge.

In this paper, we have proposed a multilevel thresholding based context awareness technique for noise removal in bandelet domain. The proposed method has been

P.C. Vinh et al. (Eds.): ICCASA 2013, LNICST 128, pp. 115–124, 2014.
DOI: 10.1007/978-3-319-05939-6_12, © Springer International Publishing Switzerland 2014

compared with earlier denoising method using complex wavelet transform [5] and curvelet transform [12]. For performance measure, we used Peak Signal to Noise ratio (PSNR), Mean Square Error (MSE) and it has been shown that the present method yields far better results.

The rest of the paper is organized as follows: in Sect. 2, we described the basic concepts of bandelet transforms. Details of the proposed algorithm are given in Sect. 3. In Sect. 4, the results of the proposed method for denoising are shown and compared to other methods. Finally in Sect. 5, we presented our conclusions.

2   Principles of Bandelet Basis

The bandelet, was constructed by Le Pennec and Mallat [1, 3], have bring optimal approximation results for geometrically regular functions. Bandelets are adapted to geometric boundaries as an orthonormal basis. The bandelets is to perform a transform on functions defined as smooth functions on smoothly bounded domains [1]. As bandelet construction utilizes wavelets, many of the results follow. Similar approaches to take account of geometric structure were taken for contourlets and curvelets.

The bandelet is an orthogonal, multiscale transform [1, 2]. The bandelet decomposition is applied on orthogonal wavelet coefficients. It is computed with a geometric orthogonal transform. We consider a wavelet transform at a fixed scale 2^j. The wavelet coefficients $<f, \psi_{jn}>$ are samples of an underlying regularized function.

$$<f, \psi_{jn}> \; = \; f * \psi_j(2^j n) \quad \text{where} \quad \psi_j(x) = \frac{1}{2^j}\psi(-2^{-j}x)$$

The coefficients $\psi_v[n]$ are the coordinates of the bandelet function $b_v \in L^2([0,1]^2)$ in the wavelet basis. A bandelet function [2] is defined by

$$b_v(x) = \sum_n \psi_v[n]\psi_{jn}(x)$$

It is a combination of wavelets and its support along a band as Fig. 1 [2]. Bandelets are as regular as the underlying wavelets. The support of bandelets overlap in the same way that the support of wavelets overlap [2]. This is particularly important for reconstructing image approximations with no artifacts. Figure 1 present a combination of wavelets along a band and its support is thus also along a band.

From an orthogonal wavelet basis with an orthogonal transformation, we are obtained from bandelets. Apply this transformation to each scale 2^j, an orthogonal basis of $L^2([0,1])^2$ defined as [2]:

$$B(T) \overset{def}{=} \underset{j \leq 0}{U} \{b_v | \psi_v \in B(T_j)\} \quad \text{where} \quad T \overset{def}{=} \underset{j \leq 0}{U} T_j$$

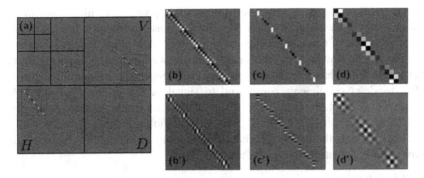

Fig. 1. (a) Localization on the wavelet domain of the squares S_i on which each Alpert wavelet vector is defined. (b)–(d) Discrete Alpert vectors ψ_{li} for various scales 2^l. (b')–(d') Corresponding bandelet functions (source: [2])

3   The Proposed Method

Denoising is the process of reducing the noise in the digital images that consists of three steps [4, 10, 12]: transform the noisy image to a new space. In new space, keep the coefficient where the signal to noise ratio is high, reduce the coefficient where the signal to noise ratio is low. A lot of work is available for the choice of suitable threshold in wavelet domain [4, 5, 7, 9]. Here, the proposed method is a two-part algorithm: bandelet coefficients computation and extraction of context aware bandelet filter.

3.1   Context-Based Soft-Thresholding Selection

The term 'context-aware', was first introduced by Schilit and Theimer [23], refer to context as location, identities of nearby people and objects, and changes to those objects.

Most of previous definitions of context are available in literature [27] that context-aware look at who's, where's, when's and what's of entities and use this information to determine why the situation is occurring. Here, our definition of context is:

"Context is any information that can be used to characterize the situation of an image such as: pixel, noise, strong edge, weak edge in medical image that is considered relevant to the interaction between pixels and pixels, including noise, weak and strong edge themselves."

In image processing, if a piece of information can be used to characterize the situation of a participant in an interaction, then that information is context. Contextual information can be stored in feature maps on themselves. Contextual information is collected over a large part of the image. These maps can encode high-level semantic features or low-level image features. The low-level features are image gradients, texture descriptors, shape descriptors information [24].

In this section, a wide range of soft-thresholding proposes to filter noise in ultrasound images. In the multiresolution analysis, the noise propagates at a higher level. For better removal of noise, especially the signal dependent noise, requires threshold at higher levels too. However, the threshold value should decrease, going from lower to higher levels. Filter-based technique features can independent of learning algorithm.

The bandelet coefficients correspond to signal of the image. The threshold T determines how the threshold is to be applied to the data. There are two popular: hard-thresholding and soft-thresholding. The soft-thresholding method shrinks all the coefficients towards the origin. The hard-thresholding shrinks only those coefficients to zero whose absolute value is less than T [25].

It is defined as:

$$w_{jk}^{soft} = sign(w_{jk}) \left(\left| w_{jk} \right| - T \right)_+$$

where,

$$sign(w_{jk}) = \begin{cases} +1, & if \ w_{jk} > 0 \\ 0, & if \ w_{jk} = 0 \\ -1, & if \ w_{jk} < 0 \end{cases}$$

and

$$(x)_+ = \begin{cases} x, & if \ x \geq 0 \\ 0, & if \ x < 0 \end{cases}$$

We estimate the threshold on the basis of statistical properties of bandelet coefficient. One of the estimates of standard deviation of noise (σ_n) in bandelet domain [25, 26] which depends on median of absolute bandelet coefficients is,

$$\widehat{\sigma_n} = Median(|w|)/0.6745$$

If $\{u_n\}$ are N independent Gaussian random variables of zero mean and variance σ^2, E (median $|u_n|_{0 \leq n \leq N}$) $\approx 0.6745 \ \sigma$. This threshold gives good result on simulated data, but this model assumes noise to be Gaussian distributed. For better removal of noise, specially the signal dependent noise, thresholding should be done at higher levels. However the amount of shrinkage should decrease, moving from lower to higher levels. Here, the level-dependent threshold T is [26],

$$T = \frac{1}{2^{j-1}} \left(\frac{\sigma}{\mu} \right) M$$

where, j is number of level at which threshold is applied.

Suppose, we have given the denoised coefficients of the $(i - 1)^{th}$ iteration step by $\widehat{X}^{i-1}[m, n]$, then the local variance of the i-th iteration step is given by [4]

$$\sigma_w^{(i)}[m,n]^2 = \frac{\sum_{j,k \in N} w_{j,k}^{(i)} \widehat{x}^{(i-1)}[j,k]^2}{\sum_{j,k \in N} w_{j,k}^{(i)}}$$

with a suitable set of weights $w^{(i)} = \{w_{j,k}^{(i)} | j, k \in N\}$. The adaptive thresholds of the i-th iteration step are define by

$$T^{(i)}[m,n] = \lambda^{(i)}(C)\sigma_n \frac{\sigma_n^2}{\sigma_w^{(i)}[m,n]^2}$$

For a coefficient-dependent of threshold, we propose a context-aware threshold selection. We use the local weighted variance $\sigma_w[m,n]^2$ of each bandelet coefficient $X^{(1,o)}[m,n]$ at level 1 using a window N, which covers a 4×4 neighborhood of $X^{(1,o)}[m,n]$ and a 2×2 neighborhood of the corresponding parent coefficient $X^{(1+1,o)}[m/2,n/2]$. Figure 2 shows one stage of the proposed context-based soft-thresholding.

3.2 Fast Bandelet Optimization

From a fast separable wavelet transform, we can be computed a fast discrete bandelet transform. We define a discrete warped wavelet transform which goes across the region boundaries. There are three steps associated to an image partition of the fast discrete bandelet transform [1]:

Firstly, we compute the image sample values in each region of the partition, we also describe its implementation together with the inverse resampling.

Secondly, a warped wavelet transform with a sub-band filtering along the flow lines is implemented. At the boundaries, warped wavelets still have two vanishing moments [1]. The wavelet coefficients of a discrete image are computed with a filter bank.

Finally, we compute bandelet coefficients along the flow lines. The transforming 1-D scaling functions into 1-D wavelets modifies a warped wavelet basis. From warped wavelet coefficients with a 1-D discrete wavelet transform along the geometric flow lines, we can compute bandelet coefficients.

The fast inverse bandelet transform includes the three inverse steps [1]:

(i)   recovers the warped wavelet coefficient along the flow lines;
(ii) an inverse warped wavelet transform with an inverse sub-band filtering;
(iii) an inverse resampling which computes the image samples along the original grid from the samples along the flow lines in each region.

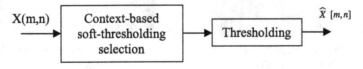

Fig. 2. Context-based soft-thresholding.

4 Experiments and Results

We applied the procedure described in Sect. 3 for our denoising experiments as briefly demonstrated in this section. For performance evaluation, we compare the proposed method based on context aware based bandelet (CABB) with the methods: the complex wavelet transform (CWT) based denoising [5], and the curvelet transform (CT) based denoising [12].

The comparison of results with other methods was done on our program and on the same images and at similar scale. The proposed method was tested using different noise levels of additive and multiplicative noise. We evaluated the performance of methods on PSNR and MSE values. MSE which requires two $M \times N$ gray-scale images, the original image I and the denoised image $\widetilde{I}$, is defined as,

$$MSE = \frac{1}{MN} \sum_{i=0}^{m-1} \sum_{j=0}^{n-1} \left| I[m,n] - \widetilde{I}[m,n] \right|^2$$

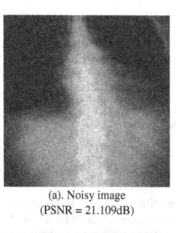

(a). Noisy image
(PSNR = 21.109dB)

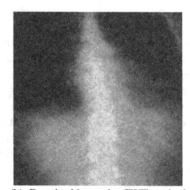

(b). Denoised image by CWT method
(PSNR = 26.093 dB)

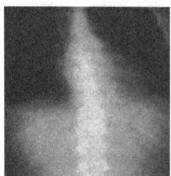

(c). Denoised image by CT
(PSNR = 29.145dB)

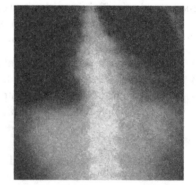

(d). Denoised image by the CABB
(PSNR = 30.583dB)

Fig. 3. Noisy image and denoised images by different methods.

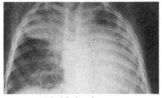

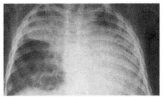

(a). Noisy image
(PSNR = 14.920 dB)

(b). Denoised image by CWT method
(PSNR = 15.415 dB)

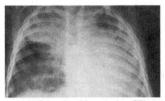

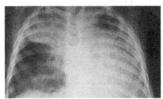

(c). Denoised image by CT
(PSNR = 16.275 dB)

(d). Denoised image by the CABB
(PSNR = 16.838 dB)

Fig. 4. Noisy image and denoised images by different methods.

The PSNR is the most commonly used as a measure of quality of reconstruction in image denoising, defined as,

$$PSNR = 20 \log_{10} \left(\frac{MAX_I}{\sqrt{MSE}} \right)$$

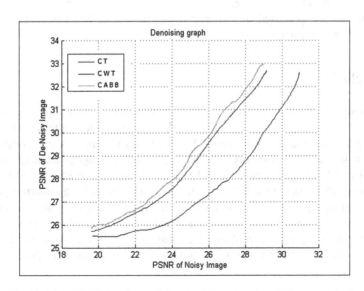

Fig. 5. Plot of PSNR values of denoised images using different methods.

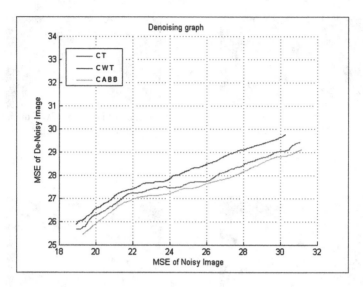

Fig. 6. Plot of MSE values of denoised images using different methods.

where, MAX_I is the maximum pixel value of the image.

Figures 3 and 4 show one representative noisy ultrasound image and denoised images by different methods as CABB, CWT and CT.

From Figs. 3 and 4, it is clear that the performance of the proposed method is better than other ones.

Figures 5 and 6 show the plot of PSNR and MSE values for different methods of the denoised images. In this figures, they can be well observed that the proposed method performs better than other methods.

To sum up, the proposed method performs better than the other methods of denoising in complex wavelet and curvelet domain.

5 Conclusions

As the above presentation, ultrasound image are generally of poor contrast. For image denoising, almost of the previous methods are frequency filtering, frequency smoothing and wavelet transformation. That methods will be lots of information in medical image and lots of memory. This paper presents an adaptive technique context-based soft-thresholding for denoising in bandelet domain. It is clear that our proposed method performs better than the other methods. The bandelet transform apply the multiscale grouping to the set of coefficient. By performing context-based soft-thresholding the largest error of a denoised image is reduced resulting in lower energy of the error which gives better denoising result. In the future work, we design an intelligent framework to select soft-threshold for another medical image.

References

1. Le Pennec, E., Mallat, S.: Sparse geometric image representations with bandelets. IEEE Trans. Image Process. **14**(4), 423–438 (2005)
2. Mallat, S., CMAP, Peyré, G., CEREMADE: Orthogonal bandelet bases for geometric images approximation. Commun. Pure Appl. Math. **LXI**, 1173–1212 (2008)
3. Le Pennec, E., Mallat, S.: Bandelet image approximation and compression. SIAM J. Multiscale Simul. **4**(3), 992–1039 (2005)
4. Khare, A., Tiwary, U.S.: Soft-thresholding for denoising of medical images – a multiresolution approach. Int. J. Wavelet Multiresolut. Inf. Process. **3**(4), 477–496 (2005)
5. Khare, A., Tiwary, U.S.: Symmetric Daubechies complex wavelet transform and its application to denoising and deblurring. WSEAS Trans. Signal Process. **2**(5), 738–745 (2006)
6. Donoho, D.L., Johnstone, I.M.: Ideal spatial adaptation by wavelet shrinkage. Biometrika **8**, 425–455 (1994)
7. Hilton, M.L., Ogden, R.T.: Data analytic wavelet threshold selection in 2-d denoising. IEEE Trans. Signal Process. **45**, 496–500 (1997)
8. Jansen, M., Malfait, M., Bultheel, A.: Generalized cross validation for wavelet thresholding. Signal Process. **56**, 33–44 (1997)
9. Weyrich, N., Warhola, G.T.: Wavelet shrinkage and generalized cross validation for image denoising. IEEE Trans. Image Process. **7**, 82–90 (1998)
10. Donoho, D.L.: Denoising by soft thresholding. IEEE Trans. Inf. Theory **41**(3), 613–627 (1995)
11. Chang, S.G., Yu, B., Vetterli, M.: Spatially adaptive wavelet thresholding with context modeling for image denoising. IEEE Trans. Image Process. **9**(9), 1522–1531 (2000)
12. Starck, J.-L., Candès, E.J., Donoho, D.L.: The curvelet transform for image denoising. IEEE Trans. Image Process. **11**(6), 670–684 (2002)
13. Coifman, R.R., Donoho, D.L.: Translation invariant denoising. In: Antoniadis, A., Oppenheim, G. (eds.) Wavelets and Statistics. Springer Lecture Notes in Statistics, vol. 103, pp. 125–150. Springer, New York (1995)
14. Strang, G.: Wavelets and dilation equations: a brief introduction. MIT numerical analysis report no. 89 (1989)
15. Gopinath, R.A.: The phaselet transform – an integral redundancy nearly shift-invariant wavelet transform. IEEE Trans. Signal Process. **51**, 1792–1805 (2003)
16. Nason, G.P., Silverman, B.W.: The stationary wavelet transform and some statistical applications. In: Antoniadis, A., Oppenheim, G. (eds.) Wavelets and Statistics. Lecture Notes in Statistics, vol. 103, pp. 281–299. Springer, Berlin (1995)
17. Simoncelli, E.P., Freeman, W.T., Adelson, E.H., Heeger, D.J.: Shiftable multiscale transforms. IEEE Trans. Inf. Theory **38**, 5587–5607 (1992)
18. Laine, A., Chang, C.-M.: Denoising via wavelet transforms using steerable filters. In: Proceedings of the IEEE International Symposium on Circuits and Systems, pp. 1956–1959 (1995)
19. Candès, E., Donoho, D.: Curvelets: a surprisingly effective nonadaptive representation of objects with edges. In: Cohen, A., Rabut, C., Schumaker, L. (eds.) Curves and Surfaces Fitting, pp. 123–143. Vanderbilt University Press, Nashville (1999)
20. Do, M.N.: Directional multiresolution image representations. Ph.D. thesis, EPFL, Lausanne, Switzerland (2001)
21. Candes, E.J.: Ridgelets: theory and applications. Ph.D. thesis, Stanford University (1998)

22. Zhang, B., Fadili, J.M., Starck, J.L.: Wavelets, ridgelets and curvelets for poisson noise removal. IEEE Trans. Image Process. **17**(7), 1093–1108 (2008)
23. Schilit, B., Theimer, M.: Disseminating active map information to mobile hosts. IEEE Network **8**, 22–32 (1994)
24. Jiang, H., Wang, J., Yuan, Z., Liu, T., Zheng, N., Li, S.: Automatic salient object segmentation based on context and shape prior. British Machine Vision Conference, pp. 1–12 (2011)
25. Donoho, D.L., Johnstone, I.M.: Ideal spatial adaptation via wavelet shrinkage. Technical report no. 400, Department of Statistics, Stanford University, Stanford, CA, November 1992
26. Donoho, D.L., Johnstone, I.M., Kerkyacharian, G., Picard, D.: Wavelet shrinkage: asymptopia? J. R. Stat. Soc. Ser. B **57**, 301–370 (1995)
27. Abowd, G.D., Dey, A.K., Brown, P.J., Davies, N., Smith, M., Steggles, P.: Towards a better understanding of context and context-awareness. In: Gellersen, H.-W. (ed.) HUC'99. LNCS, vol. 1707, pp. 304–307. Springer, Berlin (1999)

Human Object Classification in Daubechies Complex Wavelet Domain

Manish Khare[1], Rajneesh Kumar Srivastava[1], Ashish Khare[1(✉)],
Nguyen Thanh Binh[2], and Tran Anh Dien[2]

[1] Image Processing and Computer Vision Lab, Department of Electronics and
Communication, University of Allahabad, Allahabad, India
{mkharejk, rkumarsau}@gmail.com,
ashishkhare@hotmail.com
[2] Faculty of Computer Science and Engineering, Ho Chi Minh City University
of Technology, Ho Chi Minh, Vietnam
ntbinh@cse.hcmut.edu.vn, dientrananh@gmail.com

Abstract. Human object classification is an important problem for smart video
surveillance applications. In this paper we have proposed a method for human
object classification, which classify the objects into two classes: human and
non-human. The proposed method uses Daubechies complex wavelet transform
coefficients as a feature of object. Daubechies complex wavelet transform is
used due to its better edge representation and approximate shift-invariant
property as compared to real valued wavelet transform. We have used
Adaboost as a classifier for classification of objects. The proposed method
has been tested on standard datasets like, INRIA dataset. Quantitative experimental evaluation results show that the proposed method is better than other
state-of-the-art methods and gives better performance.

Keywords: Object classification · Feature selection · Daubechies complex
wavelet transform (DCxWT) · Adaboost classifier

1 Introduction

Classifying type of objects in real scene is a challenging problem for any computer
vision system with many useful applications like object tracking, segmentation of
moving object, smart surveillance etc. [1–3]. Correct video object classification is a
key component for development of a smart surveillance system. For any video surveillance application, an object classification algorithm should hold following
properties-

(i) object classification algorithm should perform under real time constraints.
(ii) object classification algorithm should be robust to the situations such as total or
partial occlusions of object, color variation in human cloths, large variation in
natural conditions, and varying lighting conditions etc.

To address the human object classification problem, different features and machine
learning techniques have been used. Selection of effective features is a crucial step for

P.C. Vinh et al. (Eds.): ICCASA 2013, LNICST 128, pp. 125–132, 2014.
DOI: 10.1007/978-3-319-05939-6_13, © Springer International Publishing Switzerland 2014

successful classification, Sialat et al. [4], in their pedestrian detection system, used Haar like features along with the decision tree. Viola et al. [5] used modified reminiscent of Haar basis function, for accomplishing object detection task. Lowe [6] used Scale Invariant Feature Transform (SIFT) as a feature descriptor for object recognition. Dalal and Triggs [7] proposed Histogram of oriented Gradient (HoG) as a feature descriptor for object detection, but HoG feature have disadvantages of having high dimensionality. Cao et al. [8] proposed a method by introducing an extension of the Histogram of oriented Gradient (HoG) features, known as boosting HoG feature. They used Adaboost scheme for boosting the HoG feature and SVM classifier for object classification. Lu et al. [9] proposed a visual feature for object classification based on binary pattern. These visual features are rotation invariant and exploit the property of pixel patterns.

All the methods discussed above depend on feature evaluation set therefore they have local advantages or disadvantage depending on the features they have used. Yu and Slotine [10] proposed a wavelet based method for visual classification. Method proposed by Yu and Slotine [10] uses real valued wavelet transform, but real valued wavelet transform is not suitable for video application because in case of video, object may be presented in translated and rotated form among different frames and coefficients of real valued wavelet transform corresponding to object region changes abruptly across different frames. Motivated by work of Yu and Slotine [10], we have proposed a new method for human object classification based on Daubechies complex wavelet transform (DCxWT) coefficients as a feature set. We have used Adaboost classifier for classifying human and non-human object classes. The DCxWT is having advantages of shift invariance and better edge representation as compared to real valued wavelet transform.

In the present work, our aim is to classify objects into two types of classes: human and non-human. We have experimented the proposed method at multiple levels of DCxWT and shown that performance of the proposed method is better at higher levels. The proposed method has been compared with the method using coefficients of discrete wavelet transform (DWT) as a feature set, and it has been shown that use of DCxWT as a feature set perform better than use of DWT coefficients as a feature set. We have compared the proposed method with other state-of-the-art methods proposed by Dalal and Triggs [7], Lu et al. [9], Renno et al. [11], and Chen et al. [12] in terms of average classification accuracy, True positive rate (Recall), True negative rate, False positive rate, False negative rate and Predicted positive rate (Precision).

The rest of the paper is organized as follows: Sect. 2 describes basics of used features (DCxWT), Sect. 3 describes Adaboost classifier and Sect. 4 describes the proposed method. Experimental results, analysis and comparison of the proposed method with other state-of-the-art methods are given in Sect. 5. Finally conclusion of the work is given in Sect. 6.

2 Feature Selection

Any object classification algorithm is commonly divided into three important components – extraction of features, selection of features and classification. Therefore, feature extraction and selection plays an important role in object classification.

We have used coefficients of Daubechies complex wavelet transform (DCxWT) as a feature for classification. A brief description of DCxWT is given in following subsection.

2.1 Daubechies Complex Wavelet Transform (DCxWT)

In object classification, we require a feature which remains invariant by shift, translation and rotation of object, because object may be present in translated and rotated form among different scenes. Due to its approximate shift-invariance and better edge representation property, we haved used DCxWT as feature set.

Any function $f(t)$ can be decomposed into complex scaling function and mother wavelet as:

$$f(t) = \sum_k c_k^{j_0} \phi_{j_0,k}(t) + \sum_{j=j_0}^{j_{max}-1} d_k^j \psi_{j,k}(t)$$

where, j_0 is a given low resolution level, $\{c_k^{j_0}\}$ and $\{d_k^j\}$ are approximation coefficients $\left[\phi(u) = 2\sum_i a_i \phi(2u - i)\right]$ and detail coefficients $\left[\psi(t) = 2\sum_n (-1)^n \overline{a_{1-n}} \phi(2t - n)\right]$.

where $\phi(t)$ and $\psi(t)$ share same compact support $[-L, L+1]$ and a_i's are coefficients. The a_i's can be real as well as complex valued and $\sum a_i = 1$.

Daubechies's wavelet bases $\{\psi_{j,k}(t)\}$ in one-dimension is defined through above scaling function $\phi(u)$ and multiresolution analysis of $L_2(\Re)$ [13]. During the formulation of general solution if we relax the condition for a_i to be real [14], it leads to complex valued scaling function.

DCxWT holds various properties [14], in which reduced shift sensitivity and better edge representation properties of DCxWT are important one.

3 Adaboost Classifier

Boosting a method to improve the performance of any learning algorithm, generally consist of sequentially learning classifier [15]. Adaboost itself trains an ensemble of weak learners to form a strong classifier which perform at least as well as an individual weak learner [11]. In our proposed work, we have used Adaboost algorithm which is firstly described by Viola and Jones [5] for their face detection system. Complete Adaboost algorithm for classifier is given below:
Adaboost algorithm for classifier-

- Given example images (I_1, J_1) (I_2, J_2),............. (I_n, J_n) where $J_i = 0,1$ for negative and positive example respectively.
  Initialize weights $W_{1,i} = \frac{1}{2n} \cdot \frac{1}{2p}$ for $j_i = 0,1$ respectively, where p and n are the number of positive and negative examples respectively.

- For t=1,2,..........T (Number of iterations)

1. Normalize the weights

$$W_{t,i} \leftarrow \frac{W_{t,i}}{\sum_{j=1}^{m} W_{t,j}}, \qquad W_t \text{ is the probability distribution}$$

2. For each feature, j, train a classifier h_j, which is restricted to using a single feature. The error (E_j) is evaluated with respect to W_t

$$E_j = \sum_i W_i |h_j(I_i) - J_i|$$

3. Choose the classifier, h_t with the lowest error E_t
4. Update the weights

$$W_{t+1,i} = W_{t,i} \beta_t^{1-\epsilon_i}$$

where $\epsilon_i = 0$, if example x_i is classified correctly
$\epsilon_i = 1$, otherwise

$$\beta_t = \frac{E_t}{1 - E_t}$$

- The final strong classifier is

$$h(I) = \begin{cases} 1, & \text{if } \sum_{t=1}^{T} \alpha_t h_t(I) \geq \frac{1}{2} \sum_{t=1}^{T} \alpha_t \\ 0, & \text{otherwise} \end{cases}$$

where, $\alpha_t = \log \frac{1}{\beta_t}$.

4 The Proposed Method

The proposed method is inspired by work of Yu and Slotine [10], which uses wavelet coefficients as a feature set. The proposed method uses Daubechies complex wavelet transform feature evaluation and Adaboost classifier for classification. For experimentation, we have considered two classes: human and non-human. Steps of the proposed method are as follows-

Step 1: Sample Collection- First step of the proposed method is to collect sample images for training the classifier. In our approach, we have taken INRIA dataset images for training purpose. The INRIA dataset [16] contains 2521 positive images and 1686 negative images of size 96 × 160. Positive images contains human object images and negative images contains any type of images in which human object is not present.

Step 2: Preprocessing of Images- The collected images are scale normalized to 256 × 256 pixel dimensions in order to reduce complexity. The scale normalized images in the RGB color space were converted to the gray level images.

Step 3: Feature Vector Calculation- For feature vector computation in the proposed method, image frames are decomposed into complex wavelet coefficients using Daubechies complex wavelet transform. After applying DCxWT, we get coefficients in four subbands namely – LL, LH, HL and HH. Values of LH, HL and HH subbands are used as feature values of different images. We skip value of LL subbands because LL subbands gives approximation coefficient of images and rest other LH, HL and HH gives detail coefficients of images.

Step 4: Human Object Classification- The calculated features are supplied into Adaboost classifier. This classifier separates, two types of images: human object image and non-human object image (do not contain any type of human). The test images have been categorized by this classifier.

5   Experimental Results

In this section, we provides experimental results of the proposed method and other state-of-the-art methods proposed by Dalal and Triggs [7], Lu et al. [9], Renno et al. [11], and Chen et al. [12] in terms of average classification accuracy, True positive rate(Recall), True negative rate, False positive rate, False negative rate and Predicted positive rate (Precision).

The proposed method for human object classification has been tested on standard dataset like – INRIA dataset [16]. INRIA dataset contains 2521 positive images and 1686 negative images of size 96 × 160. Here we present some representative images in Fig. 1.

Images shown in Fig. 1, have been taken from real scenes. By observing these images, one can observe that both frontal as well side views of human objects are

Fig. 1. Representative Human objects from INRIA dataset

taken into account. We have evaluated the proposed method for multiple levels of DCxWT coefficients (L-1,2........7). Just to compare the performance of the proposed method, we have also experimented with multilevel DWT coefficients as a feature for human object classification.

The comparative study of the proposed method and other state-of-the-art methods [7, 9, 11, 12] are shown in Table 1 in terms of six different performance metrics – average classification accuracy, True Positive Rate (Recall), True Negative Rate (TNR), False Positive Rate (FPR), False Negative Rate (FNR) and Predicted Positive Rate (PPR). These performance metrics depends on four values – TP, TN, FP and FN, which are defined as: TP (True Positive) are number of images which are originally positive images and detected as positive images, TN (True Negative) are number of images which are originally negative images and detected as negative images, FP (False Positive) are number of images which are originally negative images and detected as positive images and FN (False Negative) are number of images which are originally positive and detected as negative images.

Average classification accuracy is the proportion of the total number of predictions that were correct. True Positive Rate (also known as Recall) is the proportion of

Table 1. Performance Measure Values

Methods name	TPR (Recall) (%)	TNR (%)	FPR (%)	FNR (%)	PPR (Precision) (%)	Average Accuracy (%)
The Proposed method with DCxWT (Level-1) as a feature	94	70	30	06	75.81	82
The Proposed method with DCxWT (Level-2) as a feature	94	75	25	06	78.99	84.50
The Proposed method with DCxWT (Level-3) as a feature	98	75	25	02	79.67	86.50
The Proposed method with DCxWT (Level-4) as a feature	98	80	20	02	83.05	89
The Proposed method with DCxWT (Level-5) as a feature	99	88	12	01	89.19	93.50
The Proposed method with DCxWT (Level-6) as a feature	100	94	06	00	94.34	97
The Proposed method with DCxWT (Level-7) as a feature	100	95	05	00	95.24	97.50
DWT (Level-1) as a feature	70	65	35	30	66.67	67.5
DWT (Level-2) as a feature	75	70	30	25	71.43	72.5
DWT (Level-3) as a feature	75	70	30	25	71.43	72.5
DWT (Level-4) as a feature	80	74	26	20	75.47	77
DWT (Level-5) as a feature	85	80	20	15	80.95	82.5
DWT (Level-6) as a feature	85	82	18	15	82.52	83.5
DWT (Level-7) as a feature	92	86	14	08	86.79	89
Method used Dalal and Triggs [7]	94	92	08	06	92.16	93
Method used by Lu et al. [9]	90	70	30	10	75.00	80
Method used by Renno et al. [11]	89	69	31	11	74.17	79
Method used by Chen et al. [12]	98	96	04	02	96.08	96

positive cases that were correctly identified. True Negative Rate is defined as the proportion of negatives cases that were classified. False Positive Rate is the proportion of negatives cases that were incorrectly classified as positive. False Negative Rate is the proportion of positives cases that were incorrectly classified as negative. Predicted Positive Rate (also known as Precision) is the proportion of the predicted positive cases that were correct. These values can be determined using following formulas:

$$Average\ Classification\ Accuracy = \frac{TP + TN}{TP + FN + TN + FP}$$

$$TPR(\text{Recall}) = \frac{TP}{TP + FN}$$

$$TNR = \frac{TN}{TN + FP}$$

$$FPR = \frac{FP}{TN + FP}$$

$$FNR = \frac{FN}{TP + FN}$$

$$PPR(\text{Precision}) = \frac{TP}{TP + FP}$$

From Table 1, one can observe that the proposed method gives better performance at higher levels of Daubechies complex wavelet transform in comparison to other discrete wavelet transform and state-of-the-art methods [7, 9, 11, 12] for human object classification.

6   Conclusion

In this paper, we have developed and demonstrated a new method for classification of human object in real scenes. The approach first train Adaboost classifier by using coefficients of Daubechies complex wavelet transform as a feature set, then classify different objects into one of two categories: human and non-human. We have also experimented the classification result by using discrete wavelet transform as a feature set. We compared the proposed method with other state-of-the-art methods proposed by Dalal and Triggs [7], Lu et al. [9], Renno et al. [11], and Chen et al. [12] in terms of average classification accuracy, TPR, TNR, FPR, FNR and PPR, and found that the proposed method perform better than other methods. The main advantage of the proposed method is that, the proposed method can detect human objects of different size whether too small or too large, the proposed method can detect human objects with complex background.

Finally it could be concluded that on the basis of observed results, the proposed method for human object classification have better average classification accuracy, better TPR, TNR, FPR, FNR and PPR values in comparison to other state-of-the art methods [7, 9, 11, 12].

Acknowledgement. This work was supported in part by Council of Scientific and Industrial Research (CSIR), Human Resource Development Group, India, Under Grant No. 09/001/ (0377)/2013/EMR-I.

References

1. Hu, W., Tan, T.: A survey on visual surveillance of object motion and behaviors. IEEE Trans. Syst. Man Cybern. **34**(3), 334–352 (2006)
2. Khare, M., Srivastava, R. K., Khare, A.: Moving object segmentation in daubechies complex wavelet domain. Accepted for publication in Signal Image and Video Processing. Doi: 10.1007/s11760-013-0496-5 (2013)
3. Brooks, R.R., Grewe, L., Iyengar, S.S.: Recognition in wavelet domain: a survey. J. Electron. Imaging **10**(3), 757–784 (2001)
4. Sialat, M., Khlifat, N., Bremond, F., Hamrouni, K.: People detection in complex scene using a cascade of boosted classifiers based on Haar-like features. In: Proceeding of IEEE International Symposium on Intelligent Vehicles, pp. 83–87 (2009)
5. Viola P., Jones, M.: Rapid object detection using a boosted cascade of simple features. In: Proceeding of IEEE International Conference on Computer Vision and Pattern Recognition, vol. 1, pp. 83–87 (2001)
6. Lowe, D.: Object recognition from local scale invariant features. In: Proceeding of 7th IEEE International Conference on Computer Vision, pp. 1150–1157 (1999)
7. Dalal N., Triggs, B.: Histograms of oriented gradients for human detection. In: proceeding of IEEE International Conference on Computer vision and Pattern Recognition, pp. 886–893 (2005)
8. Cao, X., Wu, C., Yan, P., Li, X.: Linear SVM Classification using boosting HoG features for vehicle detection in low-altitude airborne videos. In: Proceeding of IEEE International Conference on Image Processing, pp. 2421–2424. (2011)
9. Lu, H., Zheng, Z.: Two novel real-time local visual features for omnidirectional vision. Pattern Recogn. **43**(12), 3938–3949 (2010)
10. Yu, G., Slotine, J. J.: Fast wavelet-based visual classification. In: Proceeding of IEEE International Conference on Pattern Recognition (ICPR), pp. 1–5 (2008)
11. Renno, J. P., Makris, D., Jones, G. A.: Object classification in visual surveillance using Adaboost. In: Proceeding of IEEE International Conference on Computer Vision and Pattern Recognition (CVPR), pp. 1–8 (2007)
12. Chen, L., Feris, R., Zhai, Y., Brown, L., Hampapur, A.: An integrated system for moving object classification in surveillance videos. In: Proceeding of IEEE International Conference on Advanced Video and Signal based Surveillance, pp. 52-59 (2008)
13. Daubechies, I.: Ten lecture on Wavelets. Society for Industrial and Applied Mathematics (SIAM) (1992)
14. Clonda, D., Lina, J.M., Goulard, B.: Complex daubechies wavelets: properties and statistical image modeling. Sig. Process. **84**(1), 1–23 (2004)
15. Zhu, Z., Zou, H., Rosset, S., Hastie, T.: Multiclass Adaboost. Int. J. Stat. Interface **2**, 349–360 (2009)
16. INRIA Person Dataset. http://pascal.inrialpes.fr/data/human Last Accessed 29 September 2013

An Efficient Method for Automated Control Flow Testing of Programs

Quang-Trung Nguyen[(✉)] and Pham Ngoc-Hung

Faculty of Information Technology, VNU University of Engineering and Technology,
Lahore, Pakistan
{trungnq.mi11,hungpn}@vnu.edu.vn

Abstract. This paper presents a method for automated control flow
testing of unit programs. The key idea of this method is to combine the
black-box and white-box techniques in order to minimize the complexity of white-box testing. Instead of performing black-box and white-box
separately, the proposed method uses the test inputs that are generated by black-box to reduce searching space of white-box testing. The
method then continually eliminates arcs in remaining space to find non-
duplicated test paths. Therefore, the proposed method is able to operate
white-box testing with less effort than the current method.

1 Introduction

Unit testing has been recognized as a key phase in improving software quality
in practice. Two techniques to operate unit testing are white-box and black-
box. Generally, black-box technique is inexpensive as well as easy to create test
cases and to test unpredictable behavior. However, it cannot detect internal
errors. On the contrary, control flow testing which has been known as a major
technique of white-box is more efficient for this problem. Unfortunately, this
technique requires deep understanding and high-level skill to analyze source
code. Because it is performed manually so it is very costly and inefficient. It is
believed that automatic testing is a solution to perform these types of testing
more effectively. Indeed, two techniques black-box and white-box have difference
pros and cons, and both of them, by them self, cannot supersede each other.
In software companies, that black-box and white-box are performed separately
takes a lot of time and effort. From the above-mentioned, what we need to find
out is how to create an efficient automatic tool combining black-box's advantages
and white-box's ones to produce a small set of test input data.

For recent years, there are many researches putting effort to minimize the
size of test inputs. For example, Gupta and Soffa [5] have studied the ways of
gathering coverage requirements so that each group can be covered by a test case,
which followed by guiding test case generation to produces a test case satisfies
multiple coverage requirements. Based on basis path testing concept [1], Ahmed
S. Ghiduk, O. Said and Sultan Aljahdali [6] introduced strategy using genetic
algorithm for automatically generating basis test paths. Bertolino and Marre [2]

P.C. Vinh et al. (Eds.): ICCASA 2013, LNICST 128, pp. 133–143, 2014.
DOI: 10.1007/978-3-319-05939-6_14, © Springer International Publishing Switzerland 2014

proposed a path generation method by using a reduced CFG. Guangmei et al [3] presented an automatic generation method of basis set of paths which is built by searching the CFG by depth-first searching method. On the other hand, with spanning sets, Martina Marre and Antonia Bertolino [4] reduced and estimated the number of test cases to satisfy coverage criteria.

This paper proposes a method to take advantage of both black-box and while-box techniques with the purpose of performing control follow testing of programs efficiently. Instead of focusing on whole CFG of the given unit, this method only uses a simplified CFG of it. The simplified CFG has been generated by removing the testing paths that are covered by the test cases of the black-box testing. Hence, the size of CFG is significantly reduced, which is followed by reducing effort in white-box testing. In addition, this method avoids duplicated paths with graph reduced before and during the searching process. It is also potentially performed to reuse test cases in the context of program evolution. Consequently, software companies have method for getting high quality set of test inputs with low cost.

The paper is organized as follows. Firstly, we introduce definitions and theorems for reducing graph in Sect. 2. The method, and two major steps of the proposed method will be shown in Sects. 3 and 4. In Sect. 5 we evaluate time complexity of two algorithms mentioned in Sects. 3, 4, and the whole of our method. Finally, Sect. 6 is conclusion.

2   Background

In this section, we show some basic definitions and theorems of graph theory that will be used through the paper.

Control flow graph which is a directed graph represents graphically the information needed to select the test cases. A control flow graph $G = (N, A)$ consists of a set N of nodes or vertices, and a set A of directed edges or arcs, where a directed edge $e = (T(e), H(e))$ is an ordered pair of adjacent nodes, called Tail and Head of e, respectively: we say that e leaves $H(e)$ and enters $T(e)$. If $H(e) = T(e')$, e and e' are called adjacent arcs. For a node n in N, $indegree(n)$ is the number of arcs entering and $outdegree(n)$ the number of arcs leaving it.

A program control flow may be mapped onto a flow graph in different ways. In this paper, we use a flow graph representation called ddgraph (decision-to-decision graph) which is particularly suitable for the purposes of branch. The following is a formal definition of ddgraph.

Definition 1. *(Ddgraph). A ddgraph is a graph $G = (N, A)$ with two distinguished nodes n_1 and n_0 (the unique entry node and the unique exit node, respectively), such that any node $n \in N$ is reached by n_1 and reaches n_0, and for each node $n \in N$, except n_1 and n_0, $(indegree(n) + outdegree(n)) > 2$, while $indegree(n_1) = 0$, $outdegree(n_1) = 1$, $indegree(n_0) > 0$, $outdegree(n_0) = 0$.*

A path P of length q in a ddgraph G is a sequence $P = (e_1, e_2, .., e_q)$ where $T(e_{i+1}) = H(e)$ for $i = 1, . . . , q\text{-}1$. P is said to be a path from e_1 to e_q, or

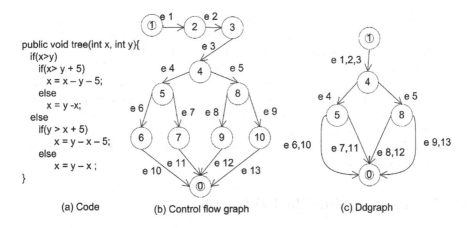

Fig. 1. Source code, control flow graph and ddgraph of tree method.

from $H(e_1)$ to $T(e_q)$. A node n reaches an arc n' if there is a path P in G from n to n'. A path, in ddgraph, is call complete path if it is path from n_1 to n_0.

Figure 1 shows the source code, traditional CFG and ddgraph form of a java unit. This method is the most complete case of ddgraph. In this case, the normal white-box technique needs select at least $|N| - 1$ path where $|N|$ is number of nodes in ddgraph for covering all branches of the unit.

Definition 2. *(Redundant arc). In ddgraph G, An arc e is call redundant arc if* $indegree(T(e) > 1, outdegree(H(e)) > 1$.

Theorem 1. *We can remove redundant arc without remove connective property of G.*

Proof. Assuming that we have a ddgraph $G = (N, A)$ with two distinguished nodes n_1 and n_0 and $e \in A$. By Definition 2, the arc e is redundant arc which $indegree(T(e)) > 1$. So, it is clear that, when we eliminate arc e in G, we can find at least one path from n_1 to $T(e)$, it mean that $T(e)$ can be reached by n_1. Similarly, because of having $outdegree(H(e)) > 1$, there is always at least one path form $H(e)$ to n_0. Thus, we can conclude that G does not loss connective property when eliminating redundant arcs.   □

Theorem 2. *In ddgraph $G = (N, A)$, with a complete path p (path from n_1 to n_0), we always reduce at least one arc $e \in p$.*

Proof. let $P = (e_1, e_2, ...e_q)$ is a complete path in ddgraph G, with $H(e_1) = n_1$ and $T(e_n) = n_0$. We assume that theorem is false. Hence, a path p has no redundant arc if any arc e of P; $indegree(T(e)) = 1$ or $outdegree(H(e)) = 1$. The arc e_1 has $H(e_1) = n_1$ so $outdegree(H(e_1)) = 1$. And because the G have no loop, we can infer that $indegree(T(e_1)) = 1$. Because of being a node of the ddgraph G, $T(e_1)$ satisfies the inequality $indegree(T(e_1)) + outdegree(T(e_1)) > 2$. So The inequality $outdegree(T(e_1)) > 1$ is true. Next, the edge e_2 has

$outdegree(H(e_2) = outdegree(T(e_1) > 1$. Likewise, the arc e_2 is not redundant arc, so $indegree(T(e_2)) = 1$. In summation, we can infer that $outdegree(T(e_2) > 1$. Similarly, by considering the other arc e_x of P (with $2 < x < q - 1$), $indegree(T(e_x)) = 1$ and $outdegree(T(e_x)) > 1$ are satisfied. At the arcs e_q where $T(e_q) = n_0$, we have $outdegree(H(e_q) > 1$ so there will be at least two arcs from the node $H(e_q)$. Because $indegree(n_0) = 1$, suppose that the arc e_y has $T(e_y) \neq n_0$. Ddgraph G has not cycles, therefore, we will always find at least one way to the n_0 which does not contain e_n from $T(e_y)$. As a result, $indegree(T(e_q)) > 1$ is true. In other words, it means that the arc e_q can be reduced and the theorem is true.   □

3   Generating Simplified Ddgraph

In order to operate control flow testing, we need to perform two major steps which are selecting paths and generating test inputs. The proposed method does not focus on selecting paths in whole CFG. Instead, it selects paths in sub CFG of program. Hence, in order to get sub ddgraph and take advantage of black-box, the first step of the proposed method simplifies the original ddgraph. Then, in the second step, the method finds test paths covering branches of sub ddgraph, followed by generating set of a test inputs corresponding to these paths.

This section presents the first step which is interested in reducing all the redundant arcs covered by black-box. The procedure named SIMPLIFY which is shown in Algorithm 1 is to operate this step. Generally, the inputs of this procedure are the test input data generated by black-box and an original ddgraph. And the output of it is a sub ddgraph of the input ddgraph. To specify, classical CFG, first, is used for symbolic execution [7] to find paths corresponding to black box test inputs. Then, the list of visited arcs will be chosen from this paths. For example, in Fig. 2, with set of black-box's path $B = \{P_1, P_2, P_3\}$, where $P_1 = (e_1, e_2, e_5)$, $P_2 = (e_1, e_2, e_4, e_7, e_8)$, and $P_3 = (e_1, e_2, e_4, e_7, e_9)$, the visited list is extracted as follow: $V = \{e | \forall e \in P_1 \bigcup P_2 \bigcup P_3\}$, so $V = \{e_1, e_2, e_4, e_5, e_7, e_8, e_9\}$.

After having V, the redundant arcs are eliminated from ddgraph. To begin, if the visited list is empty then the process stops (line 1). Conversely, each arc will be removed from the visited list and the graph if it is a redundant arc (line 2 to 7). After eliminating redundant arcs from the ddgraph, the redundant nodes which have just one arc entering and leaving on it can appear in ddgraph G. In ADJUST1 procedure presented in Algorithm 2 (line 8), all this nodes are eliminated from graph. Then the arcs binding to the redundant nodes are bound to create new arcs in both graph and visited list (line 8). Lastly, the visited list is checked to remove arcs not existing in ddgraph (line 9 to 13). After all, the process above is repeated until the visited list is empty.

When an arc is eliminated the number of outcomes in its head node and the number of incomes in its tail node will decrease by one. Hence, after that some arcs are not redundant anymore. For example, in Fig. 2(a), there are two redundant arcs from node 8 to node 1 but after one of them is removed the other is not redundant.

Algorithm 1. SIMPLIFY procedure

Input: Ddgraph G, set of visited arcs
Output: Ddgraph G' with smaller size
1: **while** visited_list is empty **do**
2:    **for** all e in visited_list **do**
3:      **if** $indegree(T(e)) > 1 \&\& outdegree(H(e)) > 1$ **then**
4:        $A = A - e$
5:        visited_list = visisted_list-e
6:      **end if**
7:    **end for**
8:    ADJUST1(G, visited_list)
9:    **for** all e in visited_list **do**
10:     **if** e $\nexists$ G **then**
11:       $visited\_list = visited\_list - e$
12:     **end if**
13:   **end for**
14: **end while**

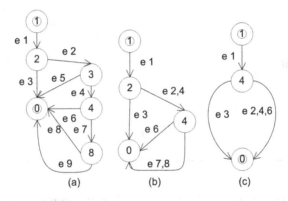

Fig. 2. Simplifying process of the ddgraph.

Figure 2 shows ddgraph in different status in three rounds of simplifying process corresponding to visited list V. In more detail, with the redundant arcs $e_5, e_8,$ and e_9 in first step, the arcs e_5, e_9, nodes 3 and 8 are reduced to generate ddgraph in Fig. 2(b). Then, the visited list V remains three arcs $\{e_1, e_{2,4}, e_{7,8}\}$. In second round, after eliminating the arc $e_{7,8}$, the visited list V consists of two arcs e_1 and $e_{2,4}$. However the arc $e_{2,4}$ does not exist in the ddgraph in Fig. 2(c), thus it is removed. The V remains one arc e_1 which is not a redundant arc thus the reducing process exits.

4   Generating Test Input Data

With the sub ddgraph, the working space of method was significantly declined. Then, in this section, the method focuses on selecting non duplicated paths and generating the set of test input corresponding to selected paths.

Algorithm 2. ADJUST1 procedure

Input: graph G, set of arcs
Output: DGraph G', set of arcs correspond to G'

```
 1: for all nodes n in N do
 2:    if indegree(n)=1 && outdegree(n)=1 then
 3:       for all e ∈ visited_list do
 4:          if T(e) = n then
 5:             eᵢ = e
 6:          end if
 7:          if H(e) = n then
 8:             eⱼ = e
 9:          end if
10:       end for
11:       e_new = (H(eᵢ), T(eⱼ))
12:       visited_list = (visited_list - eⱼ - eᵢ + e_new)
13:       for all e in A do
14:          if T(e) = n then
15:             eᵢ = e
16:          end if
17:          if H(e) = n then
18:             eⱼ = e
19:          end if
20:       end for
21:       e_new = (H(eᵢ), T(eⱼ))
22:       A = (A - eⱼ - eᵢ + e_new)
23:       N = (N - n)
24:    end if
25: end for
```

According to the Theorem 2 described in Sect. 2, a complete path always has at least one redundant arc. Thus, after finding complete paths, at least one arc may be reduced to create smaller ddgraph. In the proposed method, the selecting process continually finds complete paths and reduces redundant arcs and nodes until the ddgraph has only one arc.

The selecting process is presented in the procedure named FIND_BASIC which is shown in Algorithm 3. The following is a more detailed presentation of the method to select test paths. Initially, a set of return paths is created (line 1). Then, a path with start arc is created. If the generated path is complete (line 8), it means that the ddgraph has just one arc, then the path is added to the set of return paths (line 9) and the finding process ends (line 10). Otherwise, it is added to the stack (line 14). From line 15 to 32 is the deep-first-search process with an alteration. All redundant arcs in each found complete path are removed from the ddgraph (line 21 to 24). After the reduction, the graph is adjusted with the redundant eliminated nodes and the arcs which are bound together in ADJUST2 procedure presented in Algorithm 4 (line 26).

Algorithm 3. FIND_BASIC procedure

Input: Ddgraph G
Output: Set of complete paths covers all branches of G

```
 1: Create array of paths A
 2: while true do
 3:     Create s stack S
 4:     for all arcs e in G do
 5:         if H(e) = n₁ then
 6:             create a path p
 7:             add e to p
 8:             if p is complete path then
 9:                 add p to A
10:                 return A
11:             end if
12:         end if
13:     end for
14:     S.pop(p)
15:     while S is empty do
16:         for all arcs e in G do
17:             if e is adjacent p then
18:                 add e to p
19:                 if p is complete path then
20:                     add p to A
21:                     for all arcs e in p do
22:                         if indegree(T(e)) > 1&&outdegree(H(e)) > 1 then
23:                             A = A − e
24:                         end if
25:                     end for
26:                     ADJUST2(G)
27:                 else
28:                     S.push(p)
29:                 end if
30:             end if
31:         end for
32:     end while
33: end while
```

Figure 3 shows a ddgraph in the finding process which is implemented to generate a set of path covering all branches of it. For instance, in Fig. 3(a), after finding path $P_1 = (e_1, e_3, e_7)$, arc e_7 and node 4 are reduced. Then, in step 2, arc $e_{3,6}$ and node 2 are eliminated in path $P_2 = (e_1, e_3, e_6)$. Finally, after reducing arc e_4 and with ddgraph having only one arc $e_{1,2,5}$, the finding process is done. The process returns set of paths $S = \{(e_1, e_3, e_7), (e_1, e_3, e_6), (e_1, e_2, e_4), (e_1, e_2, e_5)\}$ covering all branches of the ddgraph.

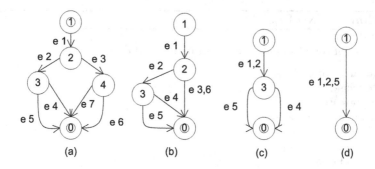

Fig. 3. Finding process.

5   Time Complexity

In this section, we estimate the time complexity of the proposed method. It can be calculated based on the time complexity of two major Algorithms 1 and 3. The time complexity of the method depends on many factors, such as the number of decision nodes, the shape of graph, and the coverage of black-box test cases. In the worst cases, if simplifying process is not operated, it may be approximately $O(n^4)$. In almost cases, when combining black-box, the time complexity of the proposed method is approximately $O(n^2 log(n))$. The following explains how the proposed method can reach time complexity $O(n^2 log(n))$.

At first glance, the time complexity of the proposed method is the maximum of the simplifying process's time complexity and the selecting process's one. So, the time complexity of generating simplified ddgraph and the one of generating simplified ddgraph are considered, respectively. First, the generating simplified ddgraph is presented in Algorithm 1. In the while loop of Algorithm 1, we can easily see that the codes from line 2 to line 7 which reduce redundant arcs have time complexity O(n). And, O(n) is the time complexity of codes eliminating not existed arcs from line 9 to 13. ADJUST1 procedure presented in Algorithm 2 has two loops. Thus, ADJUST1's time complexity is approximately $O(n^2)$. The SIMPLIFY procedure's time complexity depends on how many arcs in the visited list. In practice, when black-box's path covers all branches of the ddgraph, the SIMPLIFY procedure is not operated. But in order to estimate time complexity, we can assume that the SIMPLIFY procedure is performed when all branches are visited. So, in the worst case, in Fig. 1(c), when ddgraph has shape like complete binary tree, in each round we can reduce 1 from the height of tree when half of arcs which are connected to ending node are removed. Height H of tree is calculated as follows: $H = log(|N| - 1) + 1$. So we have time complexity of SIMPLIFY procedure is approximately $O(n^2 log(n))$.

In the FIND_BASIC procedure presented in Algorithm 3, the time complexity depends on how many arcs can be reduced from the path found by DFS. With the best case, the ddgraph which has series of condition nodes, the FIND_BASIC procedure is performed just one time. On the contrary, in the worst case, with ddgraph such as Fig. 1(c), we can reduce one arc from a found path and the loop

---

Algorithm 4. ADJUST2 procedure

Input: graph G
Output: Ddgraph G'

1: **for** all nodes n in N **do**
2:    **if** indegree(n)=1 && outdegree(n)=1 **then**
3:       **for** all e in A **do**
4:          **if** $T(e) = n$ **then**
5:             $e_i = e$
6:          **end if**
7:          **if** $H(e) = n$ **then**
8:             $e_j = e$
9:          **end if**
10:      **end for**
11:      $e_{new} = (H(e_i), T(e_j))$
12:      $A = (A - e_j - e_i + e_{new})$
13:      $N = (N - n)$
14:   **end if**
15: **end for**

Table 1. Black-box test input paths.

No.	Usage	Member score	Date	Path
1	0	50	5	e_1, e_3, e_{19}
2	0	150	25	e_1, e_3, e_{18}
3	100	50	5	e_1, e_2, e_5, e_6
4	400	150	25	e_1, e_2, e_5, e_7, e_8
5	600	50	5	$e_1, e_2, e_4, e_{11}, e_{13}, e_{17}$
6	600	50	25	$e_1, e_2, e_4, e_{11}, e_{12}, e_{15}$
7	600	150	5	$e_1, e_2, e_4, e_{11}, e_{13}, e_{16}$
8	600	150	25	$e_1, e_2, e_4, e_{11}, e_{12}, e_{15}$
9	600	300	5	$e_1, e_2, e_4, e_{11}, e_{13}, e_{16}$
10	600	300	25	$e_1, e_2, e_4, e_{11}, e_{12}, e_{14}$

will be repeated $|N| - 1$ times. Furthermore, depth-first searching algorithm is executed repeatedly. In each Depth-first searching loop, we use ADJUST2 produre so that time complexity can be calculated as $O(|A|) * O(|N| * |A|)$, approximate $O(n^3)$. Hence, when being performed just one time in the best case, it has $O(n^3)$ time complexity. And in the worst case, it has $O(n^4)$ time complexity.

Although the FIND_BASIC procedure needs a lot of time but after being simplified, the size of ddgraph is very small. We can examine the example of calculateBill method in java. The source code, CFG, and ddgraph of calculateBill is available at[1]. This method implements calculating bill task of restaurant. The input of this method are usage, member's score and date. The Table 1 shows that

---

[1] http://www.uet.vnu.edu.vn/~hungpn/calculateBill.jpg/

Table 2. While-box test inputs.

No.	Path	Constraints	Test input
1	(e_1, e_2, e_4, e_{10})	$Usage > 0$ $Usage \geq 500$ $((40) + 50 + Usage) \leq 600$	$Usage = 500.0$
2	$(e_1, e_2, e_5, e_7, e_9)$	$Usage > 0$ $Usage < 500$ $Usage > 200$ $((40) + 50 + Usage + (Usage - 50) * 0.1) < 400$	$Usage = 201.0$

10 sets of black-box test inputs covering almost of branches of the ddgraph. As a result, the ddgraph of this method was declined from graph having 11 nodes, 19 arcs to graph having 3 nodes and 3 arcs. Thus, white-box has to find two paths $S = \{(e_1, e_2, e_4, e_{10}), (e_1, e_2, e_5, e_7, e_9)\}$ for covering all branches of the sub graph. In summary, the final result is that the complexity time of whole process is approximately $O(n^2 log(n))$. The Table 2 shows the result of the while-box's test inputs corresponding with the test paths and constraints of them.

6   Conclusion

As show above, with all black-box's test paths eliminated, the control flow testing significantly reduces complexity. The time complexity of this method declines from $O(n^4)$ when performing white-box separately to $O(n^2 log(n))$ when combining with black-box. In addition, by continually removing the redundant arcs and nodes after finding complete paths, the proposed method can generate set of test inputs, which followed by yielding non duplicated paths. As a result, by take full advantage of black-box result, this method can select a small set of test inputs that cover all branches of graph with little effort. Does this method not only propose an approach get most of the black-box, it is also completely operated to reuse test cases in the context of program evolution.

Albeit, the proposed method has not supported for program unit with loop yet but in future, for solving this problem, we will focus on detecting and separating loop from graph to present it under no loop graph form. Now, this method is being implemented as a plugin of Eclipse for control flow testing java unit. In the next time, we will complete the plugin for evaluating performance of this method in practice.

References

1. McCabe, T., Thomas, J.: Structural testing: a software testing methodology using the cyclomatic complexity metric. NIST Special Publication 500–99, Washington, D.C. (1982)

2. Bertolino, A., Marre, M.: Automatic generation of path covers based on the control flow analysis of computer programs. IEEE Trans. Softw. Eng. **20**(12), 885–899 (1994)
3. Guangmei, Z., Rui, C., Xiaowei, L., Congying, H.: The automatic generation of basis set of path for path testing. In: Proceedings of the 14th Asian Test Symposium (ATS'05) (2005)
4. Marre, M., Bertolino, A.: Using spanning sets for coverage testing. IEEE Trans. Softw. Eng. **29**(11), 974–984 (1993)
5. Gupta, R., Soffa, M.L.: Employing static information in the generation of test cases. Softw. Test. Verification Reliab. **3**(1), 29–48 (1993)
6. Ghiduk, A.S., Said, O., Aljahdali, S.: Basis test paths generation using genetic algorithm. In: International Conference on Computing The Information Technology (ICCIT), pp. 303–308 (2012)
7. King, J.C.: Symbolic execution and program testing. Commun. ACM **19**(7), 385–394 (1976)

Awareness of Entities, Activities and Contexts in Ambient Systems

Bent Bruun Kristensen$^{(\boxtimes)}$

Maersk Mc-Kinney Moller Institute, University of Southern Denmark,
Odense, Denmark
bbkristensen@mmmi.sdu.dk

Abstract. Ambient systems are modeled by entities, activities and contexts, where entities exist in contexts and engage in activities. A context supports a dynamic collection of entities by services and offers awareness information about the entities. Activities also exist in contexts and model ongoing collaborations between entities. Activities and local contexts also obtain awareness information from the context about the dynamic collection of entities. Similarly activities, local contexts and entities are offered awareness information about activities and local contexts.

Keywords: Awareness · Entity · Activity · Context · Ambient system

1 Introduction

We focus on ambient systems—a combination of the reality-virtuality continuum, ubiquitous computing and robotics [1]—that are more complex than traditional systems and evolve more spontaneously. We understand ambient systems in terms of concepts and phenomena where users interact with several computations simultaneously and time and space aspects are essential. An ambient system identifies users, collaborates intelligently with the user, and supports users in their ongoing activities. We have evolved from "users communicating with information systems" to "users participating in ambient systems". Ambient systems support the participants' intentions and work tasks. However, the participants have the initiative and they deliver and request information. Users need models to understand and use ambient systems—and developers need models to design and implement ambient systems.

Ambient system models include entities, activities and contexts. A context supports a dynamic collection of entities by services and offers awareness information about this collection. Activities in contexts model ongoing collaborations between the entities. The notion of entity, activity and context used in this paper are very similar to the notion of tangible object, association and habitat used for modeling and characterization of ambient systems [1]. These concepts are abstractions with informational and physical aspects and in addition they supply each other and may be combined in descriptions and executions of collaboration. Tangible objects are autonomous and cover users, things, etc. Associations cover group activities between tangible objects like collaborations, meetings, etc. And habitats cover universes in which tangible

P.C. Vinh et al. (Eds.): ICCASA 2013, LNICST 128, pp. 144–156, 2014.
DOI: 10.1007/978-3-319-05939-6_15, © Springer International Publishing Switzerland 2014

objects and associations exist—like rooms, places, etc. [2]. The system is dynamic i.e. the instances of tangible object, association and habitat may appear and disappear. Tangible objects engage in activities and both tangible objects and associations enter and leave contexts.

Awareness means "has knowledge of existence" or in dynamic situations "becomes aware of existence". Contexts support awareness: When an element enters/leaves a context any other element in the context is notified about this—as well as the element entering/leaving is notified about any other element already in the context. Awareness is well known for traditional objects—and in this respect entities are seen as objects. However, awareness for contexts and activities is original: Context and activity are abstractions distinct to objects and entities (not only objects representing activities or contexts)—the characteristics of contexts and activities imply additional awareness support. The aim of the paper is to clarify the notion, potential, and examples of awareness support of activities and contexts (as a supplement to existing awareness of objects). The paper also includes experiments with prototypical systems and experimental implementations of awareness especially for activities and contexts.

2 Background

Habitats are conceived as some kind of locality, delimited by some boundary, comprising inhabitants and providing support to its inhabitants in the form of opportunities and services that allow its inhabitants to interact and achieve their various goals [3]. Physical habitats are close to our intuitive understanding in describing the localities where organisms and life-forms grow and live. However characterizing man-made physical environments also as habitats, rather than mere spaces, introduces the notion of thinking about how inhabitants and habitats influence each other and evolve over time. Informational habitats are those spaces that are created with and exist in information. From the definition of habitat an informational habitat is some kind of locality with inhabitants, who draw upon the support of the locality and both adapt accordingly.

Associations support associative modeling and programming through abstraction from collaborations [4]. The association abstraction integrates activity and role aspects, where the activity is between autonomous entities. The directive (sequencing rule) of an association is a central, partial description of interactions of the participating entities. An entity is autonomous, i.e. only the entity itself may execute its methods. An entity executes its contributions (e.g. a method invoked by the entity) to the activity in the context of the entity. An entity participating in various associations executes contributions from the various directives interleaved.

Related Work. Software that examines and reacts to an individual's changing context is described in [5]. Such software promotes and mediates people's interactions with devices, computers, and other people, and it helps navigate unfamiliar places. The paper defines context-aware computing, and describes four categories of context-aware applications: proximate selection, automatic contextual reconfiguration, contextual information and commands, and context-triggered actions.

When the user's situation, place or activity change the functionality of devices adapt to these changes [6]. A layered real-time architecture supports this kind of context-aware adaptation based on redundant collections of low-level sensors. A personal digital assistant and a mobile phone are used with a prototype to demonstrate situational awareness.

By means of wireless information services any social institution may structure activity in any place and thereby break down the traditional mapping between institutions and places [7]. This complicates the analysis of context for purposes of designing context-aware computing systems. Context has a physical, architectural aspect, but most aspects of context will also be defined in institutional terms. The paper includes two conceptual frameworks for the analysis of context in mobile and ubiquitous computing.

Common architecture principles of context-aware systems and a layered conceptual design framework are used to explain the different elements common to most context-aware architectures [8]. The resulting context-aware systems offer entirely new opportunities for application developers and for end users by gathering context data and adapting systems behavior accordingly.

A survey including a general analysis framework for context models and an up-to-date comparison of the most interesting, data-oriented approaches available in the literature in [9] is motivated by context-aware systems pervading everyday life. The survey provides a comprehensive evaluation framework, allowing application designers to compare context models with respect to a given target application.

A review of selected literature of context-aware pervasive computing in [10] supports the use of theory and practice to enable anywhere and anytime adaptive e-learning environments. The review particularly elaborates on context, adaptivity, context-aware systems, ontologies and software development issues.

3   Awareness

A conference information system is an example of an ambient system: Physical contexts include `seminar room`, `reception` and `coffee room`. Entities include `attendee` and `speaker`. Activities include `session`, `meeting`, `coffee break` and `conference dinner`. The `conference` is an activity in which `attendees` participate and take on roles at various events at various locations. `program committee`, `session chairs`, `speakers` are examples of informational contexts. A software agent, `desk agent`, is an example of an informational entity that offers reminders about time and place, history overview and GPS guidance. The physical entity `service robot` moves around and offers refreshments and physical guidance to `attendees`.

Figure 1 illustrates a system (static view only) with entities, contexts and activities schematically: Rectangles, stars and circles illustrate physical and informational contexts, activities and entities, respectively. Contexts are related in various ways and entities may be engaged in several activities.

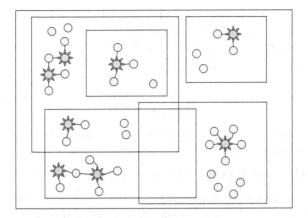

Fig. 1. Schematic example

Contexts: Services and Awareness. Contexts have two characteristic offers, namely service and awareness support:

- Services: A context has a number of services that are offered to entities contained in the context. The services are offered in various ways (in programming as methods local to the context to be invoked by the entities). For example internet and printer are offered to attendees in certain working areas.
- Awareness: Entities in the context obtain information about entities entering and leaving the context and vice versa. The information may be obtained in various ways and an entity may utilize this knowledge about other entities. For example an attendee that enters the seminar room for a session is offered information about the attendees already in the seminar room and vice versa.

We distinguish between descriptors and instances of entities, activities and contexts (similar to the distinction between classes and objects). From a description a number of instances may be created—and such instances have state. A context also contains (local) descriptors for entities, activities and contexts. In this way a context instance is not only a container of instances but by its local descriptors the context also offers potential additional instances to be created.

Figure 2 illustrates a context and entities X, Y, and Z schematically: Entity Z utilizes the services in the context, entity X enters the context and entity Y leaves the context. Entity Z becomes aware when entity X enters and entity Y leaves and entities X and Y become aware about the existence of Z. This awareness may be modified in

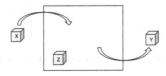

Fig. 2. Entity in, entering or leaving a context

various ways for example the notification is restricted to certain entities depending on type, state etc. Figure 2 also illustrates a generalized situation where the cube illustrates not only entities but also contexts and activities: An activity in the form of a `program committee meeting` may be interrupted shortly, moved into another location, and then continued. Similarly a context containing attendees with interest in `ambient systems` may be moved from context `attendees` to context `special interest`. Therefore awareness may include entities, activities and contexts in relation to each others, however for simplicity reasons this paper focuses specifically on awareness of activities and contexts in relation to entities.

Organization of Contexts. Contexts may be organized as follows:

- Disjoint: Two contexts are disjoint if no element is in both contexts: `seminar room` and `meeting room` are typically disjoint physical contexts.
- Overlapping: Two contexts are overlapping if some elements are in both contexts: `session chairs` and `speakers` are typically overlapping informational contexts.
- Nested: One context is nested within another context if any element in the context is also an element of the other context: `speakers` is nested within the `attendees` context.

Figure 3 illustrates the organizations of contexts schematically: Fig. 3(a) illustrates entities X and Y in disjoint contexts. Figure 3(b) illustrates entity Z in two overlapping contexts in which entity X respectively entity Y also exist. Figure 3(c) illustrates entity Y in a context that is nested in another context in which entity X also exists. Figure 3 also illustrates a generalized situation where the cube also illustrates not only entities but also context and activity.

The actual contents of context determine if the context is disjoint or overlapping: In Fig. 3(a) if an entity Z enters one of the contexts and then the other context then the organization changes from (a) to (b), and vice versa. For the nested organization in Fig. 3(c) all the contents of the local context is also in the enclosing context, i.e. entity Y is in both contexts whereas entity X is in the enclosing context only. The enclosing context offers services and awareness in Fig. 3(a). In Fig. 3(c) the local context typically has priority over the enclosing context. In Fig. 3(b) additional rules decide which context containing Z has priority.

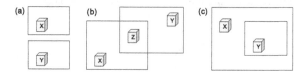

Fig. 3. (a) Disjoint, (b) Overlapping and (c) Nested contexts

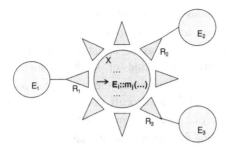

Fig. 4. Activity with directive and roles

4   Activities

Figure 4 illustrates activity X with its roles R_i, i=1...3, where entity E_i is engaged in X through role R_i. In the directive of X an arrow indicates the current position. The notation $E_i::m_j(...)$ is a request to autonomous entity E_i to execute its method m_j (because an entity is autonomous an activity cannot invoke its method but only request the entity eventually to do so) [4]. The state of X includes current position and knowledge of entities E_i, i=1...3.

Awareness of an activity includes notification of the state of the activity: An activity includes a directive, roles and entities engaged in the activity through these roles. The activity is dynamic, i.e. its state includes the current execution point of the directive. The state also includes the identity of (e.g. references to) the entities currently engaged in the activity. When an activity enters or leaves a context the state of the activity also enters/leaves. Awareness in relation to activities includes that the state of an activity is used appropriately in two situations:

- Activity awareness of entities.
- Entity awareness of activities.

Activity Awareness of Entities. An activity may be aware of entities: An activity enters or leaves a context including entities cf. Figure 5: The activity obtains information about entities in the context. Similarly an entity enters or leaves a context including activities cf. Figure 6: Also here the activities obtain information about the entity entering or leaving.

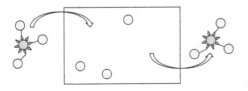

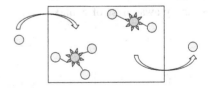

Fig. 5. Activity entering or leaving context with entities

Fig. 6. Entity entering or leaving context with activities

At the conference various activities other than `sessions` take place: Imagine a `session preparation` activity of some session between `speakers` and the `session chair`. This activity may be initiated by email interaction in an informational context supporting this kind of work. When `session chair` and `speakers` are present at the conference the `session preparation` may for practical reasons be moved to a `meeting room`. Upon its entry to the `meeting room` the `session preparation` is informed about `attendees` already in the `meeting room`—including for example additional `speakers` at the `session`. The ongoing `session preparation` is informed whenever an `attendee` (maybe yet another `speaker` at the `session`) enters the `meeting room`.

Entity Awareness of Activities. An entity may be aware of activities: Fig. 6 illustrates an entity that enters or leaves a context containing activities: The entity obtains information about activities in the context. Figure 5 illustrates entities where an activity enters or leaves the enclosing context: Also here the entities obtain information about the activity entering or leaving.

An `attendee` entering a context `seminar room` with an ongoing `session` is informed about the `session` including e.g. `session chair` and `speakers`. The `attendee` immediately is informed about the actual state of the `session` including the `paper` currently being presented and the `speaker`. The progress is also available i.e. whether the `speaker` currently presents the paper or answers questions.

5   Contexts

Figure 7 illustrates context C_G containing entity E, activity A, and local context C_L. The state of C_G includes E, A and C_L. Contexts are similar to name structures [11]: The rules of *static scoping* applies except that the organization of the contexts is modified dynamically because entities, activities and context may dynamically may enter and exit contexts (distinct from *dynamic scoping* where the scope structure is determined by the calling sequence of e.g. functions).

Awareness of a context includes notification of the state of the context: A context contains a dynamic collection of entities, activities and local contexts. When a context enters or leaves a context the state of the/now local) context—including entities activities and local contexts—also enters/leaves. Awareness in relation to local contexts includes that the state of a context is used appropriately in two situations:

- Context awareness of entities.
- Entity awareness of contexts.

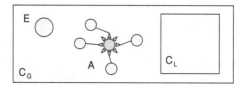

Fig. 7. Context with entity, activity and local context

Context Awareness of Entities. A context may be aware of entities: A context enters or leaves a context containing entities cf. Figure 8: This context obtains information about entities in the context. Similarly an entity may enter or leave a context containing contexts cf. Figure 9: Also here these contexts obtain information about the entity entering or leaving.

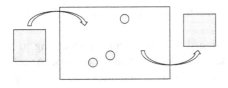

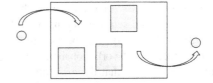

Fig. 8. Context entering or leaving context with entities

Fig. 9. Entity entering or leaving context with local contexts

A context that represents an interest group, ambient systems, may be spontaneously organized within the attendees context. At some point in time it is realized that special interest offers substantially better support and ambient systems is moved to this context. Upon its entry to the special interest the ambient systems context is informed about attendees already in the special interest (including for example attendees so far unaware of this initiative). Furthermore ambient systems is informed whenever an attendee (maybe another attendee so far unaware of this initiative) enters special interest.

Entity Awareness of Contexts. An entity may be aware of local contexts: Fig. 9 illustrates an entity that enters or leaves a context containing local contexts: This entity obtains information about local contexts in the context. Figure 8 illustrates entities where a context enters or leaves the enclosing context: Also here these entities obtain information about the context entering or leaving.

Upon entry of the ambient systems to the special interest any attendee already in this context is informed about this specific interest. Furthermore any attendee later on entering the context special interest is informed about the existence of the ambient systems context. The information includes the state of ambient systems, e.g. which events are planned and which attendees have registered so far for these events.

6 Experiments

Prototypical Systems. Various prototypical systems illustrate awareness of activities and contexts and that this additional form of awareness has shown to be useful and expressive.

Experiments include the ambient system Ubiquitous Doorman [12] where a user of a building is guided and supported in various activities in which the user takes part.

The user may enter and leave physical contexts in the form of various kinds of rooms and engage in activities such as meetings, lectures etc. At any time the user is supported by a helpful and informative ambient system. When walking in the building the user is immediately updated about the actual use of rooms and whereabouts of persons: Just outside a seminar room the user is informed which teaching activity takes place in the room and the state of this teaching activity including teacher, students and time information. Also guidance to specific locations and about upcoming events is supported: At any time and place the user is guided to a specific room or informed when a specific seminar begins or ends.

SoccerLab [13] is a soccer simulator designed and implemented according to a conceptual framework consisting of agents, activities, roles and contexts. Agents represent players that dynamically take on various roles in activities. Activities represent a soccer team's formation, tactics and styles as collaborative behavior of multiple players and prescribe sequences of player actions. Contexts represent environments in which players exist. Informational contexts represent among others groups of players, whereas physical contexts represent physical areas such as goal area and penalty area. When a team has the ball, the team is in its informational context `Ball Possession`. When the team loses the ball the team changes to context `No Ball Possession` in which the team immediately applies a service in order to instantiate appropriate activities e.g. `Pressure Play` and `Defend`. All players of the team engage in these activities simultaneously but their actions depend on their role on the team (defender, attacker, etc.) and the actual location of players and ball on the field (penalty area, own half, etc.). Furthermore different variants of these activities are available dependent on the actual location of the ball with respect to penalty area, goal area, or other physical contexts. Similarly the other team changes to context `Ball Possession` in which the team immediately applies a service in order to instantiate appropriate activities e.g. `Ball Control` and `Attack`. Similarly several variants of attack activities are available and the choice among these depends on the actual location of the ball and the players of the team.

Another exploratory prototype models collaboration of physical artifacts [14]. An artifact is a LEGO figure with basic structure and behavior—and models of collaborations between these artifacts are created. The models are executable—and the artifacts interact by e.g. moving around or sending messages. Children play with a family of dolls by making the dolls interact by creating and manipulating sequences of behavior. The family members engage as a group and individually in various activities e.g. social activities, work activities, sport activities. The environment includes physical contexts e.g. house, room, garden, neighborhood and informational contexts e.g. family, children, friends. Examples on awareness of activities and contexts are similar the other prototypes but the significant difference is that users are replaced by physical artifacts.

Experimental Implementation. A virtual environment in Java has three levels: The top part is a visualization of the system. The logical part at the bottom is an application framework with `Entity`, `Activity` and `Context` as abstract classes, i.e. (autonomous) entities (directing but not controlling) activities and contexts (with dynamic organization) are simulated. The simulator in the middle part maintains the repository of entities, activities and contexts, and supports user collaboration with the virtual environment. When entities, activities and contexts move around or a user interactively moves these around, the environment visualizes the resulting awareness support.

Figure 10 gives extracts of a simple implementation of awareness notification in abstract classes `entity`, `activity` or `context` that extend abstract class `Autonomous` and implement interface `Awareness` from Fig. 11:

- Abstract method `enters(Context c, Entity e)` informs that entity e has entered context c (similarly for methods `enters(Context c, Activity a)` and `enters(Context c, Context cc)`).
- Abstract method `exits(Context c, Entity e)` informs that entity e is contained in context c (similarly for methods `exits (Context c, Activity a)`and `exits (Context c, Context cc)`).
- Method `enter(Entity e)` of abstract class `context` is invoked when entity e enters and notifies entities, activities and contexts in `context` about e (similarly for methods `enter(Activity a)` and `enter(Context c)`).

In Figs. 12 and 13 extended abstract classes `conference_Entity` and `conference_Activity` implement some *general* reaction of `enters(...)` and `exits(...)` methods. Also extended classes of `conference_Entity` and `conference_Activity` add additional, *specific* reaction to the `enters(...)` and

```
abstract class Entity extends Autonomous
        implements Awareness {
    // ...
};
abstract class Activity extends Autonomous
        implements Awareness {
    // ...
};
abstract class Context extends Autonomous
        implements Awareness {
    public void enter(Entity e) {
      //for each Activity a in this Context:
        a.enters(this, e);
        e.exits(this, a);
      //for each Context c in this Context:
        c.enters(this, e);
        e.exits(this, c);
    };
    public void enter(Activity a) {
      //for each Entity e in this Context:
        e.enters(this, a);
        a.exits(this, e);
    };
    public void enter(Context c) {
      //for each Entity e in this Context:
        e.enters(this, c);
        c.exits(this, e);
    };
    // ...
};
```

```
abstract class Autonomous
        implements Runnable {
    protected abstract void Lifecycle();
    public void run()  {
      Lifecycle();
    };
    // ...
};


interface Awareness {
    void enters(Context c, Entity e);
    void enters(Context c, Activity a);
    void enters(Context c, Context cc);
    void exits(Context c, Entity e);
    void exits(Context c, Activity e);
    void exits(Context c, Context cc);
};
```

Fig. 10. Abstract   classes   `Entity`, `Activity` and `Context`

Fig. 11. Abstract class `Autonomous` and interface `Awareness`

```
abstract class conference_entity
                    extends Entity {
  // ...
};
class attendee extends conference_entity {
  // ...
  public void enters(Context c, Context cc) {
    super.enters(c, cc);
    // ...
  };
  public void exits(Context c, Context cc) {
    super.exits(c, cc);
    // ...
  };
  protected void Lifecycle() {
    //Autonomously execute requests
    //Also decide if notifications about
    //contexts are relevant
  };
};
class session_chair extends attendee {
  // ...
};
class speaker extends attendee {
  // ...
};
```

Fig. 12. Examples of extended classes of Entity

```
abstract class conference_activity
                    extends Activity {
  // ...
};
class session_preparation
                extends conference_activity {
  // ...
  public void enters(Context c, Entity e) {
    super.enters(c, e);
    // ...
  };
  public void exits(Context c, Entity e) {
    super.exits(c, e);
    // ...
  };
  protected void Lifecycle() {
    //Directive: Forward requests
    //Also decide if notifications about
    //entities are relevant
  };
};
class session extends conference_activity {
  // ...
  public void enters(Context c, Entity e) {
    super.enters(c, e);
    // ...
  };
  protected void Lifecycle() {
    //Directive: Forward requests
    //Also decide if notifications about
    //entities are relevant
  };
};
```

Fig. 13. Examples of extended classes of Activity

exits(...) methods. The figures illustrate among others extended classes for scenarios where an entity enters a context where an activity already exists (i.e. speaker, seminar room, session) and where an entity enters a context where a context already exist (i.e. attendee, special interest, ambient systems). The scenarios illustrate how the states of respectively activity and context are involved in awareness notification.

The activity scenario includes that the session chair and some speakers engaged in session preparation enter meeting room. Upon its entry the session preparation (through exits(Context c, Entity e)) is informed about attendees already in the meeting room, including speakers at the session. Also the ongoing session preparation is informed (through enters(Context c, Entity e)) whenever an attendee enters meeting room: session preparation can adjust to the situation so additional speakers get involved appropriately. In addition the activity scenario includes that an attendee enters a seminar room with an ongoing session and is informed about the session including session chair and speakers as well as the actual state including the paper currently being presented by the speaker. The scenario also includes that a missing speaker in the session suddenly enters the seminar room so that the ongoing session (through enters(Context c, Entity e)) is informed about this `speaker`: Because `session` directs the sequencing of the presentations either the `session` can modify the schedule appropriately and directly request this `speaker` to make a presentation—or because `session chair` is also notified about the entrance of this `speaker` the `session` can request `session chair` to reschedule the presentations.

The context scenario includes that `ambient systems` enters `special interest` where any `attendee` already in this context is informed (through `enters(Context c, Context cc)`) about `ambient systems`. Furthermore any `attendee` later on entering `special interest` is informed (through `exits(Context c, Context cc)`) about the existence of `ambient systems`. An `attendee` notified in this way may inspect the services of `ambient systems` and—if appropriate—decide also to enter `ambient systems`.

7 Summary

Awareness of contexts and activities is an essential addition to awareness of entities: Not only entities but also ongoing activities and supportive contexts become aware of not only entities but also activities and contexts. An activity is an abstraction and the state of an ongoing activity is available: The outcome is not only an entity with methods but information about execution state and entities engaged in the activity. Also a context is an abstraction and the state of a supportive context is available: The outcome is not only time, place and services offered but information about actual entities, activities and local contexts contained in the context.

Experiments with prototypes and implementation show that awareness of activities and contexts is useful and expressive—and that simple and efficient implementation techniques are available. Challenges include how awareness of activities and contexts are integrated in existing languages, platforms and tools.

Acknowledgments. We thank Palle Nowack and Daniel May for awareness and inspiration.

References

1. May D.C.-M., Kristensen, B.B., Nowack, P.: Tangible objects: modeling in style. In: Proceedings of the Second International Conference on Generative Systems in the Electronic Arts (Second Iteration—Emergence), Australia (2001)
2. May, D.C.-M., Kristensen, B.B.: Habitats for the digitally pervasive World. In: Qvortrup, L. (ed.) Applications of Virtual Inhabited 3D Worlds. Springer, London (2004)
3. May, D.C-M.: TangO: Designing for the digitally pervasive World. Ph.D. Thesis, Maersk Mc-Kinney Moller Institute, University of Southern Denmark (2003)
4. Kristensen, B.B.: Rendezvous-based collaboration between autonomous entities: centric versus associative. Concurr. Comput. Pract. Exp. **25**(3), 289–308 (2013). Wiley Press
5. Schilit, B.N., Adams, N.I., Want, R.: Context-aware computing applications. In: Proceedings of the Workshop on Mobile Computing Systems and Applications, California. IEEE Computer Society (1994)

6. Schmidt, A., Aidoo, K.A., Takaluoma, A., Tuomela, U., Van Laerhoven, K., Van de Velde, W.: Advanced interaction in context. In: Gellersen, H.-W. (ed.) HUC 1999. LNCS, vol. 1707, pp. 89–101. Springer, Heidelberg (1999)
7. Agre, P.E.: Changing places: contexts of awareness in computing. Hum. Comput. Interact. **16**(2–4), 177–192 (2001)
8. Baldauf, M., Dustdar, S., Rosenberg, F.: A Survey on context-aware systems. Int. J. Ad Hoc Ubiquitous Comput. **2**(4), 263–277 (2007)
9. Bolchini, C., Curino, C., Quintarelli, E., Schreiber, F.A., Tanca, L.: A data-oriented survey of context models. SIGMOD Rec. **36**, 19–26 (2007)
10. Soylu, A., De Causmaecker, P., Desmet, P.: Context and adaptivity in pervasive computing environments: links with software engineering and ontological engineering. J. Softw. **4**(9), 992–1013 (2009)
11. Maclennan, B.J.: Principles of Programming Languages. Design, Evaluation and Implementation, 3rd edn. Oxford University, New York (1999)
12. Jensen, S.E.: Exploration and implementation of key aspects of ubiquitous doorman. Maersk Mc-Kinney Moller Institute, University of Southern Denmark (2005)
13. Hargesheimer, B.: Design and experiments with a general model of context-dependent collaborations between autonomous participants. Maersk Mc-Kinney Moller Institute, University of Southern Denmark (2006)
14. Kristensen, B.B., May, D., Nowack, P.: Beyond playing with physical LEGO bricks: modeling interaction between behavioral artifacts. In: IADIS International Conference on Cognition and Exploratory Learning in Digital Age, Romania (2010)

A Method and Tool Support for Automated Data Flow Testing of Java Programs

Van-Cuong Pham$^{(\boxtimes)}$ and Pham Ngoc-Hung

Faculty of Information Technology, VNU University of Engineering and Technology,
Hanoi, Vietnam
{cuongpv.mi11,hungpn}@vnu.edu.vn

Abstract. This paper proposes a method and a tool support for automated data flow testing of Java programs. The key purpose of this method is to detect improper uses of data values due to coding errors. Given source code of a Java program, the proposed method analyzes and visualizes the program as a data flow graph. All test paths for covering all definition-use pairs of all variables are then generated. A test case corresponding to each generated test path is produced by identifying values to the input parameters so that the test path is executable. The expected outputs of these test cases are identified automatically. An implemented tool supporting the improved method and experimental results are also presented. This tool is promising to be applied in practice.

Keywords: Software testing · Data flow testing · White-box testing · Data flow anomaly · Data flow coverage.

1 Introduction

Software testing has been considered as the major solution in improving quality of software systems. Currently, software testing techniques can be divided into two kinds such as black-box testing and white-box testing. However, software companies focus only on the black box testing techniques in order to validate whether software products meet the customer requirements. By this approach, they only detect the errors/mistakes which can be observed by users. As a result, all potential errors of program code can be not detected. Moreover, detecting such errors has been recognized as a key difficult and expensive task in practice. In addition, the testers in charge this task are required high level knowledge and skills for analyzing source code. These issues are still open problems in software companies, especially in Vietnam.

Data flow testing has been known as a key white box testing technique that can be used to detect improper uses of data values due to coding errors [4]. These errors are inadvertently introduced in a program by programmers. For instance, a software programmer might use a variable without defining it, or he/she may define a variable, but not initialize it and then uses that variable in a predicate (e.g. int x; if(x==100);) [4]. The problem of errors in variables

P.C. Vinh et al. (Eds.): ICCASA 2013, LNICST 128, pp. 157–167, 2014.
DOI: 10.1007/978-3-319-05939-6_16, © Springer International Publishing Switzerland 2014

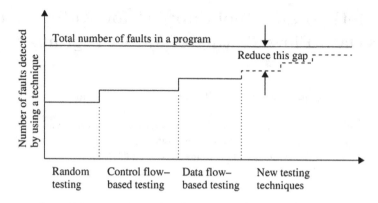

Fig. 1. Limitation of different fault detection techniques.

is common problems of programmers. In addition, Ntafos [10] has reported on the results of an experiment comparing with the effectiveness of three test selection techniques. The data flow testing, control flow testing, and random testing detected 90 %, 85.5 %, and 79.5 % respectively, of the known defects. Furthermore, Fig. 1 shows the limitation of different fault detection techniques [10]. These facts imply that data flow testing is one of the most effective methods for examining structure of programs. Although there are some methods and tools supporting data flow testing such as BPAS - ATCGS (Basic Program Analyzer System - Automatic Test Case Generation System) [8], JaBUTi [9], DFC (Data Flow Coverage) [3], etc, these methods only generate all paths for covering given source code. In fact, we need a tool that assists the tester in creating test data [5] that include expected output. Some free versions only allow testing the programs that are fixed in these tools and they are difficult to be extended in order to satisfy the specific data flow testing purposes of a certain software company.

This paper presents a method for data flow testing of Java programs. Given source code of a program, this method analyzes and visualizes the program as a data flow graph. All test paths corresponding to all paths of the data flow graph for covering all definition-use pairs of all variables in the program are then generated. All test cases of generated test paths are produced by giving values to the input parameters. The set of the values to the input parameters and expected outputs of the produced test cases are also generated automatically. In order to show the practical usefulness of the proposed method, a tool supports the method is implemented. The obtained experimental results by applying this tool for some typical programs are completely reliable in detecting all errors about using data variables. In addition, this tool is a free version, open source, and promising to be applied in practice.

The paper is organized as follows. We first review some background in Sect. 2. Section 3 describes a method for data flow testing of Java programs. Section 4 shows the implemented tool and experimental results. Finally, we conclude the paper in Sect. 5.

2   Background

This section presents some basic concepts which are used in our work as follows.

A definition of a variable x (denoted def) when the variable x is assigned a new value. When a variable x is used to compute in a statement, it is called a computation use (denoted c-use) of the variable x. Similarly, if the variable x is used in the predicate of conditional statement, it is called a predicate use (denoted p-use) of the variable x. A variable is defined in a statement and is used in another statement which may occur immediately or several statements after the definition called a definition-use (denoted def-u) pair of that variable.

Data flow graph(DFG) is a directed graph $G = \{N, E\}$, where N is a finite set of nodes and each node represents a c-use or def; E is a finite set of directed edges and each edge represents a p-use; $n_0, n_f \in N$ are entry node and exit node respectively. A path is a finite sequence of nodes connected by edges. A complete path is a path whose first node is the start node and whose last node is an exit node. A path is definition clear path (denoted def-$clear$ $path$) w.r.t a variable if it contains no new definition of that variable. A test path is a path for covering a def-u pair of a variable in a program. A complete path is executable if there exists an assignment of values to input variables and global variables such that all the predicates evaluate to true, thereby making the path executable. Executable paths are also known as feasible paths [1]. For example, source code of a program and its data flow graph are shown in Fig. 2(a) and Fig. 2(b) respectively.

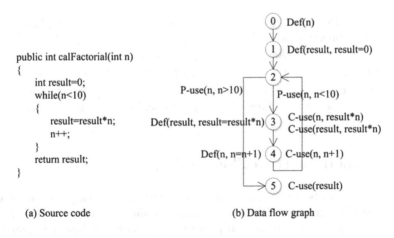

(a) Source code   (b) Data flow graph

Fig. 2. Source code and its data flow data flow graph.

Definition 1. *(DEF). A definition of a variable $v \in V$ at node $n \in N$, denoted $DEF(v, n)$, such that $DEF(v, n) = true$ if variable v is defined at node n and $DEF(v, n) = false$ otherwise.*

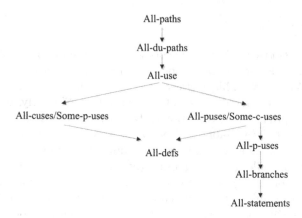

Fig. 3. Relationship among data flow testing criteria.

Definition 2. *(C-USE). A computation of a variable $v \in V$ at node $n \in N$, denoted C-USE(v,n), such that C-USE(v,n) = true if variable v is used to compute at node n and C-USE(v,n) = false otherwise.*

Definition 3. *(P-USE). A predicate of variable $v \in V$ at edge $e \in E$, denoted P-USE(v,e), such that P-USE(v,e) = true if the variable v is used at edge e and P-USE(v,e) = false otherwise.*

Definition 4. *Definition use path (du-path): A path $(n_1, ..., n_j, n_k)$ is a definition use path (denoted du-path) w.r.t. x if node n_1 has a def of x and either node n_k has a c-use of x and $(n_1, .., n_j, n_k)$ is def-c simple path w.r.t. x or edge (n_j, n_k) has a p-use of x and $(n_1, ..., n_j, n_k)$ is a def-c loop-free path w.r.t. x [1].*

Depending on the criterion selected, Frankl, Weyuker [1], and Parrish [2] have defined seven types of data flow testing criteria and relationship among them is shown in Fig. 3.

3   A Method for Data Flow Testing

This section presents a method for data flow testing of Java programs. Given source code of a program, this method analyzes and visualizes the program as a data flow graph. Next, finding all paths in the generated data flow graph for covering all *def-u* pairs of all variables in the program. Finally, all test cases corresponding to the generated test paths are created by giving values to the input parameters. The expected outputs of these test cases are also computed automatically.

Let U be a program, $V = \{v_1, v_2, .., v_n\}$ be a set of variables of U, $G = \{N, E\}$ be a data flow graph of U, and P be a set of du-path paths.

Algorithm 1. Finding all path for each variable in program

1: Initially, $P = empty$, V, G {P is a set du-paths of all variables, V is a set variables, G is a data flow graph}
2: **for** each variable v in V **do**
3:   **for** each node m in N **do**
4:     **for** each node n in N **do**
5:       **if** du-$c(v,m,n)$=$true$ **then**
6:         $P_{def-c} = P_c(v,m,n)$
7:       **end if**
8:     **end for**
9:     **for** each edge e in E **do**
10:       **if** du-$p(v,m,e)$=$true$ **then**
11:         $P_{def-c}+ = P_p(v,m,e)$
12:       **end if**
13:     **end for**
14:     **for** each path p in P_{def-c} **do**
15:       **if** p is *def-c path* **and** p is *complete path* **then**
16:         $P.add(p)$
17:       **end if**
18:     **end for**
19:   **end for**
20: **end for**
21: **return**

3.1   Test Path Generation

In this part, we propose a method for finding these paths. We are interested in finding all paths for covering all *def-u* pairs of all variables in a program U.

Definition 5. *(du-c). A variable $v \in V$ and node m and $n \in N$. du-$c(v,m,n)$ = true if $DEF(v,m) = true$ and C-$USE(v,n) = true$ else du-$p(v,m,e) = false$ otherwise.*

Definition 6. *(du-p). A variable $v \in V$, $m \in N$, and $e \in E$. du-$p(v,m,e) = true$ if $DEF(v,m) = true$ and P-$USE(v,e)$ else du-$p(v,m,e) = false$ otherwise.*

Definition 7. *(P_c). For each $v \in V$, $\forall m, n \in N$, if du-$c(v,m,n) = true$, existing a set of paths, denoted P_c, where $\forall p \in P_c$ has first node is m and last node is n.*

Definition 8. *(P_p). For each $v \in V$, $\forall m \in N$ and $\forall e \in E$ if du-$p(v,m,e) = true$, existing a set of paths, denoted P_p, where $\forall p \in P_p$ has first node is m and last edge is e.*

First, we will identify all paths which cover all *def-u* pairs of all variables. The set of these paths denotes P_{def-u}, where $P_{def-u} = P_c \cup P_p$. After that, examining all paths in P_{def-u}, $\forall p \in P_{def-u}$, if p is *def-c path* and *complete path*, then the path p is added into P.

The following is more detailed presentation of the method to find *test paths*. This method is shown in Algorithm 1. In this algorithm, we use an array data structure which contains the paths. These paths are generated by driving the path from a definition to a use of a variable in a program. Initially, the algorithm sets the array P to the *empty* (line 1). For each variable $v \in V$ (line 2), we identify a variable is defined and used at (line 5) and (line 10). Next, a set of paths is generated from a *def-u* pair (line 6 & 11). After having the set of path P, for each p in P, if p is *def-c path* and *complete path* (line 15), then add p into P (line 16). The algorithm iterates the entire process by looping from line 2 to line 20 until all variables in V are visited. The algorithm terminates and exits the program (line 21).

Depending on the criterion selected [1], we find the appropriate path for each data flow testing criteria. For example, with regard to the *All-defs* criteria, if $DEF(v, m) = true$, selecting a path $p \in P$ and path p has first node is m. Similarly, other data flow testing criteria are also identified by removing some inappropriate paths in P.

3.2   Test Case Generation

Test cases are generated by identifying the set of values to the input parameters and the set of expected outputs for each test path.

Definition 9. *(f_e). $\forall e \in E$, $\forall v \in V$, a boolean function, denoted fe, where fe:* $2^{|V|} \rightarrow \{true, false\}$.

For each $p \in P$, select a complete path p_c so that p_c contains path p. The set of edges in p_c that contains a *p-use* is $E_p = \{e | P\text{-}USE(v, e) = true, e \in p_c, v \in V\}$. Let $Fe = \{f_e | \forall e \in E_p, f_e = boolean\}$ be a set of boolean functions and $V' \in 2^{|V|}$ be a set of variable parameter. In order to p_c is an executable path, then we have to determine the values to the input parameters so that $f_e = true$, $\forall f_e \in Fe$. By improving the exhaustive search algorithm [7], the problems about generating test data have been solved partly. First, the Fe is divided into three main groups as follows.

$$Fe_1 = \{f_e(v) | v \in V', f_e(v) \in Fe, f_e(v) = C\}, \qquad (1)$$

where $\forall fe \in Fe_1$, fe only has a variable and the sign of f_e is the sign of equality($=$) and C is a constant.

$$Fe_2 = \{f_e(v) | v \in V', f_e(v) \in Fe, f_e(v) \neq C\}, \qquad (2)$$

where $\forall fe \in Fe_2$, fe only has a variable and the sign of fe is different with the sign of equality and C a constant.

$$Fe_3 = \{f_e(V') | Length(V') \geq 2, f_e(V') \in Fe, f_e(V') + A = C\}, \qquad (3)$$

where $\forall fe \in Fe_3$, fe has more than one variable, C is a constant, and A is a quantity which is added so that $fe(V') + A = C$.

Next, finding the solution of Fe_1 and Fe_2 and research spaces of Fe_3 are also the solution of Fe_1 and Fe_2. Finally, we use exhaustive research method [7] to identify final solution for whole Fe. For example, $p \in P$ has five expressions as follows: $5x = 10$, $x > 1$, $y > 1$, $y < 13$, and $x^2 + y^2 > 100$ in which x, y are parameters and $x, y \in [MIN, MAX]$. By applying the above principles, we have

$$Fe_1 = \begin{cases} 5x = 10 \\ x \in [MAX, MIN] \end{cases} \Rightarrow \{x = 2$$

After that, Let $x = \{2\}$ be a condition instead of $x = [MIN, MAX]$ in Fe_2 as follows.

$$Fe_2 = \begin{cases} x > 1 \\ y > 1 \\ y < 13 \\ x \in [MIN, MAX] \\ y \in [MIN, MAX] \end{cases} \Rightarrow \begin{cases} x > 1 \\ y > 1 \\ y < 13 \\ x = \{2\} \\ y \in [MIN, MAX] \end{cases} \Rightarrow \begin{cases} x = 2 \\ 1 < y < 13 \end{cases}$$

Finally, we use exhausted research method for Fe_3 where domain value of x is $\{2\}$ and domain value of y is $(1, 13)$ as follows.

$$Fe_3 = \begin{cases} x^2 + y^2 > 100 \\ x = \{2\} \\ y \in (1, 13) \end{cases} \Rightarrow \begin{cases} x = 2 \\ 10 \le y \le 12 \end{cases}$$

The solution of Fe_3 as well as Fe is (2, 10), (2, 11), and (2, 12).

After obtaining the values to the input parameter, we will identify the expected output base on these values. Expected results are generated by using a mechanism called test oracle. For this purpose, we have used an alternate program for generating expected results. This means that using two different functions for the same problem, each function is described in different way but they return the same result when they set the same input values. Assume that P' is a program which is built so that $U(2^{|V|}) = U'(2^{|V|})$. U' is used to identify expected output. Table 1 shows test results is created from the test path p.

Table 1. A test case of U is created from the path p

No.	Path	Input	Expected output(P')	Actual output(P)	Pass
1	$p=(e_1, e_2, e_3, e_4, e_5)$	$x = 2, y = 10$ 8	8	True
		$x = 2, y = 11$ 9	9	True
		$x = 2, y = 12$ 10	11	False

Similarly, we have to do the same for the other test paths and having a complete test suite for each data flow testing criteria.

4   Experiment and Discussion

This section presents our implemented tool for data flow testing and experimental results by applying this tool for some examples. We also discuss the advantages and disadvantages of the proposed method.

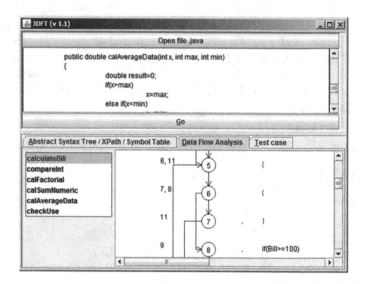

Fig. 4. Interface of the implemented tool.

Table 2. The test results of the examples for *All-du-paths* criteria

No.	Name	Number of paths	Predicate errors	Computation errors
1	calculateBill	26	7	3
2	calSumNumeric	14	3	0
3	calFactorial	11	4	2

4.1 Experiment

In order to show the effectiveness of the proposed method, we have implemented
a tool, named JDFT. The tool is developed in Java and use a third party package
name PMD (Programming Mistake Detector) [6], to analyze the given source
code and display the generated data flow graph of the program. Figure 4 shows
the user interface of JDFT. First, given source code of a Java program, this tool
analyzes and visualizes the program as a data flow graph. Second, the JDFT finds
all *def-u* pairs of all variables in the program. The test paths are then created
based on finding the paths in data flow graph for covering *def-u* pairs. Third,
this tool identifies the values to the input parameters which satisfy these test

Table 3. The test results of the examples for *All-du-paths* criteria

No.	Name	Number of paths	Predicate errors	Computation errors
1	calculateBill	28	0	0
2	calSumNumeric	16	0	0
3	calFactorial	13	0	0

paths and computing expected outputs of the test cases for the selected input. Finally, the test results are analyzed by comparing the actual output with the expected output of each test case.

We are also tested JDFT by using some typical examples in which the *calculateBill* is used to calculate the bill of a cellular service, the *calSumNumeric* is used to calculate the sum of integer divisible by 2 and the *calFactorial* is used to calculate the factorial of n. There are some common errors related to improper uses of control structure statements and computed statements in the applied examples. All examples, JDFT tool, and help document are available at the site[1]. The results for *All-du-paths* of these examples are shown in Table 2. For the *calculateBill*, this tool detects 7 errors about using control structure statements and 3 errors about using computed statements. Similarly, for the *calSumNumeric* is 3 and 0 and the *calFactorial* is 4 and 2 respectively. After fixing errors in Table 2, we use the *JDFT* to test these examples again and the obtained results of this purpose are shown in Table 3. There is not any error in the fixed programs detecting by the tool.

The above results are clear to show the practical usefulness of the implemented tool. In addition, this tool also can detect the unnecessary statements of the program under testing.

4.2 Discussion

The proposed method is a complete solution for automated data flow testing. It not only solves the key issues of white-box testing that generates test data, but also solves the problem about generating expected outputs.

Firstly, with regard to generate test data, dividing boolean functions into three main groups helps us to minimize the disadvantages of exhaustive method [7] that is running time. Generally, these functions will tend to fall into group 1 and group 2. Therefore, finding solution for these group is easy, whereas the boolean functions of group 3 is fewer and research space of this group is also solution of group 1 and group 2 hence calculation time is reduced significantly. In addition, although there are some methods to generate test data such as Genetic Algorithm [12], Ant Colony Algorithms [11], these methods are restricted about basic data types, while our method has solved all basic data types. However, it is still the restrictions as in some cases where the program includes complex boolean expressions, the calculation time is still high.

Secondly, for generating expected output, there are some automatic methods for generating expected output such as Statistical Oracle [13], Neural Network [14], and MT [15], but these methods are normally unavailable or too expensive to apply. By using an alternate program, this method is not only simple, but it is also easy to apply for software companies. Moreover, it also helps programmers have multiple perspectives on one problem, but this can also make workload of programmers as well as the volume of program code increase significantly.

---

[1] http://www.uet.vnu.edu.vn/uet/~hungpn/JDFT

Finally, comparing with other data flow testing tools has not been done, but the obtained experimental results are clear to show that the method is promising to be applied in industry.

5 Conclusion and Future Work

We have presented a method for data flow testing of Java programs. The key idea of this method is to generate all test cases such that they cover all *def-u* pairs of all variables used in the Java program under testing. The expected outputs of the generated test cases are also computed automatically by using an alternate program. A tool supports the proposed method is implemented in Java. Some typical examples are tested in order to show practical usefulness of the tool. The obtained experimental results are clear to show that the implemented tool can detect several common errors in coding.

Future work, we focus on solving the problem about test data, especially find out test paths which are not executable to remove unnecessary statements due to these statements is never executed. We are also investigating to apply some practical programs with their sizes are larger than the sizes of the applied systems in order to show the practical usefulness of the implemented tool. In addition, more experiments are needed in order to evaluate and compare the proposed method and the existing methods for data flow testing. Moreover, we also are going to apply this tool in some Vietnamese software companies.

Acknowledgments. This work is supported by the project no. QG.12.50 granted by Vietnam National University, Hanoi (VNU).

References

1. Rapps, S., Weyuker, E.J.: Selecting software test data using data flow information. IEEE Trans. Softw. Eng. **11**(4), 367–375 (1985)
2. Parrish, A.S., Zweben, S.H.: On the relationships among the all-uses, all-DU-paths, and all-edges testing criteria. IEEE Trans. Softw. Eng. **21**(12), 1006–1009 (1995)
3. Bluemke, I.: A coverage analysis tool for java programs. In: The 4th IFIP TC 2 Central and East European Conference on Advances in Software Engineering Techniques, pp. 215–228 (2009)
4. Copeland, L.: A Practitioner's Guide to Software Test Design. STQE Publishing, Massachusetts (2004)
5. Narmada, N., Mohapatra, D.P.: Automatic test data generation for data flow testing using particle swarm optimization. Commun. Comput. Inform. Sci. **95**(1), 1–12 (2010)
6. PDM Homepage, http://pmd.sourceforge.net/
7. Exhaustive research, http://en.wikipedia.org/wiki/Brute-force_search
8. BPAS-ATCGS Homepage, http://www.cs.ucy.ac.cy/~cs04pp2/WebHelp/index.htm
9. JaBUTi Homepage, http://jabuti.incubadora.fapesp.br (access, December 2007)

10. Ntafos, S.C.: On required element testing. IEEE Trans. Softw. Eng. **10**(6), 795–803 (1984)
11. Ghiduk, A.S.: A new software data-flow testing approach via ant colony algorithms. UniCSE (2010). ISSN: 2219–2158
12. Girgis, M.R.: Automatic test data generation for data flow testing using a genetic algorithm. J. UCS **11**(6), 898–915 (2005)
13. Mayer, J., Guderlei, R.: Test oracles using statistical methods. In: Proceedings of the First International Workshop on Software Quality, Lecture Notes in Informatics P-58, pp. 179–189 (2004)
14. Vanmali, M., Last, M., Kandel, A.: Using a neural network in the software testing process. Int. J. Intell. Syst. **17**(1), 45–62 (2002)
15. Hu, P., Zhang, Z., Chan, W.K., Tse, T.H.: An empirical comparison between direct and indirect test result checking approaches. In: Proceedings of the 3rd International Workshop on Software Quality ssurance (SOQUA06), pp. 6–13 (2006)

Rule-Based Techniques Using Abstract Syntax Tree for Code Optimization and Secure Programming in Java

Nguyen Hung-Cuong[✉], Huynh Quyet-Thang, and Tru Ba-Vuong

Department of Software Engineering, School of Information and Communication Technology, Hanoi University of Science and Technology, Hanoi, Vietnam
{cuongnh86,trubavuong}@gmail.com, thanghq@soict.hust.edu.vn

Abstract. Although the quality of computer software consists of many different aspects, the security and the optimization are by far the most important metrics for estimating quality of software systems. The security ensures that application will work correctly and the optimization reduces the amount of resources needed: computation, memory, size of code, etc. Those techniques can be done by applying rules in abstract syntax tree, a tree representation of the abstract syntactic structure of source code. However, the process to optimize code often makes negative effect to the security of program. This work studies about applying rules in abstract syntax tree in Java and its effect on code optimization and secure programming problems.

Keywords: Abstract syntax tree · Code optimization · Secure programming

1 Introduction and Motivation

Nowadays, computer science appears in every aspects of our life, from house to office, from industry to entertainment. One of the most important requirements when building a computer software is the reliability of system: the high-reliability system ensures that work of users will be done accurately, in different contexts and different environments. Authors use dissimilar approaches to introduce new techniques to improve the security of software and those techniques are used widely: in C/C++ [1], in UNIX [2], in Java [3,4], etc. However, the increasing of complexity system makes more many challenges that have to be overcome.

The development of software technology makes more and more compound system, so arise demand that application should be optimized. Optimization is the progress of transforming software source code to make more efficient without changing its works. In more specific, code optimization is a machine-independent optimizations that can be done in source code of project or corresponding diagram to reduces the amount of resources needed: computation, memory, size of code, etc. on many fields of computer science: compiler [5], pipeline constraints [6], embedded

P.C. Vinh et al. (Eds.): ICCASA 2013, LNICST 128, pp. 168–177, 2014.
DOI: 10.1007/978-3-319-05939-6_17, © Springer International Publishing Switzerland 2014

processors [7], etc. Many optimization problems are NP-complete and thus most optimization algorithms depend on heuristics and approximations techniques.

Normally, not good optimization technique makes some negative effects to the quality of software: developer can not control the corresponding changing between modules before and after transforming. In addition, any technique have their own application in specific context: one technique is good for this context but can make uncontrolled problems in another one. This work is going to study about the secure programming and code optimization techniques that apply rules in abstract syntax tree in Java. So give results that in this technique, code optimization process does not reduce the reliability of system.

As a important attribute of software quality, software reliability is influenced strongly by software lifecycle [8]. In the software lifecycle of a commercial applications, 50 % of errors introduced and errors detected are in coding phase, so secure programming and code optimization techniques can affect significantly to the reliability of system.

In this study, we show result about the mutuality between secure programming and code optimization in Java when applying rules in abstract syntax tree. This paper is organised as follow: after this introduction section, Sect. 2 explains definition of abstract syntax tree and some regular problems of secure programming and code optimization. Note that those problems are in common programming language, not with any specific one. Next, Sect. 3 introduces rules and how to apply rules in abstract syntax tree. Section 4 shows some experimental results, including running environment, application design and running results. Then Sect. 5 discusses some related and future problem to extend current work.

2   Basic Techniques of Java-Application Development

As mentioned earlier, in this paper we study how to improve the quality of system. This section introduces two problems of software development: code optimization and secure programming.

2.1   Code Optimization

When size of system is raised rapidly, researchers focus on optimizing the source code to save the resource needed. Aho consider [5] code optimization as a sub problem of compiler technique. Some regular techniques in code optimization will be discussed following.

1. Use length property when check emptiness of string. For example, replace

```
public boolean isEmpty(String str){
    return str.equals("");}
```

by

```
public boolean isEmpty(String str{
    return str.length()==0;}
```

2. Do not use constructor of class Integer:

```
public void fubar(){
    Integer i = new Integer(3);}
```

by

```
public void fubar(){
    Integer i = Integer.valueOf(3);}
```

Today, several compiler can optimize source code in some specific context and it is called *compile level.* Notwithstanding, code optimization should be done by programmer because it is to complex to be executed automatically. And main trade off when optimize manually is the working-cost.

2.2 Secure Programming

Secure programming relates with fault problems: detection, tolerance, back up, etc. Target of developer is building a secure system, in this work of users will be done correctly. However, it is a difficult challenges to overcome in current state of science and technology. Some regular secure problems will be discussed following.

1. Variables are set *private*

```
class Person{
    String name;
    int age;}
```

by

```
class Person{
    private String name;
    private int age;}
```

2. Let object uncloneable

```
class Person{
    /*do not use clone()*/}
```

by

```
class Person{
public final void clone()
    throws java.lang.CloneNotSupportedException{
        throw new java.lang.CloneNotSupportedException();}}
```

Many research show that most faults are made when some programming mistakes are mined, so developer need to be trained about those attacks.

2.3   Abstract Syntax Tree

Abstract syntax tree (AST), or just simply syntax tree, is a tree representation of the abstract syntactic structure of source code written in a programming language: each node of the tree denotes a construct occurring in the source code. Aho et al [5] introduce some syntax trees of basic elements as follow: each construct is represented by a node that children of it emblem the semantic meaningful components of this construct.

1. Represent blocks by AST: consider block as a single statement, AST of blocks is simply the syntax tree for the set of order statements. Then replace symbolic node in this super-AST that represent a block by corresponding sub-AST, so that link of super-AST points to root of sub-AST.
2. An AST for a statement. Operator of statement need to be defined for construction of its AST: operator of a constructs that begin with a keyword is this keyword.
   - An operator `while` for while-statements.
   - An operator `do` for do-while-statements.
   - Conditionals can be handled by defining two operators `ifelse` and `if` for if-statements with and without an else part, respectively.
3. An AST for an expression: an interior node represents an operator and corresponding operands are symbolized by children of it.

An example of AST for Euclid function:

```
int Euclid{
  while b != 0
    if a > b
      a > b
      a := a - b;
    else
      b := b - a;
  return a;}
```

is given in Fig. 1.

3   Rules and Applying in Abstract Syntax Tree

Rules are principles that modify source code to improve quality of work. They have experimental meaning and are got from practician in computer science. They contain some important information: description; "how, why and where" to apply; etc. They have to be applied on given elements in specific context, so deploying rule in real development requires combining with AST-transformation of source code.

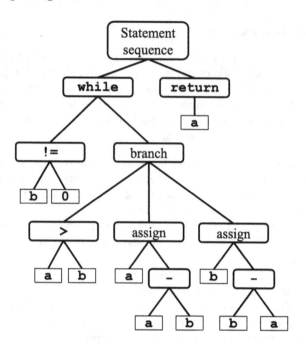

Fig. 1. Abstract syntax tree of Euclide function

3.1 Building Rules

From secure programming and code optimization problems that are discussed before, developer should synthesis a set of rules to using after. However, those techniques are used for general context and developer have to focus on techniques that adapt with Java. Furthermore, he need refer rules from secure source: from framework manufacturer, experiment developer, expert, etc... In this study, Java is a programming framework that is discussed, and then we focus on resources from Oracle, Google or AppPerfect. When apply rules in abstract syntax tree in Java to resolve secure programming and code optimization problems, developer should store them to reuse or gain experience to future work. In addition, programmer should save all information about rules that help user to lookup when needed.

3.2 Using Rules to Detect Potential Elements in Source Code

As discussed before, each rule impact to different elements of source code, and those elements are result of transform process to get AST from source code. So following 4-step strategy is used to detect potential elements:

Step 1. Transform every source code files in Java project into abstract syntax tree.

Step 2. Divide elements of each abstract syntax tree into groups, base on property of element: method calling, variable declaration, etc..

Step 3. Apply each rule to elements that are consistent: if a element is invalid with any rule, it is a potential element.

Step 4. List every potential elements and collect information that relates with each potential element. This list is supplied to developer.

Because size of set of rule is unpredicted and the application of rule on specific context is depend on semantic meaning of program, then potential elements should be listed and provided to programmer to decide apply or not.

3.3   Using Rules to Modify Source Code

After detecting potential elements, the next part is modifying source code so that rules are not violated. Developer has to decide what and how to transform by following scenario:

Step 1. Select one potential element that violates rules and all of its information.

Step 2. Check its violation again. If it is still invalid, there are two cases:
  - If this rule does not depend on program semantically, source code is changed automatically.
  - If this rule depends on program semantically, plug-in suggest developer all information to decide modify source code or not.

Step 3. Modify source code.

4   Experimental Results

4.1   Environment Descriptions

System computing performance depends on CPU Intel(R) Core(TM) i5 M520 2.40 GHz with memory RAM 4 GB. Operating system is Windows 7 Professional 64-bit and IDE is Java 6, 32-bit.

Our result is appreciated by using Java VisualVM, a tool that provides a visual interface for viewing detailed information about Java applications while they are running on a Java Virtual Machine.

Application is a Eclipse plug-in and developed by Plug-in Development Environment that supplied by Eclipse. It bases on Eclipse Juno (4.2) SR2, package "Eclipse for RCP and RAP Developers". Plug-in uses three tools of Eclipse Platform:

1. PDE (Plug-in Development Environment): providing tools to create, develop, test, debug, build and deploy Eclipse plug-ins, fragments, features, update sites and RCP products.
2. JDT (Java Development Tools): providing the tool plug-ins that implement a Java IDE supporting the development of any Java application, including Eclipse plug-ins. It allows to access, create and modify Java projects in Eclipse.
3. Eclipse Refactoring API (ERAPI): is a part of Language Toolkit (LTK) of Eclipse and is installed in two plug-ins: "org.eclipse.ltk.core.refactoring" and "org.eclipse.ltk.ui.refactoring".

4.2   Eclipse Plug-In Tool Descriptions

Product of our project is a Eclipse plug-in tool that:

+ Improve quality of application.
+ Make good programming behaviours.

Functions of tool:

1. Searching and analysing potential elements that can be impacted by code optimization and secure programming techniques.
2. Supporting method to modify those elements by showing supported information and recommending suggestions.

Data flow chart of plug-in is in Fig. 2. Our plug-in contain five modules:

1. Configuration Loader: this module saves and loads all information of rules in XML file. This configuration has to be loaded firstly and store through begin to end of session of Eclipse.
2. Preprocessor: transform every file in Java source code into abstract syntax tree and divide into groups.
3. Analyzer is one of the most important of system. It is used to detect potential elements in AST and store information of rules, including name, identity, type, priority, etc...
4. Display Problem Unit: show information about potential elements.
5. Refactoring Unit: tool that support to optimize source code.

4.3   Experimental Results

Result is got after comparing performance of system before and after using code optimization and secure programming techniques. Table 1 shows that running time of methods decrease clearly when applying code optimization and secure programming techniques. The largest slowdown is seen on method `getTopicDetailsTask()` with 33.53 % and this improvement shows that quality of source code is improved markedly.

Note. BKProfile is a intelligent web service that support to communication between lecturers, company, student and ex-student through personal profile. It is built in the form of question-answer system: users share their knowledge through making question or answering of another.

Second evaluation of this study is about system resource usage: memory and CPU. Those appreciations are got from running main functions of BKProfile system. Figures 3 and 4 show comparison of system resource using before and after optimization. Figures 3 indicates that after apply optimization techniques will decreasing CPU usage, both of maximum using and average. Figures 4 display statistical heap-using. Heap stores every objects that are created by Java in running time and is evaluated by two measures: heap-size and used-heap. In Fig. 4, we can see that there are two improvements of using memory:

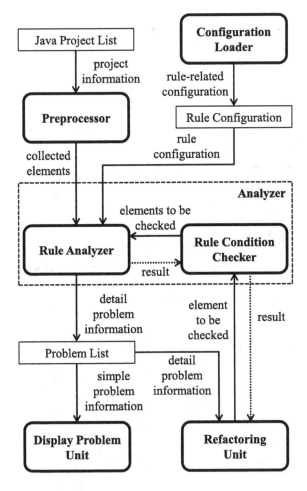

Fig. 2. Data flow chart of Eclipse plug-in tool

Table 1. Running time of methods

ID Program Method	Times	Running time(ms) Before	After	Improve(%)
1-1 QuickSort generateArray	1	2703	2671	1.18
1-2 QuickSort sort	1	36558	25362	30.63
2-1 BKProfile getTopStatsTask	10000	114	107	6.14
2-2 BKProfile getTopicDetailsTask	10000	68	45.2	33.53
2-3 BKProfile getAnswersTask	20000	1005	951	5.37
2-4 BKProfile getQuestionDetailTask	20000	135	132	2.22
2-5 BKProfile getSimilarQuestionsTask	20000	210	188	10.48
2-6 BKProfile getFollowersTask (1)	20000	266	204	23.31
2-7 BKProfile getFollowersTask (2)	20000	143	113	20.98

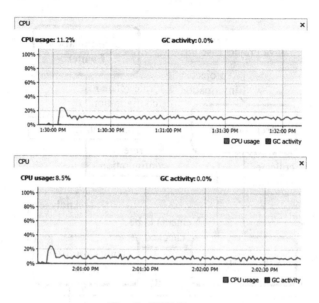

Fig. 3. CPU Usage

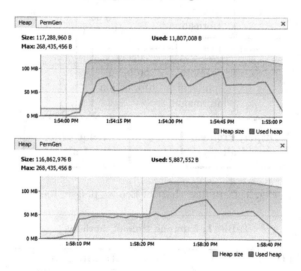

Fig. 4. Memory Usage

1. Heap-size is used less than before.
2. Used-heap is better than before with no sudden change.
3. Heap using-efficiency is better than before: average ratio between used-heap and heap-size is increased.

5   Conclusions

This study proposes architecture of a plug-in that support code optimization and secure programming techniques. After that, we build this plug-in for Java-environment Eclipse and evaluate results of performance of Java application before and after using plug-in to confirm it worth.

Code optimization and secure programming have a big number technique, and this study only works with four of them. So future works should extend set of rules to confirm application of AST on this field. Furthermore, refactoring process can be better, for example can be done automatically or semi-automatically.

References

1. Viega, J., Messier, M.: Secure Programming Cookbook for C and C++: Recipes for Cryptography, Authentication, Input Validation & More. O'Reilly Media, Inc., Sebastopol (2009)
2. Wheeler, D.A.: Secure programming for linux and unix howto (2003)
3. Oaks, S.: Java Security. O'Reilly, Sebastopol (1998). (ISBN 1565924037)
4. Bloch, J.: Effective Java. Addison-Wesley Professional, Amsterdam (2008)
5. Aho, A.V., et al.: Compilers: principles, techniques, & tools. Pearson Education India (2007)
6. Gross, T.K.R.: Code optimization of pipeline constraints (1983)
7. Leupers, R.: Code Optimization Techniques for Embedded Processors: Methods, Algorithms, and Tools. Springer Publishing Company, Incorporated, New York (2010)
8. Pham, H.: System Software Reliability. Springer, London (2006)

Overall Security Solutions for OPC UA Based Monitoring and Control Application

Nguyen Thi Thanh Tu[(⊠)] and Huynh Quyet Thang

School of Information and Communication Technology,
Hanoi University of Science and Technology, Hanoi, Vietnam
tu.nguyenthithanh@hust.edu.vn,
thanghq@soict.hust.edu.vn

Abstract. Together with the global trend, the currently popular accessing model is using Service Oriented Architecture (SOA), working based on available IT infrastructure following the industrial standard OPC UA, in order to create a new environment providing monitoring, controlling and managing industrial manufacturing system effectively. In this paper, we propose a framework based on the combination between SOA and OPC UA for the designing, improving software systems applied to monitoring, controlling and managing production assembly lines. Also, we provide secuirty solution that are proposed and applied to control and monitoring system based on OPC UA standard. Basing on the proposed framework, software developers can easily implement to design, to build monitoring, controlling systems and to manage different industry assembly lines, ensuring the characteristics of inheriting developing and improving the systems flexibly, being able to enlarge and link among different systems.

Keywords: OPC UA · SOA · PKI · Webservice · Framework

1 Introduction

Opc (Object Linking and Embedding for Process Control) is an interface standard of real time computing between monitoring devices from different factories. Protocol of Dynamic Data Exchange is the solution to exchanging the first data among applications based on Windows. Technical characters of OPC based on OLE are COM and DCOM technology developed by Microsoft for operating system Microsoft Windows in family. Technical characters determine a set of standards of objectives, interface and using methods in monitoring the process and automatic applications in manufacture, which enables to interact easily. To simplify in developing device controlling software, they remove the inconsistency between controlling software, support to change the hardware character and avoid approaching conflicts in industrial controlling systems. The organization OPC defines the standard interface allows any computers to be able to get access to any OPC compatible devices. Almost all suppliers of data collecting devices and controlling devices work with the standard of OPC [1, 2]. The common specifications of OPC are: Data Access (DA), Historical Data Access

P.C. Vinh et al. (Eds.): ICCASA 2013, LNICST 128, pp. 178–187, 2014.
DOI: 10.1007/978-3-319-05939-6_18, © Springer International Publishing Switzerland 2014

(HDA), Alarm and Events (A&E) and the latest is OPC Unified Architecture (OPC UA). OPC UA is being accepted in automatic industry [1, 2, 6].

Instead of using COM/DCOM technology of Microsoft, the latest standard of OPC Foundation (OPC UA) uses XML, Web services, SOA and the model of objective orient data to describe and perform three types of data: present data, historical data, alarm and events [6]. Invented in 2006, OPC UA has been attracting the interest of researchers of many universities, research centers and laboratories. Software developing companies hope that it will replace the traditional OPC successfully. OPC UA inherits all functions of traditional OPC. Moreover, OPC UA is independent of basement. It can run on Window, Linux or embedding device [7].

OPC standard is the technique which is applied widely all over the world and has obtained many great achievements in the field of industrial monitoring and controlling. A group of authors proposed to build a Framework based on new standards and techniques with high effectiveness combining between OPC UA and SOA [3–5]. In [13, 14] we introduced the development of an OPC UA SDK for both sides – OPC UA Server SDK and OPC UA Client SDK, based on the OPC UA specifications.

Recently, production processes of manufacturing companies are mostly based on IT systems. Production requests are initiated by Enterprise Resource Planning on IT systems, the execution of the process is managed by Manufacturing Execution Systems (MES), special HMIs used to for supervisory of the process, and the documentation of results, quality, and resource consumption are highly dependent on IT systems [1, 8]. OPC is an application layer for communication between software components for automation and control systems. It specially defines standardized interfaces through which OPC clients access the objects in OPC servers. With OPC foundation, they can design and implement the applications for automation and control system, but OPC DA based on COM/DCOM techniques. And DCOM security not enough to protect the industrial systems, because of this specification only providing the methods and properties which are applied to the OPC DA based COM productions. With the internet environment the security solutions proposed to use internal XML security approach for the control connection instead of the HTTP-S protocol, being described in XML Encrytion [15], XML Signature [16, 17] specifications.

Besides, OPC UA based framework for developing monitoring and control system applications using Internet environments is base of communication complying with XML, web services, and SOA. The XML signature is a system to encode digital signatures in an XML document. It uses the same standards and technologies of cryptography as usual digital signatures. The basis of digital signatures is symmetric or asymmetric cryptography. When using symmetric keys for encrypting and signing data, the same keys are used for decrypting and verifying the signature of the data, i.e., both parties in the client–server scenario have identical keys for certain cryptographic operations.

Security policy of OPC UA bases on public key infrastructure (PKI). UA defines a group of standard method sharing network that both Client and Server must install to encode data or sign on message. At each turn Client describes the method of security used. Then both Client and Server apply this method to ensure all messages to go through turn safely. There are 3 ways of security as following: None: no register, turn off security mode. Messages can be read and counterfeited by the third party. Register: messages are signed to ensure the entire data but the body is not encoded, so they still can be read by the third party. Register and encode: register the message and encode the body can protect the data entirely.

1.1   Service Orient Architecture in Monitoring and Controlling System

Service orient architecture (SOA) is a group of rules and designing methods, developing software as the way of interactive services. These services are designed clearly, with specific functions respectively. Service plays a roll of parts of the software and can be reused depending on certain purposes [4]. The major characters of SOA are separating the communication part and service part, communication is centre of architecture. Service is approached through communication, as the way of request – respond. A service orient interaction always includes a pair of partners: Server and Client.

SOA design separates service performing with communication calling service. This creates the consistency in communication for Client application using service that is independent of what service performing technology is. Instead of building individual and massive applications, developers build sophisticated and compact services which can be implemented and reused in the whole business process. Therefore, they have outstanding distinctions such as reusability, flexibility since developers can improve the services without affecting Client using services.

Service is the key factor in SOA. It can be considered as function formula performing certain business process. Basically, SOA is a group of services connected "flexibly" with one another (i.e one application can "talk" to another application without knowing technical details inside), there is communication defined clearly and independently of system background, and can be reused. SOA focuses on business process and uses communication standard to hide technical sophistication below. Service orient architecture (SOA) offers methods and rules to design software as the direction of interaction with service. Service is both a basic definition and the most important part of SOA. In the model of SOA, service is defined simply as a software module or a complete program structured to connect to one another through the way of exchanging messages. Each service corresponds with one business function.

In the software system, service orient architecture is a trendy design. Service is a module of software, performing a certain business function. A service orient interaction always includes a pair of partners: Server and Client. Communicating service through the pair of request - respond. Model of SOA describes service orient communication. Broker plays a part of mediating, keeping the information of server and information of services from that server. The information is registered by the server. Users request a service; they search for information from the broker. With the information obtained, they call connection to server. When connecting successfully, they can use available services. The advantages of service orient architecture are flexibility and reusability as SOA includes a group of services with high independence.

1.2 OPC UA

OPC UA developed based on service orient architecture (SOA). OPC UA Servers describe all their functions as a group of services that Client uses. OPC UA shows what these services do and how to use them. In the meanwhile, Server side provides services and Client is the side of using services. Services determine data telecommunication at level of application. Services are the ways Client uses to access to data on information model of Server. Traditional OPC standard only defines API function, but UA defines services to determine communicative interface between UA applications. Services are independent of transporting protocol and programming environment, which is basically different from traditional OP and from API defined based on certain devices.

OPC UA service is used to exchange large sized data between progresses or between internet nodes in order to reduce transmitting among applications. Service uses the form of request – respond. To call a service in Server, Client sends a request message to Server. After having processed, Server sends respond back to Client. As this message exchanging does not happen at the same time, calling service is not at the same time, either. After sending request message, Client application can handle other functions until the responding message is delivered.

OPC is the organization offering standards based on the area of industry. OPC UA is the latest generation of OPC; the first version came into life in 2006. It does not remove the former standards but inherits all of the functions that traditional OPC standards have. Moreover, OPC UA overcomes the disadvantage of depending on COM/DCOM technology of Microsoft. It can run on .NET, Linux or Embedded device [9, 10]. OPC UA is designed based on service orient architecture, after which Servers describe their function as groups of services. Client and Server exchange through the pair: request - respond.

UA Server registers to Discovery Server its information and services it provides. Discovery Server is also an OPC UA Server. Thus, not all OPC UA provide all services. Discovery Server only provides the service which saves registration and stores information of other UA Server. Client searches for information on Discovery Server. When getting the information, Client sends request to Server. Server responds to Client. Then Client can use services that Server provides [11].

Message transmitted between Client and Server will have the format of UA Binary or XML. UA Binary encodes data in turn into a plate of byte. The advantages are reducing the cost of encoding and decoding but only OPC UA Client can translate the data in this format. Therefore, people often use UA Binary to exchange data on the equipment floor due to requirement of high productivity and limitation of handling capacity. XML is a popular method to exchange data at high level. Client uses the format of XML and OPC UA Client can both read this type of data. Data in the format of XML calculate more costly than UA Binary.

OPC UA uses protocol of OPC.TCP or SOAP/HTTP(S) to transmit. OPC.TCP is a protocol based on TCP (sockets). It defines a double channel between OPC UA Server and Client. Messages are packed into a structure as the rule of binary protocol OPC TCP. Only OPC UA Client has ability of receiving data through this protocol. SOAP/HTTP (S) packs messages into SOAP and transmits through HTTP(S).

Message SOAP is a document of XML. All the messages are transmitted through HTTP or HTTPS depending on the end point and requiring security. SOAP/HTTP(S) is an industrial standard used to exchange information on the application floor. Client Web service in general can receive SOAP message through protocol of HTTP(S).

UA Binary + OPC TCP: is the most optimal method to format and transmit the data. Consequently, this is a combination with highest possibility to be used on the floor of equipment. Only OPC UA Server and OPC UA Client can exchange information through this method.

XML + SOAP/HTTP(S): this is a friendly combination and easily overcomes firewall. This method often gives priority to exchange information on the floor of application.

2 Proposed Framework Architecture for Monitoring and Controlling System

Framework for monitoring and controlling system describes all components of the system and how to communicate between the components. Apart from meeting the demand of having a joint framework designed for a monitoring and controlling system, it must follow all standards in industry. Criteria of designing framework are suggested:

- Generality: ensure spreading criterion and be a basis to design a monitoring and controlling system.
- Flexibility: ensure the flexibility in designing, operating system (system can be operated on multi-basis).
- Reusability: ensure all components be reused for other systems.
- Spread ability: inherit and develop open feature of OPC UA standard to ensure open possibility to designers and system developers.
- Advance criterion: ensure Framework be built based on advanced architecture of SOA and new industrial standard of OPC UA.
- Simplicity: the model proposed must not be too complicated, need to be easy and convenient to implement, build and design software systems.

In the architecture of Framework, Server provides services and Client uses services (Fig. 1).

Server describes all of its functions as a group of services provided for Client. Server and Client are independent on background and programming language. Interaction between them is service oriented interaction, as the pair of request – respond. Client sends request using service to Server, Server will send back the respond to Client. They do not care about which background the other side is running on, how its inside structure is, they only care about the interaction result, service. Communication between Client and Server is through protocol of SOAP/HTTP(S) or OPC.TCP. Applications of Client are various: mobile application, enterprise application, website application…

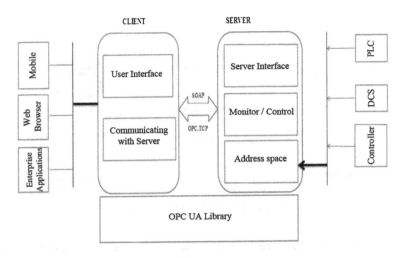

Fig. 1. Communication between Server-Client

Devices are integrated into address space of Server. In address space each device is an objective with properties and methods. Properties and methods are different from different objectives.

Tasks of the system are monitoring and controlling objectives (devices). Server provides services of monitoring and controlling them. Client searches for Server on Discovery Server, then setting connection. Communication with Server from Client allows it to use services Server provides. Users through interface of Client affect Server or devices. Client and Server programs are built based on OPC UA. It provides groups of objectives, data types, patterns of relation between nodes... as background for Server and Client. Server and Client are divided into separate components and loosely interconnect. This feature improves independence and ability of reusing components. Thus, when a certain component is changed, there will be no great influence on other components.

3 Overall Security for OPC UA

OPC UA applications will run in various environments with different security requirements, threats, and security policies. In principle, an OPC UA based framework for developing monitoring and controlling system applied for using Internet environments is base of communication complying with XML, web services, and SOA [1]. The XML signature is a system to encode digital signatures in an XML document. It uses the standard and technology encoding as other signature standard. The basic of digital signature is symmetric encryption or asymmetric encryption. However, there is important problem: How can be a secret key provided to all sides safely. There are two methods which can be used: public key and secret key (Fig. 2).

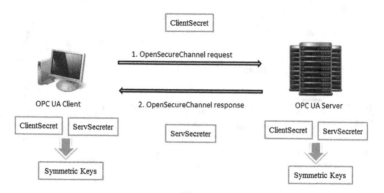

Fig. 2. Creating symmetric keys

However, there is a fundamental key problem: How a secret key can be provided to the communication partner in a secure way. In contrast to symmetric cryptography, an entity in asymmetric cryptography creates a key pair in which one of them is the public key that can be safely published. The public key can be used for encrypting data and can therefore be provided to any party intending to exchange secret data. Data can be encrypted for only the private key to decipher. The private key can be also used to generate digital signatures that are used to verify the public key. The security modes in the proposed framework are "None", "Sign", and "SignAndEcrypt" [12]. For example, in the case of Secure Channel request, if security mode Sign is used, the message is signed with the private key of the client. Signing messages allows detecting a received message that has been manipulated by an untrusted third party. If security mode SignAndEncrypt is used, then the message is additionally encrypted with the public key of the server. For example, once the secured message is received by the OPC UA server, it first validates the OPC UA client's Certificate by requesting its Validation Authority. This certificate is provided in an unencrypted part of the message and therefore can be read by the server. The message is decrypted with the associated private key of the OPC UA server and the signature is verified with the public key of the OPC UA client if the certificate is trustworthy by the server. The OPC UA server sends back the response to this request, which is similarly secured. Therefore, the same checks on the message and the server certificate are performed onthe OPC UA client side.

The connection establishment between an OPC UA client and an OPC UA server includes four steps that are: First step, an OPC UA client informs itsefl about the different configuration options of how a connection to the server can be established. The second step an OpenSecureChannel request secured in accordance to the Security Policy and the Security Mode is sent to the selected Session Endpoint of the server. The third step is to create a Session on top of the previously established Secure-Channel. If the certificates are trusted by the client, the server provides the needed capabilities and proved that it possesses the correct certificate then it proceeds to the fourth and last step [12].

In this research, when OPC UA client connect to server, server will send confirm message client, after that client create a confirmation certificate and encrypt by using public key of server and send it to server, Server will confirm OPC UA client. This message is decoded by OPC UA's secret key and the digital signature will be authenticated by public key of OPC UA client. If this message is reliable, OPC UA confirms a connection by sending other message. In the next step, client save that certificate of confirmation and it does not need to create again. The result of research from apply security mechanism namely Certificate Management for proposed architecture.

Besides, RSA is an algorithm for public-key cryptography that is based on the presumed difficulty of factoring large integers, the factoring problem. RSA involves a public key and a private key. The public key can be known by everyone and is used for encrypting messages. Messages encrypted with the public key can only be decrypted in a reasonable amount of time using the private key. In this research, security solution applied RSA authorihm, there are 2 kinds: RSA 1024 and RSA 2048 - the length of KEY. Depending on the length of KEY which is short or long, if longer, the security level will be higher (see Fig. 3). Figure 3(a): Creating Certificate of confirmation (including application name, the encryption algorithm, validity period of confirmative certificate) Fig. 3(b): Certificate of confirmation (after server accept the certificate of confirmation from client. Client will save it for the next connections):

OPC Security will define access method from client to server following a specify way to protect those data and avoid every unauthorized actions. Application OPC Security specification – Certificate Management security mechanism proposed in the framework, the author developed the authentication servers and clients through using the certificate of confirmation of clients. When this certificate is authenticated, Client got a permission to connect to server. In the next connections, client using created certificate of confirmation and does not need to create it again.

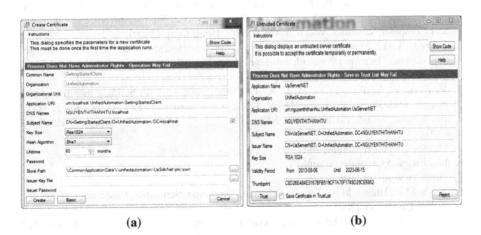

(a)   (b)

Fig. 3. (a) Create certificate (b) Untrusted certificate

4 Conclusions and Future Work

Through this research, we proposed a direction to do research, develop framework applied generally for system of monitoring and controlling automatically in industrial manufacture. We have introduced the overviews of security solutions are widely applied in automation and monitoring systems. Framework based on SOA follows the industrial standards of OPC UA to monitor, control various and complicated industrial systems bringing about flexibility in operating system, high effectiveness in management. This is a new research based on available information infrastructure of Vietnam in order to implement services of monitoring, controlling and managing manufacturing units automatically following advanced standards provided by OPC UA. Orient towards applying information technology and high technique into industrial area, which is a key area in the career of modernizing our country. Over the results of doing research and experiment, it proves that our research direction of developing framework is of highly possible implementation and brings about many practical benefits when applying in real manufacture. Orientation of future development: continue to do research and master new trends of industrial standards so as to widen and complete the model of framework much more. Coordinate with units of manufacturing automatically to implement the application of framework with a view to improving flexibility in manufacture and modernizing management, reducing cost of labor to manage and operate the system.

References

1. Damm, M., Mahnke, W., Leitner, S.-H.: OPC Unified Architecture. Springer, Berlin, 339 p. (2009)
2. Stopper, M., Katalinic, B.: Service-oriented architecture design aspects of OPC UA for industrial applications. In: Proceedings of the International Multi-Conference of Engineers and Computer Scientists, vol. II, IMECS 2009, Hong Kong (2009)
3. Leitner, S.-H., Mahnke, W.: OPC UA – Service-oriented architecture for industrial applications. http://pi.informatik.uni-siegen.de/stt/26_4/01_Fachgruppenberichte/ORA2006/07_leitner-final.pdf
4. Van Tan, V., Yoo, D.-S., Yi, M.-J.: A SOA-based framework for building monitoring and control software systems. In: Huang, D.-S., Jo, Kang-Hyun, Lee, H.-H., Kang, H.-J., Bevilacqua, V. (eds.) ICIC 2009. LNCS, vol. 5755, pp. 1013–1027. Springer, Heidelberg (2009)
5. http://www.unified-automation.com/
6. http://www.opcfoundation.org/
7. http://www.advosol.us/
8. Singh, M.P., Huhns, M.N.: Service Oriented Computing: Semantics, Processes, and Agents. Wiley, Chichester (2005)
9. Zeeb, E., Bobek, A., Bohn, H., Golatowski, F.: Service oriented architectures for embedded systems using devices profile for web services. In: Proceedings of the 21st International Conference on Advanced Information Networking and Applications Workshops, pp. 956–963. IEEE Press, Los Alamitos (2007)

10. Jammes, F., Smit, H.: Service oriented architectures for devices the SIRENA view. In: Proceedings of the 3rd IEEE International Conference on Industrial Informatics, pp. 140–147 (2005)
11. Van Tan, V.: A SOA based framework for building monitoring and control software systems, doctoral dissertation. University of Ulsan, Korea (2010)
12. Lange, J., Iwanitz, F., Burke, T. J.: OPC - From data access to unified architecture. Vde Verlag GmbH; 4. Auflage edn (July 1 2010)
13. Tu, N.T.T., Cuong, N.D., Van Tan, V., Thang, H.Q.:Research and development of OPC client – server architectures for manufacturing and process automation. In: Proceedings of SoICT, Vietnam, 27–28 August 2010, ISBN: 978-1-4503-0105-3, pp 163–170
14. Tu, N.T.T., Thang, H.Q.: Development of an OPC UA SDK based WCF-technology and Its deployment for environmental monitoring applications. First International Conference, ICCASA 2012, Ho Chi Minh City, Vietnam, 26–27 November, 2012, Revised Selected Papers. Series: Lecture Notes of the Institute for Computer Sciences, Social-Informatics and Telecommunications Engineering, vol. 109, pp. 347–356. ISBN 978-3-642-36642-0
15. XML Encryption Syntax and Processing: W3C Recommendation. http://www.w3.org/TR/2002/REC-xmlenc-core-20021210/. Accessed 10 Oct 2002
16. XML-Signature XPath Filter 2.0:W3C Recommendation. http://www.w3.org/TR/xmlenc-core. Accessed 8 Nov 2002
17. XML Signature and Processing: Recommendation. http://www.w3.org/TR/-2002/REC-xmlenc-core-20021210/. Accessed 12 Feb 2002

The Evolutionary Approach of General Systems Theory Applied to World Wide Web

Aneta Bartuskova and Ondrej Krejcar[✉]

Department of Information Technologies, Faculty of Informatics
and Management, University of Hradec Kralove,
Rokitanskeho 62, 500 03 Hradec Kralove, Czech Republic
Aneta.Bartuskova@uhk.cz,
ondrej.krejcar@remoteworld.net

Abstract. This article presents the application of general systems theory to web-based applications, with an emphasis on the evolutionary approach. The stages of web applications are discussed, according to their complexity, usage and historical appearance. Then the evolutionary approach as a framework is applied on web applications, in the meaning of their evolvement through time. This is expected to clarify a process of transformation from simple static websites to complex social web applications. The outline of these evolutional stages is followed by a suggestion of the current stage of web applications and future possibilities.

Keywords: Web applications · Evolution of the web · General systems theory

1 Introduction

Our lifestyle today is heavily influenced by available technologies, one of the most significant and also rapidly evolving is the internet. The World Wide Web undoubtedly belongs to major providers of information. It functions also as a communication platform, used by a wide range of different users [10, 11]. Considering an important role and continuous evolution of the web, it is useful to organize our knowledge of this evolvement into a known framework. With identifying individual stages of complexity in website development field, we can understand present tendencies and anticipate future possibilities. As the framework for this implementation was selected the evolutionary approach of general systems theory [5, 8].

General systems theory is a concept invented by biologist Ludwig von Bertalanffy, who identified similar principles across several fields of knowledge, such as biology, engineering, social sciences or management [7]. Yourdon applied general systems theory to the information technology and information systems [18]. Purpose of Bertalanffy's theory was to identify laws pertaining these many branches and thus create suitable conditions for their collective development [6]. One of the key aspects of this approach is investigating systems in the meaning of organizational units. Boulding defined two possible approaches to general systems theory, more of a complementary than competitive nature [4]. First of these approaches relies on picking out general

P.C. Vinh et al. (Eds.): ICCASA 2013, LNICST 128, pp. 188–197, 2014.
DOI: 10.1007/978-3-319-05939-6_19, © Springer International Publishing Switzerland 2014

phenomena across various disciplines and create relevant theoretical models. The key idea of the second approach is an arrangement of relevant constructs or empirical fields in a hierarchy, which defines organization of individual units within the system with a certain level of abstraction. We will use the second approach in this study and attempt to define a hierarchy of evolution stages of web applications according to their complexity, historical emergence and usage.

2 The Evolutionary Approach of General Systems Theory

A second approach towards general systems theory was defined by Boulding as a systematic approach leading to system of systems. Rapoport specified it as the "evolutionary approach", since levels of abstraction are of increasing complexity, marking the evolution of knowledge [3]. Each of these levels can be also defined by input, output, throughput or process, feedback, control, environment and goal or purpose, known as common elements of a system, which originated from Bertalanffy's types of finality [2, 13]. The input signifies an energy or a material which is transformed by the system through some process, resulting in an output as a product of system's processing. The feedback is also a product of the process, which returns to the system as an input. An evaluation of the input, process and input is encapsulated in a control element, an environment denotes the area around a system and a goal is a purpose of the system. Individual levels are described in (Table 1).

Similar development of stages in biology was conducted by Gerard, who did also divide concepts into nine categories of increasing complexity [9]. In this case however, entirely different approach was used. The author observes main criteria of Gerard's hierarchy as size of units, while Boulding's hierarchy can be defined as adding functional layers. Both approaches abide principle of rising complexity, yet in a different manner. In Gerard's hierarchy, every stage has defined its structural characteristics (architecture, relations, negative entropy) and equilibrium (dynamics and adaptive responses). Boulding integrated these constructs as a layers up to the third level (namely the structure level, the simple dynamic level and the control

Table 1. Arrangement of levels by Boulding [4], further specified by Rapoport [3]

Level	Name	Included entities
1	The structure level	Static structure, framework, arrangement
2	The simple dynamic level	Predetermined motions, simple machines
3	The control mechanism	Transmission and interpretation of information
4	The open system	Self-maintenance, self-reproduction
5	The genetic social level / Level of the cell	Division of labour, differentiated parts
6	The animal level	Increased mobility, teleological behaviour, self-awareness, specialized information-receptors
7	The human level	Self consciousness, self-reflexivity, speech
8	Human society	Social organizations, units as a role in society
9	The transcendental level	Ultimates and absolutes and the unknowables

Table 2. The levels of organization in biology by Gerard [9]

Level	Name	Description	*
1	Molecule	Particle made of two or more atoms	1,2
2	Organelle	Unit within a cell that has a specific function	3
3	Cell	Basic structural and functional unit of organisms	4,5
4	Organ	Unit with a common function in higher organisms	-
5	Individual	Organism with mind, feelings, consciousness	6,7
6	Small group	A small group of individuals	-
7	Species	A group of organisms capable of interbreeding	-
8	Community	Culture, community, institution	8
9	Total biota	Web of life in a space	9

* A reference to the items in (Table 1) - correspondence with the Boulding's hierarchy

mechanism). Gerard's organization is illustrated in (Table 2), including a comparison with the Boulding's hierarchy.

3 Evolution Stages of Web Applications

Essential stages of web applications are suggested and discussed in this part, in a form of an analysis on a history of the web. The stages are identified in accordance with general systems theory evolutionary approach, as an introduction to a research part of the article. Therefore, numbering of stages, which also follows a complexity of web development, comply with an arrangement of levels in general systems theory by Boulding and Rapoport [3, 4]. Identification and allocation of these levels was done according to the author's professional opinion after an elaborate analysis [24–32].

(1) World Wide Web, as an open field for web applications, had started its existence in 1993. First browsers displayed only text, next generation, starting with browser Mosaic, was capable of displaying also graphics [1]. Static structure of web applications is generally accomplished by HTML (HyperText Markup Language), eventually XML (Extensible Markup Language). Appearance of the static page is not changing after loading, until a user clicks on a link to different webpage, which is displayed next. This is considered a static webpage from a view of a user, which represents the first level of web applications.

(2) Next stage of web applications can be defined as an interactive website, which is usually powered by a combination of HTML, CSS (Cascading Style Sheets) and scripting. In this case, a scripting language is client-side, most commonly used is JavaScript, alternatives are VB Script or JScript. Purpose of CSS is mainly styling of HTML documents, but it can also convey interaction features like a hover effect. JavaScript can manipulate HTML page elements through use of DOM (Document Object Model). Combinations of these techniques (HTML, CSS, JavaScript, DOM) is commonly named as Dynamic HTML or DHTML [14].

(3) Dynamic website, as a third complexity level of web applications, features server-side scripting, which is often accompanied by a database system. Server-side scripting is accomplished through a server-side language, such as PHP (PHP: Hypertext Preprocessor), ASP (Active Server Pages), Java or Perl, and a database

system as a data source, e.g. relational database management system MySQL or MSSQL. Dynamic feature made it much easier for websites with extensive amount of content, since it enables to use the same page structure and design for dynamically loaded content from data source [15].

(4) The next stage of web applications can be characterized as a social web application, featuring a strong social aspect while technologically based on previous three stages. This advancement is covered by the term Web 2.0 and underlines foremost a socialization of the web. Popular activities include blogging, tagging and social bookmarking [1].

From the technological point of view, Web 2.0 is also associated with AJAX (Asynchronous JavaScript and XML) arrival, which enables enhanced functionality without reloading a webpage. We can summarize that core aspects of Web 2.0 are data (mash-ups), functionality (AJAX) and socialization (community) [1, 12].

(5) Fifth level of web applications can be represented by an aspiration for semantic web. Apart from Web 2.0 blogging tendency without an elaborate organization of data, semantic web aims to implement a logical structure with help of taxonomies and ontologies. The term Web 3.0 is emerging as a possibility of combining today's web with semantic technologies and architectures [16]. Embedding web content in a logical structure provides for not only machine-readable data, but also machine-understandable data [17].

A substantial feature of this level is heading towards a data integration. Web 2.0 leads to an information redundancy as the same data occur in many variations across the web. Databases contain similar data only named and formatted differently, applications are copying data from other applications and thus create another instance of this data etc. Semantic web aspires for providing information models and languages that embed semantic contexts and metadata to enable automated processing of data [1].

(6) Adaptive web applications are suggested as the sixth level of web applications. An "adaptive" has several meanings in this context. Considering an expansion of mobile devices with an internet access and other electronic devices, which can be connected to the internet in the future, an adaptation of web applications is necessary. This adaptation can be relevant to visual appearance, since desktop computers, notebooks, tablets, mobile phones etc. have different range of screen dimensions and control possibilities [22]. Evolution of web applications in this direction is closely connected to a development in ambient intelligence [33, 34], which builds on ubiquitous computing and intelligent user interfaces [19]. Web applications are in this stage becoming a context-aware pervasive systems [37], which has three basic functionalities - sensing, thinking and acting [20]. A research on sensors is thus also closely connected with this stage, e.g. sensing movement, light, location, proximity or biological signals [21].

4 The Evolutionary Approach Applied on Web Applications

Stages of web applications were suggested in Sect. 3 Evolution Stages of Web Applications, which correspond with Boulding's hierarchy. The evolutionary approach of general systems theory will be applied on web applications in this section,

Table 3. Stages of web applications in relation to the Boulding's hierarchy

Level	Type of website/output	Essential feature/input
1	Static website	Markup language, creating a static structure
2	Interactive website	Scripting client-side language, styling language (hover), creating simple dynamics
3	Dynamic website	Scripting server-side language and a database, creating a control mechanism
4	Social web application	Creating and sharing content in a community, forming a living system
5	Semantic web application	Established logical structure, ensuring differentiation of the content types
6	Adaptive web application	Adaptation and context-awareness - ability to function correctly in any environment
7	Autonomous web systems	Encapsulating functionality and decision-making with internal expert systems
8	Cooperative web systems	Communication among autonomous web systems without human intervention
9	The transcendental level	-

on the basis of an analysis from Sect. 3. Additional characteristics and underlying processes will be also described in this section. A summary of conclusions from Sect. 3, completed with remaining stages, is presented in (Table 3). The use of evolutionary approach for web applications is justified by Yourdon's four basic principles of GST [18], which can be applied to information systems and consequently also to web-based applications.

Suggested ordering of stages doesn't strictly follow a historical emergence and usage, e.g. idea about semantic web was developing rather simultaneously with Web 2.0 features, however its development will probably surpass further development of a social web. Emergence of suggested stages is also not of an equal timing. The first three stages of web applications (static, interactive and dynamic websites) occurred and came to usage nearly simultaneously, while the fourth stage with pronounced social aspect emerged in a more revolutionary way as Web 2.0. The first three stages are also based foremost on technological development, underlying principles of next two stages are rather of social nature, and the sixth stage unites both.

A timeline of usage for presented types of web applications is also different for each one of them. E.g. amount of usage for static websites goes in an opposite direction than usage of dynamic websites - while number of static websites is rapidly declining, newly created or redesigned projects are almost always of dynamic nature, which eliminates the static nature. Different situation present websites with interactive features, which can coexist with either static or dynamic websites. Interactive features also declined in usage for many years, yet they experienced rapid expansion with design trends of Web 2.0 and possibilities with AJAX techniques and JavaScript libraries such as jQuery [23]. This trend of an interaction between a user and a website is even more pronounced with an arrival of HTML5 and CSS3 specification.

(1) The first level is defined by Boulding as a static structure, also a framework or an arrangement. The static website is fully consistent with this concept. A markup

language, such as HTML or XML, forms a structure of a web document. The website is called static, as it does not change once loaded. HTML markup, such as marking the parts of a webpage or a notation of classes, creates a static base for additional styles and interactions.

(2) The evolutionary approach describes the second stage as a simple dynamic level with predetermined motions. This level is represented by simple machines. In relation to web applications, the second level corresponds with an interactive website. This type of website uses a scripting and a styling language in order to interact with a user. This interaction proceeds as a reaction of a website to a predetermined event on the client side. This reaction is usually a visual effect of a website. This effect is also predetermined, according to a triggered code, which is associated with the event.

(3) The third level is characterized as the control mechanism, with a purpose of transmission and interpretation of information. The dynamic website corresponds with this description. This type of website uses a scripting server-side language, usually accompanied by a database. This system enables inserting, updating and a retrieval of information, required by a user. It dynamically delivers information, according to the interpretation of criteria, which are defined by user's choices and behavior. It also provides mechanisms for validating inserted data. A content management system is a great example of a control mechanism, which is a fundamental description of the third level in the Boulding's hierarchy.

(4) The open system is a fourth stage according to Boulding, defined by an ability of self-maintenance and self-reproduction. A Web 2.0 application can be perceived as such an open system. Every user can be a contributor to this kind of application, so its content is growing and being maintained without directed interventions. Social networks and wiki sites are great examples on self-maintenance. Self-reproduction of applications can be viewed e.g. in the form of mash-ups. If an API or RSS is provided and application or information is worth spreading, it is usually being replicated across the web usually without control of an original source. Boulding also defined this stage as a level at which life begins to differentiate itself from not-life [4]. The social web application isn't a first type of website with pronounced social aspect. Comments and discussion forums have been popular before Web 2.0 emergence. However social networks such as Facebook creates truly living systems, which are changing our social behaviour [1]. The social web application adds an act of sharing among users into the web application mix, which can be defined as a social aspect with none or loose terms and structure [35, 36].

(5) The genetic social level is the fifth level of the evolutionary approach, defined by a division of labour and differentiated and mutually dependent parts of a system [4]. The semantic web application can represent such a model with its implementation of logical structure. By integrating and encapsulating relevant data into machine-understandable sections, they can be handled differently according to their meaning, but dependent on their context. These differentiated parts of a system enable a division of labour, since functionalities can be specific and respective to the parts they handle. Another aspect of the genetic social level and also semantic web application is a collaboration, in the meaning of a community, which needs to be active in order to

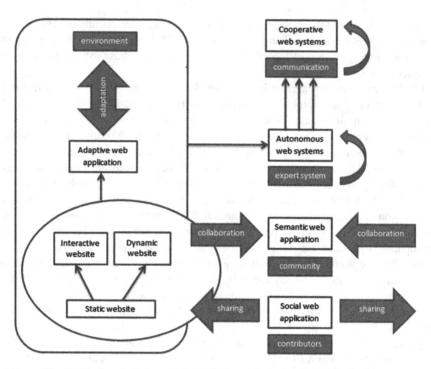

Fig. 1. Basic principles and interrelations of stages of web applications

implement linguistic and structural concepts on the web. A collaboration here represents a more elaborate social aspect with established terms and structure (Fig. 1).

(6) The sixth level as the animal level is characterized by an increased mobility, teleological behaviour, self-awareness and specialized information-receptors. Adaptive web applications correspond with this stage, as context-aware systems, with context represented by ontologies [20] from the fifth level. Mobility of a web application can be understood as an ability to function properly in different browsers, in various devices and with different screen sizes. Teleological behaviour ensures providing of different functionalities according to capabilities of chosen device. E.g. certain functionality associated with location and movement has use only for mobile devices. An adaptive web application is aware of itself, as of its capabilities, and aware of the relevant environment, which determines use of these capabilities. Web application then needs to correctly interpret information from sensors as specialized information-receptors.

According to the author, the current state of web applications can be placed past levels 1–3, in level 4 and in the beginning of both levels 5 and 6. The Boulding's hierarchy has three more levels, 7. The human level, 8. Human society and 9. The transcendental level. According to their features and a position in the hierarchy, we can roughly predict associated future stages of web applications. The seventh level as the autonomous web systems, which encapsulate wide range of functionality and are capable of complex decisions according to their implemented expert systems. The eighth level can be predicted as the cooperative web systems, capable of communication among autonomous applications and delivering desirable performance without any human intervention. Of course, throughout the evolvement of web applications, implementation of necessary hardware and infrastructure had to precede certain software development.

5 Conclusions

This article discussed web applications in relation to the evolutionary approach of general systems theory. The suggested evolutional stages of web applications were presented, according to their complexity, usage and historical appearance. The author believes that this classification approached an evolvement from simple static websites to complex web applications and clarified the framework for this evolvement. The current state of web applications was suggested in the following way: (1) Fully using qualities of the first three technological levels, with an emphasis on dynamic and interactive features, (2) in the fourth stage of social web applications, which have already changed our social behaviour, (3) progressing in the both fifth and sixth levels, with continuing efforts for semantic web and emerging requirements for adaptive web applications. Future development has been briefly suggested in a correspondence with the seventh and eighth level in the Boulding's hierarchy.

Acknowledgment. This work and the contribution were supported by: (1) the project No. CZ.1.07/2.2.00/28.0327 Innovation and support of doctoral study program (INDOP), financed from EU and Czech Republic funds; (2) project "Smart Solutions in Ubiquitous Computing Network Environments", from the Grant Agency of Excellence, University of Hradec Kralove, Faculty of Informatics and Management, Czech Republic; (3) project "SP/2013/03 - Smart-HomePoint Solutions for Ubiquitous Computing Environments" from University of Hradec Kralove.

References

1. Vossen, G., Hagemann, S.: Unleashing Web 2.0. Morgan Kaufmann, San Francisco, pp. 1-68, ISBN 9780123740342, 10.1016/B978-012374034-2.50002-2 (2007)
2. Von Bertalanffy, L.: An outline of general system theory. Br. J. Philos. Sci. 1(2), 134–165 (1950)
3. Rapoport, A.: General systems theory. Int. Encycl. Soc. Sci. 15, 452–458 (1968)
4. Boulding, K.: General systems theory – the skeleton of science. Manage. Sci. 2(3), 197–208. Reprinted in E:CO 6(1–2), Fall 2004, 127–139 (1956/2004)
5. World Wide Web Foundation (2008–2013). History of the Web. http://www.webfoundation.org/vision/history-of-the-web/
6. Hofkirchner, W., von Bertalanffy, L.: Forerunner of evolutionary systems theory. In: Gu, J., Chroust, G. (eds.) The New Role of Systems Sciences For a Knowledge-based Society, Proceedings of the First World Congress of the International Federation for Systems Research, p. 6. International Federation for Systems Research, Kobe, Japan (2005)

7. Hofkirchner, W.: General system theory. The origins of General System Theory (GST). http://www.hofkirchner.uti.at/wp-content/uploads/2010/10/GSTcombined.pdf (2010)
8. Chen, A.Q., Harper, S.: Web evolution: method and materials. Technical Report, University of Manchester. http://wel-eprints.cs.man.ac.uk/74 (2008)
9. Gerard, R.W.: Concepts and principles of biology. Behav. Sci. **3**, 95–102 (1958)
10. Shneiderman, B.: Universal design. Commun. ACM **43**, 84–91 (2000)
11. Weinreich, H., Obendorf, H., Herder, E., Mayer, M.: Not quite the average: an empirical study of web use. ACM Trans. Web **2**(1), 5:1–5:31 (2008)
12. Ankolekar, A., Krötzsch, M., Tran, T., Vrandecic, D.: The two cultures: mashing up web 2.0 and the semantic web. In: Proceedings of the 16th international conference on World Wide Web, 08–12 May, 2007, Banff, Alberta, Canada (2007)
13. Gillies, D.A.: Understanding general systems theory. Nursing Management a Systems Approach, pp. 56–74. W. B. Saunders Company, Philadelphia (1982)
14. Bates, C.: Web Programming – Building Internet Applications, 3rd edn. Wiley, Chichester, UK (2006). ISBN 978-0470017753
15. Doyle, M.: Beginning PHP 5.3. Wiley Publishing, Inc., Indianapolis ISBN 978-8126527977 (2010)
16. Wahlster, W., Dengel, A. (eds.): Web 3.0:convergence of web 2.0 and the semantic web (with contributions by Dietmar Dengler, Dominik Heckmann, Malte Kiesel, Alexander Pfalzgraf, Thomas Roth-Berghofer, Leo Sauermann, Eric Schwarzkopf, and Michael Sintek). Deutsche Telekom Laboratories, Technology Radar Feature Paper, Edition II/2006, June, pp. 1–23 (2006)
17. Berners-Lee, T., Hendler, J., Lassila, O.: The semantic web – a new form of web content that is meaningful to computers will unleash a revolution of new possibilities. Sci. Am. **284**(5), 35–43 (2001)
18. Yourdon, E.: Modern Structured Analysis. Yourdon Press, Prentice-Hall International, Englewood Cliffs, New Jersey (1989). ISBN 978-0135986240
19. Marzano, S., Aarts, E.: The new everyday view on ambient intelligence. Uitgeverij 010 Publishers, Rotterdam ISBN 978-9064505027 (2003)
20. Loke, S.: Context-aware pervasive systems: architectures for a new breed of applications. Taylor & Francis Group, UK ISBN 978-0849372551 (2007)
21. Schmidt, A.: Ubiquitous computing - computing in context. Ph.D. thesis, Computing Department, Lancaster University (2002)
22. Frain, B.: Responsive web design with HTML5 and CSS3. Packt Publishing ISBN 978-9350237885 (2012)
23. Nicholas, Z.: Professional JavaScript for Web Developers, 2nd edn (2009). Wrox. ISBN 978-0470227800
24. Longo, L., Kane, B.: A novel methodology for evaluating user interfaces in health care. In: 24th IEEE International Symposium on Computer-Based Medical Systems CBMS 2011, Bristol, England, 27–30 June 2011 (2011)
25. Kasik, V., Penhaker, M., Novák, V., Bridzik, R., Krawiec, J.: User interactive biomedical data web services application. In: Yonazi, J.J., Sedoyeka, E., Ariwa, E., El-Qawasmeh, E. (eds.) ICeND 2011. CCIS, vol. 171, pp. 223–237. Springer, Heidelberg (2011)
26. Liou, C.-Y., Cheng, W.-C.: Manifold construction by local neighborhood preservation. In: Ishikawa, M., Doya, K., Miyamoto, H., Yamakawa, T. (eds.) ICONIP 2007, Part II. LNCS, vol. 4985, pp. 683–692. Springer, Heidelberg (2008)
27. Popek, G., Kowalczyk, R., Katarzyniak, R.P.: Generating descriptions of incomplete city-traffic states with agents. Adv. Intell. Soft Comput. **122**, 105–114 (2011)

28. Penhaker, M., Stankus, M., Prauzek, M., Adamec, O., Peterek, T., Cerny, M., Kasik, V.: Advanced experimental medical diagnostic system design and realisation. Electron. Electr. Eng. **1**(117), 89–94 (2012)
29. Cheng, W.C., Liou, J.W., Liou, C.Y.: Construct adaptive template array for magnetic resonance images. In: IEEE International Joint Conference on Neural Networks, Brisbane, Australia, 10–15 June 2012 (2012). doi:10.1109/IJCNN.2012.6252560
30. Bures, V., Otcenaskova, T., Cech, P., Antos, K.: A proposal for a computer-based framework of support for public health in the management of biological incidents: the Czech Republic experience. Perspect. Public Health **132**(6), 292–298 (2012). doi:10.1177/1757913912444260
31. Machaj, J., Brida, P.: Impact of radio fingerprints processing on localization accuracy of fingerprinting algorithms. Elektronika ir Elektrotechnika **7**, 129–132 (2012). doi:10.5755/j01.eee.123.7.2391
32. Brida, P., Machaj, J., Duha, J.: A novel optimizing algorithm for DV based positioning methods in ad hoc networks. Electron. Electr. Eng. **97**(1), 33–38 (2010)
33. Mikulecky, P.: User adaptivity in smart workplaces. In: Pan, J.-S., Chen, S.-M., Nguyen, N.T. (eds.) ACIIDS 2012, Part II. LNCS(LNAI), vol. 7197, pp. 401–410. Springer, Heidelberg (2012)
34. Mikulecky, P., Olsevicova, K., Cimler, R.: Outdoor large-scale ambient intelligence, innovation vision 2020: sustainable growth. Entrepreneurship Econ. Dev. **1–4**, 1840–1842 (2012)
35. Penhaker, M., Krejcar, O., Kasik, V., Snášel, V.: Cloud computing environments for biomedical data services. In: Yin, H., Costa, J.A.F., Barreto, G. (eds.) IDEAL 2012. LNCS, vol. 7435, pp. 336–343. Springer, Heidelberg (2012)
36. Horalek, J., Sobeslav, V.: Datanetworking Aspects of Power Substation Automation, International Conference on Communication and Management in Technological Innovation and Academic Globalization, Puerto De La Cruz, Spain, November 30–December 02, 2010, pp. 147–153 (2010)
37. Behan, M., Krejcar, O.: Modern smart device-based concept of sensoric networks. EURASIP J. Wirel. Commun. Networking, Article Number: 155 (2013). doi:10.1186/1687-1499-2013-155

Impact of Mobility on the Performance of Context-Aware Applications Using Floating Content

Shahzad Ali[1,2], Gianluca Rizzo[3], Marco Ajmone Marsan[1,4],
and Vincenzo Mancuso[1(✉)]

[1] Institute IMDEA Networks, Madrid, Spain
[2] Universidad Carlos III de Madrid, Madrid, Spain
{shahzad.ali,marco.ajmone,vincenzo.mancuso}@imdea.org
[3] HES-SO Valais, Sierre, Switzerland
gianluca.rizzo@hevs.ch
[4] Politecnico di Torino, Torino, Italy

Abstract. The growth of mobile computing and the evolution of smart user devices are progressively driving applications towards "context-awareness", i.e., towards behaviors that change according to variations in context. Such applications use information that is restricted in space and time, making their communication requirements very different from those of conventional applications, so that opportunistic schemes are better suited to this case than more conventional communications. In this work we consider an opportunistic communication scheme called "Floating Content" (FC), which was specifically designed for server-less distributed context-aware applications, and we refine our previous investigation of the viability of FC for context-aware mobile applications, by considering the impact of different mobility models on the performance of FC. In particular, we consider four different mobility models, and, by using extensive simulation experiments, we investigate the performance of three different categories of context-aware applications that use FC. We also compare the simulation results to the performance predictions of our previously proposed simple analytical model. Results show that good performance can be achieved in content distribution by using FC under a variety of mobility models. They also show that a simple analytical model can provide useful performance predictions even for complex and realistic mobility models, although some application-specific characteristics might call for specialized models to improve the accuracy of performance estimates.

1   Introduction

Context is defined as "any information that can be utilized to understand the situation of an entity" and the applications which adapt their behavior according to changes in context are called "context-aware" [10]. With the pervasiveness of smart devices in the environment, such applications are becoming increasingly

P.C. Vinh et al. (Eds.): ICCASA 2013, LNICST 128, pp. 198–208, 2014.
DOI: 10.1007/978-3-319-05939-6_20, © Springer International Publishing Switzerland 2014

popular. One of the best examples of context and one of the most commonly used variables for context-aware applications is spatial and temporal locality. Locality plays an important role in a variety of applications. As an example, for a context-aware restaurant-finding application [7], information about a nearby restaurant may be of interest to an area close to the restaurant where the likelihood to find users interested in that piece of information is high, and also for a limited time, i.e., until the restaurant is open. Similar context-aware applications encompass an ever-expanding set of applications that make use of spatio-temporal locality, and wireless communications to deliver a variety of services. For many location-based context-aware applications, the scope of the generated content itself is local. This locally relevant content may be of little concern to the rest of the world, therefore moving this content from the user device to store it in a well-accessible centralized location and/or make this information available beyond its scope represents a clear waste of resources (connectivity, storage), and it may lead to the WORN (write-once, read never) problem. All these reasons make the communication requirements for context-aware applications significantly different from ordinary applications. Therefore, a careful design of the communication layer is necessary to serve such applications in the most efficient and scalable way. In this domain, opportunistic communications can play a special role. The benefit of using opportunistic communications is that they naturally incorporate context, as spatial proximity is not only associated to connectivity, but also, at the application layer, to correlation at several levels between communicating peers, between their needs, interests, etc. (the fact that they are in proximity of each other might be because they share interests and views: a same restaurant might mean same tastes for food, etc.). Indeed, connectivity to the infrastructure as a prerequisite is often limiting due to cost and capacity concerns, especially for mobile users for whom using such applications may be problematic due to high roaming charges, unavailability of data services, or simply no network coverage.

In this work we focus on a specific context-aware communication service, known as "Floating Content" (FC) [7], conceived to support server-less distributed context-aware applications. FC is a fully distributed version of ephemeral content sharing, purely based on opportunistic communications. It aims at ensuring the availability of data within a certain geographic area, and for a given duration in time (see Sect. 2 for more details).

The authors of [5] introduced the concept of FC and provided an analytical model for analyzing its feasibility. They derived a condition called "criticality condition", which can guarantee the availability of information within a given region with high probability. In [7], the authors validated the analytical results presented in [5] with extensive simulations, and showed that the criticality condition behaves well, so that floating content is feasible even when a modest number of nodes is present in the network.

The focus of both [5] and [7] was to evaluate the general feasibility of FC. However, an open issue of those works is that they do not shed light on the performance of an application that uses FC as a communication service. In contrast, in our previous work [1], the focus was on evaluating the performance of context-aware applications that use FC as a communication service. We defined *success probability*, i.e., the probability that a user obtains the content in which it is interested when it passes though the FC area, as the primary performance parameter. In [1], we assumed that content floats, i.e., that the criticality condition is satisfied, then considered the Random Direction Mobility Model (RDMM) [3] and developed a simple approximate analytical model for computing the success probability, with key parameters the node density, the node transmission range, and the radius of the area within which the content floats. However, RDMM is a very simple mobility model and does not capture the complexity of realistic movement patterns. Hence, it is important to evaluate the FC performance under different and more realistic mobility settings.

In this work our goal is to investigate the impact of different mobility models on the performance of context-aware applications using FC. In particular, in addition to RDMM, we also simulate RPGM, to account for group mobility [4], MGMM, which provides a simplistic model for vehicular mobility [2], and a synthetic mobility trace based on real vehicular traffic statistics collected in the frame of the TAPASCOLOGNE project [8] in the city of Cologne, Germany.

With our experiments, we want to verify by simulation how well FC behaves in realistic mobility settings, and how closely the values of success probability predicted by our simple analytical model match those obtained with complex mobility models. Our results show that FC is a very useful communication paradigm for a variety of context-aware applications, capable of providing good performance in terms of success probability for different mobility models. The success probability values predicted by our simple analytical model are quite close to the values obtained from simulations for very realistic mobility models. However, we also show that specific features of particular mobility models might require more accurate FC models to better predict the system performance.

The rest of the paper is organized as follows. In Sect. 2 we present the floating content service and also introduce the considered families of context-aware applications. Section 3 outlines the analytical model that was proposed in [1]. In Sect. 4 we give a brief introduction of the considered mobility models. In Sect. 5 we present a performance analysis of context-aware applications using floating content. In Sect. 6 we present our conclusions.

2   Floating Content Service

In this section we describe our system model, and the basics of operation of the Floating Content communication service, which we refer to as FC. We consider a scenario with nodes moving on a plane, and communicating with each other in ad hoc mode. Figure 1 summarizes the operation of FC. We assume that at a given point in time, a user (via a context-aware application) issues a message that is of interest only for those users that are in a given region in space, called *Anchor Zone* (AZ), and for a given duration of time. This content is spread using opportunistic communications: Whenever a node possessing this content comes within the transmission range of some other node not having that content, the content is replicated. When a node possessing the content moves out of the spatio-temporal limits for that message, we assume that it deletes the content. In this way, the content may be available on a set of nodes which moves and varies over time within the AZ, even after the node that generated the content has left the AZ, i.e., the content 'floats' within the AZ.

The basic idea behind FC is to store a given content in a spatial region without any fixed infrastructure, making it available through opportunistic communications to all users traversing the region. For this reason the performance metric we consider for the FC service is the probability that a user entering the AZ receives the floating content *timely*. We call this parameter the *success probability* of the FC service. The exact definition of this parameter depends on the way we define the time by which the content should be replicated to the new user who enters the AZ. The determination of this time is application specific, and is made with reference to a subregion of the AZ called the range of interest (ROI). We consider three cases, corresponding to three different categories of context-aware applications, and to three different definitions of success probability:

Baseline application: In this case, ROI and AZ are coincident, and the success probability is the probability that a new user entering in the AZ gets the content before leaving the AZ.

Application category 1: For this category, the message must be delivered to the new user by the time it exits the ROI. Typically, in these applications the message is expected to trigger some specific actions once the user is outside of the ROI. One example of such application can be advertising, when the fact of traversing a given area makes a user very likely to be interested in a specific offer/discount. For such applications, success probability is defined as the percentage of times a node gets content before exiting the ROI.

Application category 2: For this category of applications, the content must be delivered to users before they enter the ROI. Examples of such applications can be accident or traffic jam warnings, when a user should be notified in time to take informed decisions about alternative paths. Here success probability is the probability of getting the content before entering the ROI.

For all applications, the success probability is influenced by node density, by size, shape and relative position of the AZ and of the ROI, and node transmission range. In what follows we consider only circular anchor zones and ranges of interest, and we assume they are concentric. While ROI is strictly related to the application level definition of performance, the AZ radius can be tuned in order to get the desired success probability for all of the proposed applications.

3   An Analytical Model for Success Probability

In this section we briefly recall the main available result for the computation of the success probability for a generic application relying on FC. The derivation of this result in [1] assumes that nodes are distributed according to a planar Poisson point process with intensity λ users/Km^2, and that users move according to the Random Direction Mobility Model (RDMM) [3].

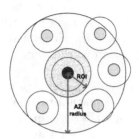 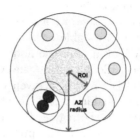 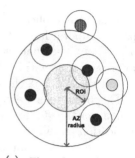

(a) A node generates a content.

(b) The content is replicated opportunistically within the AZ.

(c) Through replication, content is made available in the AZ. Nodes exiting the AZ discard the content.

Fig. 1. Operation of floating content service.

Result 1. *Consider an AZ with radius R, and nodes with transmission range r and speed v. Let Q denote the probability that two nodes successfully transfer the content while they are in contact. Then an approximated formula for the probability P_s that a node entering the AZ at time $t = 0$ gets the content by time $\tau \leq 2R/v$ is given by*

$$P_s(\tau) = \int_0^{2R} \frac{\ell^2}{\pi R^2 \sqrt{4R^2 - \ell^2}} \sum_{k=1}^{\infty} \left[1 - \left(1 - \frac{Q\overline{n}}{(\overline{m} + \overline{n})} \right)^k \right] \frac{\rho^k e^{-\rho}}{k!} d\ell, \quad (1)$$

where $\rho = 2r\lambda \cdot \min(\ell, v\tau)$, $\overline{m} = \min\left(\frac{v}{Q\nu R}, \lambda \pi R^2 \right)$, $\overline{n} = \lambda \pi R^2 - \overline{m}$, and $\nu = \frac{2rv^2}{(\pi R^2)}$. $\overline{n}$ and $\overline{m}$ are respectively the average number of nodes with and without content within the anchor zone.

The expression, which we use to compute an estimate of success probability for the three classes of applications presented in this paper, has two main parts. The first one is the probability of meeting k nodes along a path of length ℓ within the AZ, and is computed as the product of the pdf of the path lengths and the conditional pdf of the number of contacts, for a given path length. The second part is the probability that at least one out of k encounters brings to a successful transfer of content.

4   Mobility Scenarios

One of the most important aspects impacting the performance of the FC service is the way in which users move in space. In this paper we investigate this aspect, considering three different mobility models and a set of realistic vehicular traffic traces, and assessing the relationship between their characteristics and the performance of FC through extensive simulation experiments. The first mobility model we consider is the above mentioned RDMM, one of the most commonly used, and the one underlying the derivation of Result 1. In RDMM, nodes independently travel along a straight line, with an angle of movement uniformly distributed between 0 and 2π. This mobility model is simple and easily tractable analytically because the spatial node distribution remains uniform at all time instants [3]. The second model is the Manhattan Grid Mobility Model (MGMM), used to describe the mobility of vehicles in an urban area [2]. It uses a grid road topology for modeling the movements of vehicles. At each road junction, each vehicle may turn left, turn right or continue straight according to some given probability, which can be tuned to obtain different mobility behaviors. We chose it in order to analyze the impact of a grid topology, typical of a city, on the performance of FC when used by applications residing on vehicles. The third model is the Reference Point Group Mobility model (RPGM), a group mobility model [4]. We have chosen it to evaluate the impact on the performance of FC of clustering and of correlation in user mobility patterns. In RPGM, nodes move in the form of a group and each group has a geographical scope. Nodes belonging to a group are uniformly distributed within its geographical scope. Each group has a *logical center* and all the nodes belonging to that group follow the *logical center*. This logical center moves according to a group motion vector $\vec{V_g}$. For individual movement of nodes, each node is assigned a reference point which follows the group motion vector. After time τ, a new reference point is calculated by adding a random motion vector $\vec{RM}$ to the group motion vector $\vec{V_g}$. The length of $\vec{RM}$ is uniformly distributed within a certain radius centered at the reference point, and the direction is uniformly distributed between 0 and 2π. Adding a random motion vector enables a random motion behavior for each individual node. Different mobility scenarios can be modeled with RPGM. One example is groups of tourists visiting some famous attractions in a city. Another example is mobility in a disaster recovery area where different medical assistant teams, rescue teams, firemen teams are randomly moving in the area for the help and rescue operation.

For the fourth considered scenario, we use synthetic mobility traces from the city of Cologne. The Cologne dataset is one of the largest freely available realistic traces capturing both macroscopic and microscopic features [8]. It is realistic from a microscopic point of view because it captures the realistic movement of individual drivers in presence of other vehicles, traffic signals, road junctions, etc. From a macroscopic point of view, it mimics the evolution of large traffic flows across a metropolitan area over time.

5   Performance Evaluation

For all simulation experiments, we use the OMNeT++ based framework called INET [9]. The end-user transmission range is always taken to be 50 m. We evaluate the performance under the four different mobility scenarios previously described. When considering RDMM, MGMM and RPGM, each node moves

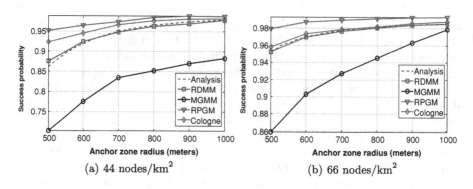

Fig. 2. Success probability for baseline application.

with a constant speed of 5 m/s, while in the Cologne dataset vehicles move at variable speed. For the case of MGMM, a block size of 200 m × 150 m is used. We simulate various values for the AZ radius, while we keep the ROI constant and equal to a circle or radius 200 m at the center of the AZ. As the Cologne dataset is very large, covering a region of 400 Km², for our simulations we considered an area of 9 Km² at the center of the city, and a two-hour time interval (from 6 AM to 8 AM) [6]. For the MGMM, the probability of turning right, turning left and going straight are, respectively, 0.25, 0.25 and 0.5, mimicking typical behavior of cars in city centers.

Figure 2 shows values of success probability as a function of the AZ radius for all the considered mobility models for the baseline application, for two values of nodes density. It can be seen that an increase in either the AZ radius or the node density improves success probability for all scenarios. The reason behind this behavior is that a larger AZ radius increases the average time a node spends inside the AZ, while a higher node density increases the contact rate, both resulting in more chances of meeting a node having content, and thus in higher success probability. For a given AZ radius and node density, RPGM yields the highest success probability, showing that clustering has a beneficial impact on the propagation of the content within the AZ and on its availability. The success probability predicted by our analytical model is very close to the ones by simulations for RDMM, for which the model was developed. We note that MGMM yields a lower success probability than RDMM in all cases. There are two main reasons behind this. First of all, if we look at the path length distribution within the AZ for MGMM and RDMM (see Fig. 3), we see that, unlike in RDMM, in MGMM shorter path lengths have a high probability as compared to relatively longer ones. For the considered block size, a high percentage of nodes traverse shorter paths inside AZ, which reduces the probability of meeting a node with content. The second reason is that, assuming that block size is much larger with respect to the node transmission range, and nodes move with a constant speed, a node can meet another node only if the other node is moving in the opposite direction (if both of them are on same road) or at the road junctions (where a node can meet other nodes traveling in other directions). This reduces the contact rate, resulting in decreased chances of meeting a node with content. MGMM and Cologne mobility traces are somewhat similar, in what they are both based on a grid of streets in a urban area. However, unlike MGMM, in a realistic setting like the one in the Cologne dataset, vehicles stop at intersections due to traffic signals, and also move according to car following model, which represents a realistic driver behavior [8]. Moreover, nodes move with variable speed, unlike in MGMM, where speed is constant. This also results in increased contact rate, and larger probability of meeting a node with content, resulting in increased success probability in the case of Cologne mobility. Moreover, MGMM keeps nodes uniformly distributed on all the area, while we have verified that mobility patterns in the Cologne dataset exhibit some correlation between vehicles mobility patterns, and some degree of clustering (traffic jams, traffic lights, etc.), which, as it happens for RPMM, improve the performance of FC.

Continuing the comparison between the results for MGMM and RDMM, an interesting observation is that, in case of application categories 1 and 2, the path length of users entering the ROI cannot be shorter than the difference between the AZ radius and the ROI radius. Therefore, we can expect that the success probabilities for application categories 1 and 2 are not impaired by the path length distribution shown for MGMM. Indeed, as shown in Figs. 4 and 5, the success probability of application categories 1 and 2 under MGMM is closer to that of RDMM, as compared to the baseline case. Under the topological settings used for the experiment reported in the figure, the minimum path length for application categories 1 and 2 is 300 m. This means that for application categories 1 and 2, the success probability is computed for paths inside the AZ with length greater than 300 m. This leads to considering longer paths as compared to the baseline case, and as a result the success probability increases and approaches the one given by the simple analytical model.

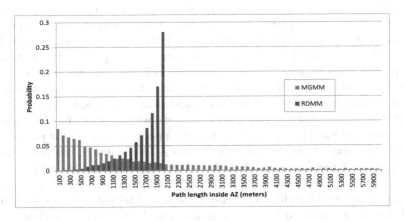

Fig. 3. Distribution of path lengths inside AZ for MGMM (1000 m AZ radius).

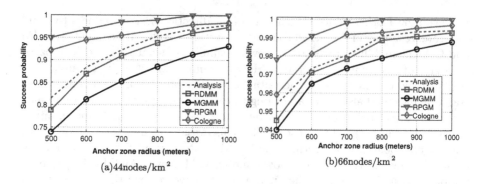

Fig. 4. Success probability for application category 1.

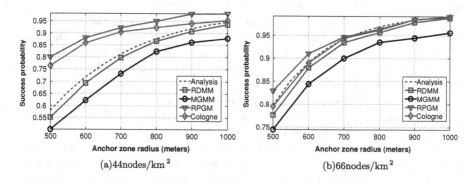

Fig. 5. Success probability for application category 2.

Specifically, Fig. 4 shows curves for success probability versus the AZ radius, for application category 1 under node densities of 44 and 66 $nodes$/km^2 respectively. For the Cologne traces, the plots have been obtained by individuating two time intervals, of 1000 s each, during which the average node density in the considered area is equal to the values of node density previously mentioned. As expected, increasing the AZ radius results in higher success probability for application category 1, under all mobility models. The reason is that increasing the AZ radius results in longer average amounts of time a node spends in AZ, resulting in increased chances of meeting a node with content. For all the considered mobility models, our analytical model predictions of success probability become more accurate for higher node densities. This is due to the assumptions underlying its derivation, which hold for a large number of nodes in the AZ.

Figure 5 shows curves for the success probability versus the AZ radius, for application category 2 under node densities of 44 and 66 $nodes$/km^2 respectively. The behavior is similar to Fig. 4. For all the considered mobility models, larger AZ radiuses translate in increased success probability for application category 2. If we consider an accident warning application, where the objective is to notify the nodes entering an area close to the accident location, so that a driver can make an informed decision, we can observe from Fig. 5 that FC is capable of providing a reasonably high success probability.

From our evaluation, we can conclude that FC is a very useful communication paradigm that can be used for a variety of context-aware applications. If parameters are carefully tuned/configured, it is capable of providing a reasonable success probability for a variety of applications and of user mobility patterns. The success probability values predicted by our simple analytical model are quite close to the values obtained from simulations for the case of RDMM. A better representation of the path lengths within the AZ is necessary to obtain comparable accuracy for the other considered mobility models, especially MGMM.

6 Conclusions

In this paper, we focused on the impact of end-user mobility models on the performance of context-aware applications using floating content as a communication paradigm. We considered three different categories of context-aware applications, and four different user mobility models. We found that FC can provide very effective performance to a variety of context-aware applications under quite diverse mobility patterns. Comparing simulation results to the performance predictions of a simple analytical model that was developed for RDMM, we found a very good agreement in the case of RDMM, as already observed in [1]. Other mobility models call for some model re-working to achieve similarly accurate estimates. For all the considered mobility models, high success probabilities can be achieved by tuning the anchor zone radii for a variety of context-aware applications, which justifies the viability of FC as an enabler for context-aware applications.

References

1. Ali, S., Rizzo, G., Rengarajan, B., Marsan, M.A.: A simple approximate analysis of floating content for context-aware applications. In: Proceedings of the Fourteenth ACM International Symposium on Mobile Ad Hoc Networking and Computing, MobiHoc '13, pp. 271–276. ACM, New York. http://eprints.networks.imdea.org/535/ (2013)
2. Bai, F., Sadagopan, N., Helmy, A.: IMPORTANT: a framework to systematically analyze the Impact of Mobility on Performance of Routing Protocols for Adhoc Networks. In: Proceedings of IEEE INFOCOM 2003, Twenty-Second Annual Joint Conference of the IEEE Computer and Communications (2003)
3. Bettstetter, C.: Mobility modeling in wireless networks: categorization, smooth movement, and border effects. SIGMOBILE Mob. Comput. Commun. Rev. 5(3), 55–66 (2001)
4. Hong, X., Gerla, M., Pei, G., Chiang, C.-C.: A group mobility model for ad hoc wireless networks. In: Proceedings of the 2nd ACM International Workshop on Modeling, Analysis and Simulation of Wireless and Mobile Systems, MSWiM'99, pp. 53–60. ACM, New York (1999)

5. Hyytiä, E., Virtamo, J., Lassila, P., Kangasharju, J., Ott, J.: When does content float? characterizing availability of anchored information in opportunistic content sharing. In: INFOCOM, Shanghai, China, April 2011 (2011)
6. Cologne mobility traces. http://kolntrace.project.citi-lab.fr/
7. Ott, J., Hyytiä, E., Lassila, P., Vaegs, T., Kangasharju, J.: Floating content: information sharing in urban areas. In: PerCom 2011, March 2011 (2011)
8. Uppoor, S., Trullols-Cruces, O., Fiore, M., Barcelo-Ordinas, J.M.: Generation and analysis of a large-scale urban vehicular mobility dataset. IEEE Trans. Mob. Comput. **99**(PrePrints), 1 (2013)
9. Varga, A.: The OMNeT++ discrete event simulation system. In: ESM 2001, June 2001 (2001)
10. Zimmermann, A., Lorenz, A., Oppermann, R.: An operational definition of context. In: Kokinov, B., Richardson, D.C., Roth-Berghofer, T.R., Vieu, L. (eds.) CONTEXT 2007. LNCS (LNAI), vol. 4635, pp. 558–571. Springer, Heidelberg (2007)

Towards Classification Based Human Activity Recognition in Video Sequences

Nguyen Thanh Binh[1(✉)], Swati Nigam[2], and Ashish Khare[2]

[1] Faculty of Computer Science and Engineering, Ho Chi Minh City
University of Technology, Ho Chi Minh City, Vietnam
ntbinh@cse.hcmut.edu.vn
[2] Department of Electronics and Communication, University of Allahabad,
Allahabad, India
swatinigam.au@gmail.com, ashishkhare@hotmail.com

Abstract. Recognizing human activities is an important component of a context aware system. In this paper, we propose a classification based human activity recognition approach. This approach recognizes different human activities based on a local shape feature descriptor and pattern classifier. We have used a novel local shape feature descriptor which is integration of central moments and local binary patterns. Classifier used is flexible binary support vector machine. Experimental evaluations have been performed on standard Weizmann activity video dataset. Six different activities have been considered for evaluation of the proposed method. Two activities have been selected at a time with binary classifier. These are walk-run, bend-jump, and jack-skip pairs. Experimental results and comparisons with other methods, demonstrate that the proposed method performs well and it is capable of recognizing six different human activities in videos.

Keywords: Human activity recognition · Classification · Feature descriptors

1 Introduction

Successful recognition of human activities enables a wide range of applications. Context aware human activity recognition generally refers to the determination of a human user's activity using camera and other contextual information that is readily available and accessible [1, 2]. The availability and accessibility of this real time contextual information creates new aspects of human activity recognition, as evidenced by Opportunity Activity Recognition Challenge [3] and Nokia Mobile Data Challenge [4]. Recognition of human activities is the final and major step of a complete human behavior analysis system and follows moving object segmentation [5], object recognition [6] and object tracking [7]. Activity recognition is important for many potential applications such as visual surveillance, biomechanical applications, human-computer interaction, clinical purposes and sports analysis, etc.

Generally, human activities can be categorized into four classes [8]. They are (i) human actions: that involve single human, (ii) human-human interactions: that involve two humans, (iii) human-object interactions: that involve human and object,

P.C. Vinh et al. (Eds.): ICCASA 2013, LNICST 128, pp. 209–218, 2014.
DOI: 10.1007/978-3-319-05939-6_21, © Springer International Publishing Switzerland 2014

and (iv) group activities: that involve multiple humans. But this is a difficult problem due to several challenges. Robustness against environment variations, robustness against actor's movement variations, robustness against various activities and insufficient amount of training videos are few of them [8].

While a number of activity recognition approaches have been explored to deal with above challenges, the proposed method takes advantage of holistic features based local descriptors and pattern classifier. In this paper, we have discussed a simple and effective unimodal approach of human activity recognition. The motivation is that the holistic features based local descriptors emphasize different aspects of activities and are suitable for different types of activity datasets. We have extracted a novel feature descriptor which is integration of moment features upon local binary features. This feature has further been classified using kernel based support vector machine classifier. While sequential classifiers, e.g. HMM [9], are common for learning from sequences, in this paper, we focus on developing a technique that enable using standard non-sequential learning technique for accurate activity recognition. This is motivated by the fact [10] that the non-sequential techniques, such as support vector machine, have good competitiveness and scalability on large-dimensional and continuous-valued activity data. Our experiments are conducted on real-world, publicly available Weizmann activity recognition video dataset [11] and we have considered six common activities and two at a time that are walk-run, bend-jump, and jack-skip pairs. There are several available activity datasets, among which the Weizmann dataset has been widely used to evaluate activity recognition approaches and many results have been reported on it.

The rest of the paper is organized as follows. Section 2 briefly explains the related work in this area, Sect. 3 describes fundamentals of the proposed feature descriptor based method, Sect. 4 explains the proposed method, Sect. 5 elaborates the experimental results and finally Sect. 6 is the conclusion of this paper.

2 Related Work

The main idea of this paper is to use holistic features based local descriptors for classification to perform human activity recognition. Therefore, we review representative papers on these features.

Several features based activity recognition techniques have been developed so far. Variants of SIFT feature, for example SIFT Flow [12] and three dimensional SIFT descriptor [13] have been successfully used for this purpose. The work done in the field of features based activity recognition can be categorized into region based and boundary based approaches. Fourier descriptor [14] is a popular boundary based feature descriptor used in literature. However, region based approaches retrieve information from boundary as well as from internal pixels. Therefore, they are preferred for general shape representation over boundary based approaches. Central moment [15] is another example of region based feature descriptors which has been used in recognition. Moment invariants [16] are well known region based features used for translation, rotation and scale invariant recognition. Flusser and Suk [17] proposed a blur and affine invariant approach for use in pattern recognition applications, e.g. activity recognition. Zernike moments [18] are rotation invariant and Legendre moments [19] are translation and scale invariant techniques for recognition.

Recognition in real scenes is a tough task due to variation in clothes, illumination conditions and poses. Dalal and Triggs [20] presented a method based on Histogram of Oriented Gradients (HOG) for handling these problems. This approach combines histogram of oriented gradients (HOG) and linear support vector machine (SVM) and provides better results. The HOG descriptors were computed and concatenated over detection window of size 16 × 16 pixels blocks. However, since the detection window slides over entire image, therefore this method is computationally expensive. Method to speed up this algorithm has been proposed in [21]. The variants of HOG include circular HOG [22] and hybrid HOG [23].

In recent years, interest is increasing to obtain local patterns of an image for better recognition. Local binary patterns (LBP) with adaptive threshold have provided excellent results for different vision applications [24]. In comparison to the gradient based features like HOG, LBP is more accurate, sparse and provides simple calculation. Moreover, LBP features can work in local color configuration and provide illumination invariant recognition. Motivated by the success of LBP features, [25] presented several variants of the original local binary pattern (LBP). To explore the discriminative ability of LBP, a window based descriptor has been proposed [26] for robust multi viewpoint recognition in different pose and under realistic environment. Center symmetric LBP in wavelet domain [27] has been computed for rapid recognition. An improved and hybrid strategy of HOG and LBP was presented in [28] for efficient and accurate recognition in real scenes.

Hence, it is clear that feature descriptors play a vital role in classification based activity recognition can be effectively used for accurate recognition of human activities.

3   Preliminaries

The purpose of this section is to provide a brief description of the Local Binary Patterns (LBP) and Central Moments (moments) used in the proposed work and to show their effectiveness towards human activity recognition.

3.1   Local Binary Patterns (LBP)

For computation of LBP, let us take an image $f(x, y)$ and g_c represent gray value of a pixel at location (x, y), i.e. $g_c = f(x_c, y_c)$. Also, let g_p represent gray level of any sample point in an equispaced circular neighborhood where P is the number of sample points within radius R. Then the general local binary pattern operator $LBP_{P,R}$ can be obtained as follows

$$LBP_{P,R}(x_c, y_c) = \sum_{P=0}^{P-1} s(g_p - g_c)2^P \qquad (1)$$

where $s(u)$ is defined as

$$s(u) = \begin{cases} 1, u \geq 0 \\ 0, u < 0 \end{cases} \tag{2}$$

3.2   Central Moments (Moments)

The geometric moment m_{pq} of order $p + q$ of an object in an image $f(x, y)$ can be defined as follows

$$m_{pq} = \sum_{x=0}^{M-1} \sum_{y=0}^{N-1} x^p y^q f(x, y) \tag{3}$$

In case of central moments

$$\mu_{pq} = \sum_{x=0}^{M-1} \sum_{y=0}^{N-1} (x - x_c)^p (y - y_c)^q f(x, y) \tag{4}$$

$$\text{where } x_c = \frac{m_{10}}{m_{00}} \text{ and } y_c = \frac{m_{01}}{m_{00}} \tag{5}$$

4   The Proposed Method

The steps of the proposed method are explained in this section.

Step 1: Read frames of a video sequence.
Step 2: Scale resize each frame.
Step 3: Convert it from RGB to gray level color space.
Step 4: Compute LBP according to following equation

$$LBP_{P,R}(x, y) = \sum_{P=0}^{P-1} s(g_p - g_c) 2^P, \quad s(u) = \begin{cases} 1, u \geq 0 \\ 0, u < 0 \end{cases} \tag{6}$$

where (x_c, y_c) is the location of center pixel in the region R, g_c is the gray value of center pixel, g_p is the gray value of the neighborhood pixels and P can take values from 0 to $N - 1$. Here N = 8.
Step 5: Compute moment-LBP according to following equation

$$MLBP_{P,R}(x, y) = \sum_{c=0}^{M-1} \sum_{c=0}^{N-1} (x - x_c)^u (y - y_c)^v LBP_{P,R}(x, y) \tag{7}$$

where $u + v = 2$.
Step 6: Classify moment-LBP features. We have computed these features in each and every frame of activity video sequence. The classification has been performed using 'rbf' kernel based binary SVM classifier. This is a two class classifier

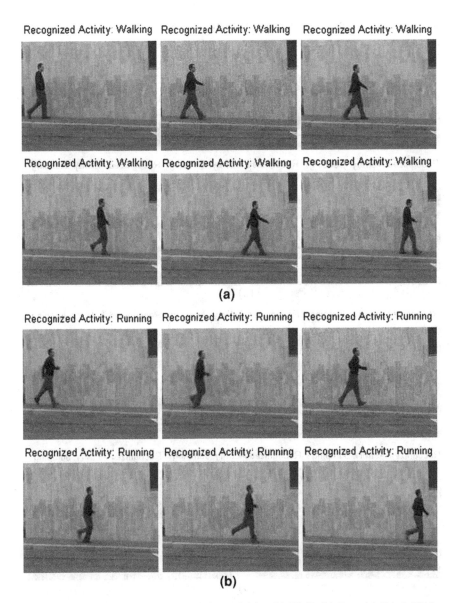

Fig. 1. Results of the proposed method for activities (a) Walk (b) Run (c) Bend (d) Jump (e) Jack and (f) Skip

Fig. 1. (continued)

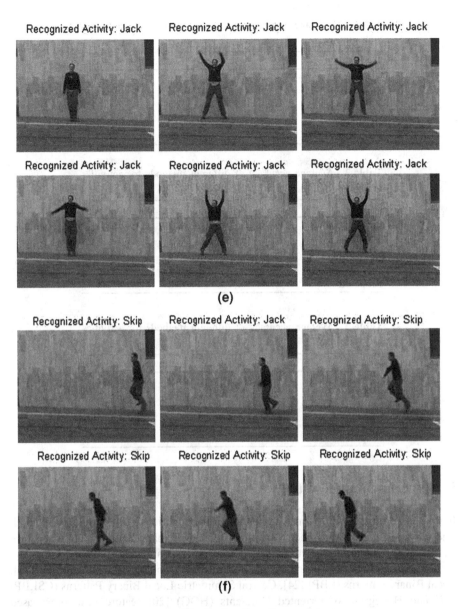

Fig. 1. (continued)

and efficiently classifies features for two activities at a time. Pair of activities have been selected for this purpose. These pairs are walk-run, bend-jump and jack-skip. First, we have selected walk-run pair of activities. Features for these activities have been computed separately. Now these features have been classified with binary SVM classifier which is an established classifier for this purpose. Other pair of activities which we have taken are bend-jump and jack-skip from Weizmann dataset.

Table 1. Average accuracy of different methods for activities walk-run pair

Method	Average accuracy (%)
Moment [15]	50.0
LBP [24]	50.0
CSLBP [27]	51.9
HOG [20]	50.0
Proposed	**72.6**

Table 2. Average accuracy of different methods for activities bend-jump pair

Method	Average accuracy (%)
Moment [15]	48.7
LBP [24]	49.1
CSLBP [27]	43.5
HOG [20]	49.1
Proposed	**56.8**

Table 3. Average accuracy of different methods for activities jack-skip pair

Method	Average accuracy (%)
Moment [15]	48.9
LBP [24]	49.5
CSLBP [27]	74.1
HOG [20]	49.5
Proposed	**77.3**

5 Experimental Results

In this section, we have performed experimental evaluations of the proposed method. The proposed method has been performed over Weizmann activity dataset and we have considered 6 different activities, two at a time, that are walk-run, bend-jump, and jack-skip pair. Also, the proposed method has been compared with Moment [15], Local Binary Patterns (LBP) [24], Central Symmetric Local Binary Patterns (CSLBP) [27] and Histogram of Oriented Gradients (HOG) [20] feature descriptor based methods. Figure 1 visually shows results of the proposed method for few representative frames.

From Fig. 1, it is observed that the proposed method recognizes different pair of activities accurately. These activities are walk-run, bend-jump and jack-skip. The recognition results of the proposed method for these activities are shown in Fig. 1(a–f). We have compared advantages and disadvantages of the proposed method with a selected number of other methods like moment [15], LBP [24], CSLBP [27] and HOG [20] based methods in terms of average accuracy, shown in Tables 1, 2, and 3.

On observing Tables 1, 2 and 3, it is clear that the average accuracy rate of the proposed method is the highest when compared to Moment [15], LBP [24], CSLBP [27] and HOG [20] based methods. Therefore, it is said that that the performance of the proposed method is better than other methods.

6 Conclusions

In this paper, we have discussed and demonstrated a classification based approach for human activity recognition. We have used novel integrated moment-local binary patterns feature descriptor and binary support vector machine (SVM) classifier. The experiments have been performed over Weizmann activity video dataset. Six activities have been considered for experimental evaluations. Among these six activities, pairs of two activities have been taken at a time for classification with binary SVM classifier. These are walk-run, bend-jump, and jack-skip pairs of activities. Performance of the proposed method has been demonstrated qualitatively and quantitatively. Quantitative results show that the proposed method outperforms other Moment [15], Local Binary Patterns [24], Center Symmetric Local Binary Patterns [27] and Histogram of Oriented Gradients [20] based methods.

Acknowledgment. This work was supported by the University Grants Commission, New Delhi, India under Grant No. F.No.36-246/2008(SR) and Council of Scientific and Industrial Research, Human Resource Development Group, India via grant no. 09/001/(0362)/2012/ EMR-I.

References

1. Zhu, Y., Nayak, N.M., Roy-Chowdhury, A.K.: Context aware activity recognition and anomaly detection in video. IEEE J. Sel. Top. Signal Process. **7**(1), 91–101 (2013)
2. Chihani, B., Bertin, E., Jeanne, F., Crespi, N.: Context-aware systems: a case study. In: Cherifi, H., Zain, J.M., El-Qawasmeh, E. (eds.) DICTAP 2011, Part II. CCIS, vol. 167, pp. 718–732. Springer, Heidelberg (2011)
3. OPPORTUNITY Activity Challenge – http://www.opportunity-project.eu/node/58 (2013). Last accessed 27 July 2013
4. NOKIA Mobile Data Challenge – http://research.nokia.com/page/12000 (2013). Last accessed 27 July 2013
5. Khare, M., Srivastava, R.K., Khare, A.: Moving object segmentation in Daubechies complex wavelet domain. Accepted for publication in Signal Image and Video Processing. ISSN: 1863-1711. Springer (2013). doi:10.1007/s11760-013-0496-4
6. Nigam, S., Deb, K., Khare, A.: Moment invariants based object recognition for different pose and appearances in real scenes. In: 2nd IEEE International Conference on Informatics, Electronics & Vision (ICIEV), pp. 1–5, Dhaka, Bangladesh, May 2013
7. Binh, N.T., Khare, A.: Object tracking of video sequences in curvelet domain. Int. J. Image Graph. **11**(1), 1–20 (2011)
8. Aggarwal, J.K., Ryoo, M.S.: Human activity analysis: a review. ACM Comput. Surv. **43**(3), article 16. http://cvrc.ece.utexas.edu/aggarwaljk/Publications/review_ryoo_hdr.pdf (2011)

9. Alemdar, H., van Kasteren, T.L.M., Ersoy, C.: Activity recognition with hidden Markov models using active learning. In: 19th IEEE Conference on Signal Processing and Communications Applications (SIU), pp. 1161–1164, Antalya (2011)

10. Cao, H., Nguyen, M.N., Phua, C., Krishnaswamy, S., Xiao, L.L.: An integrated framework for human activity classification. In: ACM Conference on Ubiquitous Computing (UbiComp'12), pp. 331–340, New York (2012)

11. Gorelick, L., Blank, M., Shechtman, E., Irani, M., Basri, R.: Actions as space time shapes. IEEE Trans. Pattern Anal. Mach. Intell. **29**(12), 2247–2253 (2007)

12. Liu, C., Yuen, J., Torralba, A.: SIFT flow: dense correspondence across scenes and its applications. IEEE Trans. Pattern Anal. Mach. Intell. **33**(5), 978–994 (2011)

13. Scovanner, P., Ali, S., Shah, M.: A 3-dimensional sift descriptor and its application to action recognition. In: ACM 15th International Conference on Multimedia, pp. 357–360 (2007)

14. Zhao, Y., Belkasim, S.: Multiresolution Fourier descriptors for multiresolution shape analysis. IEEE Signal Process. Lett. **19**(10), 692–695 (2012)

15. Flusser, J., Suk, T., Zitova, B.: Moments and Moment Invariants in Pattern Recognition. Wiley, New York (2009)

16. Hu, M.K.: Visual pattern recognition by moment invariants. IRE Trans. Inf. Theory **8**(2), 179–187 (1962)

17. Flusser, J., Suk, T.: Combined blur and affine moment invariants and their use in pattern recognition. Pattern Recogn. **36**(12), 2895–2907 (2003)

18. Chen, B.J., Shu, H.Z., Zhang, H., Chen, G., Toumoulin, C., Dillenseger, J.L., Luo, L.M.: Quaternion Zernike moments and their invariants for color image analysis and object recognition. Signal Process. **92**(2), 308–318 (2012)

19. Hosny, K.M.: Refined translation and scale Legendre moment invariants. Pattern Recogn. Lett. **31**(7), 533–538 (2010)

20. Dalal, N., Triggs, B.: Histogram of oriented gradients for human detection. In: IEEE International Conference on Computer Vision and Pattern Recognition, pp. 886–893, San Diego, CA, USA (2005)

21. Pang, Y., Yuan, Y., Li, X., Pan, J.: Efficient HOG human detection. Signal Process. **91**(4), 773–781 (2011)

22. Skibbe, H., Reisert, M., Schmidt, T., Brox, T.: Fast rotation invariant 3D feature computation utilizing efficient local neighborhood operators. IEEE Trans. Pattern Anal. Mach. Intell. **34**(8), 1563–1575 (2012)

23. Nigam, S., Khare, M., Srivastava, R.K., Khare, A.: An effective local feature descriptor for object detection in real scenes. In: IEEE Conference on Information and Communication Technologies (ICT 2013), pp. 244–248, Kanyakumari, India, April 2013

24. Pietikäinen, M., Hadid, A., Zhao, G., Ahonen, T.: Computer Vision using Local Binary Patterns. Computational Imaging and Vision, vol. 40. Springer, Heidelberg (2011)

25. Mu, Y., Yan, S., Liu, Y., Huang, T., Zhou, B.: Discriminative local binary patterns for human detection in personal album. In: IEEE International Conference on Computer Vision and Pattern Recognition, pp. 1–8, Anchorage, AK, (2008)

26. Nguyen, D.T., Ogunbona, P.O., Li, W.: A novel shape-based non-redundant local binary pattern descriptor for object detection. Pattern Recogn. **46**(5), 1485–1500 (2013)

27. Ko, B.C., Kim, D.Y., Jung, J.H., Nam, J.Y.: Three-level cascade of random forests for rapid human detection. Opt. Eng. **52**(2), 027204 (2013)

28. Shen, J., Yang, W., Sun, C.: Real-time human detection based on gentle MILBoost with variable granularity HOG-CSLBP. Neural Comput. Appl. (2012). doi:10.1007/s00521-012-1153-5

A New Fuzzy Associative Memory

Pham Viet Binh, Nong Thi Hoa[(✉)], Vu Duc Thai,
and Quach Xuan Truong

Thainguyen University of Information Technology and Communication,
Thainguyen, Vietnam
nongthihoa@gmail.com

Abstract. Fuzzy Associative Memory (FAM) is a neural network that stores associations of patterns. The most important advantage of FAM is recalling stored patterns from noisy inputs (noise tolerance). Some FAMs only show associations or content of pattern separately. Therefore, we propose a model of FAM that shows both associations and content of patterns effectively. In learning process, each pair of pattern is learned by the minimum of input and output pattern. Then, all pairs of pattern are generalized by mean of the learning results of each pair. In recalling process, a new threshold is added to improve noise tolerance. We have conducted experiments in pattern recognition to prove the effectiveness of our FAM. Experiment results show that our model tolerates noise better than previous FAMs in two types of noise.

Keywords: Fuzzy associative memory · Associative memory · Artificial neural network · Noise tolerance · Pattern recognition

1 Introduction

FAM is an artificial neural network storing pattern associations and retrieves the desired output pattern from a noisy input pattern by operators of fuzzy logic and mathematical morphology (MM) [7, 8]. FAM consists of two processes, namely, learning process and recalling process. Learning process learns and stores associations of patterns. Recalling process retrieves a stored pattern from a input pattern. FAMs have three important advantages including noise tolerance, unlimited storage, and one pass convergence in which noise tolerance is the most important advantage. It means that FAM recalls stored patterns from noisy inputs by an output function. Thus, FAM has been widely applied in many fields such as image processing, prediction, inference, and estimation.

Design of FAM has been studied to improve the ability of recalling. First, Kosko proposed the first FAM which uses the minimum of patterns in learning process and recalling process [6]. Junbo et al. used fuzzy implication operator to learn pairs of pattern and inherited output function of Kosko [5]. Fulai and Tong inherited learning process of Junbo and used a t-norm for the output function [4]. Xiao et al. proposed a new equation for learning process by using the minimum and the maximum of the input pattern and the output pattern, and applied the multiplication operator for the output function [3]. Wang et al. proposed a new model, which learned patterns by

P.C. Vinh et al. (Eds.): ICCASA 2013, LNICST 128, pp. 219–227, 2014.
DOI: 10.1007/978-3-319-05939-6_22, © Springer International Publishing Switzerland 2014

the division operator and applied the addition for the output function [2]. Sussner and Valle created a family of FAM, which are called Implicative FAM [1]. Patterns are stored by a fuzzy implication operator and computed the output function through an s-norm operator. However, previous FAMs only show content of patterns [1–5] or associations of patterns [1, 6]. Meaning that, no FAM shows both content and association of patterns.

In this paper, we propose a model of FAM presenting more effectively both associations and content of patterns. In learning process, our FAM learns and stores both content and associations of patterns. In recalling process, we improve output patterns of FAM by adding a new threshold. Experiments are conducted in pattern recognition of grey-scale images with two types of noise. Results from experiments show that proposed FAM recalls better than previous FAMs.

The rest of the paper is organized as follows. In Sect. 2, background is presented. Section 3 show the design of our novel model. The next section is experiment results to show the advantages of the proposed FAM.

2 Over View of Fuzzy Logic, Mathematical Morphology and Associative Memory

2.1 Operators of Fuzzy Logic

Let A and B are fuzzy subsets of a non-empty set X.

The **intersection** of A and B is defined as

$$\mu_{A \wedge B}(x) = \min\{\mu_A(x), \mu_B(x)\} \tag{1}$$

for all x ∈ X.

The **union** of A and B is defined as

$$\mu_{A \vee B}(x) = \max\{\mu_A(x), \mu_B(x)\} \tag{2}$$

for all x ∈ X.

The **fuzzy conjunction** of A and B is an increasing mapping C: $[0, 1] \times [0, 1] \rightarrow [0, 1]$ that satisfies

C(0, 0) = C(0, 1) = C(1, 0) = 0 and C(1, 1) = 1.

For example, the minimum operator and the product are typical examples.

A fuzzy conjunction T: $[0, 1] \times [0, 1] \rightarrow [0, 1]$ that satisfies

T(x, 1) = x for x ∈ [0, 1] is called triangular norm or t-norm.

The fuzzy conjunctions C_M, C_P, and C_L are examples of t-norms.

$$C_M(x, y) = x \wedge y \tag{3}$$

$$C_P(x, y) = x.y \tag{4}$$

$$C_L(x, y) = 0 \vee (x + y - 1) \tag{5}$$

A **fuzzy disjunction** is an increasing mapping D: $[0, 1] \times [0, 1] \rightarrow [0, 1]$ that satisfies

D(0, 0) = 0 and D(0, 1)= D(1, 0) = D(1, 1) = 1.

A fuzzy disjunction S: $[0, 1] \times [0, 1] \to [0, 1]$ that satisfies

S(1, x) = x for every $x \in [0, 1]$ is called triangular co-norm or short s-norm. The following operators represent s-norms:

$$D_M(x, y) = x \vee y \tag{6}$$

$$D_P(x, y) = x + y - x.y \tag{7}$$

$$D_L(x, y) = 1 \wedge (x + y) \tag{8}$$

An operator I: $[0, 1] \times [0, 1] \to [0, 1]$ is called a **fuzzy implication** if I extends the usual crisp implication on $[0, 1] \times [0, 1]$ with I(0, 0) = I(0, 1) = I(1, 1) = 1 and I(1, 0) = 0.

Some particular fuzzy implications:

$$I_M(x, y) = \begin{cases} 1, x \leq y \\ y, x > y \end{cases} \tag{9}$$

$$I_P(x, y) = \begin{cases} 1, x \leq y \\ \frac{y}{x}, x > y \end{cases} \tag{10}$$

$$I_L(x, y) = 1 \wedge (y - x + 1) \tag{11}$$

2.2   Basic Operators of Mathematical Morphology

A complete lattice is defined as a partially ordered set L in which every (finite or infinite) subset has an infimum and a supremum in L. For any $Y \subseteq L$, the infimum of Y is denoted by the $\wedge Y$ and the supremum is denoted by the $\vee Y$. The class of fuzzy sets inherits the complete lattice structure of the unit interval $[0, 1]$.

Erosion and dilation are two basic operators of MM. A erosion is a mapping ε from a complete lattice L to a complete lattice M that satisfies the following equation:

$$\varepsilon\left(\bigwedge Y\right) = \bigwedge_{y \in Y} \varepsilon(y) \tag{12}$$

Similarly, an operator δ: $L \to M$ is called dilation if it satisfies the following equation:

$$\varepsilon\left(\bigvee Y\right) = \bigvee_{y \in Y} \varepsilon(y) \tag{13}$$

2.3   Associative Memory

Associative memory (AM) stores pattern associations and retrieves the desired output pattern upon presentation of a noisy input pattern [9]. The associative memory is defined as follows:

Given a finite set of desired associations $(A^k, B^k), k = 1, \ldots, p$, determine a mapping G such that $G(A^k) = B^k$ for all $k = 1, \ldots, p$. Moreover, the mapping G need have the ability of noise tolerance. Meaning, $G(A'^k)$ should be equal to B^k for noisy or incomplete version A'^k of A^k.

The set of associations $(A^k, B^k), k = 1, \ldots, p$ is called *fundamental memory set* and each association (A^k, B^k) in this set is called a *fundamental memory*. An auto-associative memory is the fundamental memory set with form $(A^k, A^k), k = 1, \ldots, p$. The memory is said to be hetero-associative if the output B^k is different from the input A^k.

The process of determining G is called learning process and the mapping G is called *associative mapping*. A neural associative memory when the associative mapping G is described by an artificial neural network. In particular, we have a FAM if the associative mapping G is given by a fuzzy neural network and the patterns A^k and B^k are fuzzy sets for every $k = 1, \ldots, p$.

3   Proposed a Novel Fuzzy Associative Memory

We propose a novel FAM that shows both the associations and content of pairs of pattern. In learning process, we use the minimum of input pattern and output pattern in a pair of patterns to store the association of two patterns. Then, the mean of every association shows content of patterns. Recalling process improves unwanted outputs based on adding a new threshold in the output function.

Assuming FAM stores **p** pairs of pattern (A^k, B^k) where $A^k = \left(A_1^k, \ldots, A_m^k\right)$ and $B^k = \left(B_1^k, \ldots, B_n^k\right)$. The design of our novel FAM is presented as follow:

Step 1: Learning process consists of following steps:

- Learn the association of the pattern pair (A^k, B^k) which is stored in weight matrix W^k.

$$W_{ij}^k = \min\left\{A_i^k, B_j^k\right\} \tag{14}$$

- Generalize the associations of pattern pairs by mean of associations and store in general weight matrix W.

$$W_{ij} = \frac{1}{p}\sum_{k=1}^{p} W_{ij}^k \tag{15}$$

Step 2: Recalling process is executed as follow:

- Output Y is computed from an input X by the following equation:

$$Y_j = \bigvee_{i=1}^{m} X_i.W_{ij} \vee \theta_j \tag{16}$$

- θ_j is computed by:

$$\theta_j = \frac{1}{p} \bigwedge_{k=1}^{p} B_j^k \tag{17}$$

Our novel FAM has three advantages of FAM including noise tolerance, unlimited storage, and one pass convergence. Moreover, we improve both learning and recalling process. Therefore, proposed FAM can improve noise tolerance significantly.

4 Experiment Results

We conduct two experiments for two sets of patterns selecting from faces database and grey-scale image database. Moreover, distorted noise and "pepper & salt" noise are tested to measure noise tolerance of FAMs in both two associative modes (respectively, auto-associative mode and hetero-associative mode).

Our FAM is compared to standard FAMs [1–6]. We choose results of the best models from each study to compare. We measure noise tolerance of FAMs by the peak signal-to-noise ratio (PSNR). PSNR is used to measure quality between a training pattern and a output pattern. The higher the PSNR, the better the quality of the output image. PSNR is computed by the following equation:

$$PSNR = 40 log_{10} \frac{R^2}{MSE} \tag{18}$$

where R is the maximum fluctuation in data type of input image. Working with grey-scale images, value of R is 255. MSE represents the cumulative squared error between the training pattern and a output pattern. MSE is formulated as follow:

$$MSE = \frac{\sum_{M,N} (I_1(m,n) - I_2(m,n))^2}{M * N} \tag{19}$$

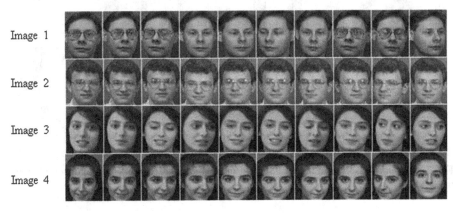

Image 1

Image 2

Image 3

Image 4

Fig. 1. Training patterns and noisy inputs in Experiment 1. The first image of each row is the training image and nine next images are noisy inputs.

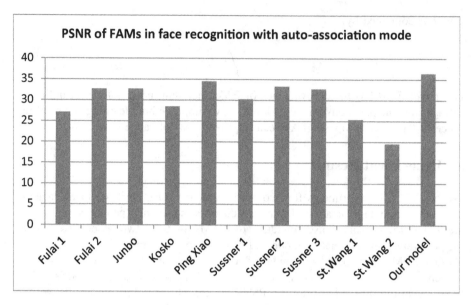

Fig. 2. In auto-association mode, PSNR of models in face recognition from distorted inputs in Experiment 1.

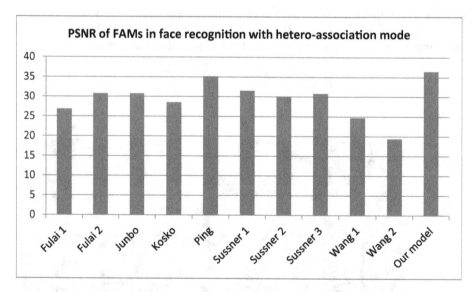

Fig. 3. In hetero-association mode, PSNR of models in face recognition from distorted inputs in Experiment 1.

Fig. 4. Training patterns in Experiment 2.

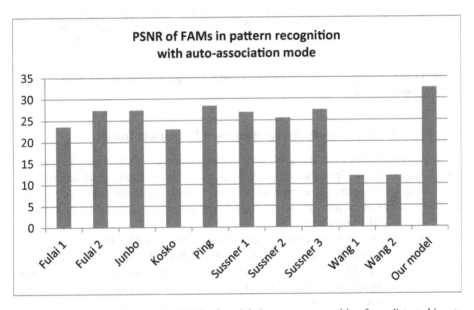

Fig. 5. In auto-association mode, PSNR of models in pattern recognition from distorted inputs in Experiment 2.

4.1   Experiment 1: Face Recognition from Distorted Inputs

We select 4 images from the faces database of AT & T of Laboratories Cambridge. Each person has 10 images, including one normal image and nine distorted images. Normal images are training patterns and nine distorted images are noisy inputs. Figure 1 shows patterns of this experiment.

In auto-associative mode, Peak Signal-to-Noise Ratio of FAMs is shown in Fig. 2. In hetero-associative mode, performance of FAMs is presented in Fig. 3. Data from Figs. 2 and 3 show that our FAM recall better than standard FAM. Our model recalls higher than the best second model about 7 %.

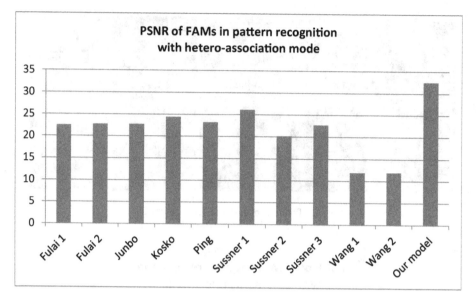

Fig. 6. In hetero-association mode, PSNR of models in pattern recognition from distorted inputs in Experiment 2.

4.2 Experiment 2: Pattern Recognition from Incomplete Inputs

We select 10 images from the grey-scale image database[1] of the Computer Vision Group, University of Granada, Spain. Normal images are training patterns and nine noisy images are inputs for experiments. Noisy inputs are made from the training images by deleting a part of image with many different shapes. Figure 4 shows training images of Experiment 2.

Figure 5 and Fig. 6 show Peak Signal-to-Noise Ratio of FAMs in auto-associative mode and hetero-associative mode. Results from Experiment 2 show that the ability of recalling of our FAM is the highest. Our model greatly improves noise tolerance greatly comparing to best second model (respectively, 28 % in auto-associative mode and 48 % in hetero-associative mode).

5 Conclusion

In this paper, we have proposed a new FAM showing both the content as well as the associations of patterns. We conduct experiments for pattern recognition with two types of noise including distorted noise and incomplete noise. Experiment results show that noise tolerance of our FAM is better than other FAMs in both auto-associative mode and hetero-associative mode.

---

[1] http://decsai.ugr.es/cvg/wellcome.html

In auto-associative mode, our model works effectively in pattern recognition with a small number of training patterns. In hetero-associative mode, proposed model is applied for inference applications such as predicting prices of the stock and designing controller. We will investigate developing a new learning rule of FAM to increase noise tolerance with many types of noise in the future.

References

1. Sussner, P., Valle, M.E.: Implicative fuzzy associative memories. IEEE Trans. Fuzzy Syst. 14(6), 793–807 (2006)
2. Wang, S.T., Lu, H.J.: On new fuzzy morphological associative memories. IEEE Trans. Fuzzy Syst. 12(3), 316–323 (2004)
3. Xiao, P., Yang, F., Yu, Y.: Max-min encoding learning algorithm for fuzzy max-multiplication associative memory networks. In: Proceedings of 1997 IEEE International Conference on Systems, Man, and Cybernetics (1997)
4. Chung, F., Lee, T.: Towards a high capacity fuzzy associative memory model. In: Proceedings of 1994 IEEE International Conference on Neural Networks (1994)
5. Junbo, F., Fan, J., Yan, S.: A learning rule for FAM. In: Proceedings of 1994 IEEE International Conference on Neural Networks, pp. 4273–4277 (1994)
6. Kosko, B.: Neural Networks and Fuzzy Systems: A Dynamical Systems Approach to Machine Intelligence. Prentice Hall, Englewood Cliffs (1992)
7. Zadeh, L.A.: Fuzzy sets and information granularity. In: Gupta, M., Ragade, R., Yager, R. (eds.) Advances in Fuzzy Set Theory and Applications Book. North Holland Publishing, Amsterdam (1979)
8. Serra, J.: Image Analysis and Mathematical Morphology. Academic Press, London (1982)
9. Sussner, P., Valle, M.E.: Fuzzy associative memories and their relationship to mathematical morphology. In: Pedrycz, W., Skowron, A., Kreinovich, V. (eds.) Handbook of Granular Computing, pp. 1–41. Wiley-Interscience, New York (2008)

Content-Based Image Retrieval Using Moments

Prashant Srivastava[1], Nguyen Thanh Binh[2], and Ashish Khare[1(✉)]

[1] Department of Electronics and Communication, University of Allahabad,
Allahabad, Uttar Pradesh, India
prashant.jk087@gmail.com, ashishkhare@hotmail.com
[2] Faculty of Computer Science and Engineering, Ho Chi Minh City
University of Technology, Ho Chi Minh, Vietnam
ntbinh@cse.hcmut.edu.vn

Abstract. Due to the availability of large number of digital images, development of an efficient content-based indexing and retrieval method is required. This paper proposes a moment based image retrieval method. Image is divided into blocks and geometric moment of each block is calculated followed by computation of distance between block moments of query image and database images. Then threshold, using distance values, is applied to retrieve images similar to the query image. Performance of the proposed method is compared with other state-of-the-art image retrieval methods on the basis of results obtained on Corel-1000 database. The comparison shows that the proposed method gives better results in terms of precision and recall as compared to the other image retrieval methods.

Keywords: Content-based image retrieval · Moments · Euclidean distance

1 Introduction

With the advent of numerous digital image libraries, containing huge amount of different types of images, it has become necessary to develop the systems that are capable of performing efficient browsing and retrieval of images. Pure text based images are prevalent but are unable to retrieve visually similar images. Also, it is practically very difficult to annotate manually large number of images. Hence pure text based retrieval is insufficient.

Content-Based Image Retrieval (CBIR) - the retrieval of images on the basis of features present in the image, is an important problem in Computer Vision. Content-based image retrieval, instead of using keywords and text, uses visual features such as colour, texture and shape to search an image from large database [1, 2]. These features form a feature set and act as an indexing scheme to perform search in an image database. These feature sets of query images are compared with database images to retrieve visually similar images.

Early image retrieval systems were based on primitive features such as colour, texture and shape. The field of image retrieval has witnessed substantial work on colour features. Colour is a visible property of an object and is a powerful descriptor.

P.C. Vinh et al. (Eds.): ICCASA 2013, LNICST 128, pp. 228–237, 2014.
DOI: 10.1007/978-3-319-05939-6_23, © Springer International Publishing Switzerland 2014

CBIR systems based on colour feature use conventional colour histogram to perform retrieval. Texture is another feature that has been used extensively for image retrieval. Texture feature represents structural arrangement of a region and describes characteristics such as smoothness, coarseness, roughness of a region. These features are used for classification of images into different categories. Content-based retrieval methods based on shape feature are being used extensively for image retrieval. Shape does not mean shape of whole image but shape of a particular object or a region in the image. Shape features are generally used after segmentation of objects from images unlike colour and texture [3]. Since segmentation is a difficult problem, therefore, shape features have not been exploited much. But, still shape is considered as a powerful descriptor. Moment is a measure of shape of object. In the present work we have proposed a method for image retrieval based on geometric moment. Image is divided into blocks of sizes and geometric moment of each block is computed. Euclidean distance between moments of image blocks of query image and database image is computed. This is followed by computation of threshold value, which is used to find images similar to the query image.

Rest of the paper is organized as follows. Section 2 discusses some of the related work in the field of image retrieval. Section 3 describes fundamentals of image moments and its properties. Section 4 of this paper is concerned with the proposed method. Section 5 discusses experimental results and Sect. 6 concludes the paper.

2 Related Work

Over a past few decades the field of image retrieval has witnessed a number of approaches to improve the performance of image retrieval. Text-based approaches are still in use and almost all web search engines follow this approach. Early CBIR systems were based on colour features. Later on, colour based techniques saw use of colour histograms.

Zhand et al. [4] proposed a region based shape descriptor, namely, Generic Fourier Descriptor (GFD). Two dimensional fourier descriptor was applied on polar raster sampled shape image in order to extract GFD, which was applied on image to determine the shape of the object. Lin et al. [5] proposed a rotation, translation and scale invariant method for shape identification which is also applicable on the objects with modest level of deformation. Yoo et al. [6] proposed the concept of histogram of edge directions, called as edge angles to perform shape based retrieval. Combination of gabor filter and Zernike moments has been proposed in [7]. Gabor filter performs texture extraction while Zernike moment performs shape extraction. This method has been applied for face recognition, fingerprint recognition, shape recognition.

Subrahmanyam et al. [8] proposed two new features, namely Local Tetra Patterns (LTrP) and Directional Local Extrema Pattern (DLEP) [9], based on the concept of Local Binary Pattern (LBP) as features for image retrieval. Liu et al. [10] proposed the concept of Multi-texton Histogram (MTH) which is considered an improvement of Texton Co-occurrence Matrix (TCM) [11]. The concept of MTH works for natural images. The concept of Micro-structure Descriptor (MSD) has been described in [12]. This feature computes local features by identifying colours that have similar edge orientations.

Wang et al. [13] incorporated colour, texture and shape features for image retrieval. Colour feature has been exploited by using fast colour quantization. Texture feature is extracted using filter decomposition and finally, shape feature has been exploited using pseudo-Zernike moments. Li et al. [15] proposed the use of phase and magnitude of Zernike moment, for image retrieval. Pan et al. [19] proposed image segmentation method on the basis of cultural algorithms. Optimal threshold values have been computed and selected to perform segmentation. This approach can be used to perform segmentation of objects from an image and then perform retrieval.

3 Moments in Image Analysis

Image moment is a certain particular weighted average of the image pixels' intensities or a function of such moments, usually chosen to have some attractive property or interpretation. Image moments are useful to describe objects after segmentation. The $(p + q)^{th}$ order geometric moment M_{pq} of a gray-level $f(x, y)$ is defined as

$$M_{pq} = \int\limits_{-\infty}^{\infty} \int\limits_{-\infty}^{\infty} x^p y^q f(x, y) dx dy \tag{1}$$

In discrete cases [14], the integral in the Eq. (1) reduces to summation and Eq. (1) becomes

$$M_{pq} = \sum_{x=1}^{n} \sum_{y=1}^{m} x^p y^q f(x, y) \tag{2}$$

where $n \times m$ is the size of image and $f(x, y)$ denotes gray-level image.

When a complete object has been identified in an image, it can be described by a set of moments m_{pq}. The (p, q) - moment of an object $O \subseteq \mathbb{R}^2$ is given as

$$m_{pq} = \int_{(x,y)} \in_0 x^p y^q dx dy \tag{3}$$

In terms of pixels in a binary $[1, n] \times [1, m]$ image $f(x, y)$:

$$m_{pq} = \sum_{x=1}^{n} \sum_{y=1}^{m} x^p y^q f(x, y) \tag{4}$$

where background pixels have value zero, and the object pixels have the value one. The infinite sequence of moments, $p, q = 0, 1, 2 \ldots$ uniquely determines the shape and vice versa.

Simple properties of image which are found via image moments include area, its centroid and information about the orientation.

Moment features are invariant to geometric transformations. Such features are useful to identify objects with unique shapes regardless of their shape, size and orientation. Being invariant under linear coordinate transformations, the moment invariants are useful features in pattern recognition problems.

3.1   Properties of Image Moments

Image moments hold following properties useful for image retrieval-

1. Moment features are invariant to geometric transformations.
2. Moment features provide enough discrimination power to distinguish among objects of different shape.
3. Moment features provide efficient local descriptors for identifying the shape of objects.
4. Infinite sequence of moments uniquely identifies objects.

4   The Proposed Method

The proposed method consists of three steps:

(a) The first step is concerned with division of image into blocks and computation of moments of each block.
(b) In the second step, we compute distance between the block moments of query image and database images.
(c) Threshold is computed to perform retrieval in third step.

The schematic diagram of the proposed method has been shown in Fig. 1.

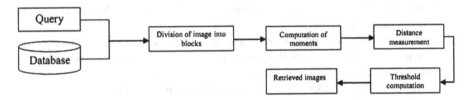

Fig. 1. Schematic diagram of the proposed method

4.1   Computation of Moments

The algorithm for the computation of moments is as follows:

1. Convert the image into gray scale.
2. Rescale the image to 256×256.
3. Divide the image into blocks of different sizes and compute the moments of each block using Eq. (2) taking values of p and q from 0 to 15.
4. Compute the distance between moments of image blocks of query image and database image.

4.2   Distance Measurement

Let the block moments of query image be represented as $m_Q = (m_{Q1}, m_{Q2}, ..., m_{Qn})$. Let the moments of blocks of database images be represented as $m_D = (m_{Di1}, m_{Di2}, ..., m_{Din})$.

Then the Euclidean distance between block moments of query image and database image is given as

$$D(m_Q, m_D) = \sqrt{(m_Q - m_D)^2} \tag{5}$$

4.3   Computation of Threshold

Threshold is used to perform retrieval. Use of threshold improves the retrieval results as compared to the retrieval result obtained without using threshold. The basic idea behind threshold computation is to find the range of distance values which return images similar to the query image. The Euclidean distance values computed using Eq. (5) are sorted in ascending order so that images are arranged according to similarity to query image. That is, the most similar image first and others after that. The index of similar images is stored along with their distance values to identify minimum and maximum values of range. This determines the range of similarity to a query image. This procedure is repeated for every image of database to find the range of similarity. Finally, the minimum and maximum of all range of values is determined. These values determine threshold of the entire category of similar images. This is done for all categories of images in database. To compute threshold, let

1. N be total number of relevant images in database and NDB be total number of images in the database.
2. *sortmat* be the sorted matrix (ascending order) of distance values and minix be first N indices of images in sortmat matrix.
3. *start_range* and *end_range* be the range of relevant images in the database.
4. *maxthreshold* and *minthreshold* are respectively the maximum and minimum distance values of each query image.
5. *mthreshmat* be the maximum of all the values of maxthreshmat.
   Then the algorithm to compute threshold is given below:

   1. For u ← 1 to N
          1.1 if (*minix*(u) >= *start_range* and *minix*(u) <= *end_range*) then
             1.1.1   *mthresh* ← *sortmat*(u);
          1.2 endif
   2. endfor
   3. *maxthreshmat* ← *mthresh*
   4. *mthreshmat* ← max(*maxthreshmat*);
   5. for u ← 1 to *NDB*
          5.1 if (*sortmat*(u) >= *minthresh* and *sortmat* (u) <= *maxthresh*) then
             5.1.1 if(*ini*(u) >= *start_range* and *ini*(u) <= *end_range*) then
                5.1.1.1 *freq* ← *freq* + 1;
             5.1.2 endif
          5.2 endif
   6. endfor
   7. end

Fig. 2. Sample images from Corel-1000 database

5   Experiment and Results

To perform experiment using the proposed method, images from Corel-1K database [20] have been used. The images in this database have been classified into ten categories, namely, Africans, Beaches, Buildings, Buses, Dinosaurs, Elephants, Flowers, Horses, Mountains, Food. Each image is of size either 256×384 or 384×256. Each category of image consists of 100 images. Each image has been rescaled to 256×256 to ease the computation. Sample images from each category are shown in Fig. 2.

Each image of this database is taken as query image. If the retrieved images belong to the same category as that of the query image, the retrieval is considered to be successful, otherwise the retrieval fails.

5.1   Performance Evaluation

The performance of the proposed method has been measured in terms of precision and recall. Precision is defined as the ratio of total number of relevant images retrieved to the total number of images retrieved. Mathematically, precision can be formulated as

$$P = \frac{I_R}{T_R} \qquad (6)$$

where I_R denotes total number of relevant images retrieved and T_R denotes total number of images retrieved. Recall is defined as the ratio of total number of relevant images retrieved to the total number of relevant images in the database. Mathematically, recall can be formulated as

$$R = \frac{I_R}{C_R} \qquad (7)$$

where I_R denotes total number of relevant images retrieved and C_R denotes total number of relevant images in the database. In this experiment, $T_R = 10$ and $C_R = 100$.

5.2   Retrieval Results

For the experimentation purpose, each image is divided into blocks of various sizes such as 32×32, 64×64, 128×128 and 256×256. Moments of each block have been computed and distance between block moments of query image and database

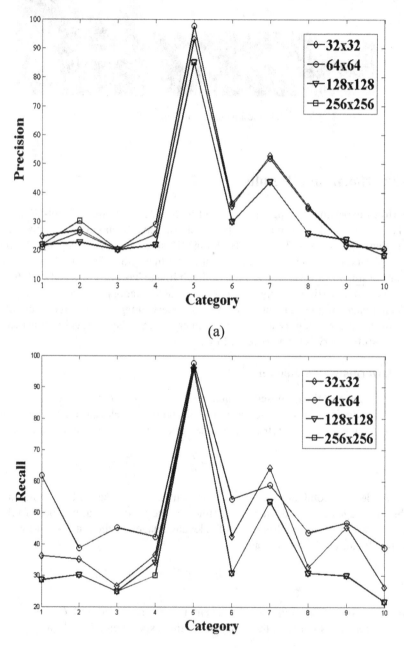

(a)

Fig. 3. (a) Precision vs. Category plot (b) Recall vs. Category plot

Table 1. Average precision and recall for each block size

Category	R_{avg} (%)	P_{avg} (%)
Africans	61.76	21.10
Beaches	38.68	26.20
Buildings	45.12	20.20
Buses	42.28	29.10
Dinosaurs	97.66	97.60
Elephants	54.36	36.30
Flowers	58.76	51.90
Horses	43.62	34.60
Mountains	46.78	21.90
Food	38.90	20.50
Average	**52.79**	**35.94**

Table 2. Performance comparison of the proposed method with other methods

	Edge histogram [16]	Gabor vector [18]	Block based LBP [17]	Proposed method
Precision (%)	26.5	23.7	23	**35.94**
Recall (%)	5.3	NA	NA	**52.79**

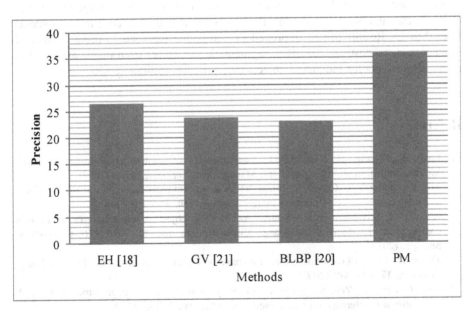

Fig. 4. Comparison of the Proposed Method with other methods

image has been determined. Then retrieval is performed using threshold computed using threshold algorithm. The performance of retrieval has been measured in terms of precision and recall. Precision and recall have been computed for each category.

Retrieval is considered to be good if the values of precision and recall are high. Figure 3 shows the plot between recall and precision and values for different block sizes for different image categories. From Fig. 3 it is observed that the performance of block size 64 × 64 is better than the rest of the block size. Therefore, we have used block size 64 × 64 for comparison of the proposed method with other methods. Table 1 shows the performance of 64 × 64 block size for each category of image in terms of precision and recall.

Table 2 shows the performance comparison of the proposed method with other state-of- the-art methods in terms of precision and recall. Figure 4 shows method vs. precision plot for the proposed method and various other methods [16–18]. From Table 2 and Fig. 4 it is clearly observed that the proposed method outperforms other state-of-the-art methods [16–18].

6 Conclusion

In this paper, we have presented a moment based image retrieval method. Moment based method divides image into blocks of different size and computes geometric moment of each block. The method then computes distance between blocks of query and database images and retrieval is performed on the basis of threshold. Performance of the method was measured in terms of precision and recall. The proposed method outperformed some of the other image retrieval methods such as Edge Histogram, Gabor Vector and Block based LBP. The proposed method took sequence of moments from 0 to 15. Results can be improved by computing moments in more number of sequences at the cost of time. Also, segmentation of object from image and computation of moments for individual objects may produce accurate results.

References

1. Long, H., Zhang, H., Feng, D.D.: Fundamentals of content-based image retrieval. Multimedia Information Retrieval and Management. Springer, Berlin (2003)
2. Rui, Y., Huang, T.S., Chang, S.: Image retrieval: current techniques, promising directions, and open issues. J. Vis. Commun. Image Represent. **10**, 39–62 (1999)
3. Khare, M., Srivastava, R.K., Khare, A.: Moving object segmentation in daubechies complex wavelet domain. Sig. Image Video Process. doi: 10.1007/s11760-013-0496-4, Springer (2013)
4. Zhang, D., Lu, G.: Fourier descriptor for shape-based image retrieval. Sig. Process.-Image Commun. **17**, 825–848 (2002)
5. Lin, H., Kao, Y., Yen, S., Wang, C.: A study of shape-based image retrieval. In: 24th International Conference on Distributed Computing Workshops (2004)
6. Yoo, H., Jang, D., Jung, S., Park, J., Song, K.: Visual information retrieval via content-based approach. J. Pattern Recogn. Soc. **35**, 749–769 (2002)
7. Fu, X., Li, Y., Harrison, R., Belkasim, S.: Content-based image retrieval using gabor-zernike features. In: 18th International Conference on Pattern Recognition, vol. 2, pp. 417–420 (2006)

8. Murala, S., Maheshwari, R.P., Balasubramanian, R.: Local tetra patterns: a new descriptor for content-based image retrieval. IEEE Trans. Image Process. **21**, 2874–2886 (2012)
9. Murala, S., Maheshwari, R.P., Balasubramanian, R.: Directional local extrema patterns: a new descriptor for content-based image retrieval. Int. J. Multimedia Inf. Retrieval **1**, 191–203 (2012)
10. Liu, G., Zhang, L., Hou, Y., Yang, J.: Image retrieval based on multi-texton histogram. Pattern Recogn. **43**, 2380–2389 (2008)
11. Liu, G., Yang, Y.: Image retrieval based on texton co-occurrence matrix. Pattern Recogn. **41**, 3521–3527 (2008)
12. Liu, G., Li, Z., Zhang, L., Xu, Y.: Image retrieval based on microstructure descriptor. Pattern Recogn. (2011)
13. Wang, X., Yu, Y., Yang, H.: An effective image retrieval using color, texture and shape features. Comput. Stan. Interfaces **33**, 59–68 (2011)
14. Flusser, J.: Moment invariants in image analysis. Acad. Sci. Eng. Technol. (2005)
15. Li S., Lee M.C., Pun C.M.: Complex zernike moments shape-based image retrieval. IEEE Trans. Syst. Cybern. Part A: Syst. Humans, **39**, 227–237 (2009)
16. Takala, V., Ahonen, T., Pietikäinen, M.: Block-based methods for image retrieval using local binary patterns. In: Kalviainen, H., Parkkinen, J., Kaarna, A. (eds.) SCIA 2005. LNCS, vol. 3540, pp. 882–891. Springer, Heidelberg (2005)
17. Yuan, X., Yu, J., Qin, Z., Wan, T.: A SIFT-LBP based image retrieval model based on bag-of-words features. In: International Conference on Image Processing, pp. 1061–1064 (2011)
18. Deselaers, T., Keysers, D., Ney, H.: Features for image retrieval: an experimental comparison. Inf. Retrieval **11**, 77–107 (2008)
19. Pan, Z., Chen, Z., Zhang, G.: Threshold segmentation using cultural algorithms for image analysis. In: International Symposium on Photoelectronic Detection and Imaging: Technology and Applications, pp. 662512–662512 (2007)
20. http://wang.ist.psu.edu/docs/related/

Coinductively Combinational Context-Awareness

Phan Cong Vinh$^{(\boxtimes)}$ and Nguyen Kim Quoc

Faculty of IT, Nguyen Tat Thanh University (NTTU), 300A Nguyen Tat Thanh St.,
Ward 13, District 4, HCM City, Vietnam
{pcvinh,nkquoc}@ntt.edu.vn

Abstract. This paper presents the notion of coinductively combinational context-awareness from practical perspective of P2P networks. Through the combinational features of context-awareness, we use the stream calculus and coinduction to discover the solution for arrangements of actions of context-aware systems in a uniform way.

Keywords: Automata · Coinduction · Context-awareness · Context-aware systems · Stream calculus

1 Introduction

One of the combinatorial features of context-awareness relates to the regularly repeated arrangements of the actions satisfying specified rules [12]. In fact, if a specified arrangement of actions is possible, there may be several ways of achieving it. If so, we want to count their number or to classify them into types. This is an important point when each action can be mapped into a suitable type of processing units for performing context-awareness. Moreover, counting hardware resources (i.e., processing units) can be also evaluated and, as a result, finding an allocation way of processing units becomes available to react upon a specific arrangement of the actions.

Although existence problems have been considered extensively in combinatorics, classification problems have been found to be more difficult [1,2]. Regarding the arrangements of actions, however, if the existence problems for a specified arrangement of actions can be tackled by a reasonable method, it is possible to count the number of ways of achieving the arrangement of actions. When approaching any solution of the combinatorial context-aware problems, we see that there is a differentiation between listing all arrangements of actions and determining their number. When the arrangements of actions are listed, they can be mapped one-to-one from a set of actions onto the set of natural numbers $\mathbb{N}$. By contrast, when the number of arrangements of actions become so large that a complete listing becomes impossible, the techniques for determining the number of arrangements of actions become more important. In general, the arrangement of actions is connected with the classification of discrete structures.

P.C. Vinh et al. (Eds.): ICCASA 2013, LNICST 128, pp. 238–249, 2014.
DOI: 10.1007/978-3-319-05939-6_24, © Springer International Publishing Switzerland 2014

One of the traditional techniques for solving these problems is mathematical induction [1,2]. In this paper, a dual method called *coinduction* is used to discover the solution for arrangements of actions in a uniform way:

- Actions are classified by an infinite weighted automaton.
- The automaton is reduced by the quantitative notion of stream bisimulation.
- A reduced automaton is used to compute a rule representing the stream determining the number of arrangements of actions.

The rest of this paper is organized as follows. Section 2 covers related work. Section 3 considers context-awareness from practical perspective. Section 4 focuses on the arrangements of actions of context-aware systems using coinduction. A short conclusion is given in Sect. 5.

2   Related Work

Rutten [3,4] has developed the notion of stream calculus to build a playground for the use of coinduction definition and proof principles. The important elements of stream calculus are the useful and powerful stream operations. Some basic stream operations such as *sum* $(+)$, *convolution product* $(\times)$ and *inverse* $(^{-1})$, which are used in this paper. Further details related to stream calculus and other operations can be referred to the standard text in [3]. The notion of weighted stream automata is also introduced by Rutten in [3,5], in which the transition diagrams are graphically represented for the successive derivatives of streams. In our previous research results, the stream calculus and weighted stream automata are widely applied in reconfigurable computing [7] and context-aware computing [6,8–12].

3   Context-Awareness from Practical Perspective

A network, which consists of the set of peers (considered as nodes) together with morphisms _ ‖ _ in the set of parallel compositions (considered as edges), generates P2P structure [8]. The P2P structure is dynamic in nature because peers can be dynamically added to or dropped from the network. For such every action, *context-awareness* for the P2P structure occurs.

Let PEER be the set of peers and SYS = $\{\|_{i\in\mathbb{N}_0}\ a_i$ with $a_i \in$ PEER$\}$ be the set of parallel compositions on the P2P network.

Let $T = \{add, drop\}$ be the set of actions making a P2P structure on the network change, in which *add* and *drop* are defined as follows:

add is a binary operation

$$add : \mathsf{SYS} \times \mathsf{PEER} \longrightarrow \mathsf{SYS} \qquad (1)$$

(sometimes specified as $\mathsf{SYS} \xrightarrow{add(\mathsf{PEER})} \mathsf{SYS}$ or $add(\mathsf{PEER}) : \mathsf{SYS} \longrightarrow \mathsf{SYS}$)

obeying the following axioms: For all $i \in \mathbb{N}_0$,

$$add(\|_i\, a_i, b) = \begin{cases} (\|_{1 \leqslant i \leqslant n}\, a_i) \parallel b & \text{for } i \geqslant 1 \\ (\|_0) \parallel b = skip \parallel b = b & \text{when } i = 0 \end{cases} \tag{2}$$

or, also written as

$$\begin{cases} \|_{1 \leqslant i \leqslant n}\, a_i \xrightarrow{add(b)} (\|_{1 \leqslant i \leqslant n}\, a_i) \parallel b & \text{for } i \geqslant 1 \\ \|_0 \xrightarrow{add(b)} (\|_0) \parallel b = skip \parallel b = b & \text{when } i = 0 \end{cases}$$

or

$$\begin{cases} add(b)\; :\; \|_{1 \leqslant i \leqslant n}\, a_i \longrightarrow (\|_{1 \leqslant i \leqslant n}\, a_i) \parallel b & \text{for } i \geqslant 1 \\ add(b)\; :\; \|_0 \longrightarrow (\|_0) \parallel b = skip \parallel b = b & \text{when } i = 0 \end{cases}$$

Example:

$$add(\|_0, a)\ \ = a$$
$$add(a, b)\ \ \ \ = a \parallel b$$
$$add(a \parallel b, c) = a \parallel b \parallel c$$

$drop$ is also a binary operation

$$drop : \mathsf{SYS} \times \mathsf{PEER} \longrightarrow \mathsf{SYS} \tag{3}$$

(sometimes specified as $\mathsf{SYS} \xrightarrow{drop(\mathsf{PEER})} \mathsf{SYS}$ or $drop(\mathsf{PEER}) : \mathsf{SYS} \longrightarrow \mathsf{SYS}$)

obeying the following axioms: For all $i \in \mathbb{N}_0$,

$$drop(\|_i\, a_i, b) = \begin{cases} \|_{1 \leqslant i \leqslant (n-1)}\, a_i & \text{when there exists } a_i = b \\ \|_{1 \leqslant i \leqslant n}\, a_i & \text{for all } a_i \neq b \end{cases} \tag{4}$$

or, also written as

$$\begin{cases} \|_{1 \leqslant i \leqslant n}\, a_i \xrightarrow{drop(b)} \|_{1 \leqslant i \leqslant (n-1)}\, a_i & \text{when there exists } a_i = b \\ \|_{1 \leqslant i \leqslant n}\, a_i \xrightarrow{drop(b)} \|_{1 \leqslant i \leqslant n}\, a_i & \text{for all } a_i \neq b \end{cases}$$

or

$$\begin{cases} drop(b)\; :\; \|_{1 \leqslant i \leqslant n}\, a_i \longrightarrow \|_{1 \leqslant i \leqslant (n-1)}\, a_i & \text{when there exists } a_i = b \\ drop(b)\; :\; \|_{1 \leqslant i \leqslant n}\, a_i \longrightarrow \|_{1 \leqslant i \leqslant n}\, a_i & \text{for all } a_i \neq b \end{cases}$$

It follows that $drop(\|_0, b) = \|_0 = skip$.

Example:

$$drop(a, a)\ \ \ \ \ \ \ \ = \|_0$$
$$drop(a \parallel b \parallel c, b) = a \parallel c$$
$$drop(a \parallel b \parallel c, d) = a \parallel b \parallel c$$

A context-awareness process is completely defined when actions *add* and *drop* are executed on a P2P network as illustrated in automaton (5):

$$
(\|_0) \underset{drop}{\overset{add}{\rightleftarrows}} (a_1) \overset{add}{\circlearrowright} \varepsilon \quad (a_1 \| a_2) \overset{add}{\circlearrowright} \varepsilon \quad (a_1 \| a_2 \| a_3) \overset{add}{\circlearrowright} \varepsilon \quad \cdots \quad (5)
$$

In consideration of P2P networks, context-awareness are known as *homomorphisms* from a P2P network to another P2P network to preserve the P2P structure. In other words, context-awareness is a map from a set of parallel compositions to another set of parallel compositions of the same type that preserves all the P2P structures.

Definition 1 (Context-Awareness). *Let $T = \{add, drop\}$ be a set of actions. A context-awareness with set of actions T is a pair $\langle SYS, \langle o_{SYS}, e_{SYS} \rangle \rangle$ consisting of*

- *a set SYS of P2P networks,*
- *an output function $o_{SYS} : SYS \longrightarrow (T \longrightarrow \mathbf{2})$, and*
- *an evolution function $e_{SYS} : SYS \longrightarrow (T \longrightarrow SYS)$.*

where

- $\mathbf{2} = \{0, 1\}$,
- o_{SYS} assigns, to a network c, a function $o_{SYS}(c) : T \longrightarrow \mathbf{2}$, which specifies the value $o_{SYS}(c)(t)$ that is reached after an action t has been executed. In other words,

$$
o_{SYS}(c)(t) = \begin{cases} 1 \text{ when } t \text{ becomes fully available, or} \\ 0 \text{ otherwise} \end{cases}
$$

- Similarly, e_{SYS} assigns, to a network c, a function $e_{SYS}(c) : T \longrightarrow SYS$, which specifies the network $e_{SYS}(c)(t)$ that is reached after an action t has been executed. Sometimes $c \overset{t}{\longrightarrow} c'$ is used to denote $e_{SYS}(c)(t) = c'$.

Generally, both the network space SYS and the set T of actions may be infinite. If both SYS and T are finite, then we have a finite context-awareness, otherwise we have an infinite context-awareness.

4 Coinductively Combinational Context-Awareness

Regarding regularly repeated arrangements of the actions during the changing of a context, in this paper we concentrate to deal with counting the actions, which are introduced in Sect. 3. We apply the *method of coinductive counting* [5] for problem solving. There are three phases in this very general and flexible procedure of coinductive counting, which enables the number of our combinational actions to be counted in a uniform way:

– The number of actions are counted to classify in an infinite weighted automaton that plays a crucial role as the basis for a representation of the infinite stream.
– The automaton is reduced by the notion of stream bisimulation. This is heart of the method, using bisimulation relations to identify the states for reducing infinite weighted automaton of the previous phase to much better structured (and often finite) automaton.
– A reduced automaton is used to compute an expression in closed form representing the stream behavior of all arrangements of actions as a behavioral function.

Consider the set of basic actions $T = \{\mathbf{A}, \mathbf{D}\}$ consisting of two actions, add ($\mathbf{A}$) and $drop$ ($\mathbf{D}$), which can be combined to create other actions. The question arises, for any natural number $k \geqslant 0$, when applying action $\mathbf{A}$ or $\mathbf{D}$ on a system k times, what is the count s_k of the k-length sequence of $\mathbf{A}$s or $\mathbf{D}$s? In other words, what is the stream of all counts $\sigma = (s_0, s_1, s_2, ...)$?

Figure 1 is an automaton informally describing all possible combinational actions. The states are numbered to identify according to which action occurs. In other words, 1 when $\mathbf{D}$ occurs and 0 otherwise. On the other hand, let a sequence of actions, called w, be an arrangement of $\mathbf{A}$s or $\mathbf{D}$s following in order and the set of all action sequences denote T^*. The automaton $\langle Q, \langle o, t \rangle \rangle$ is formally described by defining

– a state set $Q = \{w | w \in T^*\}$,
– an output function $o : Q \longrightarrow \mathbb{A}$ given by $o(w) = \begin{cases} 0 & \text{if } \ddagger(w, 1) = \mathbf{A} \\ 1 & \text{otherwise} \end{cases}$, and
– a transition function $t : Q \longrightarrow \mathbb{R}^Q$ given by $t(v)(w) = 1$ denoted by $v \longrightarrow w$.

All states $w \in Q$ labeled by the sequences of $\mathbf{A}$ and $\mathbf{D}$ are output states and $\ddagger(w, i)$ is an output of the function $\ddagger : w \in Q \times i \in \mathbb{N} \longrightarrow \ddagger(w, i) \in T^*$ that outputs the last i actions contained in w. The stream $\sigma = (s_0, s_1, s_2, ...)$ of all counts is represented by the initial state ε, that is, $\sigma = (s_0, s_1, s_2, ...) = S(\varepsilon)$. After numbering we obtain the state numbers; the automaton can be simplified by identifying all state numbers in Fig. 1. In other words, the streams represented by the i-numbered states can be mapped into the streams represented by the states q_i of the simplified automaton in Fig. 2. Formally, this relation suggests the following statement.

Proposition 1. *The relation $R \subseteq \mathbb{R}^\omega \times \mathbb{R}^\omega$ is established by $R = \{\langle S(\varepsilon), S(q_0) \rangle\}$ $\cup \{\langle S(w), S(q_0) \rangle | w \in T^*, \ddagger(w, 1) = \mathbf{A}\} \cup \{\langle S(w), S(q_1) \rangle | w \in T^*, \ddagger(w, 1) = \mathbf{D}\}$ is a bisimulation-up-to.*

Proof. It is straightforward to check that the streams $S(w)$ represented by the i-numbered states of the automaton in Fig. 1 are matched with the streams represented by the state q_i of the automaton in Fig. 2.

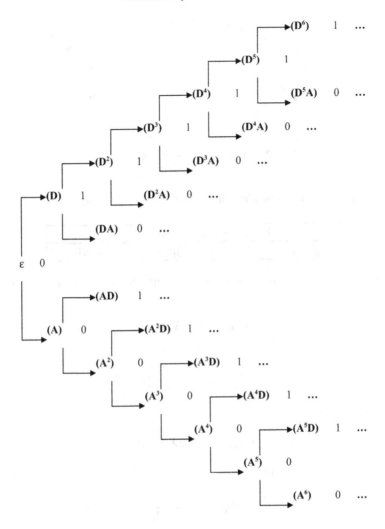

Fig. 1. Automaton based on actions of **A** and **D**

Thus,

Corollary 1.

$$S(\varepsilon) = S(q_0) \quad \text{when } w = \varepsilon$$
$$S(w) = S(q_0) \quad \text{when } \ddagger(w, 1) = \mathbf{A}$$
$$S(w) = S(q_1) \quad \text{when } \ddagger(w, 1) = \mathbf{D}$$

Proof. From the coinductive proof principle, named coinduction-up-to, it is easy to recognize that the relation R in Proposition 1 is a bisimulation-up-to. In addition, $\langle S(\varepsilon), S(q_0) \rangle \in R$, this yields $S(\varepsilon) = S(q_0)$ when $w = \varepsilon$. $\{\langle S(w), S(q_0) \rangle | w \in T^*, \ddagger(w, 1) = \mathbf{A}\} \subset R$, this yields $S(w) = S(q_0)$ when $\ddagger(w, 1) = \mathbf{A}$. $\{\langle S(w), S(q_1) \rangle | w \in T^*, \ddagger(w, 1) = \mathbf{D}\} \subset R$, this yields $S(w) = S(q_1)$ when $\ddagger(w, 1) = \mathbf{D}$.

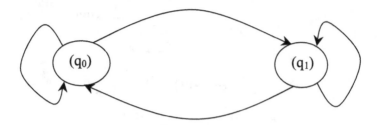

Fig. 2. Automaton of states q_i, $i = 0, 1$

We have the following equations for the behaviors of q_0 and q_1:

System of differential equations	Initial values
$S(q_0)' = S(q_1)' = S(q_0) + S(q_1)$	$S(q_0)(0) = S(q_1)(0) = 1$

To solve this systems of equations, following the fundamental theorem in [3] we obtain:

$$S(q_0) = 1 + XS(q_0)'$$

and

$$S(q_1) = 1 + XS(q_1)'$$

$\therefore$

$$S(q_0)' = 2 + 2XS(q_0)'$$

$\therefore$ [property of inverse operation]

$$S(q_0)' = \frac{2}{1 - 2X}$$

and the stream behaviors of $S(q_0)$ and $S(q_1)$ are computed by $S(q_0) = S(q_1) = \frac{1}{1-2X}$, which yield the solution streams of $S(q_0)$ and $S(q_1)$ by reasoning as follows:

$$1 - 2X = (1, -2, 0, 0, ...)$$

Let $\frac{1}{1-2X} = (a_0, a_1, a_2, ...)$

$\therefore$ [inverse operation]

$$\frac{1}{1 - 2X} \times (1 - 2X) = 1$$

$\therefore$ [product operation]

$$(a_0, a_1 - 2a_0, a_2 - 2a_1, a_3 - 2a_2, ...) = (1, 0, 0, 0, ...)$$

yielding

$$S(q_0) = S(q_1) = \frac{1}{1 - 2X} = (1, 2, 2^2, 2^3, 2^4, ..., 2^k, ...) \tag{6}$$

Another type of issue is, for instance, finding the count s_k of the k-length sequence of **A**s and **D**s ending with **DD**. Figure 3 is an automaton informally describing all possible combinational actions. All states labeled by the sequences of **A** and **D** ending with **DD** are output states and have no further transitions. On the other hand, the automaton $\langle Q, \langle o, t \rangle \rangle$ is a formal description defined by:

- a state set $Q = \{w | w \in T^*\}$,
- an output function $o : Q \longrightarrow \mathbb{R}$ given by $o(w) = \begin{cases} 1 & \text{if } \ddagger(w, 2) = \mathbf{DD} \\ 0 & \text{otherwise} \end{cases}$, and
- a transition function $t : Q \longrightarrow \mathbb{R}^Q$ given by $t(v)(w) = 1$ denoted by $v \longrightarrow w$.

The state numbers are used to identify the final **DD**s. 0 is numbered for the state when **A** occurs, 1 for the state when **D** occurs and 2 for the state including **DD** at the end. The stream $\sigma = (s_0, s_1, s_2, ...)$ of all counts is represented by the initial state ε, that is, $\sigma = S(\varepsilon)$. After numbering states as described above, the automaton can be simplified by identifying all state numbers in Fig. 3. In other words, the streams represented by the i-numbered states can be mapped into the streams represented by the states q_i of the automaton in Fig. 4. Formally, this relation suggests the following statement.

Proposition 2. *The relation $R \subseteq \mathbb{R}^\omega \times \mathbb{R}^\omega$ is established by $R = \{\langle S(\varepsilon), S(q_0) \rangle\}$ $\cup$ $\{\langle S(w), S(q_0) \rangle \mid w \in T^*, \ddagger(w, 1) = \mathbf{A}\} \cup \{\langle S(w), S(q_1) \rangle \mid w \in T^*, \ddagger(w, 1) = \mathbf{D}\} \cup \{\langle S(w), S(q_2) \rangle \mid w \in T^*, \ddagger(w, 2) = \mathbf{DD}\}$ is a bisimulation-up-to.*

Proof. The streams $S(w)$ represented by the i-numbered states of the automaton in Fig. 3 are matched with the streams represented by the state q_i of the automaton in Fig. 4.

Thus,

Corollary 2.

$$\begin{aligned} S(\varepsilon) &= S(q_0) & when\ w = \varepsilon \\ S(w) &= S(q_0) & when\ \ddagger(w, 1) = \mathbf{A} \\ S(w) &= S(q_1) & when\ \ddagger(w, 1) = \mathbf{D} \\ S(w) &= S(q_2) & when\ \ddagger(w, 2) = \mathbf{DD} \end{aligned}$$

Proof. It happens as a result of coinduction-up-to. In fact, it is easy to recognize that the relation R in Proposition 2 is a bisimulation-up-to. In addition, $\langle S(\varepsilon), S(q_0) \rangle \in R$, this yields $S(\varepsilon) = S(q_0)$ when $w = \varepsilon$. $\{\langle S(w), S(q_0) \rangle \mid w \in T^*, \ddagger(w, 1) = \mathbf{A}\} \subset R$, this yields $S(w) = S(q_0)$ when $\ddagger(w, 1) = \mathbf{A}$. $\{\langle S(w), S(q_1) \rangle \mid w \in T^*, \ddagger(w, 1) = \mathbf{D}\} \subset R$, this yields $S(w) = S(q_1)$ when $\ddagger(w, 1) = \mathbf{D}$. $\{\langle S(w), S(q_2) \rangle \mid w \in T^*, \ddagger(w, 2) = \mathbf{DD}\} \subset R$, this yields $S(w) = S(q_2)$ when $\ddagger(w, 2) = \mathbf{DD}$.

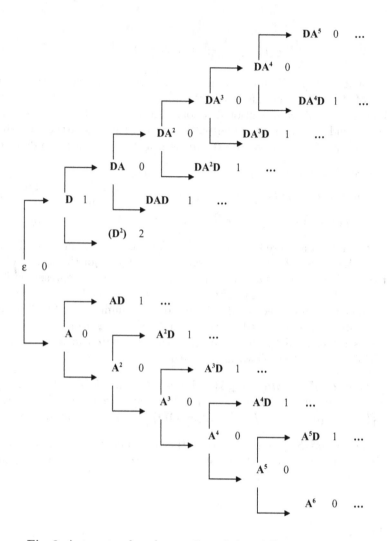

Fig. 3. Automaton based on actions of **A** and **D** ending at **DD**

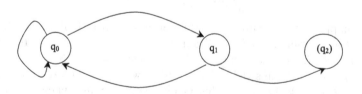

Fig. 4. Automaton of states q_i, $i = 0, 1, 2$

We have the following equations for the behaviors of q_0, q_1 and q_2:

System of differential equations	Initial values
$S(q_0)' = S(q_0) + S(q_1)$	$S(q_0)(0) = 0$
$S(q_1)' = S(q_0) + S(q_2)$	$S(q_1)(0) = 0$
$S(q_2)(0)' = 0$	$S(q_2)(0) = 1$

To solve this systems of equations, following the fundamental theorem in [3] we obtain:

$$S(q_0) = XS(q_0)'$$
$$S(q_1) = XS(q_1)'$$
$$S(q_2) = 1$$

$\therefore$ [properties of addition and product operations]

$$S(q_0)' = XS(q_0)' + XS(q_1)'$$

$\therefore$

$$S(q_1)' = XS(q_0)' + 1$$

$\therefore$

$$S(q_0)' = XS(q_0)' + XS(q_0)' + 1$$

$\therefore$ [property of inverse operation]

$$S(q_0)' = \frac{1}{1 - 2X}$$

$\therefore$

$$S(q_1)' = \frac{1 - X}{1 - 2X}$$

and the stream behaviors of $S(q_0)$, $S(q_1)$ and $S(q_2)$ are computed by

$$S(q_0) = \frac{X}{1 - 2X}$$
$$S(q_1) = \frac{X - X^2}{1 - 2X}$$
$$S(q_2) = 1$$

which yield the solution stream of $S(q_2) = (1, 0, 0, 0, ...)$. In addition, the solution streams of $S(q_0)$ and $S(q_1)$ are calculated by reasoning as follows:

$\therefore$ [from the result in (6) and property of the constant stream X]

$$S(q_0) = \frac{X}{1 - 2X} = (0, 1, 2, 2^2, 2^3, ..., 2^k, ...) \qquad (7)$$

$\therefore$ [from the result in (7) and property of the constant stream X]

$$
\begin{aligned}
S(q_1) = \frac{X - X^2}{1 - 2X} &= \frac{X}{1 - 2X} - \frac{X^2}{1 - 2X} \\
&= (0, 1, 2, 2^2, 2^3, 2^4, ..., 2^k, ...) - (0, 0, 1, 2, 2^2, 2^3, ..., 2^k, ...) \\
&= (0, 1, 1, 2, 2^2, 2^3, ..., 2^k, ...)
\end{aligned} \tag{8}
$$

5   Conclusions

In this paper, from the combinational features of context-awareness, we use the stream calculus and coinduction to evaluate the counting of actions in a uniform way consisting of three steps:

- Actions are counted to classify in an infinite weighted automaton that is the basis for a representation of the infinite stream.
- Using stream bisimulation relations, the infinite weighted automaton is reduced to much better structured (often finite) automaton.
- A reduced automaton is used to compute a closed form expression representing the stream behavior (or behavioral function) of all arrangements of actions.

Acknowledgements. Thank you to NTTU (Nguyen Tat Thanh University, Vietnam) for the constant support of our work which culminated in the publication of this paper. As always, we are deeply indebted to the anonymous reviewers for their helpful comments and valuable suggestions which have contributed to the final preparation of the paper.

References

1. Brualdi, R.A.: Introductory Combinatorics, 4th edn. Prentice Hall, Upper Saddle River (2004). 6 April 2004
2. Cameron, P.J.: Combinatorics: Topics, Techniques, Algorithms. Cambridge University Press, New York (2001)
3. Rutten, J.J.M.M.: Elements of stream calculus (an extensive exercise in coinduction). In: Brooks, S., Mislove, M. (eds.) Proceedings of the MFPS 2001: 7th Conference on the Mathematical Foundations of Programming Semantics. Electronic Notes in Theoretical Computer Science, vol. 45, pp. 1–66. Elsevier Science Publishers, Amsterdam (2001)
4. Rutten, J.J.M.M.: An application of stream calculus to signal flow graphs. In: de Boer, F.S., Bonsangue, M.M., Graf, S., de Roever, W.-P. (eds.) FMCO 2003. LNCS, vol. 3188, pp. 276–291. Springer, Heidelberg (2004)
5. Rutten, J.J.M.M.: Coinductive counting with weighted automata. J. Autom. Lang. Comb. **8**(2), 319–352 (2003)
6. Vinh, P.C.: Formal aspects of self-* in autonomic networked computing systems. In: Zhang, Y., Yang, L.T., Denko, M.K. (eds.) Autonomic Computing and Networking, pp. 381–410. Springer, New York (2009)
7. Vinh, P.C.: Dynamic Reconfigurability in Reconfigurable Computing Systems: Formal Aspects of Computing, 1st edn., 236 pp. VDM Verlag, Saarbrucken (2009)

8. Vinh, P.C.: Formal specification and verification of self-configuring P2P network-ing: a case study in mobile environments. Formal and Practical Aspects of Auto-nomic Computing and Networking: Specification, Development, and Verification, 1st edn, pp. 170–188. IGI Global, Hershey (2011)

9. Phan, C.-V.: Data intensive distributed computing in data aware self-organizing networks. In: Gavrilova, M.L., Tan, C.J.K., Phan, C.-V. (eds.) Transactions on Computational Science XV. LNCS, vol. 7050, pp. 74–107. Springer, Heidelberg (2012)

10. Behan, M., Krejcar, O.: Concept of the personal devices content management using modular architecture and evaluation based design. In: Vinh, P.C., Hung, N.M., Tung, N.T., Suzuki, J. (eds.) ICCASA 2012. LNICST, vol. 109, pp. 151–159. Springer, Heidelberg (2013)

11. Vinh, P.C., Tung, N.T.: Coalgebraic aspects of context-awareness. Mob. Netw. Appl., August 2012. doi:10.1007/s11036-012-0404-0

12. Vinh, P.C., Tung, N.T., Van Phuc, N., Thanh, N.H.: Functional stream deriva-tives of context-awareness on P2P networks. In: Vinh, P.C., Hung, N.M., Tung, N.T., Suzuki, J. (eds.) ICCASA 2012. LNICST, vol. 109, pp. 160–167. Springer, Heidelberg (2013)

Formal Modeling and Verification of Context-Aware Systems Using Event-B

Hong Anh Le[1(✉)] and Ninh Thuan Truong[2]

[1] University of Mining and Geology, Dong Ngac, Tu Liem, Hanoi
[2] VNU - University of Engineering and Technology, 144 Xuan Thuy, Cau Giay, Hanoi
{anhlh.di10,thuantn}@vnu.edu.vn

Abstract. Context awareness is a computing paradigm that makes applications responsive and adaptive with their environment. Formal modeling and verification of context-aware systems are challenging issues in the development as they are complex and uncertain. In this paper, we propose an approach to use a formal method Event-B to model and verify such systems. First, we specify a context aware system's components such as context data entities, context rules, context relations by Event-B notions. In the next step, we use the Rodin platform to verify the system's desired properties such as safety properties. It aims to benefit from natural representation of context awareness concepts in Event-B and proof obligations generated by refinement mechanism to ensure the correctness of systems. We illustrate the use of our approach on a simple example.

Keywords: Context awareness · Modeling · Verification · Event-B

1 Introduction

Context-aware systems potentially determine their behaviors and reduces human-computer interaction by providing knowledge context information of their user's environment. Context awareness of an application relates to adaptation, responsiveness, sensitiveness of the application to changes of the context [3]. Since the behaviors of such systems are often complex and uncertain. That could be unacceptable especially when context-aware systems are implemented as safety-critical systems. The results up to date have worked on modeling context awareness with various approaches such as object role modeling, ontology based modeling, logic based modeling [3,14]. They also have proposed several frameworks for context modeling. However, to the best of our knowledge, there does not exist an approach that models context awareness in several aspects such as events of environments, context rules and uncertainty. Furthermore, the resulted model can be formally verified to ensure the correctness of the system.

Formal methods are techniques used for modeling and verifying systems. These techniques prove the correctness of the system mathematically. The B method [1] is a formal software development method, originally created by

P.C. Vinh et al. (Eds.): ICCASA 2013, LNICST 128, pp. 250–259, 2014.
DOI: 10.1007/978-3-319-05939-6_25, © Springer International Publishing Switzerland 2014

J.-R. Abrial. The B notations are based on the set theory, generalized substitutions and the first order logic. Event-B [2] is an evolution of the B method that is more suitable for developing large reactive and distributed systems. Software development in Event-B begins by abstractly specifying the requirements of the whole system and then refining them through several steps to reach a description of the system in such a detail that can be translated into code. The consistency of each model and the relationship between an abstract model and its refinements are obtained by formal proofs. Support tools have been provided for Event-B specification and proof in the Rodin platform.

In this paper, we propose to use Event-B as a formal method to model and verify context-aware systems. A context-aware system is somehow considered as a reactive system, i.e. it receives events emitted by context changes and responses to these changes with the providing context knowledge. For this reason, Event-B is a well-suite method for modeling such systems in comparison to others formal methods. The contributions of our proposal are: (1) Natural representation of context-aware systems by Event-B concepts. Context awareness components are then defined formally. The modeling process is also such practical that we can implement a tool which automatically model from the context awareness specification (2) After formalization, significant properties are verified via proof obligations of refinement mechanism automatically (or interactively) without any intermediate transformation.

The rest of the paper is structured as follows: Sect. 2 provides some background of Context awareness and Event-B. In Sect. 3, we introduce an approach to model a context-aware system by formalizing its components using Event-B notations. Section 4 presents a scenario of an Adaptive Cruise Control system in order to demonstrate our approach. Section 5 summarizes some related works. We conclude and provide future works in Sect. 6.

2   Backgrounds

As we use Event-B notation to formalize context-aware systems, in this section, we introduce briefly some background of Event-B and context awareness.

2.1   Event-B

Event-B is a formal method for system-level modeling and analysis. Key features of Event-B are the use of set theory as a modeling notation, the use of refinement to represent systems at different abstraction levels and the use of mathematical proof to verify consistency between refinement levels [2]. An Event B model encodes a state transition system where the variables represent the state and the events represent the transitions from one state to another. A basic structure of an Event-B model consists of a MACHINE and a CONTEXT.

A machine is defined by a set of clauses which is able to refine another machine. We briefly introduce main concepts in Event-B machine as follows:

VARIABLES represent the state variables of the model of the specification.

INVARIANTS described by first order logic expressions, the properties of the attributes defined in the VARIABLES clause. Typing information, functional and safety properties are described in this clause. These properties are true in the whole model. Invariants need to be preserved by events clauses.

EVENTS define all the events that occur in a given model. Each event is characterized by its guard (i.e. a first order logic expression involving variables). An event is fired when its guard evaluates to true. If several guards evaluate to true, only one is fired with a non deterministic choice. The events occurring in an Event B model affect the state described in VARIABLES clause.

An Event B model may refer to a CONTEXT describing a static part where all the relevant properties and hypotheses are defined. A CONTEXT consists of the following items:

SETS describe a set of abstract and enumerated types.

CONSTANTS represent the constants used by the model.

AXIOMS describe with first order logic expressions, the properties of the attributes defined in the CONSTANTS clause. Types and constraints are described in this clause.

2.2 Context-Aware Systems

The term "context-aware" was first introduced by Bill Schilit, he defined contexts as location, identities of objects and changes of those objects to applications that then adapt themselves to the context [12]. Many works have been focused on defining terms of context awareness. Context-aware systems can be constructed in various methods which depend on requirements and conditions of sensors, the amount of users, the resource available on the devices. A context model defines and stores context data in a form that machines can process. Baldauf et al. [3] summarized several most relevant context modeling approaches such as key-value, markup scheme, graphical object oriented, logic based and ontology based models.

In this paper, we consider the environment in which a system is operating as contexts. Therefore, there are many kinds of contexts such as position, acceleration of the vehicle and/or temperature, weather, humidity, etc. The system uses sensors to capture the contexts data. Processing of the system is context-dependent, i.e. it react to the context changes (for example: if the temperature is decreased, then the system starts heating). The system's behaviors must comply with the context constraints properties (for instance: the system does not start heating, even though the operator executes heating function when the temperature is vey high).

3   Formalizing Context Awareness

In this section, we consider a simplified context-aware system and represent its components in set theory. Base upon these definitions, we then use Event-B notations to formalize a context-aware system.

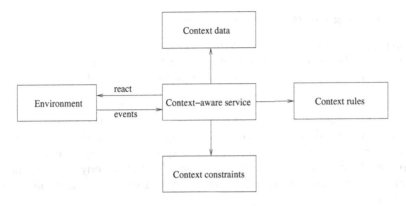

Fig. 1. A simple context-aware system

3.1 Set Representation of Context Awareness

Firstly, we introduce a simple structure of context-aware systems consisting of five components depicted in Fig. 1. A basic operation of the system is that if there is any change from the environment, it sends events to core context-aware service. This component then uses both context data entities and context rules to reason about the situation. Finally, it reacts to environment via its behaviors. During that process, the system still has to fulfill the constraints.

Definition 1 (Context-aware system). *A context-aware system is denoted by a 4-tuple, $CaS = \langle E, R, CD, CC \rangle$ where E and R represent for the environment events and context rules respectively, CD denotes context data entities and its relations and CC states the system's constraints.*

We go further for definitions of context rules and context entities. Let us assume that rules of context-awareness are in the form of ECA (event-condition-action), i.e. if an an event e occurs in condition C then do action A. Hence, we present definitions for each element $r, r \in R$ as follows:

Definition 2 (Context rules). *A rule is defined by 3-tuple $r = \langle e, a, c \rangle$, where e, c are event and condition of the rule respectively, while a states the action of the rule.*

Context data consists of context entities and their relations. This component takes a role as a data storage of the system.

Definition 3 (Context data). *Context data is denoted by a 2-tuple $CD = \langle E, R \rangle$, where E is a set of context entities and R is a set of functions mapping between sets of context entities.*

Definition 4 (Environments). *Environment is a set of events stated by a set: $E = \{e\}$, where e is an event that is sent to context aware core service.*

3.2   Modeling Context-Aware System

Event-B is based on classical set theory, we thus use it to model context-aware systems according to definitions given in Subsect. 3.1. We present transformation rules between a context-aware system and an Event-B model as follows:

- Rule 1: Recall that, we represent context data by either sets or set's elements. Hence, we formalize it as sets or constants of an Event-B Context.
- Rule 2: Each rule $r = \langle e, a, c \rangle$ is mapping to an Event-B event, since its structure is similar to ECA format. More specifically, conjunction of e and c are guards of Event-B event while a is modeled in the body of the event (see Table 1). All these events are included in either Event-B abstract machines or a refined ones.
- Rule 3: Each event that is triggered by environment is represented by an Event-B event. Example: A context-aware system includes a sensor for detecting Wind speed is high or low, it is then formalized by two events: *detectStrongWind* and *detectWeakWind*. Two events of this sensor are included in one Event-B machine.
- Rule 4: A constraint of the context-aware system is a desired property that the system should maintain. That standpoint matches to the meaning of Event-B invariants, we thus model Context constraints by a set of invariants.

We summarize transformation rules used for modeling in Table 2.

3.3   Incremental Modeling Using Refinement

In fact, the development of context-aware systems often starts from the scratch requirements, then it is built gradually when we have new requirements about context entities and reasoning. Therefore, it requires to have a suitable modeling method for incremental development. As we have described in Subsect. 3.2,

Table 1. Modeling a context rule by an Event-B event

IF (e)	
ON (c)	WHEN ($e \wedge c$)
ACTION (a)	THEN (a) END

Table 2. Transformation between context-aware systems and Event-B notations.

	Context-aware concepts	Event-B notations
Rule 1	Context data CD	Sets, constants
Rule 2	Context rules $r = \langle e, c, a \rangle$	Events
Rule 3	Environments triggers E	Events
Rule 4	Context constraints CC	Invariants

a context-aware system is transformed to abstract Event-B. It is apparently suitable for modeling initial context-aware systems. In this subsection, we answer the question how our approach fits to incremental development of such systems.

The refinement mechanism of Event-B makes it possible to model context-aware systems incrementally. We begin with abstract machines to model the very beginning system, after that we refine these machines by concrete ones to represent new requirements of the systems. It is proved through Event-B proof obligations that concrete machines are checked with invariants of abstract ones. According to Rule 4 in Subsect. 3.2, all constraints are represented by Invariants, therefore a new constructed context-aware system at any refined step preserves all constraints of the initial step.

4   An Example: Adaptive Cruise Control System

We demonstrate our approach by modeling a scenario of an Adaptive Cruise Control (ACC) system. First, we introduce the scenario, then we apply modeling method presented in Subsect. 3.2 and finally we check the significant properties.

4.1   Scenario Description

ACC controls car's speed is based on the driving conditions which are enhanced with context-aware features such as weather conditions, close target conditions, road conditions. The constructed ACC system has three sensors for detecting weather conditions, road conditions and close target. When a car travels in a raining condition or sharp bend, ACC reduces car's speed. If there is no rain or the road is not shape, then ACC resumes the preset speed. When a car detects a target close, ACC reduces car's speed to target's speed. If no target is detected, then it resumes the initial speed.

The ACC must conform to a safety property that is if driver applies the brake, then ACC stops the car in whatever condition. Immediately when the driver releases the brake, ACC resumes the initial speed.

4.2   Modeling ACC Scenario

In this scenario, there are three sensors, following the approach presented in Sect. 3, we specify the initial system with one abstract machine and three concrete machines corresponding to the car and three sensors respectively (depicted in Fig. 2).

Two events **DetectBreak** and **DetectNoBreak** are modeled by two events of the abstract machine. In Fig. 3, we formalize the context input sensor detecting weather by a concrete machine which has two events **DetectRain** and **Detect-NoRain**. These two events represent two context rules of raining conditions. Modeling context reasoning with road and target sensors are similar.

We finally specify the desired properties of the system such as safety, liveness by Event-B invariants clauses. ACC system should comply the context constraints, for example: if the weather is rain, then car's speed is slower than the

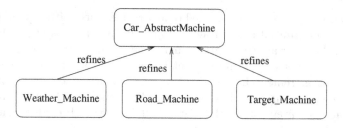

Fig. 2. ACC Event-B model overview

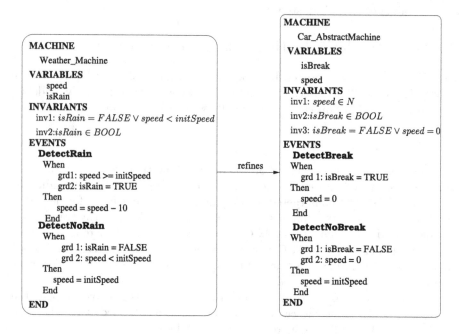

Fig. 3. Part of ACC system modeled by Event-B

initial one (stated in Fig. 3 by *inv1* of *Weather_Machine*: $isRain = FALSE \lor speed < initSpeed$). Road and Target context constraints are modeled similarly. Moreover, the system also fulfills a safety property that is if the break is applied, then the speed is zero. This property is specified by the invariant clause *inv3*: $isBreak = FALSE \lor speed = 0$.

4.3   Verifying the System's Properties

After modeling, we are able to verify the system safety properties with the Rodin tool. All desired properties are described as four invariants clauses of abstract and refined machines. The Rodin tool generates proof obligations (PO) for these invariants that are proved to be preserved through events for both refined and

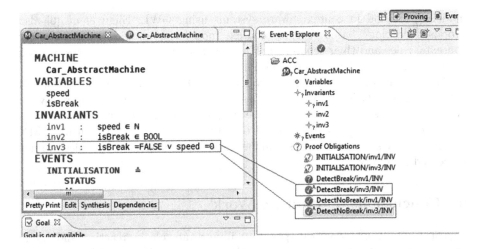

Fig. 4. Verification of safety property in Rodin

abstract machines. For instance: the generated proof obligations of the safety property (formalized by $inv3$ of the abstract machine $Car\_AbstractMachine$) are "$DetectBreak/inv3/INV$" and "$DetectNoBreak/inv3/INV$". The former is the invariant preservation PO of event $DetectBreak$, while the later is the one of event $DetectNoBreak$. The POs are presented in detail as follows:

"$DetectNoBreak/inv3/INV$": $isBreak = FALSE \land speed = 50 \vdash isBreak = FALSE \lor speed = 0$.

"$DetectBreak/inv3/INV$": $isBreak = TRUE \land speed = 0 \vdash isBreak = FALSE \lor speed = 0$.

These POs are proved trivially and done automatically with the Rodin tool as illustrated in Fig. 4.

5 Related Work

Many papers have been proposed for modeling and verifying context-aware systems with various approaches. Most research efforts that are based on markup scheme model have defined and extended markup languages. Henricksen *et al.* [7] proposed to represent contextual data by *Comprehensive Structure Context Profiles* (CSCP). Indulska *et al.* [8] extended CC/CP model to define a set of CC/PP components and attributes to express a various types of context information and context relationships.

Some researchers followed the graphical model approach to model contextual data. Mostefaoui [11] presented a three-layered data model for context. Benselim and Hassina [4] recently presented an UML extension for representing and modeling context by creating some stereotypes that are described by several tagged values and some constraints.

Almost all ontology-based approaches have used high-level ontologies to formalize context information and models. Shehzad *et al.* [13] introduced a formal modeling method in context aware systems using OWL. Ejigu *et al.* [6] also proposed ontology based reusable context model that providing structure for contexts, rules and their semantics. The problem with these two pieces of work is that there was no verification mechanism presented.

More recently, Tran *et al.* [15] introduced a ROAD4Context framework which is based on Role-Oriented Adaptive Design (ROAD) [5] to model context-aware systems. However, in order to verify the system, it takes more intermediate steps to translate a ROAD4Context model to a Petri net model and then use SPIN to check the system's behaviors. Furthermore, the transformation rules are not presented generally.

6   Conclusions and Future Work

The use of context-awareness plays an important role in reactive and interactive systems. Context aware computing is applied in many fields such as mobile, embedded systems, etc.. Modeling and verifying context-aware systems are difficult tasks due to their complex behaviors. In this paper, we introduce a proof-based approach to model and verify such systems. The advantages of our approach are natural representation of context-aware concepts to model and the use of invariant preservation proof obligations generated by refinement mechanism in Event-B to verify the correctness of the system. However, in this paper, we just consider a simple case of context awareness. Limitation of data types in Event-B method is also a weak point when modeling complex context data.

Our future research will concentrate on elaborating the modeling systems with various kinds of context data. We are working on extending this approach with modeling uncertainty in context-awareness. Developing a tool that allows to translate context-aware systems to Event-B model automatically is also one of our future aims.

Acknowledgments. This work is partly supported by the research project "Methods and tools for program analysis and their applications in education", No. QGTD.13.01, granted by Vietnam National University, Hanoi.

References

1. B method web site. http://www.bmethod.com (2013)
2. Event-b and the rodin platform. http://www.event-b.org (2013)
3. Baldauf, M., Dustdar, S., Rosenberg, F.: A survey on context-aware systems. Int. J. Ad Hoc Ubiquitous Comput. **2**(4), 263–277 (2007)
4. Benselim, M.S., Seridi-Bouchelaghem, H.: Extended UML for the development of context-aware applications. In: Benlamri, R. (ed.) NDT 2012, Part I. CCIS, vol. 293, pp. 33–43. Springer, Heidelberg (2012)
5. Colman, A.W.: Role oriented adaptive design. Ph.D. thesis, Swinburne University of Technology (2006)

6. Ejigu, D., Scuturici, M., Brunie, L.: An ontology-based approach to context modeling and reasoning in pervasive computing. In: Fifth Annual IEEE International Conference on Pervasive Computing and Communications Workshops, PerCom Workshops '07, pp. 14–19 (2007)
7. Henricksen, K., Indulska, J., Rakotonirainy, A.: Modeling context information in pervasive computing systems. In: Mattern, F., Naghshineh, M. (eds.) PERVASIVE 2002. LNCS, vol. 2414, pp. 167–180. Springer, Heidelberg (2002)
8. Indulska, J., Robinson, R., Rakotonirainy, A., Henricksen, K.: Experiences in using CC/PP in context-aware systems. In: Chen, M.-S., Chrysanthis, P.K., Sloman, M., Zaslavsky, A. (eds.) MDM 2003. LNCS, vol. 2574, pp. 247–261. Springer, Heidelberg (2003)
9. Kjaergaard, M.B., Bunde-Pedersen, J.: Towards a formal model of context awareness. In: First International Workshop on Combining Theory and Systems Building in Pervasive Computing 2006 (CTSB 2006) (2006)
10. Samulowitz, M., Michahelles, F., Linnhoff-Popien, C.: Capeus: an architecture for context-aware selection and execution of services. In: Zieliski, K., Geihs, K., Laurentowski, A. (eds.) New Developments in Distributed Applications and Interoperable Systems. IFIP, vol. 70, pp. 23–39. Springer, Heidelberg (2002)
11. Mostefaoui, S.: A context model based on uml and xml schema representations. In: IEEE/ACS International Conference on Computer Systems and Applications, AICCSA 2008, pp. 810–814 (2008)
12. Schilit, B., Adams, N., Want, R.: Context-aware computing applications. In: Proceedings of the Workshop on Mobile Computing Systems and Applications, pp. 85–90. IEEE Computer Society (1994)
13. Shehzad, A., Ngo, H.Q., Pham, K.A., Lee, S.Y.: Formal modeling in context aware systems. In: Proceedings of The 1st International Workshop on Modeling and Retrieval of Context (MRC 2004) (2004)
14. Strang, T., Linnhoff-Popien, C.: A context modeling survey. In: Workshop on Advanced Context Modelling, Reasoning and Management, UbiComp 2004 - The Sixth International Conference on Ubiquitous Computing, Nottingham/England (2004)
15. Tran, M.H., Colman, A., Han, J., Zhang, H.: Modeling and verification of context-aware systems. In: Proceedings of the 2012 19th Asia-Pacific Software Engineering Conference, APSEC '12, vol. 01, pp. 79–84. IEEE Computer Society, Washington, DC (2012)

A Method of Context-Based Services Discovery in Ubiquitous Environment

Pallapa Venkataram[✉] and M. Bharath

Protocol Engineering and Technology Unit, Electrical Communication Engineering
Department, Indian Institute of Science, Bangalore, India
{pallapa,bharathm}@ece.iisc.ernet.in
http://pet.ece.iisc.ernet.in/

Abstract. Ubiquitous services discovery without users requests (or guidance) is an important issue in ubiquitous environment. The ubiquitous systems mainly gathers the user and services context along with specific interests of users in selection right time the right services required by the user. Many of the existing service discovery schemes use a service matching process in order to offer services of interest to the users. In this work we propose a scheme to acquire the context information using CI-Constructs (Context Information Constructs) and analyze this information into observations from which beliefs are formed. The formed believes along with the users interest the system identify the user required service and guide the user to fetch the service. We propose a C-IOB (Context- Information, Observation and Belief) based service discovery model. With this formulated beliefs the required services will be provided to the users. The method has been tested with a typical ubiquitous museum guide application over different cases. The simulation results are time efficient and quite encouraging.

Keywords: Ubiquitous computing · Ubiquitous application · CI-constructs · Service discovery · Context aware

1 Introduction

Ubiquitous computing applications are heterogeneous both in terms of networking infrastructures and interaction protocols [1]. Because the users' needs change dynamically according to the user context such as position or time, an idea to compose appropriate service elements in the network dynamically based on the user context is a promising approach [2,4], as an alternative approach to the conventional way of providing services, where service providers prepare services perfectly in advance.

1.1 Context Based Services Discovery

Ubiquitous Services discovery [11] provides a mechanism which allows automatic detection of services offered by a node in ubiquitous environment. In other words,

P.C. Vinh et al. (Eds.): ICCASA 2013, LNICST 128, pp. 260–270, 2014.
DOI: 10.1007/978-3-319-05939-6_26, © Springer International Publishing Switzerland 2014

service discovery is an action of time in finding a service provider for a requested service.

Context-based [6] services that exploit information about user and environment context are becoming one of the core components in ubiquitous computing environments. The environment context information includes physical environment, system context that is being used by user, application context that is used for accessing information and social context of user which includes his/her personal data.

1.2 Some of the Existing Works

A Framework had been suggested in [7] which presents a service discovery for ubiquitous computing environment by using SLP, because the method for DA [12] discovery is based on DHCP [13] and multicast, which is more flexible and scalable architecture than Jini and SLP to extend the scope of service discovery from local to remote. Ubiquitous Service Discovery Framework for Pervasive Computing Environment [8] provides an attractive vision for accessing services anywhere, anytime. Service discovery essentially refers to the discovery of service description. It mainly comprises three components: DS [8], WSS [8] and SAP. In Service Advertisement and Discovery in Mobile Ad hoc Networks [12] the authors presented a Service Advertisement and Discovery (SAD) in Mobile Ad hoc Networks. Service advertisement and discovery is an important component for ad hoc communications and collaboration in ubiquitous computing environments.

2 The C-IOB Model

We have designed a Context-Information, Observation and Belief (C-IOB) model [14] to capture context information and perform the analysis of users in a ubiquitous environment. We discuss the model by describing each of the components of the model.

2.1 Context Information

Context describes own view of a thing or a person. For example user context gives user physical environment, what he/she has, etc. We classify the Context Information into four categories for smooth gathering. The context information is gathered from physical, system, application and social environments. The context information can be divided into four categories:

- **Physical Environment Context:** which includes the context information parameters like location, time, temperature, noise level, pressure, position, orientation, etc.
- **System Context:** gives information on device being used, operating system present in the device, supported network interfaces, output modes of the device, screen characteristics of the device, etc.

– **Application Context:** It includes the type of application, different data types in application, status of the application, resources required by the application, etc.
– **Social Context:** whose parameters include social behavior of user, preferences of the user, social identity, social trust on the user, etc.

2.1.1   Context Information Acquisition Procedure

We introduce a new procedure for acquisition of Context Information (CI) by using CI-constructs. For each type of context information we have designed a separate CI-constructs to collect the complete Context Information.

CI-Constructs

The designed CI-constructs (Context Information-constructs) enable many types of context information acquisition. Each construct is a multiway datastructure with predefined context variables. During the process of acquisition the CI-constructs gathers context information either from the devices or sensors or from the authorised persons. We have designed the following CI constructs by choosing:

a. **CI-What**: this construct asks for context information on something
b. **CI-Who**: introduces a clause of giving information on a person or people
c. **CI-When**: specify the information at or on which
d. **CI-Where**: provides information in or to what place or position
e. **CI-How**: collects information in what way or manner

These constructs in different form collects the all four types of context information. We discuss these constructs in details in the subsection on acquisition procedure.

2.2   Context Information Acquisition

We have designed templates of CI-constructs to suit to collect context information either from the devices or sensors or systems. They are PCI, SCI, ACI and SoCI Constructs to physical, system, application and social context information collection respectively.

2.2.1   Physical Environment Context Information Acquisition

We deploy the PCI-constructs (given in Appendix A) for gathering physical environment context information like location, time, temperature, pressure, etc.

Similarly, we use SCI-constructs to collect system context, ACI-constructs to collect application context and SoCI-constructs to collect user's social context information.

2.3   Observation Formulation

An observation is a summarization of various observed CI parameters of a user in a particular ubiquitous environment. The observation formulation block formulates the observations based on the existing CI of the user. The observation formulator has been designed to formulate all the observation possible, i.e., by taking the given context parameter values in 2s combination, 3s combination till K_{s-1} combination as shown in Algorithm 1. For ex., the context information for a user X gathered through CI-where(x) and CI-when(x) gives the observation: $\{X$ is CI-where at CI-when$\}$. Some of the generic observations are listed in Appendix B.

Algorithm 1. Observation Formulation in C-IOB

1: Begin
2: **Input** : K number of context values
3: **Output** : The possible observations
4: Get the Visitor Context Information values
5: We find all the possible unique composition of context information to form observation based on following formula
6: $C_K^n = \frac{n*(n-1)*....(n-k-1)}{1,2,.....,K}$
7: for $i = 1, K$ do
8: for $j = 1, i$
9: $U_{j^i} = CI(i,j) \cup CI(i,j+1) \cup ...... \cup CI(i,j = K)$
10: END

2.4   Belief Formulator

The belief formulator is a component of C-IOB which collects various temporal and symptomatic context information parameters from the environment. For a particular time of the context information corresponding observations are generated. An observation derives an activity of object or a fact from the given context information. The beliefs are deduced based on the new and available observations over a context. A belief qualifies an entity. For example (see Fig. 1), a set of observations may lead to the visitor's planning is to steal an exhibit. The beliefs $B = (b_1, b_2, \ldots, b_n)$. Where b_i is the selected belief from the set of beliefs B which contains b_1 to b_n as literals and variables used to represent various observations on which the belief will be reasoned. Algorithm 2 discusses the belief formulation method. Some examples of beliefs are given in Appendix C.

3   Services Discovery in a Ubiquitous Environment

Services discovery in a ubiquitous environment is the process by which an entity is spontaneously notified of the availability of desirable services or devices in the environment. We discuss the service discovery system by considering the museum environment where ubiquitous guide system is deployed to provide services like exhibit

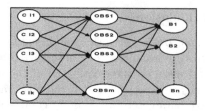

Fig. 1. Formulation of belief from observations and their context information

---

Algorithm 2. Belief Formulation in C-IOB

1: Begin
2: **Input** : K number of observation values
3: **Output** : The possible beliefs
4: We find all the possible unique composition of observations to form beliefs based on following formula
5: $C_K^n = \frac{n*(n-1)*....(n-k-1)}{1,2,.....,K}$
6: for $i = 1, K$ do
7: for $j = 1, i$
8: $U_{ji} = O(i,j) \cup O(i,j+1) \cup ...... \cup O(i, j = K)$
9: END

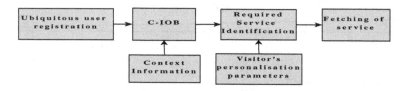

Fig. 2. Service discovery using C-IOB

information, path to exhibit, catering services, etc. The proposed ubiquitous services discovery system is given in Fig. 2. It involves the following components:

3.1 Registration of a Ubiquitous User/Visitor

Registration procedure consists of two main processes. (1) the registration process and the look-up process. Registration is used by services or their operators to provide the required service to the user, and (2). Look-up is used by visitors to find the endpoints of needed services. Different services discovery procedure architectures employ different processes for registration and look-up.

3.2 Identification of Required Service:

Identification of the service mainly depends on the system's lookup status which is offering the service, components of such systems, identifying the suitable component in the system which provides the required service, type of interface mechanism provided in the service providing entity, types of inputs and outputs of the servicing entity. Also the identification of service depends on the present context of the visitor at which the service has been requested and his/her choice/interest. This identified service must be efficient in all possible ways when compared to other servicing entities in the look-up state. Functioning of the service identification is given in Algorithm 3.

Algorithm 3. Identification of the required service

1: Begin
2: **Input** : Set of beliefs of the visitor and his/her personalised parameters
3: **Output** : Identification of the required service and path to fetch the required service
4: Identify the service based on the visitor's belief B
5: Refine the obtained services by using the visitor's belief.
6: Identify unique highly matched service based on the belief and personalised parameters of the visitor
7: Provide the service URL for fetching the required service
8: Return Service
9: END

Required service identification is done by analyzing the beliefs formed due to the present visitor's context and his/her personalised service requirements. For example, consider a well educated visitor to a museum, the present context information and visitor's personalisation parameters given in Fig. 3 enables in identifying the required service: "provide exhibit's high quality information to the visitor" (Fig. 4).

Context Information	Context Information at Particular instant	Observation	Belief	Personalisation parameters	Service
Location	at (x1,y1)	Visitor is at (x1,y1) at time t1	Visitor is spending more time near exhibit	History – Visitor is visiting museum for first time	
Time	t1				
Position	Turning towards	Visitor turning towards exhibit and moving slowly	Visitor is near Exhibit E1 and he is turning towards it	Interest – He/she is interested in science related exhibits	Provide high level exhibit information at his/her understanding level
Acceleration	Moving slowly				
Exhibit Sensor	ON	Exhibit sensor is ON and Visitor is using PDA	Visitor is using PDA and moving slowly	Personal profile– He/she is a well educated person	
Visitor Device	Laptop/PDA/ Cellphone				
Visitor Preference	Interests	Visitor interest is identified through his profile and visitor is moving in north-east direction	Visitor level is decided using his interest and movement is towards north-east direction	Preference – Understanding level is high so needs more information about exhibits	
Mobility of Visitor	Mobile/Stationary				
Direction	North/South/ East/West				

Fig. 3. Exhibit information service discovery using C-IOB model

Beliefs	Services	URL/Path
Visitor is spending more time Visitor is looking for more information	Provide exhibit information of his/her understanding level	infodb@iob.pet.ece.iisc.ernet.in
Temperature is high in museum Humidity and noise level is increasing	Provide Emergency fire exit path and call the fire extinguisher	emergency@iob.pet.ece.iisc.ernet.in
Visitor is away from exhibit Visitor is looking for service	Provide basic amenity services like path to rest rooms, etc.	basic amenity@iob.pet.ece.iisc.ernet.in
Visitor is on the move Visitor is not near to any exhibit in museum	Provide path to next exhibit according to visitor preference	Pathtoexhibit@iob.pet.ece.iisc.ernet.in
Visitor is away from exhibit Visitor preference says its his/her lunch time	Provide path to nearest restaurant and reserve a seat	pathtorestaurant@iob.pet.ece.iisc.ernet.in

Fig. 4. Service identification based on beliefs

3.3   Fetching the Required Service

Once the service required has been identified, it had to be fetched from the service providing entity. The service fetched will be based on the context, availability of the service in look-up table and current status of the service providing entity.

4   Implementation of Services Discovery System in a Ubiquitous Guide System for a Museum

The working of system is explained with an example of a Ubiquitous guide for museum application. Consider that a visitor enters the museum. The context information module collects the physical environment, system, application and social context information of the visitor's periodically. These collected context information is the input to observation formulation module where it forms different observations based on different context information. Depending on the observations formulated, the belief formulator module formulates belief based on which required services are provided to the visitor in museum.

4.1   Case Study: Services Discovery by Ubiquitous Guide in a Museum

Figure 5 illustrates all the services provided by the ubiquitous guide system in a museum. We discuss a couple of case studies for explanation of system functioning.

Case 1: Path to next exhibit service
Consider that visitor is at exhibit E_x at time t_i mins. Let us assume that according to a visitor profile calendar gives less time to spend in museum and the visitor has to visit many exhibits in the museum as per his/her interest. In such a scenario, the ubiquitous guide system comes into picture. Initially the ubiquitous guide system identifies all the exhibits and their locations in the museum as per visitor's interest. Based on the believes formulated the system is aware that the visitor has less time to visit the museum. Then based on the belief it has to take a decision of how the visitor must move on an optimal path to cover all the exhibits of his/her interest and then the system provides path to the next nearby interested exhibit soon after the visitor finishes watching the current exhibit.

Case 2: Catering and reservation services

Assume that a visitor is in a museum, and time is mid-day and the beliefs formulated suggest that "visitor needs the catering service", so the system provides the catering service. To provide the catering service to the visitor, system must know the visitor preferred dishes, which is determined from the visitor profile. Once his/her preferred dishes are determined, then the system starts searching for the nearby restaurants where these dishes are available. Once the search is complete, the system decides the best restaurant where visitor preferred dishes are available according to the visitor preference and also system reserves a table in the restaurant for the visitor to have lunch. After completing these procedures, the system informs the visitor.

Case 3: Fire emergency exit service

If there is any fire emergency in a museum or in such public places, people are more distracted due to the situation. In such a scenario the system guides the visitors to the emergency exit based on beliefs. The occurrence of fire emergency alarm can be determined by different context information such as room temperature, humidity, noise level in a room. The corresponding observations for this context informations: sudden increase in room temperature, increase in humidity level and noise level is high; leads to the belief that there is some fire disaster. Once this belief has been formulated, then the system decides that the visitor needs emergency fire exit service and it provides the path to emergency exit as well as it informs the fire extinguisher service to control the fire.

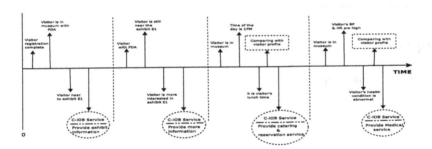

Fig. 5. Providing different services based on context

5 Results

The designed services discovery system is tested with the Ubiquitous museum guide system. With the results obtained, we can conclude that more than 75% of visitors are satisfied with the services provided, which is performance measure of the C-IOB based services discovery system in a ubiquitous environment.

From the statistics given, we can conclude that as the number of requests increases, the time taken to service the requests by C-IOB based service discovery system is less when compared to traditional service discovery system, which makes the system efficient and to perform well in real time environment.

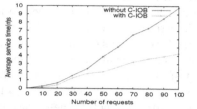 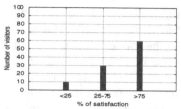

(a) Average service time taken to number of requests from visitor

(b) Average visitor satisfaction to the number of requests from visitor

6   Conclusion

C-IOB based services discovery is a new concept in discovering the required services for the ubiquitous computing users. The C-IOB model proposes to exploit useful contextual information within ubiquitous computing environments to discover the most appropriate and relevant services for the requesting user. The key feature of the C-IOB model is that context information is used not only to select the most appropriate service instance, but also to improve the dissemination of service requests across heterogeneous ubiquitous environments, thus minimizing the resource consumption.

Appendix

A   CI-Constructs

See Fig. 6.

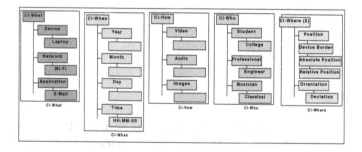

Fig. 6. Context Information(CI)-constructs

B   Observations

See Fig. 7.

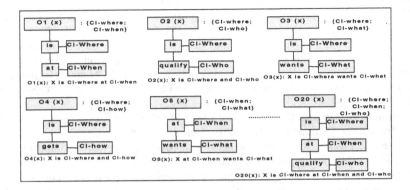

Fig. 7. Formulation of observations from Context Information-constructs

C   Beliefs

Consider observations $O_1(x)$ and $O_3(x)$ of Appendix B. From those observations the formulated belief is:

In the museum environment if <u>CI-where = near the exhibit</u> wants <u>CI-what =</u> <u>path to next similar exhibit</u> at <u>CI-when = after 5 min</u>.

References

1. Weiser, M.: Ubiquitous computing. Commun. ACM **36**(1), 75–84 (1993)
2. Gribble, S., et al.: The Ninja architecture for robust internet-scale systems and services. Comput. Netw. **35**(4), 473–497 (2001)
3. Lei, H., Sow, D.M., John, I., Davis, S., Banavar, G., Ebling, M.R.: The design and applications of a context service. SIGMOBILE Mob. Comput. Commun. Rev. **6**(4), 45–55 (2002)
4. Dey, A.K.: Understanding and using context. Pers. Ubiquit. Comput. **5**(1), 4–7 (2001)
5. Liu, Q., Linge, N.: Towards a new context representation, maintenance and discovery in mobile ad hoc networks. www.cms.livjm.ac.uk/pgnet2009/Proceedings/Papers/2009028.pdf

6. Takemoto, M., et al.: A service-composition and service-emergence framework for ubiquitous-computing environments. In: SAINT 2004, January 2004, pp. 313–318 (2004)

7. Gu, X., Shi, H., Ye, J., Zhu, Z.: A service discovery framework for ubiquitous computing. In: 8th International IEEE 2007 (2007)

8. Xu, T., Ye, B.: A Gnutella Inspired Ubiquitous Service Discovery Framework for Pervasive Computing Environment, Tokyo, 163–0914, Japan. IEEE (2008)

9. Cheng, L.: Service advertisement and discovery in bobile ad hoc networks, In: Proceedings of Workshop on Ad hoc Communications and Collaboration in Ubiquitous Computing Environments, in conjunction with the ACM 2002 Conference on Computer Supported Cooperative Work, New Orleans, Louisiana, USA, November 2002, pp. 16–20

10. Guttman, E., Perkins, C., Veizades, J., Day, M.: Service location protocol. Version 2, Request for Comments (RFC) 2608, June 1999 (1999)

11. Miller, B., Pascoe, R.: Salutation service discovery in pervasive computing environments. Technical report, IBM White Paper (2000)

12. Choi, O., Han, S.: Ubiquitous computing services discovery and execution using a novel intelligent web services algorithm. Sensors **7**, 1287–1305 (2007). ISSN: 1424–8220

13. Kang, S., Kim, W., Lee, D., Lee, Y.: Group Context-aware Service Discovery for Supporting Continuous Service Availability. In: Proceedings of ubiPCMM 2005, Tokyo, Japan pp. 62–63 (2005)

14. Venkataram, P., Bharath, M.: Context based service discovery for ubiquitous applications. In: International Conference on Information Networking (ICOIN) 2011, pp. 311–316 (2011). ISBN: 978-1-61284-661-3

Towards an Adaptive Visualization System in Context-Aware Environments

Xiaoyan Bai[(✉)], David White, and David Sundaram

Department of Information Systems and Operations Management,
University of Auckland, Auckland, New Zealand
xbai008@aucklanduni.ac.nz,
{d.white,d.sundaram}@auckland.ac.nz

Abstract. To provide good visibility of present and potential future contexts and improve system usability and effectiveness, context-aware systems need support for developing effective visualizations of both context and user problem data. However, it is quite difficult to maintain visualization effectiveness across different problem domains, stakeholders, purposes and/or time. Although many existing visualization techniques can provide reasonable support for developing visualizations effective under a certain context, they are still weak for maintaining visualization effectiveness under varying contexts. To address these problems and requirements, this paper discusses contextual factors that may affect visualization effectiveness and proposes a context adaptive visualization framework to guide the development of visualization systems that can be embedded in or used together with context-aware systems in order to develop and maintain effective visualizations. Furthermore, it demonstrates an implementation of the proposed framework through a sequence of context-driven visualizations.

Keywords: Context adaptive visualizations · Context-aware systems · Visualization context · Context adaptability · Framework · Implementation

1 Introduction

Context-aware systems refer to information systems that can sense problem and user contexts of use, detect contextual changes and proactively respond to the changes by adapting system operations and services at runtime [1, 2]. They are often applied to deliver useful relevant information and services to the right users in the right time at the right place. Typical applications of context-aware systems are mobile systems, tour guide, and smart homes, hospitals and class rooms [3]. An essential goal of context-aware systems is to improve usability and effectiveness by explicitly taking the context of use into account [3, 4]. This requires system designers and developers to obtain a thorough understanding of possible contextual situations, reasoning rules and system adaptation alternatives at design and compile time, and also requires context-aware systems to be capable of inferring user intent based on the context input as well as selecting appropriate system operations to execute at runtime [1, 3, 4]. In addition, it is important that context-aware systems support functionalities such as informing users of

P.C. Vinh et al. (Eds.): ICCASA 2013, LNICST 128, pp. 271–282, 2014.
DOI: 10.1007/978-3-319-05939-6_27, © Springer International Publishing Switzerland 2014

the present contextual situations, providing feedback/confirmation to users, enforcing user identity and action disclosure and allowing users to control system behaviors [1].

The above goal and requirements highlight the need of having effective visualization systems embedded in and/or designed separately to support context-aware systems in order to visualize the present contextual situations, future context alternatives inferred from the context of use and data of the decisional problem(s) to be addressed. To support this, a common practice is to apply appropriate visualization techniques to visually encode and present the context and problem data and enable users to interact with the data. Reviews on representative visualization techniques and applications can be found in [6–8]. Although many existing visualization techniques and applications can provide reasonable support for developing visualizations that are effective under a certain context, they are still weak for maintaining visualization effectiveness when the underlying context changes. The same visualization may attract stakeholders with different background knowledge, cognitive characteristics and visual preferences, and can be applied to address different decisional problems for fulfilling different purposes. However, Visualizations effective for one problem domain/stakeholder/purpose and/or time may be ineffective or even inapplicable for others. For example, a beginner-level user may prefer visualizations dealing with smaller chunks of data at one time and require step-by-step support for how to manipulate visualizations, while an expert-level user may be interested in more sophisticated visualizations presenting larger volumes of data and need support for advanced information analysis and pattern discovery.

To address the above problems and issues, context-aware systems need include visualization subsystems or be used together with separate visualization systems that can offer flexible support for creating/manipulating/transforming/improving/disposing visualization solutions. The visualization systems also need to explicitly consider the impact from the relevant contexts. To address these requirements, we propose a context adaptive visualization (CAV) framework, which employs a mechanism of designing and developing visualizations through integrating and manipulating appropriate context-related and visualization-related data, models, solvers and scenarios and maintains visualization effectiveness by adjusting these building blocks.

The goal of this paper is to provide guidance on designing and implementing visualization systems for context-aware environments. In this paper, we explore principal contextual factors affecting visualization effectiveness in Sect. 2. Then, in Sect. 3, we proceed to discuss the CAV framework and how context profiles and visualization scenarios can cooperate with each other to develop effective context adaptive visualization solutions. To validate the CAV framework, we implemented a prototypical system, and in Sect. 4 we provide a context-driven description of the system to demonstrate its support for maintaining visualization effectiveness.

2 Contextual Factors Affecting Visualization Effectiveness

Context is a broad term and can be articulated in many different ways depending on the underlying research domains. For example, from the perspective of human-computer interaction, context is considered as any situational information that characterizes a user, system application and user-system interaction [2]. In the area of mobile computing, context is treated as knowledge determining the status of users or IT devices such as surroundings, situation, task and location [9]. In the domain of context-aware systems, Vrbaski et al. [4] consider context as any contextual information associated with the computing, user and physical environments.

With a specific focus on information visualization, we define visualization context as the information of any environmental entities that can influence visualization design, implementation, application and evaluation. Visualization context is concerned with three essential aspects, that is, the decision problem(s) of interest, the stakeholders and the visualization purposes that they intend to accomplish. These aspects may involve contextual information about relevant problem situations, time, space, social context, and technological context (including hardware and software). They can also encompass the information regarding the visualization profiles of stakeholders such as their cognitive styles, personal characteristics and preferences, pre-knowledge, age, gender and even their mood when making decisions. The effectiveness of a visualization depends upon the context where it is applied. It is the visualization context that determines what visual designs are most effective for aiding visualization stakeholders to address their decisional problems of interest and to fulfill their intended purposes. The design elements (e.g. border, background, joint of elements, etc.) involved in a visual design can have significant influences on its stakeholders' understanding and interpretation of the underlying data [10].

By reviewing and synthesizing the existing context classifications and visualization contextual information (e.g. [11–14]), we propose a visualization context model (Fig. 1) to highlight four principal visualization dimensions, that is, problem, stakeholder, purpose, and time. Each dimension consists of a series of contextual factors. More specifically, the problem dimension is concerned with the contextual information in regard to the problem situation to be supported and potential solutions.

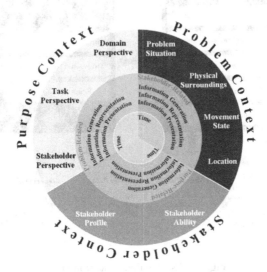

Fig. 1. Visualization context model

The stakeholder dimension involves any stakeholder-related aspects that can affect the design, development, cognition, interpretation and/or evaluation of a visualization by different kinds of stakeholders. The purpose dimension incorporates the contextual information about what a visualization stakeholder is trying to achieve through applying the visualization in a particular domain to address/accomplish a certain problem/task respectively. The time dimension concerns the time data (such as year, season, month, week, day, time, etc.) associated with decisional problems, stakeholders and purposes.

Based on understanding of visualization context, we introduce the CAV framework to help with handling context complexities in the following section.

3   Context Adaptive Visualization Framework

To support developing and maintaining effective visualizations under changing contexts, we propose a three-tier context adaptive visualization framework (Fig. 2). This framework is a conceptual level sense and respond model demonstrating the key building blocks of a context adaptive visualization system, and reveals the mechanisms of how these building blocks could relate together for creating and managing context adaptive visualizations. It leverages context profiles and visualization scenarios to aid in (1) the sensing of contextual changes (2) the analysis, transformation

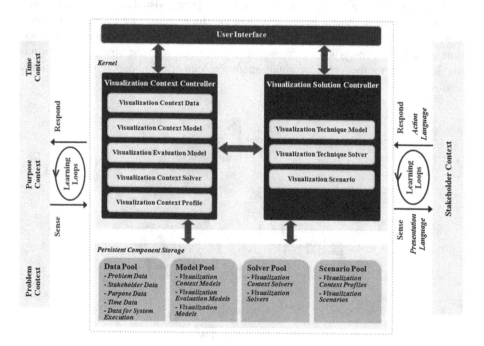

Fig. 2. Visualization context model

and learning of the new contexts and (3) responding to the contextual changes and the associated visualization requirement changes.

As illustrated in Fig. 2, this framework supports sensing the problem/stakeholder/ purpose/time contexts and responds to it through the creation and adaptation of visualization. We envisage it as a two-stage process. In the initial stage, the visualization context/real world is sensed through various mechanisms such as real time feeds from context-aware systems, databases, and human input which together contribute to CAV understanding the problem, purpose, surrounding, state, time, tasks, etc. This understanding by CAV and subsequently by users enables them together to respond to what has been sensed through a variety of measures. The responses could be at different levels: parametric change (single loop learning), introduction/modification/deletion of variables of model (double loop learning), and/or transformational changes at a deep and broad level (triple loop learning). Triple loop learning is especially important when the context changes significantly. Furthermore, CAV mediates between visualization problems and users through the explicit provision of action and presentation languages. Users may engage with CAV through a proper visual presentation language which enables them in understanding and sensing the contexts and responding appropriately through a visual action language. Obviously what is presented to the users is adapted according to their visualization profile, ability and ultimate purpose(s).

More specifically, the top tier in CAV is the interface through which users can communicate their requirements/feedback and interact with the system. The middle tier is responsible for supporting users to design and generate context-adaptive visualization solutions via two important controllers, i.e. visualization solution controller and visualization context controller. The former manages the creation, modification, transformation, implementation, initialization, execution and retirement of visualization solutions, while the latter focuses on the development lifecycle of context profiles.

With CAV, a visualization solution can be constructed by selecting and integrating appropriate visualization scenario(s) and context profile(s). A visualization scenario can be created by integrating appropriate visualization data, model(s) and solver(s). A visualization model describes how data can be represented and presented by a certain visualization technique, which can be manipulated by visualization solvers (algorithms that manipulate how the visualization model behaves). A visualization context profile can be developed by selecting and mapping appropriate context data, context model(s), evaluation model(s) and context solver(s). A context model is used to define the context where the visualization solution is to be applied, for example, what contextual factors are relevant, their weights in terms of their impact on the visualization solution design, and how they can be structured to describe and represent the visualization context. In contrast, the evaluation model defines the way of how the effectiveness of the generated visualization solution will be measured and monitored. Both the context and evaluation models are manipulated by context solvers. A component view of a visualization solution is presented in Fig. 3. All the context and visualization related data, models, solvers and scenarios are stored in their corresponding resource pools located at the bottom tier.

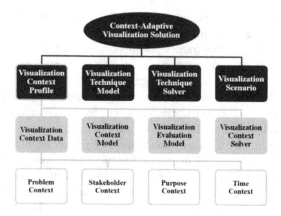

Fig. 3. Context adaptive visualization solution decomposition

4 Implementation

As a proof of concept, we implemented a prototype based on a multi-tier object oriented system architecture which is designed to support the CAV framework. This vertical prototypical system leverages a set of Microsoft technologies, that is, Microsoft Bing map, Windows Presentation Foundation, ADO.NET entity framework, and SQL Server. However, a similar system could be developed by utilizing equivalent technologies from other vendors such as Oracle and IBM. The prototype enables the sensing of contextual changes through accessing a number of historical and/or real-time data streams. The prototype can be applied to help a context-aware system with responding to the contextual changes through creating or adjusting visualization solutions. To demonstrate the support for adapting to the changing context and maintaining visualization effectiveness, we apply the prototype to the case of managing network reliability performance in electricity distribution businesses. This case is representative because it involves a wide range of stakeholders with shared/specific visualization interests, preferences, purposes and requirements, for example, electricity engineers, service/network operators, network pricing analysts, asset investment managers, senior finance managers, etc.

In this section, we delineate the case background Sect. 4.1 and demonstrate the support for adapting to various problem/stakeholder/purpose/time context changes and the associated visualization requirements changes in Sects. 4.2–4.5.

4.1 Case Background

A common requirement of electricity distribution businesses is to measure and analyze their network reliability performance so as to direct maintenance and replacement programmes, meet operational targets, comply with regulatory reporting requirements and enable demonstrably prudent and efficient network asset management decision-making. To support this, electricity distribution companies are often required to monitor and report both the frequency and duration of interruptions through the internationally recognized measures of SAIDI (system average interruption duration index) and SAIFI (system average interruption frequency index). Targets for SAIDI and SAIFI are set by regulatory requirements. One of their strategic goals is to deliver network reliability that meets these targets and also to meet customer expectations, which are reflected in customer service levels. Both operational and management staff within the companies may have the requirement to monitor network faults and investigate their impact on the network so as to direct maintenance efforts and identify trends and anomalies in performance. Apart from this, the companies may be required to disclose their performance against its SAIDI and SAIFI targets in an annual quality compliance statement, which could be subjected to external audit, in order to establish a high level of assurance in the reported information. In some countries like Australia and New Zealand, failure to meet the annual agreed performance targets can incur significant penalties. Therefore, it is quite important to deliver right network fault information to the right users in the companies at the right time and place.

4.2   Problem Context Adaptability

The CAV prototype supports adapting to various problem contexts by creating and manipulating appropriate visualization solutions. For example, a typical problem context in network reliability management is about supporting service/network operations engineers to monitor daily network faults and investigate their impact on the network so as to assist in isolating/removing the faults. Another one is about helping customer relations managers run customer surveys from time to time in order to understand customer experiences/expectations about the network performance and services. To support network fault management, the prototype allows designing and developing visualization solutions showing daily network faults distribution (Fig. 4).

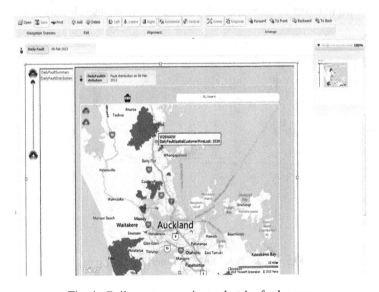

Fig. 4. Daily customer minutes lost by feeder area

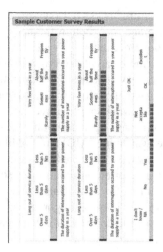

Fig. 5. Sample customer survey results

When the problem context changes to customer satisfaction management, it allows creating visualizations displaying customer survey results (Fig. 5).

4.3 Purpose Context Adaptability

In electricity distribution businesses, monitoring and investigating network faults may aid in fulfilling various purposes (Fig. 6). It can benefit service/network operations engineers to facilitate minimizing risks to the health and safety of people and network equipment and to direct maintenance efforts in a timely manner. It may also assist the

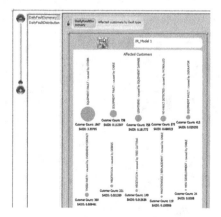

Fig. 6. Daily affected customers by fault type

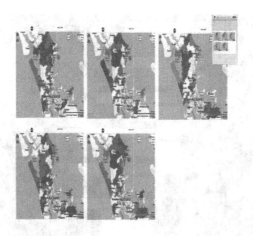

Fig. 7. Yearly SAIDI distributions from 2007 to 2011

senior management to analyze and identify patterns, trends and anomalies in performance including exceptions to service level agreements. With CAV, multiple-layer visualization solutions can be created to support the purpose of service/network operations engineers. For example, it could be helpful to have a two-layer solution presenting both the overview and detailed view of daily network faults. The top layer applies small multiples to represent the number of customers affected by different types of network faults on a selected date (Fig. 7). The size of each bubble represents the affected customers count. In the second layer (Fig. 4), Bing map is utilized to present the distribution of feeder areas affected by the faults and map polygon colors indicate the amount of customer minutes lost in each affected feeder area. The darker the color is, the larger the amount of customer minutes is lost.

When it comes to support the purpose context of discovering patterns of problematic network areas, the prototype can be used to create visualizations allowing users to compare SAIDI distributions cross years (Fig. 8).

4.4 Stakeholder Context Adaptability

CAV can support users with different cognitive and skill acquisition characteristics, prior knowledge and visual preferences. For example, it allows beginner-level users to work with less number of network reliability KPIs during shorter time-periods (normally involving less volumes of performance data) while for proficient users it supports to plot and compare multiple network reliability KPIs in the same timeline viewer (Fig. 9) and zoom in to view relevant details. It also allows users and/or context-aware systems to leverage the efforts already put into developing visualization solutions. Existing visualization solutions can be reused by replacing or adjusting the underlying data, models and solvers settings of the involved visualization and context components to support new visualization requirements.

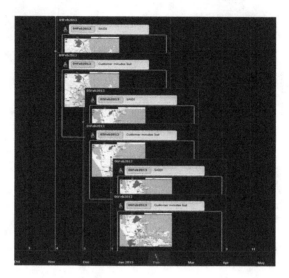

Fig. 8. Comparing network reliability KPIs of different periods

4.5 Time Context Adaptability

With CAV, users can show network reliability performance in different time periods and drill up/down to display the performance data in long-term/short-term periods. For instance, in the visualization solution below, users can display the distribution of network faults with map polygon color indicating the monthly SAIDI (Fig. 9). The darker the color is, the more significant the monthly SAIDI is to be. If needed, users can drill down to view the relevant daily SAIDI and customer minutes lost that contribute to the monthly KPI.

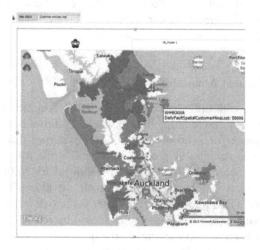

Fig. 9. Monthly SAIDI by feeder area (Color figure online)

5 Conclusion

To achieve high usability and effectiveness, context-aware systems need to provide users a good visibility of the present contextual situations, potential future context alternatives, the decisional problem(s) to be addressed, and how they adapt to contextual changes. These requirements highlight the need of having effective visualization systems embedded in and/or designed separately to support context-aware systems. Such visualization systems need to enable users and/or context-aware systems to flexibly create, manipulate, transform, improve and dispose visualization solutions and maintain their effectiveness under the changing/evolving visualization context. This paper introduces the context adaptive visualization framework, which employs context profiles to model the relevant contextual data and to serve as an input to visualization technique models in order to explicitly mange the impact from contextual changes. CAV supports the flexibility required by developing and maintaining effective visualization solutions through allowing users and/or context-aware systems to integrate and manipulate appropriate visualization components. Furthermore, this paper describes an implementation of CAV through the case of managing and reporting electricity network reliability and demonstrates its support for adapting to various problem/stakeholder/purpose/time context changes and the associated visualization requirement changes. It deserves to be pointed out that the current prototype has only been tested within a limited number of application domains. The application and realization of CAV in a variety of scenarios ranging from business to art to history to engineering to science will be accomplished in our future research.

References

1. Bellotti, V., Edwards, K.: Intelligibility and accountability: human considerations in context-aware systems. Hum. Comput. Interact. **16**, 193–212 (2001)
2. Dey, A.K.: Understanding and using context. Pers. Ubiquit. Comput. **5**(1), 4–7 (2001)
3. Hong, J., Suh, E., Kim, S.J.: Context-aware systems: a literature review and classification. Expert Syst. Appl. **36**(4), 8509–8522 (2009)
4. Vrbaski, M., Mussbacher, G., Petriu, D., Amyot, D.: Goal models as run-time entities in context-aware systems. In: 7th Workshop on Models@run.time (MRT '12), pp. 3–8. ACM, New York (2012)
5. Mori, M.: A software lifecycle process for context-aware adaptive systems. In: 19th ACM SIGSOFT Symposium and the 13th European Conference on Foundations of Software Engineering (ESEC/FSE '11), pp. 412–415. ACM, New York (2011)
6. Spence, R.: Information Visualization: Design for Interaction, 2nd edn. Prentice Hall, Saddle River (2007)
7. Card, S.K., Mackinlay, J.D., Shneiderman, B.: Readings in Information Visualization: Using Vision to Think. Morgan Kaufman, San Francisco (1999)
8. Heer, J., Shneiderman, B.: Interactive dynamics for visual analysis. Commun. ACM **55**(4), 45–54 (2012)

9. Schmidt, A., Aidoo, K.A., Takaluoma, A., Tuomela, U., Van Laerhoven, K., Van de Velde, W.: Advanced interaction in context. In: Gellersen, H.-W. (ed.) HUC 1999. LNCS, vol. 1707, pp. 89–101. Springer, Heidelberg (1999)

10. Ziemkiewicz, C., Kosara, R.: Implied dynamics in information visualization. In: The International Conference on Advanced Visual Interfaces, pp. 215–222. ACM, New York (2010)

11. Schilit, B., Adams, N., Want, R.: Context-aware computing applications. In: IEEE Workshop on Mobile Computing Systems and Applications, Santa Cruz, California, pp. 85–90 (1994)

12. Wu, Z., Chen, Y.: Context awareness and modeling in self-adaptive geo-information visualization. In: 24th International Cartographic Conferences, Santiago (2009)

13. Dreyfus, H.L., Dreyfus, S.E.: Mind over Machine: The Power of Human Intuition and Expertise in the Era of the Computer. Free Press, New York (1986)

14. IBM Many Eyes, Visualization Options Available in Many Eyes. http://www958.ibm.com/software/analytics/manyeyes/page/Visualization_Options.html (2013)

Human Sensing for Tabletop Entertainment System

Hafizuddin Yusof[1]([⊠]), Eugene Ch'ng[1], and Christopher Baber[2]

[1] IBM Visual and Spatial Technology Centre, do.collaboration,
University of Birmingham, Edgbaston, Birmingham B15 2TT, UK
hafizuddin.yusof@gmail.com, e.chng@bham.ac.uk
[2] School of Electronic, Electrical and Computer Engineering,
University of Birmingham, Edgbaston, Birmingham B15 2TT, UK
c.baber@bham.ac.uk

Abstract. Tabletop displays are gaining interests in gaming environments. Computer Game in the genre of board games, competitive actions, real-time strategies are amongst those that are suitable for tabletop displays. Currently most games developed for tabletops use physical objects with markings as the controllers and standard touch and gestures as the inputs. To extend the present limits of gestures and touch, we present an implementation of high performance sensor-based input modality as an extension to tabletop displays. The additional input modality has the capability to sense and track users' bodies while they are interacting with the table. This paper outlines the configuration of the sensors, the tracking accuracy test result and informal evaluations of the system. We emphasise the simplicity of sensor configuration, cost, robustness and high performance in the design of tabletop sensor systems. To demonstrate the capability of our system, we developed a computer game "Body Pong" where each player controls a paddle assigned automatically to him/her by moving his/her position left and right. The game demonstrates how context-awareness adapts when number of users changes during game play.

Keywords: Human-aware · Tabletop · Games · Input devices · Interaction modality · Sensor · Proximity

1 Introduction

Entertainment systems designed in the present generation's tabletop computers consist of a horizontal computer screen or monitor and CPU unit. Players normally interact with the system via input devices such as the conventional keyboard and mouse, or with gestures and touch [9]. Players sit or stand around the table facing other players similar to traditional games played on a physical table. In this sense, tabletop systems are suitable for competitive or cooperative multi-player gaming [11]. Computer games in public entertainment outlets provide various interaction styles that involves body and limbs movements; these are dance mat, card based input and controllers such as joystick, gun, steering wheel, and etc. [9]. Tabletop entertainment systems however, are currently restricted to inputs from forelimbs such as hands, fingers and tangible

P.C. Vinh et al. (Eds.): ICCASA 2013, LNICST 128, pp. 283–292, 2014.
DOI: 10.1007/978-3-319-05939-6_28, © Springer International Publishing Switzerland 2014

objects with markers. To explore research in tabletop interaction modalities, we investigated a new interaction technique that uses players' positional information around the tabletop. Our proposed system is aware of human presence and is able to track the number of users standing at proximity from the table, with accurate positional information for each user. Two pieces of information is available for game use:

1. The presence of a player at allocated spots.
2. The continuous body position of a player along its defined path on the table's edges.

This extended modality can potentially provide for new forms of player experience. In our experiments, we performed an accuracy test on the sensor setup to observe the optimum interaction envelopes around the table. This is presented in the later section of the paper. To demonstrate the robustness of the system, we developed a game application called "Body Pong" to evaluate the robustness, responsiveness, accuracy and smoothness of the application using the tracking system we developed. Body Pong is a tabletop game inspired by the popular classic Pong game. The plan was to demonstrate the capability of the table's tracking system by allowing a maximum of six persons to play simultaneously. In summary the game has the following features:

- The user's body (or torso) is the controller for the game. The paddle position derives its position directly from the user's body along the edges of the table. The paddle is always positioned at the front of the player.
- The game can have up to 6 players due to the size of the tabletop display (65" diagonal, 138 cm length and width of 76 cm). The game changes its state automatically depending on the number of players playing at the time. As an example, if two players are playing at the long sides of the table (Fig. 1), the game keeps scores only for each player. If a new player joins in on the long side of the table (say the left side), the game automatically divides the table's side into two equal sections and begins to keep the scores for the new player.
- The objective of the game is to collect as many points as possible by preventing the ball from hitting the edge of the table. Two scores are collected for each player: (1)

Fig. 1. Two players playing the BodyPong game. Dashed arrows indicate players' moving direction.

the reward points are awarded when the ball bounces off the paddle, (2) one penalty point is given when the player misses the ball.

2 Related Work

Tabletop gaming was mostly developed for multiplayer to encourage social interactions utilising the large display space it offers. It can be observed that multiplayer tabletop gaming has been a popular topic of research on tabletop since decades ago and we try to look at how sensing technology has been developed for tabletops to enhance users' experience when working on them.

2.1 Multiplayer Tabletop Gaming

Aside from information retrievals and educational applications in museums and public spaces [4, 5], tabletop games are increasingly becoming popular as tabletop displays becomes affordable. Social gaming experience can be improved with a tabletop setup that combines the advantages of a digital environment [15] and tabletops are generally well suited for games due to its similar setting with traditional board games [6]. Examples of tabletop game prototypes developed for tabletop includes False Prophets [16], Tankwar [17], Entertaible [10], Marble Market [13], PAC-PAC [9], RealTim-eChess [6], Weathergods [2], Surface-Poker [7] and SIDES [18]. Existing digital tabletop games mostly use turn-based interaction as in traditional games where each player must wait before others have finished their turn. Our literature review reveals that there is very little research on synchronous interactions for tabletop games. This is unfortunate as the effects of simultaneous interactions can be used as an advantage to support good collaboration [12]. However we think that although the many aspects of simultaneous interactions is important, they may not necessarily be the most beneficial for computer games as they are for work. Synchronous interactions on a tabletop may be better executed if the system is aware of the identity of the users or at the very least, the number of users and their positions around the table.

2.2 Proximity-Aware Tabletop

Research in human sensing systems are not new [3]. There have been a number of developments in the sensing of human presence in tabletop human-computer interaction research. Here, we will briefly list these related developments. Bootstrapper [20] recognises users by their shoes. The table needs to be raised from the floor with lights fitted at the bottom of the table to allow the cameras to 'see' the shoes. A total of four Kinect sensors are used around the table to get the depth and color image of the shoes as a method of identifying the users. Others, such as Ewerling et al.'s system [8] detects and tracks the hands and fingers of users of a table. The system heuristically locates the positions of users around the table. The system however only suits tables with projection displays as it uses optical infrared cameras fitted at the back of the screen. Another vision-based tabletop systems named "See Me See You" [25] uses

Finger Orientation (FO) of the touch gesture to deduce the location of the user around the table. The system assumes that users perform touches with a certain angle of orientation and this is a known limitation of the system. Carpus [19] recognises users through the observation of the dorsal region of users' hands with a high-resolution camera mounted above the table. One of the limitations of the system is the difficulty of installation at places with high ceilings, mobility is another issue. Ewerling *et al.* [8], Zhang *et al.* [24] and Ramakers *et al.* [19] require users to perform touch gestures on the table before the system begins to locate users' positions.

DiamondSpin [21] was one of the earliest systems that tracked users' positions around a tabletop but requires users to be seated statically on a chair fitted with sensors. Tanase *et al.'s system* [23] tracks users with a very low resolution of five user positions on each side using twelve infrared (IR) sensors, three on each side facing away from the table's edges. Medusa [1] was constructed to sense users' presence and track users' positions around a tabletop using an array of 38, out of the total 138 IR sensors. The other 100 sensors are used to track the upper limbs (hands and arms) above the display. The cost and the crowded arrangements of sensors make it difficult to duplicate on alternate tables. A similar system, Klinkhammer *et al.* [14] uses a similar configuration as Medusa's but with an additional 58 IR sensors in order to achieve a higher resolution of user tracking).

3   Methodology: Human-Aware Sensor-Based Architecture

The proposed technique recognises users' positions when they are at proximity, along the edges of the tabletop display. The system continuously tracks user's position by sensing the torsos as they stand or move along the edges of the table. The sensors coordinate the body positions and stream the information to a separate game application via UDP sockets. Our tracking system is designed with simplicity, low cost, and ease of assembly in mind. A simple do-it-yourself (DIY) instruction is sufficient to have this tracking system attached to a tabletop display. Our experience showed that the system could be installed within an hour.

Our prototype setup was configured on a 65-inch multitouch table. The measurement of the table is 172 cm (length) × 108 cm (width) with screen's length of 138 cm and width of 76 cm. A total of 12 Sharp IR distance sensors are used, 8 of which are for medium range 10–80 cm (**2Y0A21**), and the remaining 4 are for long range 20–150 cm (**2Y0A02**). The reason for using two types of range sensors was to combine the optimum working distance from both types of sensors. All the sensors connect to I/O processing boards, **PhidgetInterfaceKit 8/8/8.** Figure 2 illustrates the sensors setup.

The algorithms for processing signals from the sensors are programmed in C# with the Phidgets library for Windows environment. Two Phidgets I/O boards (PhidgetInterfaceKit 8/8/8) are used to connect all the sensors. The eight medium distance IR sensors are connected to the first I/O board and the remaining four long range sensors are connected to the second I/O board. The sensors are sampled at 20 Hz and a simple Moving Average [22] filter was applied to the readings with a window size of 5 readings used to minimise noise and stabilise tracking. A Moving Average Filter was

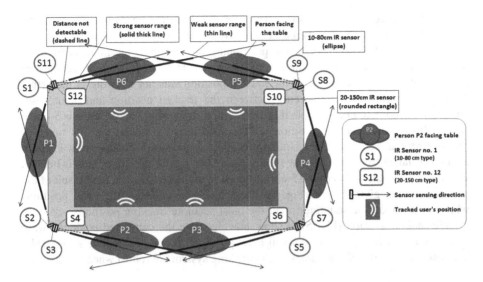

Fig. 2. Diagram shows placement of sensors around the table and range of sensing distance for each sensor.

found to give acceptable performance (compared to other more complex filters) and was used because of its simplicity. Window size of 5 is selected to maintain the responsiveness of the system while giving smooth and stable sensor readings.

4 Sensor Accuracy and Interaction Scenarios

4.1 Tracking Accuracy

We performed an evaluation test to measure the accuracy of body position when a user standing around the table. The purpose of this test is to find the ideal positions where users should be standing around the tabletop display to get the most accurate tracking. The floor parallel to the edges of the table is labeled with the white stickers separated by 5 cm horizontally, and 10 cm between the first row and the second, first row being the closest to the table's edge (Fig. 3).

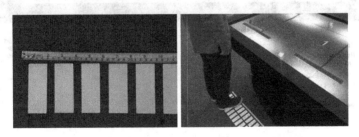

Fig. 3. Left: User positions spaced by 5 cm labeled with white stickers. Positions displayed on screen are recorded for each user position. Right: User is standing on one of the labels.

The test procedure is as follows: The user stood at the bottom left corner of the table at the start. The user is then asked to move right on the side by an increment of 5 cm each step. The accuracy of the positioning in relation to the markers is determined by visual inspection. If the tracked position matched exactly with actual user position, then "0" is recorded. If the tracked position was not showing at the actual position, then the offset (difference between the tracked position and actual user position) is recorded. For example if the tracked position shown on the table is 5 cm to the left from the actual user position, we recorded it as "5". After the first round of measurement, a second test with similar procedure is measured. The user now keeps at a larger distance from the table, at 10 cm away from the table's edge. This is iterated with a further 5 cm (to become 15 cm) distance in the third test. The final result of the accuracy test is given below (Fig. 4). The white area indicates the ideal positions where users should be standing to get the most accurate tracking positions.

We plotted a graph (Fig. 5) to show how accurate the computed positions were when compared to the actual physical body position on one of the table's long side. The test confirms that the accuracy of the tracking system are robust when the distance

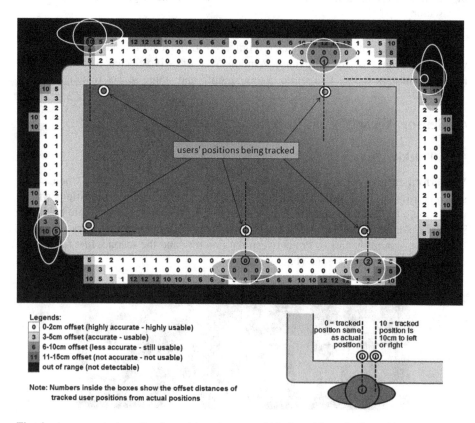

Fig. 4. Accuracy test results show the optimum and ideal positions (indicated by white area) where users should be standing when using the tracking system of the table.

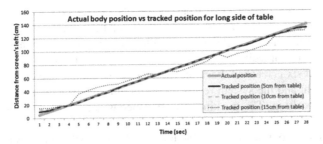

Fig. 5. Graph showing distance (recorded every second) of actual body positions versus tracked (computed) positions when user moves from left of table to the right.

between table's edge and the user is less than 15 cm. Tracking accuracy drops from a distance of 15 cm and beyond because of the design arrangement of the sensors.

4.2   Interaction Scenarios

In this section, we demonstrate the different scenarios of the human-aware sensor-based tabletop system using the game we developed. The table is programmed to allow six maximum players playing synchronously. Each of the players gets equivalent space partitions of the table when they play the game (Fig. 6: Top left).

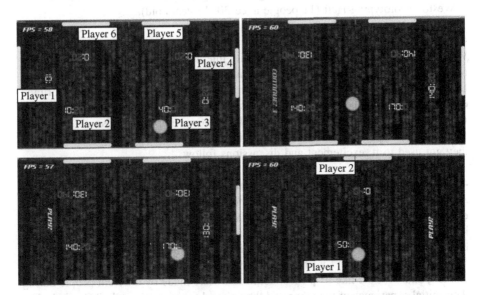

Fig. 6. (Top left): Six players standing around the table playing. **(Top right)**: Player 1 steps back from the table, a *"Continue?"* message is displayed at his position. **(Bottom left)**: 10 seconds has elapsed, a *"Play?"* message is displayed to invite new player to join. **(Bottom right)**: Two players are playing. The game automatically keeps scores for Player 1 and Player 2 if there are two players playing, one on each long side of the table. The same applies if there are two players playing, each on the left and right of the table (Color figure online).

Individual scores are displayed in front of the player (Reward scores are coloured white, and penalties are red. *10:20* means 1 ball-paddle hit collected and 2 misses).

When a player joins the table, a new paddle is created and positioned in front and his/her score starts immediately. New paddles are created for additional players until the maximum of six is reached. Each player interacts with the game by moving his/her body left or right and the system reacts by positioning the paddle at the centre of the player's body position. The tracking is instantaneous and continuous throughout the gameplay.

If a player steps out of the game, the message "Continue?" prompts the player for action to continue the game with his current scores. After 10 seconds have elapsed the message switches to a "Play?" prompt that invites new players. Figure 6 illustrated some of the game scenarios.

4.3   Evaluation and Observation

Behaviours of the participants are observed from several informal tests where the game was demonstrated:

- The Heritage and Cultural Learning Hub's Open Day 2013 (28 people aged 20–50 years old)
- Birmingham Science and Art Festival 2013 (16 people aged 20–45 years old).
- CAKE (Collaboration and Knowledge Exchange) events at Chowen and Garfield Weston Prototyping Hall (11 people aged 30–45 years old).

4.3.1   Interactions

We found that the users' past experience with interaction modalities with touch-based interfaces were transferred. When visitors first played the game, there was a tendency for some to attempt to move the paddle by the touch even though they were briefed earlier on the body-movement interactions. A short period of time (2–3 min) were needed for them to get used to the new style of interaction. It was also observed that they moved around and seemed to use their hips as if they were 'hitting' the ball. Once they got used to it, excitement and discussions follow.

4.3.2   Subjective Evaluation (Participants' Responses)

All initial users were surprised at the new interaction modality and expressed excitement at the possibility of application areas. The responses were positive: "This is cool!", "This could be turned to an exercise game", "I want this game at my home", "This is weird, swaying my hip left and right like this, but it's pretty cool", "This is so much fun", "I wish I could have more time playing this", "This is very clever", and "Wow I like it!". Most comments were made by different people during their initial experience of the game and they played for approximately 3–4 min before moving on to check out other exhibits in the hall.

5 Conclusion and Future Work

In this article, we proposed a new interaction modality within the research area of human-aware systems. The proposed area of research attempts to extend the functionality of tabletop computers to modalities that are beyond touch gestures. We proposed a system that uses twelve low cost IR distant sensors attached to the corners of a tabletop display. Adaptive algorithm uses distance information to continuously track human body along the edges of the table and streams the coordinates of bodies' positions to other application via UDP. Our system when compared to existing systems uses minimal sensors but provides for maximum resolution and efficiency in user positional tracking due to our method of coupling sensors and algorithms.

This low cost setup has a simple configuration making it easy to implement and assemble on existing tabletops. We developed a game application using the tracking system and the system has been on display at several events such as University of Birmingham's Heritage and Cultural Learning Hub's Open Day 2013 and Birmingham Science and Art Festival 2013.

The implications of the robustness, reliability, accuracy, and cost effectiveness that we have demonstrated showed great potentials in the system's potential application in gaming, and also other areas that involve the personalisation of user experience in shared public spaces such as Galleries, Libraries, Archives and Museums (GLAMs).

Future work will involve the extension of the tabletop's spatial functionality to include a much larger context of sensing equipments for enhancing inter-table and inter-room interaction modalities.

References

1. Annett, M., Grossman, T., Wigdor, D., Fitzmaurice, G.: Medusa: a proximity-aware multi-touch tabletop. In: Proceedings of UIST 2011, pp. 337–346 (2011)
2. Bakker, S., Vorstenbosch, D., van den Hoven, E., Hollemans, G., Bergman, T.: Weathergods: tangible interaction in a digital tabletop game. In: Proceedings of TEI 2007, pp. 151–152 (2007)
3. Ballendat, T., Marquardt, N., Greenberg, S.: Proxemic interaction: designing for a proximity and orientation-aware environment. In: Proceedings of ITS 2010 (2010)
4. Ch'ng, E.: New ways of accessing information spaces using 3D multitouch tables. In: Proceedings of the Art, Design and Virtual Worlds Conference, Cyberworlds2012, 25–27 September 2012 (2012)
5. Ch'ng, E.: The mirror between two worlds: 3D surface computing interaction for digital objects and environments. In: Digital Media and Technologies for Virtual Artistic Spaces. IGI Global (2013)
6. Chaboissier, J., Cnrs, L.: RealTimeChess: lessons from a participatory design process for a collaborative multi-touch, multi-user game. In: ITS 2011 (2011)

7. Dang, C.T., Andr, E.: Surface-poker: multimodality in tabletop games. In ITS'10, pp. 251–252 (2010)
8. Ewerling, P., Kulik, A., Froehlich, B.: Finger and hand detection for multi-touch interfaces based on maximally stable extremal regions. In: Proceedings of ITS 2012, p. 173 (2012)
9. Fukuchi, K., Sato, T., Mamiya, H., Koike, H.: PAC-PAC: pinching gesture recognition for tabletop entertainment system. In AVI 2010, pp. 267–273 (2010)
10. Hollemans, G.: Entertaible: the best of two gaming worlds. MST NEWS 3, 9–11 (2006)
11. Gerard, H., Bergman, T., Buil, V., van Gelder, K., Groten, M., Hoonhout, J., Lashina, T., van Loenen, E., van de Wijdeven, S.: Entertaible: multi-user multi-object concurrent input. In: Proceedings of the 19th Annual ACM Symposium on User Interface Software and Technology, pp. 55–56 (2006)
12. Isenberg, P., Fisher, D., Morris, M.R., Inkpen, K., Czerwinski, M.: An exploratory study of co-located collaborative visual analytics around a tabletop display. In: 2010 IEEE Symposium on Visual Analytics Science and Technology, pp. 179–186 (2010)
13. Kentaro Fukuchi, J.R.: Marble market: bimanual interactive game with a body shape sensor. In: ICEC'07 Proceedings of the 6th International Conference on Entertainment Computing, pp. 374–380 (2007)
14. Klinkhammer, D., Nitsche, M., Specht, M., Reiterer, H.: Adaptive personal territories for co-located tabletop interaction in a museum setting. In: Proceedings of ITS 2011, p. 107 (2011)
15. Leitner, J., Haller, M., Yun, K., et al.: Physical interfaces for tabletop games. Comput. Entertain. 7(4), 1 (2009)
16. Mandryk, R.L., Maranan, D.S., Science, C., Inkpen, K.M.: False prophets: exploring hybrid board/video games. In: CHI 2002, pp. 640–641 (2002)
17. Nilsen, T.: Tankwar - AR Games at GenCon Indy 2005. In ICAT 2005, pp. 243–244 (2005)
18. Piper, A.M., Brien, E.O., Morris, M.R., Winograd, T.: SIDES: a cooperative tabletop computer game for social skills development. In: Proceedings of CSCW 2006, pp. 1–10 (2006)
19. Ramakers, R., Vanacken, D., Luyten, K., Coninx, K., Carpus, J.S.: A non-intrusive user identification for interactive surfaces. In: Proceedings of User Interface Software and Technology 2012 (2012)
20. Richter, S.R., Holz, C., Baudisch, P.: Bootstrapper: recognizing tabletop users by their shoes. In: Proceedings of SIGCHI 2012, pp. 2–5 (2012)
21. Shen, C. DiamondSpin: an extensible toolkit for around-the-table interaction. In: Proceedings of CHI '04 6, 1 pp. 167–174 (2004)
22. Smith, S.W.: The Scientist and Engineer's Guide to Digital Signal Processing, 2nd edn. California Technical Publishing, San Diego (1999)
23. Tănase, C.A., Vatavu, R., Pentiuc, Ş., Graur, A.: Detecting and tracking multiple users in the proximity of interactive tabletops. Adv. Electr. Comput. Eng. 8, 2 (2008)
24. Zhang, H., Yang, X., Ens, B.: See me, see you: a lightweight method for discriminating user touches on tabletop displays. In: Proceedings of CHI 2012, pp. 2327–2336 (2012)
25. Zhang, H., Yang, X.-D., Ens, B., Liang, H.-N., Boulanger, P., Irani, P.: See me, see you: a lightweight method for discriminating user touches on tabletop displays. In: Proceedings of CHI 2012. ACM Press, p. 2327 (2012)

Adaptive Sustainable Enterprises: A Framework, Architecture and Implementation

Gabrielle Peko[✉], Ching-Shen Dong, and David Sundaram

Department of Information Systems and Operations Management,
University of Auckland, Private Bag 92019, Auckland, New Zealand
{g.peko,j.dong,d.sundaram}@auckland.ac.nz

Abstract. Enterprises that want to compete in today's dynamic markets need to be able to respond to the ever-increasing rates of change. At the same time enterprises strive to be ever more sustainable in terms of economic, environmental, societal, and cultural concerns. Enterprises are being challenged at all levels to meet the demands for sustainability and in a manner that can handle the complexity that is present. In this paper we suggest that enterprises need to integrate sustainability objectives with adaptive approaches to manage complexity and uncertainty. The overarching objective of the research is to explore how an enterprise can become both adaptive and sustainable by interweaving the deliberate and emergent in the context of strategy, organization, process, and information. This research seeks to model and develop several artefacts that assist with responses to complexity and uncertainty while also supporting goals of sustainability. In particular, we propose context aware adaptive and sustainable concepts, framework, lifecycle, architecture, and a prototypical implementation.

Keywords:: Enterprise · Adaptive · Sustainable · Strategy · Organization · Process · Information · Framework · Architecture · Lifecycle

1 Introduction

We live in a world that is characterized by complexity and uncertainty. Enterprises that want to compete in today's dynamic markets need to respond to ever-increasing rates of change. Simultaneously, enterprises are being challenged at all levels to meet demands to be more sustainable in terms of economic, environmental, societal, and cultural concerns and in a manner that can handle the ever present business volatility. The subject of organizational adaptation as a means to survive has been a research topic for researchers over the past two decades. There is a good amount of published literature that supports the theme of organizations being adaptive. However, this research goes beyond to explore how adaptive enterprises can incorporate the four dimensions of sustainability to become not only adaptive but sustainable as well. This research seeks to model and develop several adaptive enterprise artefacts that assist with responses to complexity and uncertainty while also exploring four dimensions of sustainability. The research explores the resources and constraints of an adaptive and sustainable enterprise. We will look into research lacunas of sustainability in terms of

P.C. Vinh et al. (Eds.): ICCASA 2013, LNICST 128, pp. 293–303, 2014.
DOI: 10.1007/978-3-319-05939-6_29, © Springer International Publishing Switzerland 2014

adaptive strategy, organization, process, and information while attempting to address the question; how can an enterprise become more sustainable and adaptive? And can it be done by interweaving deliberate and emergent aspects in the context of strategy, organization, process, and information? In the next section we first explore adaptive enterprises (Sect. 1.1) followed by an investigation of what it means to be a sustainable enterprise (Sect. 1.2). Integrating ideas, theories, and models from these two concepts we propose a model of an Adaptive Sustainable Enterprise in Sect. 2. The framework (Sect. 3), architecture (Sect. 4), and implementation (Sect. 5) that supports these theories, models, and concepts are the subject of discussion in the remainder of the paper.

1.1 Adaptive Enterprises

Scott-Morton [1] suggests that an organization can be thought of as a complex system comprised of interrelated forces that is constantly adapting to influences from its external and internal environment. This interrelated organizational system can be thought of in terms of strategy, organization (individuals and roles), process, and information. These elements, together with the influence of culture and the external socioeconomic and technological environment, enable an organization to function and evolve. Scheer [2] proposes a model which illustrates the intensity of control versus connectivity between internal and external organizational groups. He suggests that organizations with top down, hierarchical management structures have high levels of control and low connectivity. These organizations, although inflexible, succeed in stable environments and follow a deliberate approach. Conversely, organizations that follow an emergent approach are very flexible and reactive. Their levels of connectivity are high while control is low. Scheer [2] argues that the best place to be is on the edge of chaos where organizations balance flexibility and stability. This equates to a balance between the deliberate and emergent approach, which in this research we define as the adaptive approach. The adaptive approach is applied to the four key elements proposed by Scott-Morton [1].

1.2 Sustainable Enterprise

Sustainability is about the ability to continue, to endure, and to strategize for the present and future. In economic terms, that means an enterprise takes the necessary measures for it to stay in business. In terms of the influence an enterprise may have on the environment, to be sustainable means to attempt to be a caretaker of the planet, to maintain the natural world, and be responsible for not harming the environment. In terms of societal sustainability, it means an enterprise should make decisions based on the knowledge of how those decisions will affect people and society in general. Cultural sustainability encompasses ideas as broad as other cultures and basic human rights [3]. Many societies have cultural, religious, and community beliefs and practices that are very important to them. To be truly sustainable an enterprise needs to successfully balance the four dimensions of sustainability, namely the economic, environmental, societal, and cultural dimensions.

2 Adaptive Sustainable Enterprises

There is little understanding of how adaptive and sustainable systems can be leveraged and interwoven with enterprise systems designed around strategy, organization, process, and information. There is sparse literature on how to design and support such systems along with their development. We propose a new model of an Adaptive Sustainable Enterprise that attempts to interweave the adaptive, sustainable, and enterprise dimensions in a seamless way (Fig. 1). The overarching objective of our research is to explore how, "an enterprise can become both adaptive and sustainable by interweaving the deliberate and emergent in the context of strategy, organization, process, and information along with enterprise systems that support the four main sustainability dimensions" In the following sections we explore each of these components in more detail. First, we explore the enterprise dimension (strategy, organization, process, and information) in terms of deliberate, emergent, and adaptive approaches. And finally, we explore how the four sustainability dimensions can be interwoven into the enterprise and adaptation dimensions.

Strategy: In rapidly changing environments managers struggle to develop an approach that allows an enterprise to maintain its chosen strategy while providing the necessary flexibility required to avoid organizational decline [4, 5]. Mintzberg, Lampel and Ahlstrand [4] introduced the idea of a strategy as consisting of two elements: deliberate strategy and emergent strategy. Deliberate strategy is when the enterprise develops a strategic plan that is realized as intended. Emergent strategy is an unintended set of consistent actions that form patterns of behavior over time.

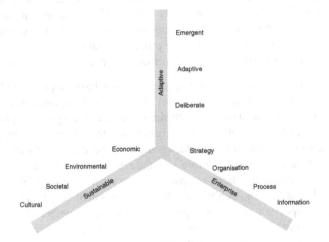

Fig. 1. Adaptive sustainable enterprise

The key concepts of a deliberate, intended strategy (plan and position) and emergent, unplanned strategy (as a pattern in a stream of decisions) are positioned at each end of the strategy formation continuum. Essentially, the main difference between deliberate and emergent strategy is the degree of intent about action. To create an effective strategy an interwoven adaptive approach is required that blends the deliberate approach with the emergent approach. It involves both intuitive and strategic thinking.

Organisation: An organizational structure exists for management and control purposes. It defines the work roles and how activities are grouped together [7]. Many enterprises are structured as functional organizations that support the deliberate approach [8]. An emergent organization structure is one where the enterprise employees interact with each other continuously. It allows for high levels of connectivity among individual members of the enterprise and with the environment. It is an extremely flexible structure that enables an enterprise to be reactive and innovative [9]. A matrix organizational structure supports both an emergent and deliberate management orientation. It consists of the horizontal management and control lines of a product orientated structure combined with the vertical lines of a functional structure. A matrix type structure supports an adaptive approach. It facilitates a project orientation and brings together the required expertise from different parts of the enterprise.

Process: Process is a way for an enterprise to organize work and resources to accomplish its goals [10]. Given that a business process exists to serve the customer, it can therefore be perceived as a key to remain competitive and sustainable. In dynamic business environments new business processes are constantly emerging [11]. In traditional enterprises the presence of rigid organizational structures and rules and a lack of communication and interaction mean work processes are set and people isolated. The management of processes is deliberate and the enterprise will be unable to react to change in a timely way. Conversely, there are enterprises with low levels of process control that are very reactive, connectivity between parties and the external environment is very high. They are constantly sensing the environment and trying to respond to change. Neither of these extreme positions is good. An enterprise should balance deliberate approaches to managing processes that support stable evolutionary growth with flexible approaches that support more opportunistic growth.

Information: Over the past twenty years enterprises have implemented enterprise resource planning (ERP) systems to support informational requirements. These ERP systems have replaced the stand alone business information systems applications in many enterprises [12]. They follow a very rigid structure and are predominantly based on a very deliberate approach to the management of the enterprise's transaction and business processes requirements. More common today are systems that support a purely emergent approach. These systems possess what is termed in literature and industry as an Event Driven Architecture (EDA). They enable event processing in real time and thus support an emergent approach. There are a number of systems architectures that support the adaptive approach. For instance, there are hybrid systems architectures such as Oracle's, which support both the emergent and deliberate approaches. These systems possess a whole host of components that explicitly support the EDA paradigm and explicit components that support the deliberate approach through business process management. In addition, most enterprise system vendors are advocating the implementation of systems based on a service-oriented architecture (SOA), which is defined as "a technology neutral architectural concept based on generally re-useable services". The SOA directly supports the adaptive approach.

In the following paragraph we explore how the sustainability dimensions of economic, environmental, societal, and cultural can be interwoven into the enterprise and adaptation dimensions discussed previously.

Economic, Environmental, Societal, and Cultural Dimensions: Truly economically sustainable enterprises are those with resilient visions, "built to last". Our interpretation of what an adaptive sustainable enterprise is takes into account a local and a global focus, a deeper appreciation for the environmental, social, and cultural dimensions of sustainability along with the economic sustainability of the enterprise itself – the ability to continuously adapt and generate wealth. Social and cultural sustainability encompasses ideas as broad as other cultures and basic human rights. We can speak of social and cultural sustainability that promotes the capabilities of present people without compromising capabilities of future generations. Moreover, social and cultural sustainability is closely connected with economic sustainability. It relates to the internal and external stakeholders of an enterprise and the products and services it provides. The social, cultural, and economic dimensions of business involves the ability to attract, retain, and make best use of the skills and talent for the betterment of everyone involved on a community scale. Environmental sustainability involves the oceans, freshwater systems, land and atmosphere but following the sustainability principle of scale it can be equally applied to any ecosystem.

3 Adaptive Sustainable Enterprise Framework and Lifecycle

To synthesize the ideas proposed above and address the requirements of adaptive sustainable enterprises, we propose a framework and lifecycle approach that integrates ideas from management, operations, information systems, and computer science (Fig. 2).

Context-Aware: A key aspect of the framework is the emphasis on being aware of the context. The framework is cognizant of external and internal contexts from the economic, societal, environmental, and technological to the managerial and cultural contexts. Being aware of the context is crucial in being able to adapt in time. It is also vital in being aware of emergent phenomena – phenomena at the macro, meso, and micro levels.

Deliberate and Emergent: The framework integrates the top-down deliberate approach along with the bottom-up emergent approach into a middle-out adaptive approach. This approach balances the deliberate strategy and formal organizational structures, roles, and processes with emergent strategy and informal roles and processes. This interweaving at the edge of chaos between stability and flexibility is crucial for an enterprise to be adaptive.

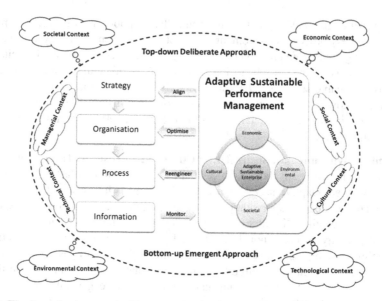

Fig. 2. Adaptive sustainable enterprise framework and performance lifecycle

Context-Adaptive: The framework suggests that context is adapted through a sense-interpret-respond approach. The various contexts are sensed through a variety of mechanisms (formal and informal) and informational inputs (internal, external, structured, and unstructured). These are then interpreted by cybernetic systems made up of managers, analytical processes, and decision technologies. Based on the interpretation the cybernetic system responds at different organizational levels. This could either be an optimization of the organization structures and roles or it could be a reengineering of the processes or it could be an alignment or even a reformulation of the vision and strategy of the enterprise. The alignment, optimization, and reengineering are guided by sustainability principles keeping in balance the economic, environmental, societal, and cultural dimensions. Thus, the organization will adapt sustainably using a variety of mechanisms from organizational roles to processes to strategies and ultimately even the vision.

Adaptive Sustainable Performance Management Lifecycle: Beyond providing a framework the figure also illustrates a lifecycle approach whereby one could interweave the deliberate with the emergent through adaptive sustainable performance management. Adaptive sustainable performance management enables us to monitor the health of the enterprise (in terms of adaptively and sustainability) and correct, optimize, and align the organization, business processes, and strategy respectively on a continuous basis. Obviously an enterprise cannot achieve adaptively and sustainability overnight, it is an evolutionary maturing process. A cyclical process that involves (a) discovery and learning through information sensing, interpretation, and synthesis (b) strategizing (c) design of new and improved processes, organizational structures, and systems (d) transformation of the enterprise, and ultimately (e) monitoring and controlling in a holistic fashion.

4 Adaptive Sustainable Enterprise System Architecture

We propose an Adaptive Sustainable Enterprise architecture (Fig. 3) which realizes the proposed framework (Fig. 2) using context-aware technologies. In this architecture an adaptive sustainable enterprise is implemented through dynamic and open context-aware strategic management, business processes, and information systems. Business requirements and their support systems at different levels of an enterprise need to be addressed.

Strategic Adaptive and Sustainable planning and management requirements are manifold. They include the activities to create, manage, and change business strategies based on the goals derived from the vision and sustainability objectives. In the lifecycle of strategies, new strategies may emerge over a period of time. The emerging strategies need to be identified and integrated into deliberate strategies as adopted strategies. The implemented strategies are used to govern the business requirements at the lower levels.

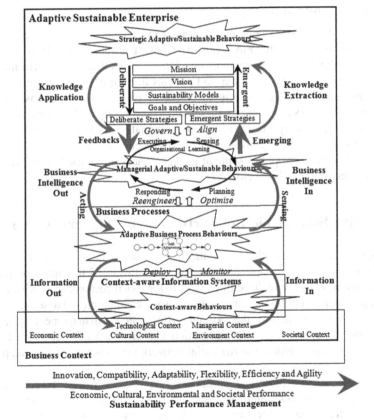

Fig. 3. Adaptive sustainable enterprise architecture

Integral to *Managerial Adaptive and Sustainable* operations is learning. Organizational learning involves single, double, and triple loop learning. Single loop learning involves reviewing operations to identify possible improvements in business rules. Double loop learning involves reviewing business operations and rules to identify possible improvements in organizational policies. Triple looping learning involves reviewing business operations, rules, and policies to identify possible improvements in strategies. These organizational learning loops are performed through Sense-Respond and Plan-Execute adaptive processes. The learning is implemented through adaptive business processes.

Adaptive Business Processes enable the business activities to be re-engineered easily and quickly in order to satisfy customers in a dynamic business environment. These business processes can be optimized automatically and manually to support and advance the enterprises sustainability objectives. Pre-set business rules and software agents support business processes to adapt automatically. Knowledge workers are also required to adapt business processes through manual interventions. The building blocks of business processes are enterprise services that are assembled and re-assembled into applications based on the contextual information collected from the internal and external environment.

Context-aware Mechanisms continually monitor events and harvest information from business processes and the environment. Context aware technologies facilitate information collection and dissemination. Managers evaluate the performance of enterprise and make changes to rules and policies if required. This bottom-up review and interpret process is in response to emergent phenomena. The sense-interpret-respond process occurs at the micro, meso, and macro levels of the enterprise keeping in mind the sustainability imperatives. This culminates in the reengineering of processes, optimization of organization, and alignment of strategy. A prototypical implementation that exemplifies some of the key concepts espoused in the framework and architecture is described below.

5   Adaptive Sustainable Enterprise System Implementation

The adaptive and sustainability requirements of strategy, organization, process, and information in the framework and architecture are illustrated through a prototypical implementation. They are realized through utilizing cloud computing, service oriented architecture, social networking, and context-aware technologies. These technologies are used to build and deploy the (a) enterprise strategic management systems (b) business process composition and integration platforms (c) context-aware business activity monitoring systems, and (d) social network systems that in turn support the enterprise requirements.

The design of the prototype components is shown in Fig. 4. The *Strategic Adaptive and Sustainable* component and the *Sustainability Performance Management* component of the architecture are implemented by Software as a Service (SaaS) deployed on a private cloud. The *Managerial Adaptive and Sustainable* component are implemented by Platform as a Service (PaaS) deployed on a hybrid cloud.

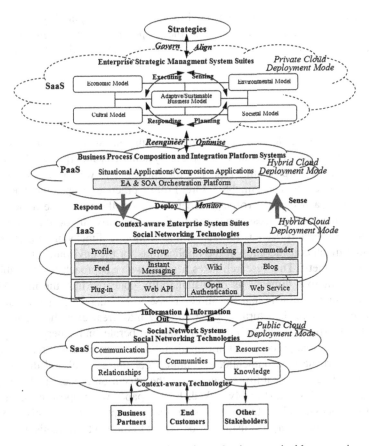

Fig. 4. The implementation design of an adaptive sustainable enterprise

The *Adaptive Business Process* is realized by business process composition, integration, and management systems, which are implemented by Infrastructure as a Service (IaaS) deployed on a hybrid cloud. The *Context-aware Mechanisms* component is implemented by Software as a Service (SaaS) deployed on a public cloud.

The following systems and applications are used to build the prototype and to perform the business scenarios:

- Virtual workstation: VMware Workstation 9.0
- Host System: Ubuntu Linux 11.10 and Windows 7
- Cloud Computing platform: Openstack Nova Server and Windows Azure
- Business Process Application: ProcessMaker
- Web Services: Restful Web service
- Web Server: Apache 2.2.20 (Ubuntu) with PHP 5.3.6-13ubuntu3.2
- Database System: MySQL 5.1.58-1ubuntu1
- Social Networking Site: Elgg 1.8.1
- J2EE Web Application
- SAP Discovery System for SOA HP ProLiant ML370

A vertical prototype was implemented to validate the adaptability aspects of the architecture. The sustainability aspects of the proposed framework and architecture have been implemented as part of our ongoing research agenda into adaptive and sustainable systems.

6 Conclusion

Industry experts and academics have been researching and writing about adaptive and sustainable enterprise systems and how these systems can incorporate the core ideologies, values, and purposes that represent the enterprise as well as the processes and procedures to adhere to a sustainable future. From a practice perspective, the adaptive sustainable approach is still evolving to better support the enterprise dimensions of strategy, organization, process, and information. Virtually all of the literature on adaptability of an enterprise has focused on the economic dimension of sustainability only without much consideration of the implications for the environment or the effect on culture or society. This research takes a much wider approach to adaptability by incorporating all four dimensions of sustainability concerns into the mix. The significance of our research is that for an enterprise to be adaptable and sustainable it should focus on more than turning great strategy into great execution. An adaptive sustainable enterprise needs to interweave the deliberate and emergent aspects of strategy, organization, process, and information. Such enterprises will require systems that also support the environmental, economic, societal, and cultural dimensions of sustainability. Real sustainability occurs when the execution process and the strategy process are viewed as inextricably linked. In this paper we propose concepts and a framework, process, architecture, and system that attempts to proactively support an adaptive sustainable enterprise using deliberate and emergent mechanisms.

References

1. Scott-Morton, M.: The Corporation of the 1990s: Information Technology and Organizational Transformation. Oxford University Press, Oxford (1991)
2. Scheer, C. H.: Jazz improvisation and management. Expert J. (2007)
3. Sen, A.K.: The ends and means of sustainability. In: Keynote Address at the International Conference on Transition to sustainability, Tokyo, May 2000
4. Mintzberg, H., Lampel, J., Ahlstrand, B.: Safari: A Guided Tour Through the Wilds of Strategic Management. The Free Press, New York (2005)
5. Eisenhardt, K.M., Shona, L.B.: Competing on the edge: strategy as structured chaos. Long Range Plan. 31(5), 786 (1998)
6. Hamel, G., Prahalad, C.K.: Strategic Intent. Harvard Bus. Rev. 83(7,8), 148 (2005)
7. Lasher, W.: Strategic Planning for a Growing Business. Thomson/South-Western (2005)
8. Bryan, L.L., Joyce, C.I.: Better strategy through organizational design. McKinsey Q. 2(07), 21–29 (2007)
9. Weick, K.E.: Making Sense of the Organization: The Impermanent Organization, vol. 2. Wiley, New York (2012)

10. Sharp, A., McDermott, P.: Workflow Modeling: Tools for Process Improvement and Application Development. Artech House Publishers, London (2001)
11. Marjanovic, O.: Towards is supported coordination in emergent business processes. Bus. Process Manag. J. **11**(5), 476–487 (2005)
12. Al-Mashari, M., Al-Mudimigh, A.: ERP implementation: lessons from a case study. Inf. Technol. People **16**(1), 21–33 (2003)

A Stability-Aware Approach to Continuous Self-adaptation of Data-Intensive Systems

Marco Mori[1]($\boxtimes$), Anthony Cleve[1], and Paola Inverardi[2]

[1] PReCISe Research Center, University of Namur, Namur, Belgium
{marco.mori,anthony.cleve}@unamur.be
[2] Dipartimento di Informatica, University of L'Aquila, L'Aquila, Italy
paola.inverardi@di.univaq.it

Abstract. Nowadays data-intensive software systems have to meet user expectations in ever-changing execution environments. The increasing space of possible context states and the limited capacity of mobile devices make no longer possible to incorporate all necessary software functionalities and data in the system. Instead, the system database has to be adapted to successive context changes, in order to include all the information required at each stage. This adaptation process may translate into frequent and costly reconfigurations, in turn affecting negatively system stability and performance. This paper presents an approach to context-dependent database reconfiguration that aims to improve system stability by anticipating future information needs. The latter are specified by means of an annotated probabilistic task model, where each state is associated with a database subset. Experiments suggest that this approach has a positive impact on the stability of the system, the gain depending on the degree of similarity of the successive tasks in terms of database usage.

1 Introduction

In the era of ubiquitous environments, modern *data-intensive systems* are highly dynamic with respect to different aspects: they have to provide different software functionalities according to changing environmental conditions and changing user needs (i.e., context). Consequently, they have to provide users with the information that are suited for their current context of operation in a resource-constraint environment. The literature of *self-adaptive systems* [3,7,17] promotes the creation of self-adaptable applications by means of different software alternatives that satisfy different sets of requirements based on the current context. Different software alternatives, created for different contexts, possibly need different portions of data belonging to a big data source. Keeping all these data on the server and making them available through the *cloud* is not a good solution for variants running in resource-constraint environments. Indeed, continuous interactions with the server require an always-on Internet connection, which in turn consumes device resources. Further, in case of data that are rarely changed or

P.C. Vinh et al. (Eds.): ICCASA 2013, LNICST 128, pp. 304–315, 2014.
DOI: 10.1007/978-3-319-05939-6_30, © Springer International Publishing Switzerland 2014

whose modifications do not negatively affect competing accesses, frequent interactions with the server are even not necessary. For this reasons, we consider a local copy of the database available to the application at a specific context. Ubiquitous resource-constraint environments where these applications run, suffer from the limited capacity (storage and computational) of devices and from the large number of context situations for which different portions of data are necessary. This implies that it is not feasible to include the global database within the storage-constraint device thus making it necessary to provide adaptivity not only for applications but also for data and their manipulation mechanisms. In addition, even privacy concerns should prevent users, under certain conditions, to access sensitive information. To this end, the literature of *context-aware databases* includes the support to provide the application with the subset of the database according to current context, user tasks and user preferences [1,5,9].

Variability of accessing data poses the interest towards new data-intensive systems for ubiquitous environments that are able to perform run-time reconfigurations to data-related artifacts [12]. Data adaptations occurring in nonstationary environments suffer from performance degradations and furthermore they negatively affect *stability* of data, i.e., the capacity of the system to have the lowest possible variation of data with respect to the variations of tasks [8,14]. In this paper, we provide a framework for improving the stability of the database reconfiguration process by exploiting a predictive task model which expresses probable future variation of the application requirements in terms of variation of the information needs. Upon task variation we determine which are the *admissible* configurations of the database, i.e., the ones that fit into the device and that provide at least the minimum set of data required for the current task. Among those *legal* configurations, we then choose the one that allows reaching the highest level of stability. To this end, we consider two criteria: (i) how good each solution is with respect to future variations to the current task (and required data) and (ii) how good each solution is with respect to the operations to perform over the current database instance. It is worth noticing that a good configuration for the future may be too costly to reach from the current one. Conversely, a configuration that is easy to obtain may not constitute a good choice for the future. In light of this, we have formalized the two conflicting criteria and we have combined them in a single utility function with the aim of choosing the best admissible one by means of a future-aware and a future un-aware decision-making approach. Experimental results evaluate the stability for the two approaches with different input task models, each providing a different level of shared information needs and different memory occupancy among states.

Motivating Scenario. We consider an e-health system to support the doctor activities within and outside the hospital. A doctor works at the cardiology and orthopedy department either as physician or as director. Based on the current context, i.e., current location, role and activity, the doctor is interested in different excerpt of data. As physician performing check-up visits, the doctor needs to access a complete set of patient information with sensitive data, while if he performs check-up visits at the patient home (outside the hospital) he visualizes only basics patient information without sensitive data. Indeed, for security reasons, the application prevents the access to sensitive data in case of remote accesses. Only in case of operations at the surgery room, the doctor has to visualize information supporting the specific operation he is performing. As director, the doctor needs to access information about other doctors such as actual working time and operations performed during the week. In addition he may be interested in checking performance at the hospital level such as the average time of surgery for patients and the current stock of healthcare materials. Finally, in case of an emergency the doctor should only access basic patient information concerning particular diseases affecting the patient.

All the heterogeneous data that are necessary to perform all the doctor activities are included in a global data source. In a certain context, the doctor only requires a partition of the global data to perform its current activity. These activities are performed following a certain schedule, e.g., the doctor issues orders to healthcare manufacturer after he has discovered that a particular healthcare material is ending or he performs surgery operations after he performed check-up visits. Determining a deterministic scheduling for these activities is not possible since they depend on un-predictable conditions such as patients' behavior and materials usage. Nevertheless predicting how context changes (along with required data), may support the reconfiguration process in anticipating reconfiguration needs and assuring a better stability to data provided to the device.

2   Basics Models

Our approach supports the reconfiguration of the current subset of data based on the current and probable future contexts. We support the context-dependent variability of the conceptual schema following a feature engineering perspective. We model *features* as the basic functionalities of the system each corresponding to a certain *requirement*, a *contextual presence condition*, and a *data excerpt* expressed in terms of a set of entity types belonging to the global *conceptual schema*. We exploit a *probabilistic task model* where each state represents a different task for which a set of features with the corresponding data are required. Based on the current task we determine the *admissible* subsets of data and we apply a multi-objective optimization problem in order to choose the best possible reconfiguration which optimizes the overall system stability.

2.1   Data, Context and Features

Conceptual Schema. We represent *data* through a conceptual schema CS defined as a set of entity types and relationships. We model the variability of data by means of views, i.e., $V \subseteq CS$. Our granularity of adaptation is currently limited to entity types and relationships.

Context. We define the context as a set of dimensions affecting the interest of the user towards different portions of data, i.e., user role, task, location, device characteristics, etc. each of which can assume a finite set of domain values. In our e-health scenario we defined three context dimensions, i.e., user role ($d_1 = \{Doctor, Director\}$), user location ($d_2 = \{Cardiology, Orthopedy, Outside\}$) and activity ($d_3 = \{Surgery, Check-up, HospitalManagement, IssuingOrders, StockManagement, Emergency\}$).

Feature. We represent the context-dependent variability of data based on features, each defined as a triple $f = (Q, P, E)$ where Q is a functional, non-functional or a specific quality requirement (context independent), e.g., $f_x.Q$: *The system manages check-up visits*; P is the presence condition, i.e., a contextual constraint requirement which expresses the applicability of the feature, e.g., $f_x.P$: *Activity=Check-up AND Role=Doctor*, meaning that f_x is required in case of Check-up visits of the doctor, while E is the subset of entity types of the conceptual schema of interest for the feature, e.g., $f_x.E$: $\{Patient, Disease, Therapy, Diagnosis\}$. Among the features for the e-health scenario, *Surgery Operation* supports the operations at the surgery room, *BasicInfo* manages basic personal information of the patient, *Cardiology* and *Orthopedy* features provide the support for managing patients belonging to the corresponding department, *SensitiveInfo* manages sensitive patient information such as HIV test results and genetic screening information, *Hospital Dashboard* and *Doctor Dashboard* features support the direction activity of the doctor by providing useful information about care processes.

Given a subset T over the complete set of features we derive its corresponding database view V_T by creating a consistent excerpt of the global conceptual schema. In [11] we have formalized this process which consists of collecting together the entity types belonging to each feature in T and in adding relationships types and is-a relationships in order to produce a consistent view of the conceptual schema. Finally, we define function $M(T)$ to assesses the space required by the database instance corresponding to view V_T.

2.2 Probabilistic Task Model

Given a set of features F, the probabilistic task model is defined as $PTM = (S, L, Z)$ where $S = \{S_0, ..., S_t\}$ is the set of states with the required features, i.e., $S_i \subseteq F$ for $i = 1, ..., t$; L is the set of transition probabilities from one state to another; $Z : S \times L \rightarrow S$ is the probabilistic transition function. This automaton can be obtained by mining the past data accesses of the system. Such a mining process is out of the scope of this paper, which assumes the availability of the probabilistic task model. We introduce the notion of uncertainty in switching from one state to another. Following the idea of the PageRank algorithm we consider a low factor d of moving from one state to another while we consider with weight $1 - d$ the transition probabilities as obtained by the mining process. This allows us to partially consider transitions that have never occurred in past

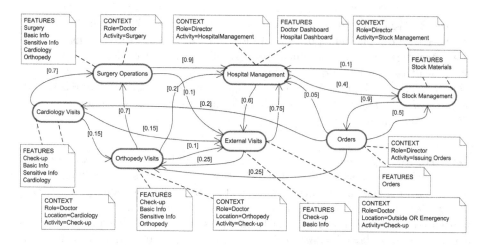

Fig. 1. Task model

executions and to have a fully connected automaton where infinite cycles are not
possible (thus making it possible to evaluate a steady-state probability vector).
Figure 1 shows the automaton for the e-health scenario. Among task states,
Hospital Management manages care processes concerning a single doctor and
the whole hospital thus it requires features *Doctor Dashboard* and *Hospital
Dashboard*; *Surgery Operations* task supports the operations and it requires
features *Surgery, Basic Info, Sensitive Info, Cardiology* and *Orthopedy*; state
External Visits supports check-up visits of the doctor at the patients home and
it requires features *Check-up* and *Basic Info*; *Cardiology Visits* and *Orthopedy
Visits* states support check-up visits at the corresponding two hospital depart-
ments. Transition probabilities leaving from a state express the future tasks for
the doctor/director, e.g., after *Cardiology Visits* he will either perform *Orthopedy
Visits* or *External Visits* with equal probability or he will perform *Surgery
Operations* with an higher probability.

Database Reconfiguration Cost. Reconfigurations to the current database
instance come at some cost which affects the performance of the application.
This cost depends on the operations that have to be performed over the current
database and it can be approximated with the number of operations that have
to be performed over the conceptual schema. To this end, we have implemented
an algorithm that given two subsets of features $F_i, F_j \in 2^F$ and their corresponding views V_i, V_j, it evaluates $C(F_i, F_j)$ as the number of entity types and
relationships to add and to delete to switch from V_i to V_j.

Stability. Our definition of stability takes into account observed reconfiguration
costs along with the variations of data required at a certain context. Given a
certain path of states of the probabilistic automaton $Path = \{S_0, S_1, ..., S_n\}$

each containing a set of required features $S_i \subseteq F$ for $i = 1, ..., n$, we define *stability* as the ratio between observed database reconfiguration costs (output) and required database reconfiguration costs (input) (Eq. 1). The component at the numerator sums the costs for reconfiguring the *best* configuration T_i at step i while the denominator sums costs between states of the path.

$$st = \frac{\sum_{i=0}^{n-1} C(T_i, T_{i+1})}{\sum_{i=0}^{n-1} C(S_i, S_{i+1})} \qquad (1)$$

Sharing Index. The nature of the task model is essential for evaluating the best approach for improving stability during the reconfiguration process. To this end, given two subsets of features $F_i, F_j \in 2^F$ and their corresponding views V_i, V_j, we define the *data-requirement sharing* as the number of their shared elements $D_{Equal}(F_i, F_j) = |V_i \cap V_j|$. Starting from this metric, we define the sharing index sh as the average number of shared elements among states of the probabilistic automaton (Eq. 2). For each state we sum the data-requirement sharing D_{Equal} with respect to any of the possible next states weighted with the probability of moving towards any of those. Then we sum these quantities weighted with the importance of each state according to the steady-state probability vector r. Finally, we divide this quantity by the maximum number of elements per state $MaxES$.

$$sh = \frac{\sum_{i=1}^{t} r_i \cdot \sum_{j=1}^{t} p(i,j) \cdot D_{Equal}(S_i, S_j)}{MaxES} \qquad (2)$$

Memory Occupancy Index. We also characterize the automaton according to the percentage of memory required at each state (Eq. 3) as the ratio between the total space required by the features of each state S_i (weighted with its importance according to vector r) and the space available at the device $MaxSpace$.

$$mo = \frac{\sum_{i=1}^{t} r_i \cdot M(S_i)}{MaxSpace} \qquad (3)$$

Data-Requirement Distance. In our approach we consider how good a certain configuration is with respect to future states of the task model. To this end, given two set of features F_i, F_j and their views V_i, V_j, we define their *data-requirement distance* $D_{Miss}(F_i, F_j) = |V_j - V_i|$ as the number of elements that lack to V_j with respect to V_i.

3   Approach to Stability

Upon task variation we have to determine the best possible reconfiguration of data. In Eq. 4 we formalize this decision-making problem as a minimum optimization problem to assess the most suitable configuration of features among the ones that fit the memory space limit $MaxSpace$ while providing the set of features required at the current task S_{curr}. The utility function evaluates the best T that minimizes two conflicting objectives: its reconfiguration cost with respect to the current one T_{curr} and its distance with respect to probable future states.

$$\min_{T \in 2^F} \quad \alpha \cdot C(T_{curr}, T) + (1 - \alpha) \cdot D_{Future}(w, T)$$
$$\text{subject to} \quad M(T) \leq MaxSpace, S_{curr} \subseteq T \tag{4}$$

To weigh two conflicting objectives we introduce the parameter $\alpha = [0, 1]$. Setting values closer to 1 we give more importance to the current reconfiguration cost, while setting values closer to 0 we give more importance to future states. Based on the values assigned to α and w we compare different approaches to the decision-making problem. By setting $\alpha = 1$ we obtain a *future un-aware technique* where only the current state and the cost between source and target configuration are considered. On the contrary, by setting a value of α lower than 1, we obtain a *future-aware technique*. In this case we exploit w to consider till one step ahead, till two steps ahead, and so on. We evaluate the fitness of a configuration with respect to future states by considering a variable number of steps ahead in the future. If we consider one step ahead ($w = 1$) we evaluate the sum of the data-requirement distances between the target configuration and each next state weighted with the probability of moving from the current state to each next state:

$$D_{Future}(1, T) = \sum_{i=1}^{t} p(S_{curr}, S_i) \cdot D_{Miss}(T, S_i) \tag{5}$$

If we consider two steps ahead ($w = 2$) we augment the previous sum with the relevance for states that are two steps ahead:

$$D_{Future}(2, T) = D_{Future}(1, T) + \sum_{i=1}^{t} \sum_{j=1}^{t} p(S_{curr}, S_i) \cdot p(S_i, S_j) \cdot D_{Miss}(T, S_j) \tag{6}$$

We have also defined a technique to consider an increasing number of states by evaluating the fitness of each T as the sum of its distances to each state S_i weighted according to the steady-state probability vector r:

$$D_{Future}(fixpoint, T) = \sum_{i=1}^{t} r_i \cdot D_{Miss}(T, S_i) \tag{7}$$

Example. We suppose that the doctor is at state *Orthopedy Visits* (Fig. 1) since he is performing check-up visits at the Orthopedy department of the hospital. Upon task variation towards *Hospital Management* we have to reconfigure data to include features required in the new state, i.e., *Doctor Dashboard* and *Hospital Dashboard*. Since the space for data is limited, we have to discard almost all the features that are not anymore required at the new state in order to give room for the data required by the two new features. Among the admissible configurations that contain the new two features we choose the one that minimizes stability considering current and future context changes. Indeed, by looking at future tasks we discover that with high probability (0.6) feature *Check-up* will be required again by the task *External Visits*, thus we maintain it by choosing among the admissible configurations one that contains features *Doctor Dashboard*, *Hospital Dashboard* and *Check-up*. Thus, we improve stability of data by keeping a feature that is likely to be required by future tasks.

4 Validation

We have implemented a simulator of the theoretical framework with the aim of measuring the impact of future-aware and future un-aware approaches on the stability of the system. We consider as input to the simulator two different large conceptual schema: *OsCommerce* conceptual schema which supports the management of an e-commerce web store[1], and *Oscar* conceptual schema which supports the management of heterogeneous care processes within a hospital[2]. *OsCommerce* conceptual schema, which contains 330 entity types and 813 relationships, is available at http://www.info.fundp.ac.be/~mmo/osCommerce.use through the UML-based tool USE [6]. *Oscar* conceptual schema which contains 455 entity types and 267 relationships, is available at http://www.info.fundp.ac.be/~mmo/Oscar.lun through the data-modeling tool DB-MAIN[3]. Starting from the above schemas we have considered a set of different experiments with the following characteristics. We have generated 12 features by assigning to each of them 12 different entity types. Then we have created different automata by randomly selecting 4 features for each state and a distribution of random probabilities each one between 0.1 and 0.3. For each automaton we have experimented a set of 100 paths each one with 1000 hops representing variations to the current task state. For each path we have measured its stability and we have computed an average stability value among all paths. We have repeated the same experiment with different combinations of values for α and w to compare future-aware and future un-aware approaches.

We have obtained different stability values based on the nature of the input automaton, depending on its sharing index sh and its memory occupancy index mo. Figure 2 shows the stability measure obtained according to six different automata which are good representative over the set of experiments we carried out. These automata have an average of either 33 % ($sh = 0.33$) or 45 % ($sh = 0.45$) of shared elements between states and either 90 % ($mo = 0.90$) or 70 % ($mo = 0.70$) or 40 % ($mo = 0.40$) of memory required at each state. The stability curves refer to the *future un-aware* ($\alpha = 1$) approach and to future-aware approaches, i.e., $1-step\ ahead$ ($w = 1$), $2-step\ ahead$ ($w = 2$) and *fixpoint*. If the memory required at each single state is almost equal to the memory available ($mo = 0.9$), it follows that st is approximately equal to 1 for both future-aware and future un-aware approaches. In this case, each time a state requires

---

[1] OsCommerce technical guide, http://guifre.lsi.upc.edu/OSCommerce.pdf.
[2] Oscar official website, http://www.new.oscarmanual.org/.
[3] DB-MAIN official website, http://www.db-main.be.

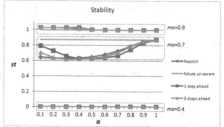

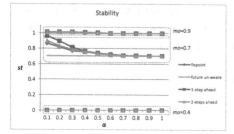

Fig. 2. *Stability* of future un-aware and future-aware ($w = 1$, $w = 2$, $w = fixpoint$) techniques depending on utility objective weights α with 33 % and 45 % of sharing and 90 %, 70 % and 40 % of memory occupancy.

database elements that were not required at the previous state it is necessary to perform the corresponding operations to change the schema. This behavior holds independently to the percentage of shared elements among states. If the memory occupancy among states is equal to 70 % ($mo = 0.7$), we obtain different results depending on the sharing index. First, with $sh = 33$ the best stability is obtained by applying the *future un-aware* technique; in particular, while after $\alpha \geq 0.6$ we have similar stability values, with $\alpha \leq 0.6$ future-aware approaches produce higher values for st, meaning that on average given the same paths of task variations, they required higher database reconfiguration costs. This occurs because the gain of loading features that will be required in future states is less than the gain obtained by choosing the less costly reconfiguration. Second, results gained with $sh = 45$ show that future-aware approaches produce better stability than future un-aware ones; in particular with $\alpha \geq 0.6$ already look-ing one-step ahead we get on average the lowest database reconfiguration costs given the same paths of task variations. Finally, the stability curves with 40 % of memory occupancy ($mo = 0.4$) show that there is space for keeping a big set of features which is enough to satisfy almost each future task. Even though future un-aware approaches will load this set of features gradually (as needed), while future-aware approaches load them in advance (before they are needed), both approaches produce a stability close to 0 meaning that on average almost no reconfigurations to the schema are performed.

As we observed in the three different cases of memory occupancy, we claim that if the required memory at each different state is too near ($mo = 0.9$) or too far ($mo = 0.4$) from the total capacity, it is not convenient to apply a future-aware approach because the same level of stability can be already obtained with a simple future un-aware approach. In both cases, the level of sharing elements of the automata does not affect the level of stability. Conversely, if the memory required at each state is far from both the maximum and the minimum capacity (e.g., $mo = 0.7$) it may be convenient to adopt a future-aware approach. In particular, we observed that adopting future-aware techniques is convenient if states share a high number of elements, as it can be evaluated with our sh

index. Furthermore, these approaches are particularly suitable in case of unstable contexts with frequent and intensive variations from one task to another.

5   Related Work

Task based models are receiving an increasing attention in supporting the adaptivity of systems with the aim of providing better performance to the reconfiguration process [18]. Task models are not fixed during the whole lifecycle process but they may change as a consequence of context variations [16] or user preferences variations [10,19]. Different approaches provide adaptivity to data based on context or user preferences variations. In [2] the authors propose a methodology to extract and to merge portions of the relational and logical schema based on a hierarchical context model. In [5] the authors propose an approach to select the most suitable portion of the relational database based on context-dependent user preferences. In [20] the authors define a filtering technique for extracting the excerpt of the conceptual schema based on a set of entity types that are required in a certain context. All these approaches to database adaptivity [2,5,20] provide the subset of the database based on a certain input context. Nevertheless continuous reconfigurations of the database are not supported, i.e., a certain excerpt of the database is produced based on context and kept for all the system lifetime. Applications for ubiquitous environment need continuous self-adaptations while taking into account device capacity limits and multi-objective criteria (costs and performance) in choosing the best possible reconfiguration [15]. Moreover, in order to achieve reconfigurations of data resilient to changes it is important to consider future context variations. This problem has been addressed in the literature of self-adaptive systems, e.g., in [4] predictive availability of context resources are exploited to achieve system adaptations, while in [13] adaptations are achieved based on a probabilistic user preferences model. Differently from these approaches, we provide adaptivity to data and we achieve reconfigurations of the current database that are resilient to future probable changes of information requirements as annotated in a predictive task model.

6   Conclusion and Future Work

We presented a framework to support continuous reconfigurations of data-intensive systems in resource-constraint environments. We formalized a decision-making problem to select the best possible reconfiguration of data according to a predictive task model expressing future probable variations of data accesses. Results showed that it makes sense to consider a predictive task model for improving stability of the reconfiguration process and they showed under which conditions of the task model it is convenient to adopt either a future-aware or a future un-aware approach. As for future work, we will implement the reconfiguration process by adopting the DB-MAIN tool for creating sub-schemas of the global schema and a relational DBMS for propagating these variations to actual data. We will adopt higher level of granularity for adapting the schema by considering variations of attributes beyond concepts and relationships. Furthermore, we will introduce further variability dimensions to the reconfiguration process such as the addition of un-anticipated features with data, the addition of new states and the variation to the probabilities of the task model.

Acknowledgment. This work has been partially supported by first author's FSR Incoming Post-doctoral Fellowship of the *Académie universitaire 'Louvain'*, co-funded by the Marie Curie Actions of the European Commission.

References

1. Bolchini, C., Curino, C., Orsi, G., Quintarelli, E., Rossato, R., Schreiber, F.A., Tanca, L.: And what can context do for data? ACM **52**(11), 136–140 (2009)
2. Bolchini, C., Quintarelli, E., Tanca, L.: Carve: context-aware automatic view definition over relational databases. IS **38**(1), 45–67 (2012)
3. Cheng, B.H.C., de Lemos, R., Giese, H., Inverardi, P., Magee, J. (eds.): SEFSAS 2009. LNCS, vol. 5525. Springer, Heidelberg (2009)
4. Cheng, S.-W., Poladian, V.V., Garlan, D., Schmerl, B.: Improving architecture-based self-adaptation through resource prediction. In: Cheng, B.H.C., de Lemos, R., Giese, H., Inverardi, P., Magee, J. (eds.) SEFSAS 2009. LNCS, vol. 5525, pp. 71–88. Springer, Heidelberg (2009)
5. Ciaccia, P., Torlone, R.: Modeling the propagation of user preferences. In: Jeusfeld, M., Delcambre, L., Ling, T.-W. (eds.) ER 2011. LNCS, vol. 6998, pp. 304–317. Springer, Heidelberg (2011)
6. Gogolla, M., Büttner, F., Richters, M.: Use: a UML-based specification environment for validating UML and OCL. SCP **69**(1–3), 27–34 (2007)
7. Inverardi, P., Mori, M.: A software lifecycle process to support consistent evolutions. In: de Lemos, R., Giese, H., Müller, H.A., Shaw, M. (eds.) Self-Adaptive Systems. LNCS, vol. 7475, pp. 239–264. Springer, Heidelberg (2013)
8. Karsai, G., Lédeczi, A., Sztipanovits, J., Péceli, G., Simon, G., Kovácsházy, T.: An approach to self-adaptive software based on supervisory control. In: Laddaga, R., Shrobe, H.E., Robertson, P. (eds.) IWSAS 2001. LNCS, vol. 2614, pp. 24–38. Springer, Heidelberg (2003)
9. Martinenghi, D., Torlone, R.: A logical approach to context-aware databases. In: D'Atri, A., De Marco, M., Braccini, A.M., Cabiddu, F. (eds.) Management of the Interconnected World, pp. 211–219. Physica-Verlag HD, Heidelberg (2010)
10. Miele, A., Quintarelli, E., Tanca, L.: A methodology for preference-based personalization of contextual data. In: EDBT, pp. 287–298 (2009)
11. Mori, M., Cleve, A.: Feature-based adaptation of database schemas. In: Machado, R.J., Maciel, R.S.P., Rubin, J., Botterweck, G. (eds.) MOMPES 2012. LNCS, vol. 7706, pp. 85–105. Springer, Heidelberg (2013)
12. Mori, M., Cleve, A.: Towards highly adaptive data-intensive systems: a research agenda. In: Franch, X., Soffer, P. (eds.) CAiSE 2013 Workshops. LNBIP, vol. 148, pp. 386–401. Springer, Heidelberg (2013)
13. Mori, M., Li, F., Dorn, C., Inverardi, P., Dustdar, S.: Leveraging state-based user preferences in context-aware reconfigurations for self-adaptive systems. In: Barthe, G., Pardo, A., Schneider, G. (eds.) SEFM 2011. LNCS, vol. 7041, pp. 286–301. Springer, Heidelberg (2011)

14. Nzekwa, R., Rouvoy, R., Seinturier, L.: A flexible context stabilization approach for self-adaptive application. In: PerCom, pp. 7–12 (2010)
15. Parra, C., Romero, D., Mosser, S., Rouvoy, R., Duchien, L., Seinturier, L.: Using constraint-based optimization and variability to support continuous self-adaptation. In: SAC, pp. 486–491 (2012)
16. Quintarelli, E., Rabosio, E., Tanca, L.: Context schema evolution in context-aware data management. In: Jeusfeld, M., Delcambre, L., Ling, T.-W. (eds.) ER 2011. LNCS, vol. 6998, pp. 290–303. Springer, Heidelberg (2011)
17. Salehie, M., Tahvildari, L.: Self-adaptive software: landscape and research challenges. TAAS **4**(2), 1–42 (2009)
18. Sousa, J.P., Poladian, V., Garlan, D., Schmerl, B., Shaw, M.: Task-based adaptation for ubiquitous computing. Trans. Sys. Man Cyber (C) **36**(3), 328–340 (2006)
19. Sykes, D., Heaven, W., Magee, J., Kramer, J.: Exploiting non-functional preferences in architectural adaptation for self-managed systems. In: SAC, pp. 431–438 (2010)
20. Villegas, A., Olivé, A.: A method for filtering large conceptual schemas. In: Parsons, J., Saeki, M., Shoval, P., Woo, C., Wand, Y. (eds.) ER 2010. LNCS, vol. 6412, pp. 247–260. Springer, Heidelberg (2010)

A Comprehensive View of Ubiquitous Learning Context Usage in Context-Aware Learning System

Raoudha Souabni[1(✉)], Ines Bayoudh Saadi[1], Kinshuk[2],
and Henda Ben Ghezala[1]

[1] RIADI Research Laboratory - ENSI, Manouba University, Manouba, Tunisia
souabni_raoudha@yahoo.fr,
{ines.bayoudh,henda.benghezala}@ensi.rnu.tn
[2] School of Computing and Information Systems, Athabasca University,
Athabasca, Canada
kinshuk@ieee.org

Abstract. Research related to context-aware u-learning system has prolifer-ated during last decades. Systems identified in literature are developed in ad-hoc manner to resolve a specific problem in a given context; however, u-learning systems developers need to have a clear and a general view of how their intended systems make use of the ubiquitous context. The paper details a general descriptive view of context usage within learning systems through three different view-points inspired from Dowson's work [1]. Each view is capturing a particular aspect of context handling. Then a set of facets is associated to each given aspect in order to study, understand and appropriately describe it. This work would be useful for context-aware u-learning system developers in order to have a clear understanding of the context usage in such systems and to underline the requirements of the u-learning environment to respond. This research is also aimed to establish a structured baseline to help in comparing and evaluating context-aware u-learning systems according to the descriptive system views.

Keywords: Context-awareness · Ubiquitous learning · Context modeling · Context analyzing and management · Context execution

1 Introduction

The quality of distance learning is strongly linked to its degree of adaptation to the learning context [2]. This has led to the evolution of distance learning environments into context-aware environments, particularly into ubiquitous ones [3], with particular focus on learning context. These environments aim to provide the necessary means to take into account the context and assist learners in following a learning situation personalized to their contexts. However, current context-aware u-learning applications are often developed in ad-hoc manner to resolve a specific problem in a given context. Such ad-hoc approaches did not dictate general requirements of ubiquitous context usage; subsequently developed applications rarely fulfill environmental requirements.

P.C. Vinh et al. (Eds.): ICCASA 2013, LNICST 128, pp. 316–326, 2014.
DOI: 10.1007/978-3-319-05939-6_31, © Springer International Publishing Switzerland 2014

Hence, u-learning system developers need to have a clear view and understanding of the different aspects of u-learning context usage.

The context usage world in u-learning environments deals with the locations where the context is established and handled. Three interactive domains are inspired in this research from Dowson's work [1] - to describe processes in process centered software engineering environment - dealing with the three aspects of the context usage: *context modeling, context analyzing and managing,* and *context execution domain.*

The *context modeling domain* contains the model of the ubiquitous learning context and describes how the context is represented. A context model defines and describes the context information and associated relationships.

The *context analyzing and managing domain* enables following functionality:

- *Building the ubiquitous learning context*: In order to build the current context instance, the *context analyzing and managing domain* has to (1) capture the context information; and, (2) instantiate the context model as shown in Fig. 1.
- *Analyzing the context information*: The *context analyzing and managing domain* has to interpret low-level sensor information, detect the imperfection of the detected information, and detect the evolution of the learner context.
- *Managing the context*: The management of the context consists of the aggregation of new context information, the summarization of the history information, the resolution of the detected imperfection, the adaptation of the learning system and the context model, and, the evolving of the context model.

The *context execution domain* concerns the learning environment, the actors and their activities conducted during the learning process.

The interactions between described domains (numerated in Fig. 1) are as follows:

- **Context information traces and feedback**: The *context analyzing and managing domain* uses traces and feedback captured from the *context execution domain*. When feedback is negative, the system has to adapt the learning situation to meet the learner needs and preferences (arrow 3 in Fig. 1). Concerning the context information traces, an update or an evolution could be detected. In case of update detection, the context instance is updated and adaptation techniques are applied to

Fig. 1. Ubiquitous learning context usage world

guide the learning situation (arrow 3 in Fig. 1). In case of context evolution detection, the model has to be improved (arrow 4 in Fig. 1).

- **Context model instantiation**: Having detected context information, the *context analyzing and managing domain* has to create the context instance via the instantiation of the context model.
- **Adaptation**: The *context analyzing and managing domain* applies adaptation techniques in order to adapt the learning situation to the learning context information traces and feedback.
- **Context model evolution**: When capturing unanticipated context information from traces, the *context analyzing and managing domain* has to improve the context model so that it could model the newly detected information.

In this paper, a description of the three aspects of context usage is given via three viewpoints associated to the previously mentioned domains. Each view is described with a set of facets; each facet is illustrated with a set of sub-facets or valued attributes suitable to characterize a given aspect of context handling. Attribute values are defined within a domain. The later could be a predefined type such as *Integer*, *Boolean* and so forth, an enumerated type noted as *Enum{a, b, c}* (the attribute takes its values in the list *{a, b, c}*), or a structured type designated by *Set*.

Sections 2, 3 and 4 present faceted descriptions of each domain according to their associated views. Section 5 illustrates a comparative analysis documenting the instantiation of views' facets to evaluate a list of systems and to identify new research issues. Finally, Sect. 6 concludes the paper.

2 The context Modeling View

The representation of learning context is studied in terms of the following points:

- Q_a: What should be represented?
- Q_b: What are the properties of what is represented?
- Q_c: To what extent the context model is faithful to the real world?

The *coverage* facet deals with the object to be represented (Q_a). The *description* facet treats the properties of what is represented (Q_b). The *faithfulness of the context model* facet concerns with the capacity of the context model to be able to model the real learning context (Q_c).

2.1 Coverage Facet

This facet answers the question *"What should be represented?"* It concerns with the contents of the ubiquitous learning context to be modeled. The real context of learning is composed of a set of information and semantic relationships among those information pieces. Thus, this facet is characterized by the attribute *coverage* as follows:

Coverage: Set (Enum {information, relationship})

2.2 Description Facet

The *description* facet treats the properties of what is represented. It is described via its two sub-facets: the *context information properties* facet and the *relationships properties* facet. Table 1 summarizes the content of the current facet.

2.3 Faithfulness of the Context Model Facet

This facet describes the extent to which the established model describes faithfully the real world. The attribute *faithfulness degree* indicates whether the model is faithful, moderately faithful or unfaithful to the learner's real context. So this attribute takes on values from the enumerated domain {*faithful, moderately faithful, unfaithful*}.

Faithfulness degree: Enum{faithful, moderately faithful, unfaithful}

3 Context Analyzing and Managing View

The current view is studied in terms of the following three questions:

- Q_a: How to construct the u-learning context?
- Q_b: How to analyze it?
- Q_c: How to manage the analyzed context?

The *construction* facet indicates the construction technique used for building the current context instance (Q_a). The *analyzing* facet describes how the *analyzing and managing domain* analyzes detected learning context information (Q_b) in order to generate more abstract context information and to detect the imperfection of the captured information. Finally, the *managing* facet illustrates used techniques to manage information (Q_c). It consists of the reuse of the history information, the resolution of the detected imperfection, the adaptation of the learning system and the context model, the recommendation of useful materials and the evolution of the context model based on the detection of the evolution of the learner context.

3.1 Construction Facet

Using the context information traces detected by the *execution domain* and the instantiation of the context model built by the *modeling domain*, the *analyzing and managing domain* has to construct the current learning context. The *construction* facet indicates whether the context instance is built centrally or in a distributed way [8].

Construction technique: Enum{central, distributed}

Table 1. Summary of the description facet

Context information properties facet

Sub-facet	Description	Sub-facet details
Heterogeneity	Context information sources are classified in three groups: physical sensors, virtual sensors and logical sensors [4]. Context information can be categorized into three classes: sensed, profiled and derived.	- Information source: Set (Enum {physical, virtual, logical }) - Information type: Set (Enum {sensed, profiled, derived})
Mobility	Changing context information is retrieved from local and remote providers. In [5] three types of update are identified in order to guarantee correct and updated information: periodical update, update on change and update on request.	- Provider: Set (Enum {local, remote}) - Update type: Set(Enum{periodical update, update on change, update on request})
Quality	Due to its dynamic and heterogeneous nature, the information may be of varied quality. To model the quality of data, following QoC (Quality of Context) parameters will be used as proposed by [7]: up-to-dateness, trustworthiness, completeness and significance.	- QoC parameter: Set(Enum {up-to-dateness, trustworthiness, completeness, significance})
Subjectivity	Subjectivity is a main characteristic of context [6]. Learning context entity can be perceived from different viewpoints (teachers, learners and/or systems) and consequently have different quantitative or qualitative subjective ratings.	- Multi viewpoint: Boolean - Subjectivity_viewpoint: Set(Enum {system, learner, teacher}) - Subjective_rate_type: Set(Enum{quantitative, qualitative})
History	Recorded information pieces may be useful for predicting learner behavior, detecting learning style, and inferring other information. The provision of a complete history of the dynamic learning context is a difficult issue and may in fact not be feasible. Therefore, summarization function may need to be applied.	- History_recording: Boolean - Recorded_information: Set (Object) - History_record_format: Enum {Set (Object), function}
Abstraction	U-learning systems are able to treat low-level sensor information pieces, to use interpreted ones or to combine them for more significant data (e.g. learning situation).	- Abstraction_level: Set(Enum {low-level, interpreted, aggregated })
Granularity	Context information elements are of different levels of detail qualitatively measured as low, medium or high. Information with high granularity may lead to a more appropriate adaptation decision.	- Granularity_level: Enum {low, medium, high}

Relationships properties facet

Description		Facet details
It is necessary to represent not only the context information values but also the context information relationships. The main types of semantic relations that are considered in this work are: association, dependency, hierarchy, composition, aggregation and instantiation. Besides to that, constraints may be indicated on modeled relationships.		- Relation type: Set (Enum {association, dependency, hierarchy, composition, aggregation, instantiation}) - Constraints on relation: Boolean

3.2   Analyzing Facet

The *analyzing* facet illustrates the used techniques by the *analyzing and managing domain* to analyze context information. Associated sub-facets are given in Table 2.

3.3   Managing Facet

The *managing* facet illustrates the used techniques by the *analyzing and managing domain* to manage context information. Associated sub-facets are given in Table 3.

4   Context Execution View

The exploitation of the current context information and users' feedback is used to guide the system's operation and to adapt and evolve the context model. The current view has to be described with reference to the *context change* facet and *feedback* facet responding respectively to the following two questions.

Table 2. Summary of the analyzing facet

Sub-facet	Description	Sub-facet details
Information processing	Low-level sensor information is processed in order to generate more abstract information using processing techniques such as interpretation and aggregation.	- Processing technique: Set (Enum {interpretation, aggregation})
Imperfection detection	The dynamic and heterogeneous collected information may be imperfect. The imperfection detection techniques are based on QoC evaluation policies. In [7], five types of QoC evaluation policies are detailed: up-to-datedness, trustworthiness, completeness, significance and combinations based policy. The imperfection detection could occur at different levels [7]. It may occur when making the selection of low level context information among different sensors, processing, and applying the context information.. The detected imperfection may be of different types: incorrect, inconsistent, incomplete or redundant. The imperfection detection strategy could be of two types: static (anticipated at the design time) or dynamic (occurs at the runtime).	- Detection technique: Set(Enum{up-to-datedness based, trustworthiness based, completeness based, significance based, QoC combinations}) - Detection level: Set (Enum{context acquisition, context processing, context appliance} - Imperfection type: Set (Enum {incorrect, inconsistent, incomplete, redundant}) - Detection strategy: Set (Enum {Static, Dynamic})

Table 3. Summary of the managing facet

Sub-facet	Description	Sub-facet details
History reuse	U-learning systems need to deal with history reuse in order to predict future context values. The reused objects need to be considered to evaluate the extent to which the system takes into account the reuse of saved history in the adaptation process.	-History reuse: Boolean -Reused objects: Set(Object)
Imperfection resolution	U-learning systems need to use resolution techniques to avoid the use of imperfect data. Resolution policies have been defined, based on user preferences [7], QoC parameters [7], discarding the entire conflicting context, the last received or the bad context information [10]. Resolution could occur at the design time [9] or at the execution time [11]. Given that the system has to cope with the dynamic context, runtime resolution has to be applied. U-learning systems may allow user intervention to resolve conflict situations.	-Resolution technique: Enum{user preferences based, QoC parameters based, drop-latest, drop-all, drop-bad} -Resolution time: Enum{design time, execution time} -User intervention: Boolean
System adaptation	Context-aware learning applications use context data to evaluate whether there is a change in the learner's situation and whether any adaptation to that change is necessary. This amounts to adapting certain context information piece(s) (adapted object(s)) based on other one(s) (adaptation factor(s)). Adaptation may occur at three levels: presentation, content and behavior level. Systems can be classified into adaptable (static adaptation) and adaptive (dynamic adaptation) systems. They may allow mixing automatic and static adaptation.	-Adaptation factor: Set(context object) -Adaptation level: Set (Enum{presentation, content, behavior}) -Adapted objects: Set (context object) -Adaptation type: Enum{adaptativity, adaptability, mixed}
Recommendation	U-learning systems could recommend different objects that may possibly meet the learner's needs. Recommended objects may be internally designed by the system tutor, or externally collected and integrated into the system. In literature, four recommendation techniques have been identified [12]: collaborative, content-based, and knowledge-based techniques. Recent research works have proposed hybrid ones.	-Recommended material: Set(object) -Material type: Enum {internal, external} -Recommendation technique: Enum {collaborative, content-based, knowledge-based, hybrid}
Context model adaptation	U-learning systems need to dynamically adapt the context model in order to represent only the useful runtime context data and relation to reduce the monitoring overhead [13].	-Runtime model adaptation: Boolean
Context model evolving	The system has to evolve the context model in order to cope with unanticipated changes [13]. The model could be evolved after interrupting the system execution. However, the more efficient the learning systems are, the better they have to perform in a highly dynamic environment, and therefore have to improve dynamically the context model.	-Model evolving: Boolean -Evolving type: Enum{Dynamic, Static}

- Q_a: What kind of change occurs while execution?
- Q_b: What are the learners' feedbacks?

4.1   Context Change Detection Facet

When detecting a change in context information, the *context execution domain* returns the detected information to the *context analyzing and management domain* for exploitation. The detection of new information is due to the dynamic nature of the environments. In such case, the system has to cope with the unanticipated context changes that were not considered at the design time by evolving the context model. However, when detecting updates, only the context instance is modified.

Context change type: Set (Enum {new information, updated information})

4.2   Feedback Detection Facet

Feedback is considered to be of great importance knowing that it helps in adapting the learning system to the learner performance. Learning systems could allow qualitative and/or quantitative feedback for assessing the relevance of learning and may allow the learner to express him/herself through comments and suggestions [14].

Feedback detection: Boolean

Feedback type: Set (Enum {quantitative, qualitative, comment, suggestion})

5   Review of 6 U-Learning Systems

In this section, the use of the context usage world is illustrated for u-learning systems via the evaluation of six systems: PERKAM [14], TSUL environment [15], JAMI-OLAS 3.0 [16], JAPELAS [17], LOCH system [18] and TANGO system [19]. The instantiation of the description of the context usage world within listed systems (Table 4) allows their evaluation by bringing out their main features and limits.

Majority of developed systems does not cover modeling the relationships between context information pieces. PERKAM and TSUL environment take into consideration the modeling of only associations and/or aggregations. Dependency relationships are ignored by all systems. Subsequently the used context model by each system is moderately faithful to the real world. JAPELAS, LOCH and TANGO do not detect any type of context change from the *execution domain* and subsequently do not take into consideration neither update types when modeling the context nor imperfection detection and resolution when treating the learning context. Studied systems, expect TSUL environment, use only interpreted information pieces and/or low-level sensor ones. JAMIOLAS and LOCH didn't deal with system adaptation. The remaining four systems use very few context information pieces as adaptation factors and tend to adapt only one or two contextual elements. The adaptation of the presentation and

Table 4. Systems' evaluation according to the context usage world

Modeling view

					PERKAM	TSUL	JAMIOLAS	JAPELAS	LOCH	TANGO
Coverage	Coverage				Information Relationship	Information Relationship	Information	Information	Information	Information
Description	Context information properties	Heterogeneity	Information source		Physical Virtual	Physical Virtual	Virtual	Physical Virtual	Physical Virtual	Physical Virtual
			Information type		Sensed Profiled Derived	Sensed Profiled Derived	Sensed Profiled	Sensed Profiled Derived	Sensed Profiled	Sensed Profiled Derived
		Mobility	Provider		Local	Local	Local Remote	Local	Local Remote	Local
			Update type		Periodical update Update on change	Periodical update	Periodical update	Periodical update	-	-
		Quality	QoC parameter		Up-to-datedness	Up-to-datedness	-		-	
		Subjectivity	Multi viewpoint		true	False	true	true	False	False
			Subjectivity viewpoint		System Learner	Learner	Teacher System	System Learner	Learner System Teacher	System Learner
			Subjective rate type		Quantitative Qualitative	Qualitative	Qualitative	Qualitative	Qualitative	Qualitative
		History	History recording		true	True	False	true	true	true
			Record format		Set (Object)	Set (Object)	-	Set (Object)	Set (Object)	Set (Object)
			Recorded information		Learner's experience	Learner's capability		Learner conversation	Learner's location Task activities	Learner's experience
		Abstraction	Abstraction level		Low-level Interpreted	Low-level Interpreted Aggregated	Low-level	Low-level	Low-level	Low-level Interpreted
		Granularity	Granularity level		Low	High	Low	Low	Low	Low
	Relationship properties	Relation type			Association	Association Aggregation	-	-	-	-
		Constraints on relation			False	False	False	False	False	False
Faithfulness of the CM	Faithfulness degree				Moderately faithful	Moderately faithful	Moderately faithful	Moderately faithful	Moderately faithful	Moderately faithful

Analyzing and managing view

				PERKAM	TSUL	JAMIOLAS	JAPELAS	LOCH	TANGO
Construction	Construction technique			Central	Central	Central	Central	Central	Central
Analyzing	Information processing	Processing technique		Interpretation	Interpretation Aggregation	-	Interpretation	-	-
	Imperfection detection	Detection technique		Up-to-datedness based	Up-to-datedness based	-	-	-	-
		Detection level		Acquisition	Acquisition	-	-	-	-
		Imperfection type		Incorrect	Incorrect	-	-	-	-
		Detection strategy		Dynamic	Dynamic	-	-	-	-
Managing	History reuse	History reuse		true	true	False	true		true
		Reused objects		Learner's experience	Learner's capability	-	Learner conversation	Learner's location Task activities	Learner's experience
	Imperfection resolution	Resolution technique		QoC parameters based	QoC parameters based	-	-	-	-
		Resolution time		Execution time	Execution time	-	-	-	-
		User intervention		False	False	-	-	-	-
	System adaptation	Adaptation factor		Learner's profile Learner's location Learner's social network	Learner's capability	-	Hyponymy Social distance Situation's formality	-	Learner's comprehensive level Learner's location
		Adaptation level		Content	Content	-	Content	-	Content
		Adapted objects		Peer helper Educational material	Learning task Peer assistant	-	Japeneese polite expression	-	Expression
		Adaptation type		Adaptability	Adaptability	-	Adaptability	-	Adaptability
	Recommendation	Recommended material		Peer helper Educational material	Learning task Peer assistant	-	Japeneese polite expression	-	-
		Material type		External	External	-	Internal	-	-
		Recommendation technique		Knowledge-based	Knowledge-based	-	Knowledge-based	-	-
Model adaptation	Runtime adaptation			False	False	False	False	False	False
Context model evolving	Model evolving			False	False	False	False	False	False
	Evolving type			-	-	-	-	-	-

Execution view

		PERKAM	TSUL	JAMIOLAS	JAPELAS	LOCH	TANGO
Context change detection	Context change type	Updated information	Updated information	Updated information	-	-	-
Feedback detection	Feedback detection	true	False	False	False	False	False
	Feedback type	Quantitative-Qualitative Comment -Suggestion					

system behavior are not taken into consideration. None of evaluated systems evokes runtime model adaptation to reduce monitoring overhead. None of the systems evokes the detection of new context information from the *execution domain* and thus none of the systems evokes the evolution of the context model.

Subsequently, main research issues could be summarized as follows:

- U-learning systems need to model a very complex and dynamic learning situation including context information pieces and relationships.
- In order to serve learners with personalized learning, systems need to enable learning in a very complex situation combining online and offline information pieces and relationships. Hence, adaptation factors should cover the combination of situation entities, and adaptation should take into consideration adaptation of the content, the presentation and the system behavior.
- Context model covers very large context information pieces and relationships which are not all needed based on the runtime detected situation. Hence, runtime model adaptation could be applied to reduce monitoring overhead.
- A main issue for u-learning systems is to cope with the runtime learning context, especially with unforeseen changes that could occur during system execution.

6   Conclusion

In this paper, a descriptive view of the context usage in context-aware u-learning systems is detailed. A comparative analysis within this description is established for a non exhaustive list of u-learning systems in order to highlight their strengths and limitations and to demonstrate the implications of this research.

The suggested description was build to respond to the following purposes: to establish a structured baseline from which the three aspects of context usage can be easily identified within every studied u-learning system, to identify its drawbacks and to analyze the possibility to propose new research issues. In this paper, the focus was maintained on how the u-learning context should be used; however, there is still no consensus on *what is learning context, how it should be represented*, and *how its representation should be developed*. Hence, next work will focus on the establishment of a common evaluating framework for u-learning systems along four complementary worlds (including the usage world) capturing the four mentioned aspects of context.

Acknowledgment. The authors acknowledge the support of NSERC, iCORE, Xerox, and the research-related gift funding by Mr. A. Markin.

References

1. Dowson, M.: Software process themes and issues. In: IEEE 2nd International Conference on the Software Process, pp. 54–62. IEEE Computer Society (1993)
2. Liu, H.I., Yang, M.N.: QoI guaranteed adaptation and personalization in e-learning systems. IEEE Trans. Edu. **48**(4), 676–687 (2005)

3. Ogata, H., Akamatsu, R., Yano, Y.: Computer supported ubiquitous learning environment for vocabulary learning using rfid tags. In: Workshop on Technology Enhanced Learning, pp. 121–130. Springer ,US (2005)
4. Baldauf, M., Dustdar, S., Rosenberg, F.: A survey on context-aware systems. Int. J. Ad Hoc Ubiquitous Comput. **2**(4), 263–277 (2007)
5. Ismail, I.: Contextual data description and management in ubiquitous environments. In: 1st Taibah University of International Conference on Computing and Information Technology, pp. 427–432 (2012)
6. Pascoe, J.: Adding generic contextual capabilities to wearable computers. In: 2nd International Symposium on Wearable Computers, pp. 92–99. IEEE Computer Society (1998)
7. Manzoor, A., Truong, H.-L., Dustdar, S.: Using quality of context to resolve conflicts in context-aware systems. In: Rothermel, K., Fritsch, D., Blochinger, W., Dürr, F. (eds.) QuaCon 2009. LNCS, vol. 5786, pp. 144–155. Springer, Heidelberg (2009)
8. Bolchini, C., Curino, C.A., Quintarelli, E., Schreiber, F.A., Tanca, L.: A data-oriented survey of context models. SIGMOD Rec. **36**(4), 19–26 (2007)
9. Park, I., Lee, D., Hyun, S. J.: A dynamic context-conflict management scheme for group-aware ubiquitous computing environments. In: 29th Annual International Computer Software and Applications Conference, pp. 359–364. IEEE Computer Society (2005)
10. Xu, C., Cheung, S. C., Chan, W. K., Ye, C.: Heuristics-based strategies for resolving context inconsistencies in pervasive computing applications. In: 28th International Conference on Distributed Computing Systems, pp. 709–717. IEEE Computer Society (2008)
11. Capra, L., Emmerich, W., Mascolo, C.: Carisma: context-aware reflective middleware system for mobile application. IEEE Trans. Softw. Eng. **29**(10), 929–945 (2003)
12. Adomavicius, G., Tuzhilin, A.: Towards the next generation of recommender systems: a survey of the state-of-the-art and possible extensions. IEEE Trans. Knowl. Data Eng. **2**(4), 734–749 (2005)
13. Hussein, M., Han, J., Colman, A.: A system-context relationship oriented survey of context-aware adaptive systems. Technical Report, Faculty of Information and Communication Technologies, Swinburne University of Technology, Australia (2010)
14. El-Bishouty, M., Ogata, H., Rahman, S., Yano, Y.: Social knowledge awareness map for computer supported ubiquitous learning environment. J. Educ. Technol. Soc. **13**(4), 27–37 (2010)
15. El-Bishouty, M., Ogata, H., Ayala, G., Yano, Y.: Context-aware support for self-directed ubiquitous-learning. Int. J. Mob. Learn. Organ. **4**(3), 317–331 (2010)
16. Hou, B., Ogata, H., Miyata, M., Li, M., Yano, Y.: Development of web-based japanese mimicry and onomatopoeia learning assistant system with sensor network. In: 6th International Conference on Wireless, Mobile and Ubiquitous Technologies in Education, pp. 117–121 (2010)
17. Yin, C., Ogata, H., Yano, Y.: JAPELAS: supporting Japanese polite expressions learning using PDA(s) towards ubiquitous learning. Int. J. Inf. Syst. Edu. **3**(1), 33–39 (2005)
18. Ogata, H., Hui, G.L., Yin, C.U., Oishi, Y., Yano, Y.: LOCH: supporting Mobile Language Learning Outside Classrooms. Int. J. Mob. Learn. Organ. **2**(3), 271–282 (2008)
19. Ogata, H., Akamatsu, R., Mitsuhara, H., Yano, Y., Matsuura, K., Kanenishi, K.: TANGO: supporting vocabulary learning with RFID tags. In: International Workshop Series on RFID (2004)

Context-Based
Recommendation Systems

Data Mining Assisted Resource Management in Wide WLANs

Thuy Van T. Duong[1]($\boxtimes$), Dinh Que Tran[2], and Cong Hung Tran[2]

[1] Faculty of Information Technology, University of Ton Duc Thang,
No. 19 Nguyen Huu Tho Street, Tan Phong Ward, District 7,
Ho Chi Minh, Vietnam
vanduongthuy@tdt.edu.vn, vanduongthuy@yahoo.com
[2] Faculty of Information Technology, Post and Telecommunication
Institute of Technology, Ho Chi Minh, Vietnam

Abstract. WLANs are currently being considered for use in the context of a larger geographical area such as a city or a campus due to their convenience, cost efficiency, and ease of integration with other networks. Due to support large numbers of portable devices and their dynamic relocation, wide WLANs must face problems of location management and network resource allocation. In order to solve these challenges, future mobility information of all mobile users in the network is required to accurate estimation of network resource demands at future time toward more efficient network resource management. Therefore, mobility prediction has played a crucial role in the resource management of wide WLANs and it has attracted recently a great deal of research interests. However, since most of the current approaches are based on personal movement profile for predicting the next location of mobile users, these techniques may fail to make a prediction for new users or ones with movements on novel paths. In this paper, we propose a prediction model which is based on group mobility behaviors to deal with such the lack of information of individual movement histories. Our proposed prediction approach makes use of clustering techniques in data mining to classify mobility patterns of users into groups. Experiments will be performed to demonstrate that using group mobility behaviors may significantly enhance the accuracy of the mobility prediction.

Keywords: Movement group · Mobility pattern · Mobile user · Prediction · Wireless network

1 Introduction

WLANs may allow users access Internet applications from where they want and still remain connected to the Internet whilst on the move, using smart phones, iPads, iPods, tablets, laptops and other portable devices, they are no longer limited by the length of the cable. Due to their convenience, cost efficiency, and ease of integration with other networks, WLANs are growing fast. WLANs have often deployed to variety of limited coverage areas, such as coffee shops, buildings, etc before. But now, its coverage area is extended across a larger geographical area such as a city or a campus and called wide WLAN. In fact, some cities such as New York and London have started to offer

P.C. Vinh et al. (Eds.): ICCASA 2013, LNICST 128, pp. 329–338, 2014.
DOI: 10.1007/978-3-319-05939-6_32, © Springer International Publishing Switzerland 2014

wide WLANs to enable people access the Internet even outside their normal work environment, for example when they ride the train home. Some colleges and universities have also deployed campus-wide WLANs to open higher-learning environments with many educational facilities and enable both students and faculty use portable communication devices as learning and teaching tools. The portable devices such as IP phones, smartphones, iPads, iPods and tablets are light enough to walk-and-talk, so these users often leave their devices on most of the time for accessing Internet applications, for example Voice over IP (VoIP) or realtime multimedia data transmission, etc. Due to campus-wide WLANs provide wireless availability not only in the classroom but also at every corner of the campus - communal spaces, cafeterias, campus retail outlets, libraries, on-campus living accommodation and also temporary or mobile study areas, these portable device users may still remain connect to the Internet during they moving around the campus. For example, Dartmouth College has about 550 APs providing 11 Mbps 802.11 b coverage to the entire campus of about 190 buildings, including all administrative, academic, and residential buildings, and most athletic facilities [1]. Dartmouth College has about 5,500 students, 4,200 undergraduate students and 1,215 full-time professors. Most of the undergraduate students live on campus and use wireless devices on most of the time. That mean, there are a large numbers of mobile and wireless users active in any given day, about 3,500 users in 2003.

Due to support large numbers of portable devices and their dynamic relocation, wide WLANs must face problems of location management and network resource allocation. In reality, whenever a mobile user moves from one cell to another, called *handover* or *handoff*, the network resources must be reallocated for his device at the new cell to continue the service. The required network resources are not available or not sufficient in the new cell force the network to terminate service to the user. Dropping a service in progress is considered to have a more negative impact from the user's perspective than blocking a newly requested service, thus handoff services are normally assigned higher priority over the new services. This requires future mobility information of all mobile users in the network to accurate estimation of network resource demands at future time. Therefore, mobility prediction has received a great deal of attention of research community [2–10] to provide useful mobility information for reserving resources in such cells where the users are likely to be in toward more efficient network resource management.

Among the proposed approaches, data mining has been widely used for mobility prediction based on the past mobility behaviors of WLAN users. Because mobility history hides useful knowledge patterns that describe typical behavior of mobile users, many approaches [2–4, 9, 10] make use of such mined knowledge patterns, which are represented in the form of mobility rules, to predict future movement of mobile users. Although these current studies are effective in predicting next cells for majority of mobile users, most of them are only based on individual mobility behaviors that cause false prediction for new users or ones with movements on novel paths due to the lack of information on personal movement profile.

Unlike most previous approaches [2–4, 9, 10], which have utilized personal profile to predict the next locations visited by a mobile user, our premise is that applying group mobility behaviors to facilitate the predicting in the case of new users or ones with movements on novel paths. In reality, even though human movement and mobility patterns have a high degree of freedom and variation, they also exhibit mobility behaviors in groups due to geographic, social and friendship constraints [11, 12]. For instance, mobile users in a university campus network can be categorized as students, graduate students, departmental staffs, lecturers and so on. Students often move to classrooms, laboratories, library, etc whereas departmental staffs spend most of the day near the administrative offices. In order to fully exploit the similar movement characteristics, it is crucial to determine the movement groups, where the mobile users belong to the same group have the same mobility behaviors. In other words, the group mobility behavior reflects the fact that mobile users often behave as groups. Discovering such group mobility behaviors is a key issue for predicting future movement of a new user based on the mobility behaviors of members in a group.

In this paper, we propose a four-phase mobility prediction technique which is able to deal with the lack of information on personal profile. We first make use of data mining techniques to discover frequent mobility patterns from histories of all users in the network. The second phase is to cluster discovered mobility patterns into movement groups. The third phase determines which group the user's current path belongs to. And the last makes use of mobility rules derived from that group to predict the next location for the user. The efficacy of the proposed approach is verified on the synthetic dataset and experimental results show that the group mobility behavior may significantly enhance the accuracy of mobility prediction.

The remainder of this paper is constructed as follows. Section 2 describes a typical wide WLAN architecture and the mobility model in this network. In Sect. 3, a novel model of mobility prediction based on the group mobility behavior is investigated and proposed. Section 4 is devoted to describing experiments and results for evaluating the proposed mobility prediction approach. Finally, Sect. 5 draws concluding remarks and further research work.

2 Modeling Mobility in Wide Wireless Local Area Network

In a typical wide WLAN, such as a academic campus WLAN or a city WLAN, the radio coverage region is partitioned into many potentially overlapping cells. Each cell is covered by a wireless access point (AP) which is base station (BS) for the wireless network. APs transmit and receive radio frequencies for wireless devices such as laptops, personal digital assistants (PDAs), iPads, iPods, tablets, IP phones or other smartphones to communicate with. All APs in the same building are connected through a switch, called Access Controller (AC), which is used to control all the APs in the building for performing their jobs. Every building's AC is wired to the campus back-bone network which is managed by some servers [1]. Figure 1 shows a typical wide WLAN architecture.

It is assumed that the radio coverage region is presented by a hexagonal shaped network as in Fig. 2. Each hexagon is a cell which is served by a AP in the communication space. The mobile users can travel around the coverage region. In order to illustrate the mobility model of WLAN users, we use an unweighted directed graph $G = (V, E)$, where the vertex-set V is the set of cells in the coverage region and the

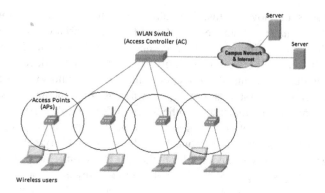

Fig. 1. A typical campus-wide WLAN architecture

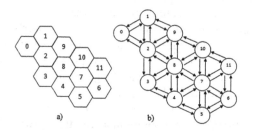

Fig. 2. The coverage region (a) and corresponding graph G (b)

edge-set E represent the adjacence between pairs of cells. These bidirected edges illustrate the fact that WLAN users may move from one cell to another directly and vice versa.

In this paper, we focus on WLAN users who use portable devices such as IP phones, smartphones, iPads, iPods or tablets. This is because that these users leave their devices, which are light enough to walk-and-talk, on most of the time. That means, they show a more mobile characteristic while connected to the network than WLAN users who use laptops or other heavy devices. On the other hand, such portable device users not only connect to the Internet but also use various services such as VoIP and realtime multimedia data transmission, e.g., streaming audio and video. Hence, they may frequently change their associated APs for network access, depending on their locations. Every time a wireless user roams from one AP to another, a syslog message is recorded thereby it is possible to collect sequences of associated APs for each WLAN user. That means, the handoff history of all WLAN users is maintained in the network. The main purpose of this paper is studying WLAN users' handoff history for mobility prediction which has played a crucial role in the resource network management. The following is the formalization for mobility patterns of WLAN users.

Let c be the ID number of the cell to which the mobile user connected at a predefined timestamp t, a point is defined as follows:

Definition 1. *Let C and T be two sets of ID cells and timestamps, respectively. The ordered pairs p = (c, t), in which $c \in C$ and $t \in T$, is called a point. Denote P to be the set of all points $P = C \times T = \{(c, t) \mid c \in C$ and $t \in T\}$.*

Two point $p_i = (c_i, t_i)$ and $p_j = (c_j, t_j)$ are said to be equivalent if and only if $c_i = c_j$ and $t_i = t_j$. Point $p_i = (c_i, t_i)$ is defined to be earlier than point $p_j = (c_j, t_j)$ if and only if $t_i < t_j$, and it is denoted as $(c_i, t_i) < (c_j, t_j)$ or $p_i < p_j$.

Definition 2. *The trajectory of the mobile user is defined as a finite sequence of points $<p_1, p_2, ..., p_k>$ in $C \times T$ space, where $p_j = (c_j, t_j)$ are points for $1 \leq j \leq k$ and ID cells of two consecutive points must be neighbors in the coverage region. A trajectory composed of k elements is denoted as a k-pattern.*

Note that the ascending order of a mobility pattern's points is sorted by t. For example $<(c_1, t_1), (c_2, t_2), (c_3, t_3), (c_4, t_4)>$ is a 4-pattern, where $t_1 \leq t_2 \leq t_3 \leq t_4$.

3 Mobility Prediction Based on Group Mobility Behaviors

3.1 Discovering Frequent Mobility Patterns

Even though human movements have a high degree of freedom, no one move randomly all day and every user's movement is based on some regular habits. It's easy to see that the mobility prediction can only work well with regular movements and its accuracy degrades with increasing random movements. Therefore, random movements should be eliminated from the trajectory database as much as possible. This phase takes responsibility for mining frequent mobility patterns (or mobility patterns for short) from trajectory databases of all mobile users in the coverage region. The algorithm for discovering all mobility patterns is the modified version of the Apriori technique [13, 14]. We have used spatial and temporal constraints to reduce the number of generated candidates. That is, the mobility pattern and the candidate derived from it must satisfy the neighbor constraint and ascending time constraint. The detail of the mining algorithm has been presented in our previous work [10].

3.2 Clustering Mobility Patterns into Groups

Our purpose in this work is to discover group mobility behaviors of a population of mobile users for predicting future movement of individuals, who are new users or ones with movements on novel paths. To get such group information of mobility behaviors, we first collect frequent mobility patterns which are discovered from histories of all mobile users and then classify them into groups of similar behaviors. The subsection presents briefly our proposed dissimilarity measure [15], which is the basis for constructing the clustering procedure to identify groups of similar mobility patterns.

Suppose that given two mobility patterns $P_a = <(c_{a1}, t_{a1}), (c_{a2}, t_{a2}), ..., (c_{an}, t_{an})>$ and $P_b = <(c_{b1}, t_{b1}), (c_{b2}, t_{b2}), ..., (c_{bm}, t_{bm})>$.

Definition 3. *Let f: $S \times S \rightarrow R$ be a function representing the number of uncommon cells in two mobility patterns P_a and P_b. Then, f is determined by the formula:*

$$f(P_a, P_b) = card(\{c_{ai}|c_{ai} \notin P_b\}) + card(\{c_{bi}|c_{bi} \notin P_a\}) \tag{1}$$

The spatial dissimilarity measure can be defined in terms of spatial dissimilarity between two mobility patterns. The more uncommon cells there are in two patterns, the more spatially dissimilar they are.

Definition 4. *The spatial dissimilarity measure $D_{space}(P_a, P_b)$ between two mobility patterns P_a and P_b with length n and m, respectively, is defined as follows:*

$$D_{space}(P_a, P_b) = \frac{f(P_a, P_b)}{n + m} \tag{2}$$

For determining the temporal dissimilarity between the two mobility patterns, we need to calculate the total of temporal difference between the timestamps of the common cells in two patterns. The smaller the total time difference is, the less temporally dissimilar the two patterns are:

Definition 5. *The temporal dissimilarity measure $D_{time}(P_a, P_b)$ between two patterns P_a and P_b with length n and m, respectively, is given by*

$$D_{time}(P_a, P_b) = \frac{1}{k} \sum_{i=1,j=1}^{n,m} \frac{|t_{ai} - t_{bj}|}{\max(t_{ai}, t_{bj})} \text{ where } c_{ai} = c_{bj} \tag{3}$$

where k is the number of common cells of P_a and P_b.

In order to fully exploit the characteristics of mobility patterns, it is crucial for weighted combination of two dissimilarity measures on space and time.

Definition 6. *The composition dissimilarity measure between two patterns P_a and P_b is given by*

$$D(P_a, P_b) = W_{space}.D_{space}(P_a, P_b) + W_{time}.D_{time}(P_a, P_b) \tag{4}$$

in which W_{space} and W_{time} are respectively weights of spatial and temporal dissimilarity measures, such that $W_{space} + W_{time} = 1$.

The purpose of this phase is to classify the set of mobility patterns into groups such that patterns within the same group have a high degree of similarity, whereas patterns belong to different groups have a high degree of dissimilarity. We extend the traditional k-means approach to partition the set of mobility patterns into k clusters in order to take its advantages of simplicity and computational speed [16–19]. Our alternative clustering algorithm focuses on applying our proposed dissimilarity measures for finding cluster centers and assigning mobility patterns to clusters. After initialization for k cluster centers, each pattern in the set of mobility patterns is assigned to the nearest cluster based on the proposed dissimilarity measure. Then, the center of each cluster will be updated and further each mobility pattern will be reassigned to the nearest cluster by also using our similarity measures. The processes of center updating and pattern reassigning are repeated until no mobility pattern has changed clusters via a test cycle of the whole set of mobility patterns.

3.3 Determining the Movement Group of a Path

The previous phase takes responsibility for discovering movement groups such that mobile users in the same group have the same movement behaviors. Finding such grouping information of mobile users, based on the similarity among their movement behaviors, play a crucial role in predicting future movement to deal with the lack of mobility behaviors of individuals. Hence, for predicting the future locations of a mobile user, we first determine which movement group his current path belong to and then using mobility rules derived from that group to forecast. Since each cluster of mobility patterns is represented by a cluster center, the movement group of a current path is the cluster such that the similarity between its center and the path is the largest. Due to both cluster center and path are mobility patterns, the similarity between them are also measured by Definition 6. The process of group determining is outlined as follows:

1. Calculating the similarity between the current path P and each cluster center C_i, $D(P, C_i)$;
2. Choosing C_i such that $D(P, C_i)$ is minimized;
3. Returning the cluster that is represented by C_i.

3.4 Using Mobility Rules in Groups to Predict Future Movement

Due to geographic and friendship constraints, human movements express similar movement characteristics. It is clear that with good knowledge of groups to which a mobile user belongs, we can derive common behaviors among objects during their moving. Therefore, this phase focuses on discovering mobility rules from multiple users whose mobility behaviors are similar to facilitate the predicting future movement of a new user or with movements on novel paths.

In order to address the issue, this phase is first interested in generating a set of mobility rules from the movement group which the current path belongs to. Each generated rule has a confidence value and only rules which have confidence values higher than the predefined confidence threshold $conf_{min}$ are selected for predicting future locations of the current path. Then, we match the current path to the head of rule and find the best matching using the time constraint.

4 Experimental Evaluation

4.1 Evaluating the Proposed Prediction Model

This section is devoted to studying how effective the proposed mobility prediction approach is. We first mine the trajectory dataset $DS500$ which is produced by a dataset generator into discover all mobility patterns which have support values higher than the predefined minimum support threshold. Second, all mobility patterns are clustered into k groups and then generating mobility rules for each group of mobility patterns. For evaluating, we use a test set $TS10$ which consists of 7 trajectories with label 1, 2 trajectories with label 2 and 1 trajectories with label 3 from the dataset $DS500$.

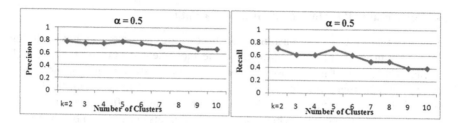

Fig. 3. The effect of the generated number of clusters k on prediction accuracy

The next location of each trajectory in *T10* is predicted and the results are used to calculate precision and recall. Varying k from 2 to 10 on 1 incremental steps, we obtain experimental results as in Fig. 3.

Figure 3 shows that the recall decreases slightly whereas precision is not affected as the number of clusters k increases from 2 to 5. However, when k is larger than 5, although the precision is still not affected, the recall is strong reduced. That is due to that the probability of having some no-prediction cases becomes higher as k increases.

By considering the experimental result, the unchangeability of the precision values as k increases implies that our clustering procedure is good. This is because that each mobility pattern has assigned to the nearest group and further mobility patterns within the same group have a high degree of similarity, so the best matched rules of the current path are always found, even when k increases. Moreover, reducing the recall as k increases suggest that using personal profile to predict his future locations will return no-predictions and thus affect prediction accuracy if he is a new user or his current paths are novel. Therefore, it is necessary to group mobility behaviors of mobile users according to their similarity for reducing the probability of having some no-prediction cases.

As another results of this experiment, reducing the time cost of computation as k increases implies that we should classify the set of mobility patterns into as many groups as possible such that the prediction accuracy is still guaranteed. In this experiment, the best value of k is 5, which is the same as the number of movement groups of the dataset *DS500*.

4.2   Comparing with Prediction Models based on Personal Profile

The question now is that whether or not using group mobility behaviors to predict future movement. In order to answer this question, we perform two prediction approaches:

- *Case 1*: The prediction model based on group mobility behaviors
- *Case 2*: The prediction model based on individual mobility behaviors [8, 10]

For generating dataset of *Case 2*, we randomly select 50 trajectories with label 1 from the dataset *DS500* to create a set of trajectories of the same mobile user and

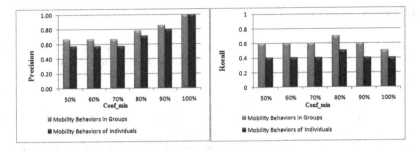

Fig. 4. The difference of prediction accuracy between the two models

name *DS50*. In *Case 1*, we also use *DS500* and fix the number of clusters at 5. For comparing the prediction accuracy of two approaches with respect to both precision and recall, we use the test set *TS10* and obtain experimental results as in Fig. 4. The prediction accuracy in the case based on group mobility behaviors is always better than that in the case based on individual mobility behaviors. This is because that if the current path is novel, *Case 2* will return no-prediction whereas *Case 1* may return correct prediction. In addition, Case 1 and Case 2 will have the same results with movements on old paths due to the similar mobility patterns have been classified into the same group.

In conclusion, we can say that group mobility behaviors may facilitate the predicting future locations of new users or ones with movements on novel paths and further contribute considerably to the improvement in prediction accuracy.

5 Conclusions

In this paper, we have presented a novel approach for predicting future movement of mobile users in wide WLANs, which is based on clustering technique for group behaviors. The proposed approach may deal with the lack of information on personal profile which is the drawback of making use of conventional prediction techniques. We first discover mobility rules from multiple users whose mobility behaviors are similar to each other. And then, we make use of mobility rules derived from the movement group to which the current path belongs for predicting the next point-of-attachments of users. In order to demonstrate the necessity and effectiveness of the proposed approach, we have conducted experiments to evaluate the approach with respect to both precision and recall measures as well as to compare the approach with the model based on individual mobility behaviors. We are currently constructing a real life dataset which is collected from campus-wide WLAN of Dartmouth College to verify the efficacy of the proposed approach. Moreover, such the real dataset enable us to compare the proposed approach with other ones which are also based on group mobility behaviors. These research results will be presented in our future work.

References

1. Kotz, D., Essien, K.: Analysis of a Campus-wide Wireless Network. In: Proceedings of the 8th Annual International Conference on Mobile Computing and Networking (ACM MOBICOM'02), pp. 107–118 (2002)
2. Yavas, G., Katsaros, D., Ulusoy, O., Manolopoulos, Y.: A data mining approach for location prediction in mobile environments. J. Data Knowl. Eng. **54**, 121–146 (2005)
3. Kang, J., Yong, H.-S.: A Frequent pattern based prediction model for moving objects. Int. J. Comput. Sci. Netw. Secur. **10**(3), 200–205 (2010)
4. Lee, J.W., Paek, O.H., Ryu, K.H.: Temporal moving pattern mining for location-based service. J. Syst. Softw. **73**, 481–490 (2004). (Elsevier)
5. Hung, C., Peng, W.: Clustering object moving patterns for prediction-based object tracking sensor networks. In: Proceedings of the 18th ACM conference on Information and knowledge management, pp. 1633–1636, USA (2009)
6. Avasthi, S., Dwivedi, A.: Prediction of mobile user behavior using clustering. Int. J. Sci. Res. Publ. **3**(2), 1–5 (2013)
7. Bergh, A.E., Ventura, N.: Prediction assisted fast handovers for mobile IPv6. IEEE MILCOM 2006 Unclassified Technical Sessions, Washington D.C. (2006)
8. Duong, T.V., Tran, D.Q., Tran, C.H.: Spatiotemporal data mining for mobility prediction in wireless network. In: Proceedings of the National Conference of Fundamental and Applied IT Research (FAIR), pp. 224–235, Vietnam (2011)
9. Wanalertlak, W., Lee, B., Yu, C., Kim, M., Park, S.M., Kim, W.T.: Behavior-based mobility prediction for seamless handoff in mobile wireless networks. Wirel. Netw. **17**, 645–658 (2011). (Springer Science + Business Media)
10. Duong, T.V., Tran, D.Q.: An effective approach for mobility prediction in wireless network based on temporal weighted mobility rule. Int. J. Comput. Sci. Telecommun. **3**(2), 29–36 (2012)
11. Cho, E., Myers, S.A., Leskovec, J.: Friendship and mobility: user movement in location-based social networks. In: Proceedings of the 17th ACM SIGKDD International Conference on Knowledge Discovery and Data Mining, pp. 1082–1090, USA (2011)
12. Somayeh, D.: Exploring movement similarity analysis of moving objects. Doctor thesis, University of Zurich, Switzerland (2011)
13. Yao, X.: Research issues in spatio-temporal data mining. In: Workshop on Geospatial Visualization and Knowledge Discovery, University Consortium for Geographic Information Science, Virginia (2003)
14. Shekhar, S., Vatsavai, R.R., Celik, M.: Spatial and Spatiotemporal Data Mining: Recent Advances. Symposium, Next Generation of Data Mining, pp. 549–584 (2008)
15. Duong, T.V., Tran, D.Q., Tran, C.H.: A weighted combination similarity measure for mobility patterns in wireless networks. Int. J. Comput. Netw. Commun. **4**(3), 21–35 (2012)
16. Huang, K., Yu, T.H., Kao, T.: Analyzing structural changes using clustering techniques. Int. J. Innovative Comput. Inf. Control **4**(5), 1195–1202 (2008)
17. Ranjan, M., Anna, D.P., Arka, P.G:. A systematic evaluation of different methods for initializing the K-means clustering algorithm. IEEE Trans. Knowl. Data Eng. **38**, 522–537 (2010)
18. Hartigan, J.A., Wong, A.: A k-means clustering algorithm. Appl. Stat. **28**, 100–108 (1979)
19. Berkhin, P.: A survey of clustering data mining techniques. Grouping Multidimensional Data in Grouping Multidimensional Data, pp. 25–71 (2006)

Social Context-Based Movie Recommendation: A Case Study on MyMovieHistory

Yong Seung Lee[1], Xuan Hau Pham[1], Duc Nguyen Trung[1], Jason J. Jung[1][(✉)], and Hien T. Nguyen[2]

[1] Department of Computer Engineering, Yeungnam University, Gyeongsan, Korea
{lceose,pxhauqbu,duc.nguyentrung,j2jung}@gmail.com
[2] Faculty of Information Technology, Ton Duc Thang University, Ho Chi Minh City, Vietnam
hien@tdt.edu.vn

Abstract. Social networking services (in short, SNS) allow users to share their own data with family, friends, and communities. Since there are many kinds of information that has been uploaded and shared through the SNS, the amount of information on the SNS keeps increasing exponentially. Particularly, Facebook has adopted some interesting features related to entertainment (e.g., movie, music and TV show). However, they do not consider contextual information of users for recommendation (e.g., time, location, and social contexts). Therefore, in this paper, we propose a novel approach for movie recommendation based on the integration of a variety contextual information (i.e., when the users watched the movies, where the users watched the movies, and who watched the movie with them). Thus, we developed a Facebook application (called MyMovieHistory) for recording the movie history of users and recommending relevant movies.

Keywords: Recommendation systems · Social contexts · Facebook · User history · Timeline

1 Introduction

Social networking sites are places such as Facebook, Twitter, and Google+ where people post their thoughts and share their ideas. They are growing rapidly, becoming a part of our lives. A lot of applications have been using metadata from social networks in application development. The systems can understand and discover several important things about specific users and their friends. Information sharing among the systems is a new trend on the Internet. For example, IMDB[1] data has been integrated into the movies feature on social network and different movie-related systems. In addition, some authors have proposed new approaches to deal with the cold-start problem in recommendation systems by using social user profiles [1,2].

---

[1] http://www.imdb.com

P.C. Vinh et al. (Eds.): ICCASA 2013, LNICST 128, pp. 339–348, 2014.
DOI: 10.1007/978-3-319-05939-6_33, © Springer International Publishing Switzerland 2014

Several applications to integrate contextual information have been used and have proved that context modeling is a potential opportunity for all types of applications [3]. Within these growing social networks, social context is a new approach to user profiling [4]. In traditional recommendation systems, we can build an individual user profile. However, in recommendation systems on social networks, not only can we build a specific user profile but we can also build group profiles [5].

Social contexts contain a set of particular situations for a user or a user group. Thus, social context extraction is an important process in understanding user activities on social networks. This not only offers user-friendly interactions to the user but it also provides useful information for social context-based applications. There are several applications that have been integrated into social networks. Facebook is a social service where users share information with family, friends, and the online community. Many kinds of data are uploaded and shared via the website, and the amount of data continues to grow incessantly.

Recommendation systems are support tools to help users choose products they may be interested in. Furthermore, the number of movie repositories on the Internet is increasing rapidly. This offers many opportunities for everyone to watch and share movies. Thus, movie recommendation systems have been developed as an application on Facebook that brings together users who share a passion for movies.

Movie recommendation systems are personalization techniques to overcome the information overload problem by recommending movies based on a user's preferences. There is a movie section on Facebook. Using this feature, users can choose which movie they want to watch, and it shows a list of movies that the user has watched. Users can share these movie lists with friends and others. The section also suggests a list of movies of potential interest to the user. However, Facebook has not taken into account contextual information, such as when you watched the movie, who watched with you, and where you watched the movie. Studying a user's preference in a particular situation is very important for predicting a list of movies that may be interesting to that user at any one moment. A system can be developed based on the user's current situation, emotions, and other contextual information, which may bring more satisfaction to the user. We consider Table 1.

Table 1 contains 3 users u_1, u_2, u_3, 6 movies $i_1, .., i_6$. The pair c_{ij} expresses that u_i watched movie j within social context c.

Table 1. Context-based user model

	i_1	i_2	i_3	i_4	i_5	i_6
u_1	c_{11}		c_{13}	c_{14}		
u_2	c_{21}	c_{22}		c_{24}		c_{26}
u_3			c_{33}	c_{34}	c_{35}	

Assume that u_1 is current user. This person watched the same two movies with other users. How do we recommend movies of potential interest to these users? It is difficult to find suitable movies. Thus, in this paper, we propose a new approach for movie recommendation based on social context information. We apply collaborative filtering by computing the similarity between two users based on social context. We also developed a new application on Facebook for our idea, called (MyMovieHistory). In this application, you can describe your movie history as a timeline of movie watching.

The outline of this paper is organized as follows. In Sect. 2, we represent related work. In Sect. 3, we discuss social context and recommendation modeling based on social context. In Sect. 4, we show recommendation process. Finally, in Sect. 5, we conclude our proposal and suggest future work.

2   Related Work

Recommendation systems have been applied to social networks. However, social context-based systems for recommending have not yet been considered. In [6–9], they presented about contextual information and applied it to recommendation systems. In addition, the investigation of context parameters in the movie domain was also mentioned. In [10], author have focused on analyzing interactions among characters based on emotional similarity in movie stories to discover the relationships. In [11], they proposed a method to extract underlying relations among entities from social networks. They found contexts in which two entities co-occur, and the given collective context was clustered based on similarity.

In [12], they introduced a group recommendation system as a Facebook application. They made recommendations for user groups based on three factors: personality, social trust and previous recommendations. However, they did not show this application on Facebook. The number of user groups on Facebook is increasing more and more. It is difficult for a user to select the right group to join. In order to solve this problem, Baatarjav et al. [13] introduced a group recommendation system using a combination of hierarchical clustering and a decision-tree technique based on users' profiles.

Movie recommendation systems have also been considered in social networks. In [14], they presented their video recommendation system on YouTube. They proposed a recommendation framework based on a user's previous activity on the site and a top-N algorithm is applied to find high-quality videos relevant to the user's interests. Using a network of reviewers of videos and extracting information from them to make recommendations was proposed by Qin et al [15]. Social network profile-based systems for recommendations have been applying to deal with the cold-start problem [16,17].

3   Social Context in Movie Recommendation

In this section, we discuss various contexts in social network. Also, particularly, social context-based movie recommendation will be explained. We also present

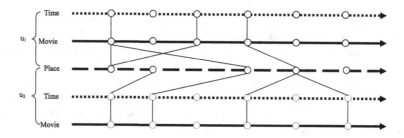

Fig. 1. Movie history as Timeline

formal definitions for social contexts. Social context can provide content such as a user's location, activity, surrounding people, agenda [18], and emotion [10]. Other definitions about social context refer to interactions wherein people react to events differently, depending on their immediate situation. For example, some people do not like to watch comedy movies alone, but if their friends invite them to watch this kind of movie, they might agree to join the group and they may be interested in this movie.. Social context is contextual information describing where you are, what you are doing and who you are with.

Contextual information is mentioned in social network sites as interaction data between user and system, or user activities. Depending on the kind of application, context is considered to have different aspects. In [3], they proposed the categories of context parameters such as User&Role, Process&Task, Location, Time and Device. In [7], they considered contextual information in music recommender systems such as environment context (e.g., location, time, weather and so on), user context (e.g., activity, demographical, emotional and so on). We assume that users with the same social context may have a sense of social consensus.

From Table 1, we can depict the movie histories of two users in the form of Timeline, as shown in Fig. 1.

The relationship between user and movie within a social context is defined formally as follows.

Definition 1 (Social context). *Given a set of users $\mathcal{U}$, a social context $\mathcal{SC}$ is represented as:*

$$\mathcal{SC} = \langle \mathcal{U}, \mathcal{I}, \mathcal{C} \rangle \tag{1}$$

where, $\mathcal{I}$ is a set of items and $\mathcal{C}$ is a set of contextual information.

For each user $u \in \mathcal{U}$, a social context for an individual user is expressed as follows: $sc(u) = \{(i,c) | i \in \mathcal{I}_u, c \in \mathcal{C}\}$.

In Fig. 1, we can see that the location for each user is the same. It means that these users watched different movies in the same location. In the social network, the relationship among users is very important. The mission of a social network is to share information and help people connect. Each user may find out about common characteristics of other people on the network in order to make friends. For example, if you like James Cameron movies and I do, too, we can become friends on Facebook even though we did not know each other before. The following definition presents the relationship between users based on user movie history

Definition 2 (Social relationship). *$G(u)$ is a set of users who are the user's friends. $\forall u' \in G(u)$, the relationship based on watched-movie history, is denoted as $r(u)$ and is represented as follows:*

$$r(u, u') = \begin{cases} w(u, u') & \text{if } I(u) \cap I(u') \neq \emptyset \\ 0 & \text{otherwise} \end{cases}$$

where, $w(u, u')$ is weight of the relationship between u and u' $I(u)$ and $I(u')$ are watched movies sets of users u and u', respectively.

The weight of the relationship is defined as follows:

Definition 3 (Weight of the relationship). *Weight of the relationship between two users is computed as follows:*

$$w(u, u') = \frac{card(I(u) \cap I(u'))}{card(I(u))} \tag{2}$$

For example, we have $I(u) = \{i_1, i_2, i_5, i_7, i_8\}$ and $I(u') = \{i_2, i_3, i_4, i_5, i_7, i_9, i_{10}\}$.

The weight of the relationship between u and u' is computed as: $w(u, u') = \frac{3}{5} = 0.6$ and $r(u, u') = 0.6$.

In a social network, we usually consider two kinds of information. The first is individual user information. This information is complied by a user. This person will be the "inviter". The second is group information. This information is accepted and shared by the user's friends. The friends will be the "invitees". Hence, there are two kinds of user profile [5].

- Individual user history profile
- Group history profiles

A user movie history consists of two parts. One part contains a dominant values by extracting a set of watched-movies attributes and a set of attribute values. The other part contains contextual information depending on the user's situation. A context-based user profile is considered according to two aspects:

- Time-based: We consider the time that a user accesses Facebook. This is very important in order to identify the user's situation. For example, a user who accesses in the morning is be different from a user who accesses at night, and recommendation results will be different.
- Location-based: Depending on the user's current location, the system adapts different recommendations. For example, one user has taken a trip to other country; the system will recommend a list of movies that may be related.

Group profile expresses the group preference. This means that it contains a list of movies that each user in the group shares with others and also a list of locations, and times that they watched together.

- List of friends who shared a list of movies
- List of watched movies
- Weight of inter-relationship between friends

The main goal of context-based movie recommendation is not only to suggest a list of movies that each user may be interested in but also that are suitable for a particular situation. In the next section, we will present our framework for recommending.

4   Recommendation Process

4.1   Context-Based Movie Recommendation Systems

Social context-based movie recommendation systems suggest a list of movies to users by using a set of user-context information. For a particular situation, the system will provide a specific recommendation. Social networks offer a lot of advantages for developing recommendation services. The services can access a user's profile, a user's interests or the user's activities for extracting overall user preferences. Figure 2 provides an overview of a movie recommendation process. In order to make the recommendation process, we have the following definitions.

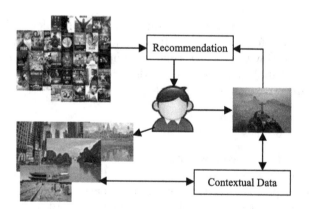

Fig. 2. Place-based recommendation process

Definition 4 (Movie history). *Given social context SC, $\forall u \in U$, a movie history is defined as follows:*

$$Hist(u) = \{(i, c, f)|\forall i \in I, c \in sc(u), f \in U\} \tag{3}$$

In this paper, we apply a collaborative filtering technique by computing the similarity between two users based on social context. Assume that we take into account two elements of social context: time and location. We have the following definition.

Definition 5 (Similarity). *Let $c \in C$, given two users $u, u' \in U$. The similarity between two users based on social contexts is defined as follows:*

$$sim(u, u') = \frac{1}{card(C)} \sum_{c \in C,} (sim(u, u')_c) \qquad (4)$$

where $card(C)$ is a function that returns a number of social context elements and $p \in P$

$$sim(u, u')_c = \frac{\sum_{i=1}^{n}(sc_u^{hist(u)} \times sc_{u'}^{hist(u')})}{\sqrt{\sum_{i=1}^{n}(sc_u^{hist(u)})^2} \times \sqrt{\sum_{i=1}^{n}(sc_{u'}^{hist(u')})^2}} \qquad (5)$$

where sc_u and $sc_{u'}$ are vectors of certain context elements of u and u', respectively.

According to Definition 5, the similarity between users based on social context is computed by using similarities in social context elements. For example, if a set of contexts consisting of three elements $Time, Location, Friend$, denoted t, p, f, we have:

$$sim(u, u') = \frac{1}{card(3)}(sim(u, u')_t + sim(u, u')_p + sim(u, u')_f)$$

A recommendation result is computed as follows:

$$Rec(u) = TopN(\Pi_{u' \in U}(sim(u, u'), w(u, u'))) \qquad (6)$$

where $TopN$ is a function to find out the number of potential movies that may be suitable for the user's situation. The list of movies depends on who has the highest similarity and the Π function supports selecting the candidates.

4.2 My Movie History as Watching Timeline

Facebook's application is a new trend to apply services to the social network. Facebook is discussed as a nation by in [19]. There are a lot of applications that have been developed by using the Facebook API. Facebook is the first in the list of most visited social networking sites. According to statistics[2], in March 2013, there were 655 million daily active users, 751 million monthly active users who used Facebook mobile products and 1.11 billion monthly active users. Total number of Facebook apps is about 10 million, and the average number of friends per Facebook user is about 142.

---

[2] http://newsroom.fb.com/Key-Facts

In this section, we introduce our recommendation system, called *MyMovieHistory*, which is a Facebook application for movie recommendation. The application provides a better recommendation process based on extracting social context. In order to use our application, users must have a Facebook account and run *My Movie History* in the *APPS* section. Another way to use our application is to access the link[3]. This social context-based movie recommendation system consists of components as follows:

- Creating the user history: each user talks about his/her watched movie history. Each user can add their story as a timeline. Each watched movie includes the following information:
    - Which movie they watched
    - When they watched this movie
    - Who they watched the movie with
    - Where they watched this movie
- Extracting the user's social context: the system collects the user's contextual information that is related this movie. The contextual information in the application consists of three elements: time, location, and friends. If a user does not select any friend(s) who watched a movie with him, it means that he/she watched this movie alone.
- Discovering user's relationship: the system extract a list of user's friends from the Facebook profile. When a certain user adds his/her friends into history, the application will send automatically the notification to them.
- Extracting the dominant attribute values: the dominant attribute values will be identified by using attributes-values pairs from the list of watched movies [20]. In this application, we focus on three movie attributes: *Genre*, *Actor* and *Director*. The statistics are shown to the user.
- Editing movie history: the system helps users change their history. For each event, a user can share it with friends who watched this movie with them; the user can change the time that he/she watched this movie; and the user can delete the event. Each user has a list of friends. Users can share history events with their friends. When a user shares certain events with his/her friends, the system automatically identifies the inviter and the invitees. It is important to extract the relationships among users for the movie.
- Recommendation: When users log in to our application, a list of potential movies will be recommended. If you know a user's history, you can know what he/she may be interested in. Depending on the user context, the systems can recommend different sets of movies to the user. We will recommend movies to individual users. In this process, we have applied collaborative filtering method to find out the highest similarity between current the user and the other friends.
- Integrated data: The information about movies from IMDB is also extracted and presented to users.

---

[3] https://apps.facebook.com/mymoviehistory/

5 Concluding Remarks

Social networks have become a global phenomenon. Content and number of users in these communities grows rapidly. Users can share information and make new friends without considering location and time. Thus, developing a movie recommendation system as a Facebook application based on contextual information is a new approach, bringing a new opportunity to provide user satisfaction. Social context provides useful information for making recommendations, such as where you are, who your friends are and so on. In this paper, we propose a new framework for such an application. The recommendation process is generated by computing similarity among users based on social context and dominant attribute values. Our application is also available on Facebook, allowing users to record about their watched movie history and to share their histories with friends. We applied the Facebook API to develop our application, called *MyMovieHistory*.

In future work, we will present our experimental results after collecting data. We will also consider user activities on Facebook and develop our application to make it more comfortable to use. We will also try to use the Facebook mobile API to develop a mobile application.

Acknowledgement. This work was supported by the National Research Foundation of Korea (NRF) grant funded by the Korean government (MEST) (No. 2011-0017156).

References

1. Heitmann, B., Hayes, C.: Using linked data to build open, collaborative recommender systems. In: AAAI Spring Symposium: Linked Data Meets Artificial Intelligence (2010)
2. Hassanzadeh, O., Consens, M.: Linked movie data base. In: Workshop on Linked Data on the Web (LDOW 2009) (2009)
3. Kaltz, W.J., Ziegler, J., Lohmann, S.: Context-aware web engineering: modeling and applications. RIA - Revue d'Intelligence Artificielle (Special Issue on Applying Context-Management) **19**(3), 439–458 (2005)
4. Baldauf, M., Dustdar, S., Rosenberg, F.: A survey on context-aware systems. Int. J. Ad Hoc Ubiquitous Comput. **2**(4), 263–277 (2007)
5. Thomsen, J., Vanrompay, Y., Berbers, Y.: Evolution of context-aware user profiles. In: Ultra Modern Telecommunications, pp. 1–6 (2009)
6. Kaminskas, M., Ricci, F.: Location-adapted music recommendation using tags. In: Konstan, J.A., Conejo, R., Marzo, J.L., Oliver, N. (eds.) UMAP 2011. LNCS, vol. 6787, pp. 183–194. Springer, Heidelberg (2011)
7. Kaminskas, M., Ricci, F.: Contextual music information retrieval and recommendation: state of the art and challenges. Comput. Sci. Rev. **6**(2–3), 89–119 (2012)
8. Adomavicius, G., Tuzhilin, A.: Context-aware recommender systems. In: Ricci, F., Rokach, L., Shapira, B., Kantor, P.B. (eds.) Recommender Systems Handbook, pp. 217–253. Springer, New York (2011)
9. Braunhofer, M., Kaminskas, M., Ricci, F.: Recommending music for places of interest in a mobile travel guide. In: Proceedings of the Fifth ACM Conference on Recommender Systems. RecSys '11, pp. 253–256. ACM, New York, NY, USA (2011)

10. Jung, J.J., You, E., Park, S.B.: Emotion-based character clustering for managing story-based contents: a cinemetric analysis. Multimed. Tools Appl. **65**(1), 29–45 (2013)

11. Mori, J., Tsujishita, T., Matsuo, Y., Ishizuka, M.: Extracting relations in social networks from the web using similarity between collective contexts. In: Cruz, I., Decker, S., Allemang, D., Preist, Ch., Schwabe, D., Mika, P., Uschold, M., Aroyo, L.M. (eds.) ISWC 2006. LNCS, vol. 4273, pp. 487–500. Springer, Heidelberg (2006)

12. Sánchez, L.Q., Recio-García, J.A., Díaz-Agudo, B., Jiménez-Díaz, G.: Happy movie: a group recommender application in Facebook. In: Murray, R.C., McCarthy, P.M. (eds.) Proceedings of the 24th International Florida Artificial Intelligence Research Society Conference (FLAIRS), 18–20 May 2011, Palm Beach, FL, USA. AAAI Press, Menlo Park (2011)

13. Baatarjav, E.-A., Phithakkitnukoon, S., Dantu, R.: Group recommendation system for Facebook. In: Meersman, R., Tari, Z., Herrero, P. (eds.) OTM-WS 2008. LNCS, vol. 5333, pp. 211–219. Springer, Heidelberg (2008)

14. Davidson, J., Liebald, B., Liu, J., Nandy, P., Van Vleet, T., Gargi, U., Gupta, S., He, Y., Lambert, M., Livingston, B., Sampath, D.: The YouTube video recommendation system. In: Proceedings of the Fourth ACM Conference on Recommender Systems. RecSys '10, pp. 293–296. ACM, New York, NY, USA (2010)

15. Qin, S., Menezes, R., Silaghi, M.: A recommender system for YouTube based on its network of reviewers. In: Proceedings of the 2010 IEEE Second International Conference on Social Computing. SOCIALCOM '10, pp. 323–328. IEEE Computer Society, Washington, DC, USA (2010)

16. Fijalkowski, D., Zatoka, R.: An architecture of a web recommender system using social network user profiles for e-commerce. In: Computer Science and Information Systems (FedCSIS), 2011 Federated Conference on, pp. 287–290 (2011)

17. Kandhan, R., Teletia, N.: !Trendz: recommender system using Facebook profile (2009)

18. Joly, A., Maret, P., Daigremont, J.: Context-awareness, the missing block of social networking. Int. J. Comput. Sci. Appl. (Special Issue on Networking Mobile Virtual Knowledge) **4**(2), 50–65 (2009)

19. Lee, N.: Facebook Nation: Total Information Awareness. Springer, New York (2012)

20. Pham, X.H., Jung, J.J.: Preference-based user rating correction process for interactive recommendation systems. Multimed. Tools Appl. **65**(1), 119–132 (2012)

Understanding Effect of Sentiment Content Toward Information Diffusion Pattern in Online Social Networks: A Case Study on TweetScope

Duc Nguyen Trung[1], Tri Tuong Nguyen[1], Jason J. Jung[1(✉)], and Dongjin Choi[2]

[1] Department of Computer Engineering, Yeungnam University,
Gyeongsan 712-749, Korea
{duc.nguyentrung,tuongtringuyen,j2jung}@gmail.com
[2] Department of Computer Engineering, Chosun University, Gwangju, Korea

Abstract. Understanding customers' opinion and subjectivity is regarded as an important task in various domains (e.g., marketing). Particularly, with many types of social media (e.g., Twitter and FaceBook), such opinions are propagated to other users and might make a significant influence on them. In this paper, we propose a method for understanding relationship between sentiment content corresponding with its diffusion degree in Online Social Networks. Thereby, a practical system, called *TweetScope*, has been implemented to efficiently collect and analyze all possible tweets from customers.

Keywords: Sentiment analysis · Opinion mining · Online social media · Information diffusion

1 Introduction

It is important for businesses to collect customers' feedbacks about their products and services in direct and more importantly indirect manners [15,16]. Online users have been creating a large amount of information (e.g., personal experiences and opinions) in various forms (e.g., rating [1–3], reviews [5], comments, and articles). Such "personal opinions" among users have be efficiently processed by using various learning methodologies (e.g., decision tree [10], clustering, and so on) [20].

Since many social networking services (SNS) have been emerged, they have enabled the customers to share and exchange their personal opinions. Then, these customers can either make a significant influence on others or get influences from the others [12,13]. For example, if some of friends (or family) have shown any positive (and negative) comments against a certain item (e.g., news and products), one will have a similar feeling regardless of their own personal opinion [6–8,14]. More importantly, the SNS has shown significant power on information diffusion. Once a new piece of information is generated, the information can be propagated to a very large number of other users in a short time.

P.C. Vinh et al. (Eds.): ICCASA 2013, LNICST 128, pp. 349–358, 2014.
DOI: 10.1007/978-3-319-05939-6_34, © Springer International Publishing Switzerland 2014

The outline of this paper is as follows. Section 2 describes our research issues about the effect of sentiment content toward its diffusion degree from the original source to another social members via their friendship links on Online Social Networks. Sentiment classification method and analysis method for classifying relationship between information diffusion pattern and sentiment content of microtexts posted in Online social networks, are introduced in Sects. 3 and 4. In Sects. 5 and 6, we show the experimental data collection, data preprocessing. The experimental results and evaluations are also discussed. Section 7 draws our conclusion of this work and presents next research directions in the future.

2   Problem Description

A SNS is an open environment where people build their social network or social relations, information from one person can be diffused to another via his/her social links or friendship links. Most social network services are web-based and provide means for user to interact over the Internet, such as Facebook, Google+ and Twitter widely used worldwide. Each SNS has a way of organizing social relation and a mechanism for passing news between a related group of member, Twitter is one of the most popular SNS that enables its users to send and read text-based messages of up to 140 character, know as "tweet" or microtext. Social relations in Twitter is organizing by *"following"* or *"followed"* relationship, a member can follow or be followed by many another members. Followers can read and be notified about tweets, whenever it is posted by who he/she are following, so news can be transmitted among related members. Besides that, Twitter has a powerful and unique news transmission mechanism called *"retweet"* action or RT for short, by which a member can easily copy a tweet from a "following" friend then posts in his/her own timeline. The action has effect to diffuse news from the original author to followers of the author's followers.

In our work, we focused on analysis the relationship between sentiment polarity of tweet content and its diffusion among related Twitter members based *retweet* mechanism. The main research questions are

- Is there any relationship between sentiment content and how information diffuse through social media?
- Is it possible for businesses to employ sentiment opinion to increase effect of the information propagation?

So, there are two main tasks in this work: in the first task, tweets are classified as positive, negative or neutral depend on author's opinion embedded in it; and the second task is to characterize information propagation between Twitter members by measured features, known as information diffusion patterns. Such classification and specification allows us to clarify relationships between distinct sentiment groups of tweets and how it diffused.

For experimenting, we evaluate a case study on a practical system named TweetScope. The application monitors and analyzes data fetched from a text stream provided by Twitter by filtering tweets on the timeline of certain famous accounts who have a quite enough number of statuses and followers. It's capable of extracting and visualizing the feasible information on marketing [21]. We expect that the visual interface of this system can help decision makers to understand the diffusion patterns on Twitter [9,11].

3 Sentiment Classifier

As description in the above sections, the first task of this work is classification each tweet in to sentiment classes respectively into "positive", "negative" and "neutral". We use common classifier model which has system structure shown as Fig. 1, the model is described detail in the book of Steven Bird et al. [22] with base implemented algorithms packed in a library named "Natural Language Toolkit"[1].

3.1 Naive Bayesian Classifier

The Naive Bayes classifier is often used in text classification due to its speed and simplicity [17–19]. It provides a flexible way for dealing with a number of attributes or classes based on probability theory. The method assumes that the presence or absence of a particular feature is unrelated to the presence or absence of any other feature, given the class variable. For given set of classes, it estimated the probability of a class c, given a document d with terms t as

$$P(c|d) = P(c) \prod_{\forall t \in d} P(t|c) \tag{1}$$

Using the rule 1, the Naive Bayes classifier labels a new document as a class c with a decision rule. One common rule is to pick the hypothesis that is most probable, this is know as the maximum a posteriori. The classifier returns a class

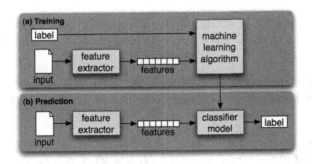

Fig. 1. Common structure of classifier system

---

[1] Natural Language Toolkit package can be downloaded at http://nltk.org.

level with the highest probability given the document. In our case, the value of class is might be *Positive, Negative* or *Neutral*, these classes are assigned a integer value 1, -1 or 0 respectively. In addition if a tweet is granted label *Positive* or *Negative* with a low probability, which is below a threshold ϵ, we considered the tweet is belonged to the neutral class. Therefore, we use following function to classify all tweets in our collected dataset.

$$\text{classify}(d) = \begin{cases} argmax_c\ P(c|d) & \text{if } \exists c\ P(c, d) > \epsilon \\ 0 & \text{Otherwise} \end{cases} \tag{2}$$

4   Diffusion Patterns

4.1   Network Formalization

In order to formalize the information diffusion patterns, we have to define the following notations and show an example. In this paper, we call statuses or news on SNS as microtexts, since they are usually short.

Definition 1 (Microtext). *A microtext twt is a piece of textual information. It is composed of three main features given by*

$$twt = \langle TF, \tau, \Psi \rangle \tag{3}$$

which are (i) term frequencies TF (how many times each term appears in the microtext), (ii) timestamps τ (when the microtext was generated), and (iii) a set of neighbors Ψ (who has been involved in the microtexts).

Given a microtext t, a set of term features $TF(twt, w_k)$ can be extracted by measuring term frequencies in the vector-space model. It can be represented as

$$TF_{twt} = \begin{bmatrix} w_1 & w_2 & \cdots & w_{|t|} \\ \frac{count(w_1)}{|t|} & \frac{count(w_2)}{|t|} & \cdots & \frac{count(w_{|t|})}{|t|} \end{bmatrix}^T \tag{4}$$

where $w_i \in twt$ is a list of words in twt, and function *count* returns the number of occurrence of a term w_k. Also, $|twt|$ is the length of twt (i.e., the total number of words).

Definition 2 (Directed Social Network). *A Directed Social Network S is a network where information is diffused from one to other users via their relationship. It is represented as*

$$S = \langle U, N \rangle \tag{5}$$

where U is a set of users and $N \subseteq |U| \times |U|$ is a set of relationship betweens the users.

4.2   Diffusion Patterns

In our previous work [4], we have defined a RT network $\mathcal{S}^{twt}_{RT(t)}$ to represent information diffusion network of a specified tweet twt, and also the diffusion pattern of twt by coverage rate ϕ^{twt}.

Definition 3 (Coverage rate). *A coverage rate ϕ can be measured as*

$$\phi^{twt}_{(t)} = \frac{\kappa \times \rho^{twt}_{(t)}}{(1 - \kappa) \times \tau^{twt}_{(t)}} \tag{6}$$

where (t) is a certain timestamp for understanding temporal dynamics; $\rho^{twt}_{(t)}$ is a coverage value represent degree of where the target tweet had diffused; $\tau^{twt}_{(t)}$ is a sensitivity known as a response time since the target tweet has been generated, it indicates how quickly users have retweeted [4]. Also, κ is a weighting parameter for emphasizing either coverage (i.e., $0.5 \leq \kappa \leq 1$) or sensitivity (i.e., $0 \leq \kappa < 0.5$).

4.3   Characteristic of Diffusion Patterns

Each Retweet Network of a certain tweet twt has its own a diffusion pattern $g(twt)$ by coverage rate ϕ^{twt} that indicates how many users have diffused twt to others within a unit time. The interesting issue is that some $g(twt)$ can reach its own highest value of ϕ more quick than another; and their maximum value are distributed in various ranges, i.e. In Fig. 2, $g_1(twt_i)$ has a peak later than $g_2(twt_j)$. Besides that, the average value of $g(twt)$ on series of "retweet" times also provide a perspective about the diffusion pattern, so to compare between diffusion patterns, we represent the maximum value of a diffusion pattern $g(twt)$, its time and average value of $g(twt)$ as following

$$\Phi^{twt} = [\phi_{max}, \phi_{avg}, d] \tag{7}$$

where ϕ_{max} is highest value of $g(twt)$ and d is timestamp or retweet position when ϕ_{max} is occurred, ϕ_{avg} is average value of $g(twt)$ over series of "retweet" times.

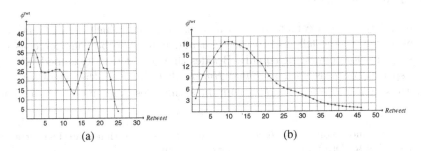

Fig. 2. Two diffusion patterns by (a) $g_1(twt_i)$ of @Windowsphone account, (b) $g_2(twt_j)$ of @SamsumMobile accounts

5   Data Collection

Several famous Twitter accounts which are most popular with high quantity of followers[2], are selected to collect status from 2013, March 1st to 2013, August 1st. Twenty six Twitter accounts are grouped in 3 categories (*Industry*, *Entertainment* and *News*) depend on the accounts' activities. In this section we describe the data, data collection method and data pre-processing step.

5.1   Training Data Set

The performance of classification depends on the subject of data as well as the size of training data set. So, for training the classifier we collect a lot of sentiment microtext from different corpora that are available on previous sentiment analysis studies.

5.2   Data Collection

This work has focused on understanding relationship if any between information diffusion pattern of the tweets and its sentiment content, so there are two sub-tasks can be done independently: The first one is classifying sentiment class of tweets as positive, negative or neutral based on its content, so does not require any other than pure tweet's text posted on Twitter; the second one is building information diffusion patterns of each tweet. This step require data about relationship between authors of the tweets and who re-tweeted it. Although, these data are available on Twitter and can be fetched easily via Twitter API[3], however there is limits with these functions, so it makes collection task is difficult to obtain data, especially fetching information of retweet action and also friendship relationship. Each Twitter API have a rate limit feature that limit number of the API calling in a small range of time; and number records of returned result is also fixed to each functions. So that, we have no other way to request all necessary data immediately from Twitter rather than building an application to download necessary information from time to time.

5.3   Data Preparation

In this study, each tweet are defined as a list of word which are not enclosed by non-letters to the left and to the right and it need to be considered as not case sensitive for comparing equally. Besides that, tweet usually embedded with some special patterns such as *Short Hyperlink* link to another resource with pattern $<http \| https>: // <Linkcontent>$ that describes more detail about

---

[2] http://twitaholic.com - *Twitterholics* is an online service that scan Twitter a few times a day to determine who is the biggest account.

[3] https://dev.twitter.com/docs provides a detail description about the latest version 1.1 of Twitter API.

content of tweet, but it is not necessary for us analysis even it is good to understand author's opinion; *Mention* is a specified feature of Twitter using pattern @<*username*> that refer to another relevant account however it only help to identity who is mentioned rather than sentiment of the status; and *Hashtag* using pattern #<*hashtag*> that can be used to grouping statuses with similar topic and also giving us some useful information for understand author's opinion e.g., *#romantic, #bestphone, #incrediblecamera*, etc. Therefore unlike data about information diffusion among users, the content of tweets request to be pre-processed before any analysis task is executed. The data pre-processing is done by the following steps

- *Case-insensitive*: For similar in string comparing method, all tweet is converted to lower case.
- *Hyperlink*: All hyperlink in tweets are replace with a special constant 'LINK'.
- *Mention*: Replace all mentions with a special constant 'USER'.
- *Hashtag*: Because it can contain some useful information for sentiment detection, so we remove symbol '#' from any hashtags to get it original content e.g., '#bestphone' will become 'bestphone'.
- *Numeric*: Numeric string is not prove clearly effect in sentiment expression, so it will remove for the tweets.
- *Special symbol*: Remove all punctuations and other special symbols even if punctuations can help to detect sentiment of the tweet in some cases.
- *Normalization*: The tweets will be rewritten in a form where no space character at either the beginning or end, each words are separated by a single space character.

6 Experimental Results and Discussion

Our *TweetScope* application can collect tweets from Twitter efficiently by using Twitter Stream service; user can access and generate useful data what represent how information diffused from original source to followers on Twitter, Table 1 show a statistic report about our collected dataset.

Using computational result obtained from sentiment classifying task and information diffusion pattern building task, the tweet dataset is classified into

Table 1. Statistics about the data used for the experiment

No		Industry	News	Entertainments
1	Number of twitter accounts	14	5	7
2	Number of tweets	3572	6755	11187
3	Number of feature words	1748	36250	47128
4	Number of stop words	1202	15548	34302
5	Number of hashtags	518	818	981
6	Number of urls	2890	4880	8407
7	Number of mentions	426	849	1703

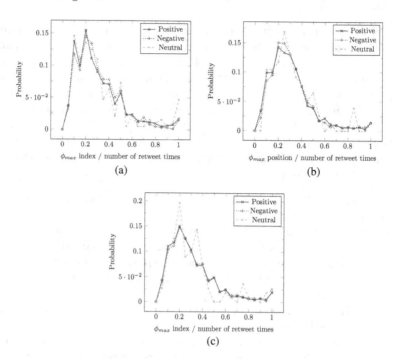

Fig. 3. Probability distribution of ratio between position of ϕ_{max} and number of "retweet" times (a) Industry group, (b) News group, (c) Entertainment group

three group based on its class labels, then we compare difference between characteristic of each polarity groups of tweets. In general we want to compare the data statistically, so ratio between ϕ_{avg}/ϕ_{max} is used as measuring value to show characteristic of diffusion patterns. The ratio value indicates an average rate of information diffused from original source to followers per an unit of time, it is mapped into range [0..1]. By splitting the range [0..1] into a list of small segments, we calculate probability appearance of ϕ_{avg}/ϕ_{max} in each inner range by dividing number of elements in the inner range and number of tweet in each sentiment polarity respectively. These charts indicate that the diffusion patterns of *positive/negative* class have probability of the average rate of information diffusion higher than another of *neutral* class, especially at high value segments. The result is consistent with the assumption that the sentiment content have a certain attraction for related users. However, there are not much difference between chart of classes at some ranges, this can be explained by the influence of noise data, the accuracy of classifier or the novelty of information has its own effect to draw attention of users.

In addition, we consider the time of occurrence of the ϕ_{max} by calculating a factor of retweet index Φ_t^{twt}, where the diffusion pattern get highest peak, and total number of retweet times of the considering tweet. The histogram charts of probability distribution of Φ_t^{twt} / *Number of retweet times* are shown as Fig. 3.

Most of diffusion patterns have a hight probability to reach highest value of coverage rate ϕ_{max} at the one-third of the early stage in series of "retweet" actions. This is quite consistent with the fact that a given news shared on social networks only attracting attention of users in short time around its posting time. The similarity of the graphs shows that shared information on social networks have same chance to spread quickly to related user regardless its sentiment polarity. Once again, may be the novelty of information can play an important role in information diffusion phenomena.

7 Conclusion

In this paper, we developed a method and a practical system to collect and analyze the relationship between sentiment polarity and information diffusion pattern of tweets, which are posted by three group of Twitter users. The experimental result showed a clear potential chance that tweet had sentiment polarity as *positive* or *negative*, have higher probability to diffuse to more users in a given unit of time, even though all kind of tweets are capable to reach highest peak of its diffusion pattern in a short time around posting time regardless its sentiment polarity.

We also recognize that the sentiment polarity and the novelty of news play the same crucial role in attracting attention of users. However, due to the limitations of this work, it will be the target of our next work in the future.

Acknowledgement. This work was supported by the BK21+ Program of the National Research Foundation (NRF) of Korea.

References

1. Brown, J., Broderick, A.J., Lee, N.: Word of mouth communication within online communities: conceptualizing the online social network. J. Interact. Mark. **21**(3), 2–20 (2007)
2. Brunelli, M., Fedrizzi, M.: A fuzzy approach to social network analysis. In: Proceedings of the 2009 International Conference on Advances in Social Network Analysis and Mining, ASONAM '09, pp. 225–230. IEEE Computer Society, Washington, DC (2009)
3. Dang-Xuan, L., Stieglitz, S.: Impact and diffusion of sentiment in political communication - an empirical analysis of political weblogs. In: Proceedings of the Sixth International AAAI Conference on Weblogs and Social Media, pp. 427–430. The AAAI Press, Dublin (2012)
4. Trung, D.N., Jung, J.J., Lee, N., Kim, J.: Thematic analysis by discovering diffusion patterns in social media: an exploratory study with tweetScope. In: Selamat, A., Nguyen, N.T., Haron, H. (eds.) ACIIDS 2013, Part II. LNCS, vol. 7803, pp. 266–274. Springer, Heidelberg (2013)
5. Huffaker, D.: Dimensions of leadership and social influence in online communities. Human Commun. Res. **36**(4), 593–617 (2010)

6. Jung, J.J.: An empirical study on optimizing query transformation on semantic peer-to-peer networks. J. Intel. Fuzzy Syst. **21**(3), 187–195 (2010)

7. Jung, J.J.: Ontology mapping composition for query transformation on distributed environments. Expert Syst. Appl. **37**(12), 8401–8405 (2010)

8. Jung, J.J.: Reusing ontology mappings for query segmentation and routing in semantic peer-to-peer environment. Inf. Sci. **180**(17), 3248–3257 (2010)

9. Jung, J.J.: Service chain-based business alliance formation in service-oriented architecture. Expert Syst. Appl. **38**(3), 2206–2211 (2011)

10. Jung, J.J.: Attribute selection-based recommendation framework for short-head user group: an empirical study by MovieLens and IMDB. Expert Syst. Appl. **39**(4), 4049–4054 (2012)

11. Jung, J.J.: Computational reputation model based on selecting consensus choices: an empirical study on semantic wiki platform. Expert Syst. Appl. **39**(10), 9002–9007 (2012)

12. Jung, J.J.: ContextGrid: a contextual mashup-based collaborative browsing system. Inf. Syst. Front. **14**(4), 953–961 (2012)

13. Jung, J.J.: Discovering community of lingual practice for matching multilingual tags from folksonomies. Comput. J. **55**(3), 337–346 (2012)

14. Jung, J.J.: Evolutionary approach for semantic-based query sampling in large-scale information sources. Inf. Sci. **182**(1), 30–39 (2012)

15. Jung, J.J.: Semantic annotation of cognitive map for knowledge sharing between heterogeneous businesses. Expert Syst. Appl. **39**(5), 1245–1248 (2012)

16. Jung, J.J.: Semantic optimization of query transformation in a large-scale peer-to-peer network. Neurocomputing **88**, 36–41 (2012)

17. Kim, M., Xie, L., Christen, P.: Event diffusion patterns in social media. In: Breslin, J.G., Ellison, N.B., Shanahan, J.G., Tufekci, Z. (eds.) Proceedings of the 6th International Conference on Weblogs and Social Media (ICWSM 2012). The AAAI Press, Dublin (2012)

18. Pham, X.H., Jung, J.J., Hwang, D.: Beating social pulse: understanding information propagation via online social tagging systems. J. Univers. Comput. Sci. **18**(8), 1022–1031 (2012)

19. Salmeron, J.L.: Fuzzy cognitive maps for artificial emotions forecasting. Appl. Soft Comput. **12**(12), 3704–3710 (2012)

20. Sen, S., Lerman, D.: Why are you telling me this? an examination into negative consumer reviews on the web. J. Interact. Mark. **21**(4), 76–94 (2007)

21. Strapparava, C., Mihalcea, R.: Learning to identify emotions in text. In: Proceedings of the 2008 ACM Symposium on Applied Computing, SAC '08, pp. 1556–1560. ACM, New York (2008)

22. Bird, S., Loper, E., Klein, E.: Natural Language Processing with Python. O'Reilly Media Inc., Sebastopol (2009)

A Method for Normalizing Non-standard Words in Online Social Network Services: A Case Study on Twitter

Dongjin Choi, Jeongin Kim, and Pankoo Kim[(✉)]

Department of Computer Engineering, Chosun University, 375 Seoseok-dong,
Dong-gu, Gwangju, Republic of Korea
{dongjin.choi84,jungingim}@gmail.com, pkkim@chosun.ac.kr

Abstract. Due to the big developments of Smartphone devices and online social network services, people can share diverse information about what they have been experienced during a day with no constrain to time or location. This fact has changed entire previous online system. We simply insert a query to search engine or OSNSs by using Smartphone devices. Because of this effectiveness, text data in OSNSs is getting bigger including many noisy data especially non-standard words. People are likely to type a text in short format such as abbreviation, acronym, and more when they using Smartphone to send a message to their friends in order to save time and data usages. As a result of these reasons, non-standard words on the web is extremely increasing so it has to be normalize into standard words in order to enhance performance of Natural Language Processing. When we analyze plain text data to extract semantic meaning, this nosy data has been ignore even though it has valuable information. In order to overcome this problem, we address a method for normalizing non-standard words in OSNSs, particularly for Twitter text data. We analyzed more than fifty million tweets which was collected by Stanford University and normalized non-standard words into standard English words by using diverse coefficient method such as dice, jacard, ochiai, sorgenfrei, and more. We finally conclude this paper by comparing those coefficient methods with our proposed one.

Keywords: Words normalization · Online social network services · Twitter

1 Introduction

There are many kinds of contents described in diverse forms such as text, audio, images, and more on the World Wide Web. Particularly, text data is the most common type of data and the volume of this data is extremely huge. Due to this text data was written by human, many researchers have been studying to discover semantic meanings from human written text data by using diverse kinds of approaches such as statistical, machine learning, knowledge

P.C. Vinh et al. (Eds.): ICCASA 2013, LNICST 128, pp. 359–368, 2014.
DOI: 10.1007/978-3-319-05939-6_35, © Springer International Publishing Switzerland 2014

based approaches, and so on [1–3]. Although, scientists have been applied highly advanced approaches for a long time, it is still challenging that the performance of Natural Language Processing (NLP) is not always increasing due to the fact that human written data has many noisy texts. For instance, miss spelled word 'univercity,' abbreviation 'st.' acronym 'WSD' are normally considered as a unimportant data for extracting semantics even though those words has valuable information. Moreover, special characters such as #, @, &, and more are normally removed in a preprocessing step in order to reduce the size of test data and enhance the performance ratio. However, these special characters do indicate specific actions in Twitter system. There is a policy in Twitter that people can share information by sending text-based message restricted to only 140 characters, known as tweets. As a result of this policy, non-standard words on the web is extremely increasing so it has to be normalize into standard words in order to machine can analyze non-standard words. Besides, there is a high possibility that people are likely to type a text in short format such as abbreviation, acronym, or no-standard English form when they using Smartphone to send a message to their friends in order to save time and data usages. This issue brings huge obstacle when scientists conduct an experiment by using NLP techniques. In order to overcome this problem, we introduce a method to normalize non-standard words in online social network services particularly for Twitter data by using several coefficient approaches. The reminder of the paper is organized as follows: Sect. 2 describes what Twitter is and related works; Sect. 3 explains a method for normalizing non-standard words in Twitter based on several coefficient approaches; Sect. 4 gives experimental results; and finally Sect. 5 conclude this paper with future works.

2   Related Works

Twitter is one of the most common online social network services (OSNSs) platform which let people share information, interests, and knowledge among others by sending text-based message restricted to only 140 characters, known as a tweet [4]. Because of this limitation of text size and inconvenience of Smartphone text input system, people type a text message as short as possible in order to save time and usage. As a result, Twitter is full of non-standard words which machine cannot detect as important terms. Besides, there are few interesting functions which operated by special characters in Twitter. The following Table 1 shows examples of tweets written by certain online user A.

According to Twitter policy, there are interesting functions which is described by special characters such as @, #, and RT. The @ sign is used to call out (mention) usernames in Tweets and it becomes a link to a user profile. The # indicates hashtags which is used to mark keywords or topics to categorize messages. RT represents retweet which is a re-posting someone else tweets to spread news or share valuable information with others [5]. Therefore, these non-standard words have not to be removed in pre-processing step. Non-standard words have been interested by many researchers for long time. Before we introduce other

Table 1. Examples of tweet messages in Twitter

Text messages in Twitter
RT @fanfusionblog: RT this message to win $ 50 Gift Card! 100th to do so wins!
@AllSelenaGomez Blah, I'm tired, good. You?
#dumbquestions (calling the house phone) WHERE ARE YOU?!
@MrsBieber69 love you too, and #ofcourse #betheresoon

Table 2. Examples of non-standard words

Taxonomy	Example
Contraction	Im, cant, wont, havent, ...
Abbreviation	uni., dept., ref., max., ...
Acronym	SCUBA, ROM, NLP, NER, FBI, ...
Mixed	WS99, x220, MS-Dos, ...
Funny spelling	cooool, hooooot, lol, :), b4, ...
Misspelling	geogaphy, univercity, knowlege, ...

researches approaches to normalize non-standard words, we describe examples of non-standard words shown in Table 2.

A contraction word is a shortened form of word created by using apostrophe such as {*let us: lets, I am: Im, cannot: cant, have not: haven*}. This contraction is defined in English grammar so it is not difficult to normalize into standard words. An abbreviation is a shortened form of word or phrase to omit when the length of a word is too long such as ad for advertisement. Abbreviation is also defined in many English dictionaries so it can be normalized by using dictionary and rule based approaches [6,7]. An acronym is an abbreviation formed which is composed of initial components of multiple words such as {*CEO: Chief Executive Officer, SCUBA: Self-Contained Underwater Breathing Apparatus, FAQ: Frequently Asked Question, BBC: British Broadcasting Corporation*}. The problem is that acronyms can have several kinds of different expansion words, in other words it has a word sense disambiguation problem. For example, acronym NER indicates not only Named Entity Recognition in computer science area but also North Eastern Railway which was an English railway company. According to Wikipedia[1], there are 14 different kinds of entities indicating acronym NER. This is huge obstacle when we faced this polysemous acronym in test data. In order to overcome this obstacle, Hwang [8] proposed a method for normalize terminologies by using Wikipedia labels to enhance the performance. This research based on the assumption that labels in Wikipedia is the standard terms for terminologies. However, they did not cover the acronyms which have multiple expansion words. Non-standard words such as a mixed form would not be fully detected when we only applied rule-based approaches. Because, there are no particular patterns to represent mixed formed words. Funny spelling words are new type of words to

---

[1] http://www.en.wikipedia.org/wiki/NER

emphasize adjective by repeating certain characters or emoticons. These words are created due to the fact that people want to express their emotional status far beyond normal English words. Misspelled words are commonly appeared in online text messages, email, short message service (SMS), blog, Twitter, Facebook, and more. Misspelled words can be normalized by using n-gram based approaches [9, 10]. As we can see in this section, English words are not always expressed by perfect standard format. Especially, online text messages are full of non-standard words. Hence, we propose a method for normalizing non-standard words appeared in OSNSs especially for Twitter text messages.

3   Twitter Data Set

Twitter text messages which we are going to deal with were collected by Stanford University [11] contains entire text messages on November in 2009 approximately 8.27 GB by more than 5.5 million users. In order to find active users not spammers, we focused on users who exposed someones birthday by using simple linguistic rule [12]. So we can obtain 24,922 candidate active users. This data set consists of three kinds of information which are time, user URL, and tweet message shown in Table 3.

Table 3. Examples of the Twitter data set

Type	Information
T	2009-11-01 00:43:19
U	http://twitter.com/ivoryshorty
W	@iamdorkster you the effin' best ...
T	2009-11-01 01:10:46
U	http://twitter.com/ivoryshorty
W	@documentedmusic very dope...I like your flow ...
T	2009-11-01 02:49:53
U	http://twitter.com/ivoryshorty
W	@PinkRoyaltie Aww how cute! Yeah ours was yesterday ...

As we can see in Table 3, the tweet messages are full of non-standard words which are needed to be normalized. We randomly choose five thousands users from Twitter data set and analyzed how many non-standard words are by using PyEnchant[2] module which is a spellchecking library for Python. The total number of tweets for 5,000 users is 365,967 which contain 5,748,586 words. According to PyEnchant spellchecking library, there are more than 40 percent of non-standard words in this tweet text messages. This will bring big obstacle if we analyze natural language processing by using this Twitter text messages. This is the main reason why we want to normalize non-standard words in Twitter.

---

[2] http://www.pythonhosted.org/pyenchant/

4   Normalization for Non-standard Words in Twitter

This section describes a method for normalizing non-standard words into standard words in Twitter text messages by using several coefficient methods. As we introduced in the previous section, we prepared test data set which contains non-standard words. These non-standard words are consisted of contractions, abbreviations, acronyms, mixed words, funny spelling words, and misspelling words. We put those words into PyEnchant module to find standard words of them. The following Table 4 shows the results of this step.

Table 4. Results of suggestions for non-standard words by using PyEnchant

Taxonomy	NSW	Suggestions
Contraction	havent	haven, haven't, havens, ha vent, haven t'
Contraction	youre	yourself, your, you're, you've
Mixed	MS-Dos	None
Funny spelling	freee	free, freeze, frees, freer, freed, free e
Funny spelling	need2know	needlework, needlewomen, needlewoman,needlepoint
Misspelling	definately	definitely, definably, determinately, definable, definitively

Although, PyEnchant is powerful module to check English spelling, it does not always give a perfect suggestion for non-standard words. PyEnchant module cannot find expansion words for abbreviations, acronyms, and mixed words. However, it does recommend candidate standard words for contractions, funny spelling words, and misspelling words. The problem is that we cannot guarantee whether suggested words for funny spelling words are correct or not. Therefore, we want to find the most appropriate words by using Dice, Jaccard, Ochiai, and proposed coefficient approaches. The non-standard words we want to focus on are contraction, funny spelling, and misspelling words in this paper.

Dice coefficient is a statistic approach for comparing the similarity of two samples developed by *Lee Raymond Dice* [13]. Let us assume that we have two samples 'havent' and 'haven't'. Bigrams of these two words can be represented by as follows: $bigram_{havent} = \{ha, av, ve, en, nt\}$ and $bigram_{haven't} = \{ha, av, ve, en, n','t\}$. Dice coefficient of these two words can be calculated by following the Eq. 1.

$$Dice\_coeff(w_i, w_j) = \frac{2 \times |bigram_{w_i} \cap bigram_{w_j}|}{|bigram_{w_i}| + |bigram_{w_j}|} \qquad (1)$$

where, $|bigram_{w_i}|$ and $|bigram_{w_j}|$ are the number of total bigram of given words $|w_i|$ and $|w_j|$. $|bigram_{w_i} \cap bigram_{w_j}|$ denotes the number of bigrams which appeared in $|w_i|$ and $|w_j|$ at the same time.

Jaccard coefficient which was developed by *Paul Jaccard* is statistic used for measuring similarity and diversity of samples followed by the Eq. 2 [13].

$$Jaccard\_coeff(w_i, w_j) = \frac{|bigram_{w_i} \cap bigram_{w_j}|}{|bigram_{w_i} \cup bigram_{w_j}|} \qquad (2)$$

Ochiai coefficient or also known as Ochiai-Barkman coefficient, or Otsuka-Ochiai coefficient was considered as a superior coefficient measurement in research [13] which can be calculated by the following Eq. 3.

$$Ochiai\_coeff(w_i, w_j) = \frac{|bigram_{w_i} \cap bigram_{w_j}|}{\sqrt{|bigram_{w_i}| \times |bigram_{w_j}|}} \tag{3}$$

Our proposed coefficient measurement is performed well when two given words has the same number of characters such as words {'Seoul' and 'Seuol'} followed by the Eq. 4.

$$Proposed\_coeff(w_i, w_j) = \frac{|bigram_{w_i} \cap bigram_{w_j}|}{avg(|bigram_{w_i}| + |bigram_{w_j}|)} \tag{4}$$

We hereby measure the similarities between non-standard word and suggested words by PyEnchant module in order to address what the weakness of this

Table 5. Similarity results between non-standard words and suggested words

NSW	Suggestions	Dice	Jaccard	Ochiai	Proposed
freeee	freezer	0.667	0.375	0.548	0.545
	freemen	0.667	0.375	0.548	0.545
	freeze	**0.75**	**0.428**	**0.6**	**0.6**
	freeness	0.6	0.333	0.507	0.5
	free	1.0	0.6	0.774	0.75
definately	**definitely**	**0.778**	**0.636**	**0.778**	0.889
	definably	0.706	0.545	0.707	**0.941**
	definable	0.588	0.417	0.589	0.823
	subordinately	0.571	0.4	0.577	0.762
Thinking	**Thinking**	**0.909**	0.625	0.771	0.769
	Thinkable	0.615	0.4	0.577	0.714
	Thinkably	0.615	0.4	0.577	0.714
	Thinker	0.727	0.5	0.667	**0.833**
	Think	0.889	**0.667**	**0.816**	0.8
havent	**haven't**	0.727	0.571	0.730	**0.909**
	Haven	**0.889**	**0.8**	**0.894**	0.889
	haver	0.667	0.5	0.670	0.889
bday	Hobday	**0.75**	**0.6**	**0.774**	0.75
	Bayda	0.571	0.4	0.577	**0.857**
	birthday	0.4	0.25	0.436	0.6
	daybed	0.5	0.33	0.516	0.75
thnks	methinks	0.545	0.375	0.567	0.727
	think	0.5	0.333	0.5	0.75
	thank	0.5	0.333	0.5	0.75
	thunk	0.5	0.333	0.5	0.75
txt	**text**	0.4	0.25	0.408	**0.8**
	twixt	0.333	0.2	0.353	0.667
	TX	**0.667**	**0.5**	**0.707**	0.667

system and how can we applied our proposed coefficient measurement. Table 5 indicates the results of similarities between non-standard words and suggested words by using four kinds of coefficient methods.

According to the results of Table 5, the proposed method does not always give the best standard words for NSWs. However, it does give the best words if the type of non-standard words is the contraction such as *'havent'*. As we can see in the Table 5, the candidate words for *'havent'* are {*havent, Haven, haven, haver*}. If we applied the Dice, Jaccard, and Ochiai coefficient methods, we cannot find the right words for *'havent'*. However, we could find the most likely reasonable word if we applied the proposed coefficient method.

The non-standard word *'freeee'* is the funny spelling words for a word *'free'*. However, as we can see in the Table 5, PyEnchant suggested four kinds of words {*'freezer,' 'freemen,' 'freeze,' 'freeness'*} except *'free'*. If PyEnchant can recommend a word *'free'* the similarities between words *'freeee'* and *'free'* might be the highest values by using four kinds of coefficients. Therefore, we have concluded that this module is not suitable for normalizing funny spelling words. In

Table 6. Similarity results between funny words and suggested words

Funny words	Suggestions	Dice	Jaccard	Ochiai	Proposed
happpppy	happily	0.6	0.3	0.462	0.615
	happening	0.5	0.25	0.400	0.4
	happiness	0.5	0.25	0.400	0.4
	happy	**1.0**	**0.571**	**0.755**	**0.727**
freeee	freezer	0.667	0.375	0.548	0.545
	freemen	0.667	0.375	0.548	0.545
	freeze	**0.75**	**0.428**	**0.6**	**0.6**
	freeness	0.6	0.333	0.507	0.5
juuuust	justness	0.545	0.3	0.462	0.461
	justest	**0.666**	**0.333**	**0.5**	**0.5**
	justing	0.6	**0.333**	**0.5**	**0.5**
	Justice	0.6	**0.333**	**0.5**	**0.5**
truuueee	trusteeing	0.428	0.230	0.377	0.5
	trusteeship	0.4	0.214	0.358	0.470
	Truckee	**0.545**	**0.3**	**0.462**	**0.615**
	trustee	**0.545**	**0.3**	**0.462**	**0.615**
gooooole	**Google**	0.666	0.333	0.507	0.5
baaaad	Baal	0.666	0.333	0.516	0.5
weeeeird	weekender	0.307	0.153	0.267	0.266
	weirdness	0.615	0.363	0.534	0.533
	weedkiller	0.285	0.142	0.251	0.375
	weirdie	**0.727**	**0.444**	**0.617**	**0.615**
hellllooo	hellebore	0.461	0.25	0.400	0.533
	Hellespont	0.428	0.230	0.377	0.5
	hellhole	0.5	0.272	0.428	0.571
	hellion	**0.545**	**0.3**	**0.462**	**0.615**

Table 7. Similarity results between normalized funny words and suggested words

Normalized words	Suggestions	Dice	Jaccard	Ochiai	Proposed
happy	**happy**	**1.0**	**1.0**	**1.0**	**1.0**
free	**free**	**1.0**	**1.0**	**1.0**	**1.0**
	frees	0.857	0.75	0.866	0.857
	freer	0.857	0.75	0.866	0.857
	freed	0.857	0.75	0.866	0.857
juust	**just**	**0.857**	**0.75**	**0.866**	**0.857**
	Justen	0.666	0.5	0.670	0.666
	juster	0.666	0.5	0.670	0.666
	justed	0.666	0.5	0.670	0.666
	Justis	0.666	0.5	0.670	0.666
truuee	trustee	0.5454	0.375	0.547	0.727
	Truckee	0.5454	0.375	0.547	0.727
	truelove	0.5	0.333	0.507	0.666
	trueness	0.5	0.333	0.507	0.666
	true	**0.75**	**0.6**	**0.774**	**0.75**
goole	**Google**	**0.666**	**0.5**	**0.607**	**0.666**
	goober	0.444	0.285	0.447	0.444
	gooier	0.444	0.285	0.447	0.444
	Goober	0.444	0.285	0.447	0.444
baad	Baal	0.666	0.5	0.666	0.666
	baa	**0.8**	**0.666**	**0.816**	**0.8**
	ballad	0.5	0.333	0.516	0.5
	Baden	0.571	0.4	0.577	0.571
	bad	**0.8**	**0.666**	**0.816**	**0.8**
weeird	**weird**	**0.888**	**0.8**	**0.894**	**0.888**
	weirdie	0.727	0.571	0.730	0.727
	weirdo	0.8	0.666	0.8	0.8
	weeing	0.6	0.428	0.6	0.6
	weirdness	0.615	0.444	0.632	0.615
helloo	**hello**	**1.0**	**1.0**	**1.0**	**0.75**
	weirdness	0.888	0.8	0.894	0.666

order to find the most appropriate word for *'freeee'*, we defined a rule based on the linguistic patterns of the funny spelling words. In case of the funny spelling words, certain character is normally repeated for emphasizing a word. For example, {*happppppy, freeee, juuuust, truuueee, gooooole, baaaaad, weeeeird, hellllooo*} these words are the funny spelling words when people used for giving emotional status in text messages. A funny spelling word can be represented by following Eq. 5 where, w_i denotes a funny spelling word and c_j denotes an English character.

$$w_i = (c_j + c_{j+1} + c_{j+2} + ... + c_n) \tag{5}$$

If c_j and c_{j+1} are the same, it is not a funny word. However, if c_j, c_{j+1}, ... c_{j+n} are the same, we can simply normalize this word into standard word due to the fact that the maximum number of the same character in an English word is two.

When we simply put funny spelled words without the normalizing step into our system, the results will not be reasonable as show in Table 6. As we can see in Table 6, we only can find two correct words (happy and Google) for funny spelled words. PyEnchant suggested words based on the length of word and their characters so the suggested words for funny spelled words are not always adequate. Therefore, we need to normalize funny spelled words by using Eq. 5 in order to reduce their complexities. As a result, we can obtain more precise candidate words for the funny spelled words described in Table 7. We cannot find a standard word for '*juuuust*' shown in Table 6 however, we are able to find '*just*' by using our proposed approach. Therefore, we can normalize the funny spelled words which commonly considered as a noisy data into the standard English word successfully. If we do not normalize the funny spelled word such as '*baaaad*', computer is not able to find the standard word '*bad*'.

5   Conclusion and Future Works

This paper proposed a method for normalizing non-standard words to standard English words in online social network services especially for Twitter text messages. Although, Twitter provides great convenience to user for sharing their interest, experience, knowledge and more, there are full of non-standard words in Twitter due to the restricted input policy and users have to text a message by using smartphone devices. Non-standard words bring huge obstacle when we analyze human written language in order to find semantic meanings from given texts or documents. There is a powerful NLP module based on Python named PyEnchant which is a spellchecking library. It suggests words to users when input words are not in standard English form based on the length of words and combination of words characters. The problem is that we cannot guarantee whether those suggested words are the precise one or not. Therefore, we introduced a method for finding the most appropriate word from suggested words by using Dice, Jaccard, Ochiai, and proposed coefficient similarities. We can conclude that our proposed method is strongly able to distinguish contraction and funny spelled type of NSW compared with other methods. However, the proposed approach is mainly depending on the PyEnchant. If PyEnchant does not suggest candidate words for NSW, we cannot find the standard type of words at all. Hence, we need to develop more strongly system to find the candidate word for NSW without PyEnchant's help. This is the next goal of our research.

Acknowledgments. This research was supported by Basic Science Research Program through the National Research Foundation of Korea (NRF) funded by the Ministry of Education (No. 2013R1A1A2A10011667) and financially supported by the Ministry of Education, Science Technology (MEST) and National Research Foundation of Korea (NRF) through the Human Resource Training Project for Regional Innovation.

References

1. Hwang, M., Choi, C., Kim, P.: Automatic enrichment of semantic relation network and its application to word sense disambiguation. IEEE Trans. Knowl. Data Eng. **23**(6), 845–858 (2011)
2. Steyvers, M., Tenenbaum, J.B.: The large-scale structure of semantic networks: statistical analyses and a model of semantic growth. Cogn. Sci. **29**, 41–78 (2005)
3. Choudhury, M., Saraf, R., Jain, V., Mukherjee, A., Sarkar, S., Basu, A.: Investigation and modeling of the structure of texting language. Int. J. Doc. Anal. Recogn. **10**(3), 157–174 (2007)
4. http://www.en.wikipedia.org/wiki/Twitter
5. http://www.support.twitter.com/articles/166337-the-twitter-glossary
6. Cook, P., Stevenson, S.: An unsupervised model for text message normalization. In: Proceedings of the Workshop on Computational Approaches to Linguistic Creativity, pp. 421–432 (2009)
7. Han, B., Cook, P., Baldwin, T.: Automatically constructing a normalisation dictionary for microblogs. In: Conference on Empirical Methods in Natural Language Processing, pp. 421–432 (2012)
8. Hwang, M., Jeong, D., Kim, J., Song, S., Jung, H., Shin, J., Kim, P.: A term normalization method for efficient knowledge acquisition through text processing. Multimedia Tools Appl. **65**(1), 75–91 (2013)
9. Henriquez, C.A., Hernandez, A.: A ngrambased statistical machine translation approach for text normalization on chatspeak style communications. In: Proceedings of CAW2.0, pp. 1–5 (2009)
10. Sproat, R., Black, A.W., Chen, S., Kumar, S., Ostendorf, M., Richards, C.: Normalization of non-standard words. Comput. Speech Lang. **15**(3), 287–333 (2001)
11. Yang, J., Leskovec, J.: Patterns of temporal variation in online media. In: ACM International Conference on Web Search and Data Mining, pp. 177–186 (2011)
12. Choi, D., You, I., Kim, P.: Syntactic analysis for monitoring personal information leakage on social network services: a case study on twitter. In: Mustofa, K., Neuhold, E.J., Tjoa, A.M., Weippl, E., You, I. (eds.) ICT-EurAsia 2013. LNCS, vol. 7804, pp. 253–260. Springer, Heidelberg (2013)
13. Jackson, D.A., Sombers, K.M., Harvey, H.H.: Similarity coefficients: measures of co-occurrence and association or simply measures of occurrence? Am. Nat. **133**(3), 436–453 (1989)

Combining Heuristics and Learning
for Entity Linking

Hien T. Nguyen(✉)

Ton Duc Thang University, Ho Chi Minh, Vietnam
hien@tdt.edu.vn

Abstract. Entity linking refers to the task of mapping name strings in a text to their corresponding entities in a given knowledge base. It is an essential component in natural language processing applications and a challenging task. This paper proposes a method that combines heuristics and learning for entity linking by (i) learning coherence among co-occurrence entities within the text based on Wikipedia's link structure and (ii) exploiting some heuristics based on the contexts and coreference relations among name strings. The experiment results on TAC-KBP2011 dataset show that our method achieves performance comparable to the state-of-the-art methods. The results also show that the proposed model is simple because of using a classifier trained on just two popular features in combination with some heuristics, but effective.

Keywords: Entity linking · Entity disambiguation · Wikification

1 Introduction

The task of identifying *surface forms* – strings used mentioning to entities in text – and linking them to their corresponding knowledge base (KB) entries that provide background information about the referent entities is an essential component in natural language processing applications. This task was well-known as entity disambiguation [1] or entity linking [2]. When the used KB is Wikipedia, the task is also known as wikification [5]. This work pursues the entity linking task that is to annotate/map surface forms in text with/to their corresponding entries in a given KB, i.e., Wikipedia. For instance, given the mention *Jim Clark* in the context "Jim Clark took pole position for the Monaco Grand Prix", a good entity linking method will recognize Jim Clark as the British Formula One racing driver, but in another context "Netscape cofounder Jim Clark returns to the Forbes Billionaires List", that method will recognize Jim Clark as the cofounder of Netscape. From now on, we use entity linking in place of both entity disambiguation and wikification.

Entity linking (EL) is challenging due to surface forms ambiguity. That is because one surface form may refer to different entities in different occurrences and one entity may be referred to by different surface forms in different contexts. For example, the surface form *Michael Jordan* in different occurrences may refer to the basketball player (who had ever played for Chicago Bulls), the professor working at UC Berkeley, etc.; or surface forms *Michael Jordan* and *Jordan* in different contexts can referred to the same person. In particular, given a document d, let $S = \{s_1, s_2, ..., s_N\}$ be

P.C. Vinh et al. (Eds.): ICCASA 2013, LNICST 128, pp. 369–378, 2014.
DOI: 10.1007/978-3-319-05939-6_36, © Springer International Publishing Switzerland 2014

the set of surface forms in d; the goal is to produce annotations of the set of surface forms with the set of KB entries $A = \{a_1, a_2, ..., a_N\}$. When the used KB is Wikipedia, A is a set of Wikipedia articles.

Since 2009, the entity linking shared task yearly held at Text Analysis Conference (TAC) [2] has attracted more and more attention of research groups all over the world and many approaches to entity linking have been proposed. In TAC entity linking, given a query consisting of a surface form and a background document where the surface form occurs, the EL system is required to provide the identifier (ID) of the KB entry of that surface form; or *NIL* if there is no such KB entry [2]. Figure 1 shows an example in which *Georgia* is the surface form targeted disambiguation. The figure also shows that co-occurrence name strings such as "US" and "Atlanta" actually help to clarify which entity Georgia actually refers to.

In this paper, we propose an entity linking method that tries to model how human beings disambiguate a surface form. When reading a text and encountering a surface form, one may rely on his/her knowledge accumulated in the past and the context of the text to identify which one is the underlying entity of that surface form. Indeed, our method exploits prior knowledge about entities and analyzes the context to perform linking decisions. Our proposed model was presented in Fig. 2 with three key steps: (1) candidate generation, (2) linking by heuristics, and (3) linking by learning. As showed in Fig. 2, our entity linking system receives an input as a query that consists of a surface form and the document where that surface form occurs, and then outputs the ID of the KB entry that the surface form actually mentions.

The contribution of this paper is three-fold as follows: (i) we propose a model that combines heuristics and learning for entity linking; (ii) we show that the proposed model is simple with several heuristics and a classifier trained on just two popular features, but effective in that it gives performance comparable to the state-of-the-art methods; and (iii) we evaluate the proposed method on a public dataset and show that it gets good performance.

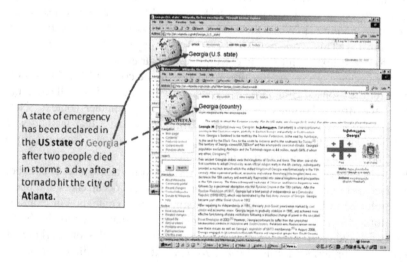

Fig. 1. Wikification

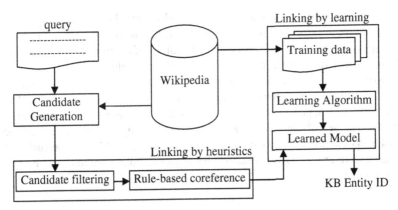

Fig. 2. Our entity linking system

The rest of this paper is organized as follows. Section 2 presents how our method generates candidates for a surface form. Sections 3 and 4 present linking by heuristics and learning respectively. Experiments and results are presented in Sect. 5. Section 6 presents related work. Finally, we draw conclusion and perspectives for future work.

2 Candidate Generation

Wikipedia is a free encyclopedia written by a collaborative effort of a large number of volunteer contributors. There are many meaningful resources of information in Wikipedia that we can exploit for entity linking. Our method proposed in this paper exploits the following resources.

Articles. A basic entry in Wikipedia is an *article* that defines and describes a single entity. It is uniquely identified by its title that is considered as its ID and includes a surface form of that entity. When the surface form is ambiguous, the title may contain further information that we call *title-hint* to distinguish the described entity from others. The title-hint is separated from the surface form by parentheses, e.g. "John McCarthy (computer scientist)", or a comma, e.g. "Columbia, South Carolina".

Categories. The category hierarchy of Wikipedia is a kind of collaborative tagging system that enables the users to categorize the content of the encyclopedic entries. Each article in Wikipedia belongs to some categories. For instance, from the categories of the article describing John McCarthy (computer scientist) in Wikipedia, we extract its category labels as follows: Stanford University faculty; Lisp programming language; Artificial intelligence researchers; etc.

Redirect Pages. A redirect page typically contains only a reference to an article. The title of a redirect page is an alternative surface form of the described entity or concept in that article. For example, from redirect pages of the United States, we extract alternative surface forms of the United States such as "US", "USA", "United States of America", etc.

Links. Each page consists of many outgoing links (outlinks) and ingoing links (inlinks). Each link is associated with an anchor text that represents the surface form of the corresponding entity. We collect candidates of a surface form based on outlinks in all articles in which the surface form occurs as labels of the outlinks.

We extract surface forms from the titles of articles and the titles of redirect pages to build a dictionary in which each entry is a surface form. Each entry surface form in the dictionary is mapped to the set of entities that the surface form may denote in Wikipedia. The set of entities is identified by exploiting outlinks in all articles in Wikipedia. As a result, an entity e is included in that set if and only if the surface form can be used to refer to e. Given a surface form, its candidates are retrieved by looking up the dictionary.

3   Linking by Heuristics

Co-occurring entities in a text may have relation with each other. Furthermore, the referent of a surface form can be inferred from nearby entities that have already been identified in the text. For example, when "Michael Jordan" occurs with "Chicago Bulls" or "NBA" in a text, it is more likely that the surface form "Michael Jordan" refers to the former player of Chicago Bulls basketball team. In reality, an entity may have several different surface forms. Therefore, when referring to a certain entity, one can use one or more of its surface forms. We observed that some surface forms co-occurring in a text and referring to the same entity is common. So this method exploits coreference relations among co-occurring surface forms for entity linking.

- Candidate filtering: We employ heuristics, H_1, H_2, and H_3 proposed by Nguyen and Cao (2012) [23] to filter candidates of surface forms. If the number of a surface form is reduced to 1, it is considered as disambiguated and linked to its corresponding entity in the KB.
- Coreference: We employ some of orthomatcher rules proposed in [16] to identify if two certain surface forms are coreferent and then coreference chains among surface forms in the query document are established.

Note that to produce a reliable coreference relation between two mentions, we prohibit the transitive property. That is because in many cases transitivity in coreference relations causes failure. In particular, assume we know that $\{m_1, m_2\}$ and $\{m_2, m_3\}$ are coreferent pairs, we do not imply that m_1 and m_3 are coreferent. An example in [16] showed that assuming transitivity and two coreferent pairs {BBC News, News} and {News, ITV News} imply wrongly that {BBC News, ITV News} are coreferent.

4   Linking by Learning

Milne and Witten [10] employed some classification algorithms to train classifiers using three features namely: commonness (CM), semantic relatedness (SR), and context quality (CQ). The authors showed that Bagged C4.5 give the best performance. In this section, we re-present features proposed by Milne and Witten [10] for representing entities and how to rank candidate entities of a surface form.

4.1 Commonness

Let s be a surface form, CE_s be a set of candidate entities of s. Commonness [11] of an entity $e \in CE_s$ is the probability of s to link to e. The commonness of a certain pair of the entity e and the surface form s is computed based on Wikipedia as a KB, with different occurrences of s linked to (i.e., referring to) different entities (i.e., Wikipedia articles) including the entity e and defined as follows:

$$Commonnes(e) = \frac{counts_s(e)}{\sum_{e_i \in CE_s} counts_s(e_i)}$$

where $counts_s(e)$ is a function that returns the number of times the surface form s is used to refer to entity e in a certain KB. For instance, assuming that in a KB, a surface form s occurs 10 times and refers to three different entities a, b, c, in which 7 times s refers to a, 2 times s refers to b respectively; then commonness $(a) = 7/10 = 0.7$, commonness $(b) = 2/10 = 0.2$, commonness $(c) = 1/10 = 0.1$; therefore, a is considered as more popular than b and c in the given KB.

4.2 Semantic Relatedness

Given two entities e_1 and e_2, let A_1 be the set of all Wikipedia articles, each of which has a link to e_1, A_2 be the set of all Wikipedia articles, each of which has a link to e_2, and W is the set of all articles in Wikipedia; semantic relatedness between the two entities, e_1 and e_2, called $sem(e_1,e_2)$ is defined as follows:

$$Sem(e_1, e_2) = 1 - \frac{\log(\max(|A_1|, |A_2|)) - \log(A_1 \cap A_2)}{\log(|W|) - \log(\min(|A_1|, |A_2|))}$$

Let E be the set of entities that have already been identified, which are called context entities. We calculate semantic relatedness of an entity e, denoted $SR_w(e)$ and $SR(e)$, as respectively *weighted* average and average of its semantic relatedness to context entities.

$$SR_w(e) = \frac{\sum_{e' \in E} weight(e') \times Sem(e, e')}{\sum_{e' \in E} weight(e')}$$

$$SR(e) = \frac{\sum_{e' \in E} Sem(e, e')}{|E|}$$

The weight of each entity $e' \in E$ of the surface form s in $SR_w(e)$ was used as the third features in [10] to balance between commonness and semantic relatedness; and is calculated as follows:

$$weight(e) = \frac{\alpha SR(e) + \beta IM(s)}{\alpha + \beta}$$

The $IM(s)$ function estimates the important of the surface form s. We observed that not all surface forms, as well as their referents, play an equally importance role in disambiguation decision of a certain surface form. In other word, some surface forms are more informative than other ones. $IM(s)$ is calculated as follows:

$$IM(s) = \frac{|A'(s)|}{|A(s)|}$$

where $A(s)$ is the set of Wikipedia articles in which s occurs and $A'(s)$ is the set of Wikipedia articles in which s occurs as a label of an outgoing link.

4.3   Linking by Expanding Candidate Set

Our proposed method utilizes coreference relations among surface forms to expand the set of candidates of a certain surface form and then ranks those candidates to choose the best one. It firstly ranks candidates of the surface form to be linked and choose the candidate that having the rank higher a threshold; otherwise, the set of candidates of that surface form is expanded by all candidates of all its coreferent surface forms. For instance, assume that two surface forms s and s' are coreferent and s is the surface form to be linked; let $\{c_1, c_2, c_3\}$ be the set of candidates of s and $\{c'_1, c'_2\}$ be the set of candidates of s'; assume that after being ranked, c_1 has the highest rank and the rank of c_1 is lower than a threshold, our proposed method will rank c'_1 and c'_2 and if the highest rank between those of them is greater than a threshold, s is linked to the corresponding candidate, otherwise, s is linked NIL. Note that the detected list of candidates for each surface form might not be complete; therefore, our method does not require two certain referent candidates c_i and c'_j of s and s' respectively must be the same.

Note that the method presented in [10] considers a surface form that has only one candidate as an unambiguous one and the mapping between that surface form and its sole candidate as the final linking decision. However, in reality, the sole candidate of a surface form may not be the entity that the surface form actually refers to. Our proposed method can overcome this drawback by exploiting the coreference relations. Indeed, for a surface form that having only one candidate, our method may link the surface form to an entity other than its sole candidate. For example, assume that two surface forms s and s' are coreferent and s is the surface form to be linked; let c_1 be the sole candidate of s and $\{c'_1, c'_2\}$ be a set of candidates of s'; assume that c'_1 has the highest rank among those of c_1, c'_1, c'_2, our method will link s to c'_1 instead of c_1.

5   Evaluation

We employ the Bagged C4.5 classification algorithm to train a classifier using the features presented in Sect. 4. As in [10], we train our system on a collection of 500 Wikipedia articles and use 100 other Wikipedia articles that do not appear in the training set to tune parameters. We evaluate our proposed method on TAC-KBP2011 dataset. This dataset consists of 2250 entity mention queries, in which 1124 entity mentions refer to entities described by Wikipedia articles. The evaluation metrics we use are micro-average accuracy (MAA) and B-Cubed+ [2]. We conducted two experiments: (1) without expanding candidate set, namely *Exp1* and (2) with expanding candidate set, namely *Exp2*. Tables 1 and 3 show MAA overall results of *Exp1* and *Exp2* on TAC-KBP2011 dataset respectively. Tables 2 and 4 show B-Cubed+ F1 overall results of *Exp1* and *Exp2* on TAC-KBP2011 dataset respectively. Table 5 show the performance of our method among top 5 best systems in TAC 2011 [2].

The results show that our proposed method is simple, but its performance is comparable to sophisticated methods proposed in top 5 best systems submitted to TAC 2011. Tables 3 and 4 show that expanding candidate set using coreference relations among co-occurrence surface forms improves about 9 % in the best cases when combining commonness and semantic relatedness for training the classifier.

Table 1. The MAA overall results of *Exp1* on TAC-KBP2011 dataset

Feature sets	All (2,250) (%)	NIL (1126) (%)	Non-NIL (1124) (%)
CM	68.3	90.6	46.0
CM+SR	72.7	96.6	48.7
CM+SR+CQ	**73.4**	**94.8**	**52.0**

Table 2. The B-Cubed+ F1 overall results of *Exp1* on TAC-KBP2011 dataset

Feature sets	All (2,250) (%)	NIL (1126) (%)	Non-NIL (1124) (%)
CM	65.5	87.6	44.9
CM+SR	69.6	93	47.3
CM+SR+CQ	**70.4**	**91.4**	**50.6**

Table 3. The MAA overall results of *Exp2* on TAC-KBP2011 dataset

Feature sets	All (2,250) (%)	NIL (1126) (%)	Non-NIL (1124) (%)
CM	75.3	87.8	62.8
CM+SR	**82.5**	**95**	**69.9**
CM+SR+CQ	81.7	92.5	71.0

Table 4. The B-Cubed+ F1 overall results of *Exp2* on TAC-KBP2011 dataset

Feature sets	All (2,250) (%)	NIL (1126) (%)	Non-NIL (1124) (%)
CM	72.7	85	61.5
CM+SR	**79.5**	**91.3**	**68.4**
CM+SR+CQ	78.8	88.9	69.4

Table 5. Our method among top 5 best systems in TAC 2011 [2]

Systems	MAA (%)	B-Cubed+ F1 (%)
LCC [19]	86.1	84.6
NUSchime [18]	86.3	83.1
Ours	**82.5**	**79.5**
Stanford_UBC [20]	79.0	76.3
CUNY [22]	77.8	77.1
CMCRC [21]	77.9	75.4

6 Related Work

To date, many approaches have been proposed for EL using Wikipedia. All of them can fit into three disambiguating strategies: *local*, *global*, and *collective*. Local methods disambiguate each mention independently based on local context compatibility between the mention and its candidate entities using some context features. Global and collective methods assume that linking decisions are interdependence and there is coherence between co-occurrence entities in a text, enabling the use of measures of semantic relatedness for disambiguation. While collective methods simultaneously perform disambiguation decisions, global methods disambiguate mentions in turn.

As a local approach, the method proposed in [12] uses an SVM kernel to compare the lexical context around a certain mention to that of its candidates, in combination with estimating correlation of the contextual words with the candidates' categories. Each candidate of a mention is a Wikipedia article and its lexical context is the content of the article. In [15] the authors implemented and evaluated two different disambiguation algorithms. The first one was based on the measure of contextual overlapping between the local context of a mention and the content of candidate Wikipedia articles to identify the most likely candidate. The second one trains a Naïve Bayes classifier for each mention using three words to the left and the right of outlinks in Wikipedia articles, with their parts-of-speech, as contextual features. In [7] the authors employed classification algorithms that learn context compatibility for disambiguation. The authors in [8] and [9] employed learning-to-rank techniques to rank all candidates and link the mention to the most likely one. The method presented in [4] improved the one proposed in [7] by a learning model for automatically generating a very-large training set and training a statistical classifier to detect name variants. The main drawback of the local approaches is that they do not take into account the interdependence between linking decisions.

Global approaches assumed interdependence between linking decisions and exploited two main kinds of information that are disambiguation context and semantic relatedness. Cucerzan [13] was the first to model interdependence among disambiguation decisions. In [13], a disambiguation context consists of all Wikipedia contexts that occur in the text and semantic relatedness is based on overlapping in categories of candidates, where each candidate corresponds to a mention. Wikipedia contexts are phrases that comprise inlink labels, outlink labels, and title-hints of all Wikipedia articles. The limitation of this approach is to add irrelevant cues to the disambiguation context.

The proposed method in [14] extended the work in [10] by resolving jointly optimization problem of overall disambiguation decisions using two approximation solutions. Ratinov [5] proposed an approach that combines both local and global methods. Kataria [6] proposed a weakly semi-supervised Latent Dirichlet Allocation model for modeling correlations among words and among topics for disambiguation. Sen [1] adapted topic models for EL. His method exploited proximity to learning word-entity association with observations that a word appears closer to a mention to be stronger indicator of its referent. In [17] the authors mined word-entity association for named entity disambiguation.

Han and Sun [3] proposed a collective approach that firstly builds a referent graph for a text based on local context compatibility and coherence among entities and then disambiguates mentions by a collective inference method using the referent graph. A referent graph is a weighted and undirected graph $G = (E, V)$ where V contains all mentions in the text and all possible candidates of these mentions. Each node represents a mention or an entity. The graph has two kinds of edges: (i) A mention-entity edge is established between a mention and an entity and its weight is calculated using cosine similarity implemented in a bag-of-words model as in [12]; and (ii) An entity-entity edge is established between two entities and its weight is calculated using semantic relatedness between these entities. The author adopted the formula presented in [10] to calculate the semantic relatedness between two entities. The collective algorithm collects initial evidence for each mention and then reinforces the evidence by propagating them via edges of the referent graph.

7 Conclusion

Entity linking is an essential task in natural language processing applications such as semantic web, information retrieval, question answering, or knowledge base population. This paper proposes a method that links surface forms in a text to entries of a given knowledge base. The method combines heuristics and learning for entity linking. The method exploits some heuristics based on the contexts and coreference relations, and learns coherence among co-occurrence entities within the text based on Wikipedia's link structure. The experiment results show that our proposed method is simple and effective. The results also show that expanding candidate set using coreference relations among co-occurrence surface forms significantly improves the performance of entity linking systems.

References

1. Sen, P.: Collective context-aware topic models for entity disambiguation. In: WWW 2012 (2012)
2. Ji, H., Grishman, R., Dang, H.T.: An overview of the TAC2011 knowledge base population track. In: Proceedings of Text Analysis Conference (TAC 2011) (2011)
3. Han, X., Sun, L., and Zhao, J.: Collective entity linking in web text: a graph-based method. In: Proceedings of SIGIR 2011, pp. 765–774 (2011)

4. Zhang, W., Sim, Y.C., Su, J., Tan, C.-L.: Entity linking with effective acronym expansion, instance selection and topic modeling. In: Proceedings of the 20th IJCAI (IJCAI 2011), pp. 1909–1904 (2011)
5. Ratinov, L., Roth, D., Downey, D., Anderson, M.: Local and global algorithms for disambiguation to Wikipedia. In: Proceedings of ACL-HLT 2011 (2011)
6. Kataria, S., Kumar, K., Rastogi, R., Sen, P., Sengamedu, S.: Entity disambiguation with hierarchical topic models. In: KDD 2011
7. Zhang, W., Su, J., Tan, C.-L., Wang, W.: Entity linking leveraging automatically generated annotation. In: Proceedings of COLING 2010 (2010)
8. Zheng, Z., Li, F., Huang, M., Zhu, X.: Learning to link entities with knowledge base. In: Proceedings of HLT: NAACL 2010 (2010)
9. Dredze, M., McNamee, P., Rao, D., Gerber, A., Finin, T.: Entity disambiguation for knowledge base population. In: Proceedings of COLING 2010 (2010)
10. Milne, D. and Witten, I.H.: Learning to link with Wikipedia. In: Proceedings of the 17th ACM CIKM (CIKM 2008), pp. 509–518 (2008)
11. Medelyan, O., Witten, I.H., Milne, D.: Topic indexing with Wikipedia. In: Proceedings of Wikipedia and AI Workshop at the AAAI-2008 Conference (2008)
12. Bunescu, R., Paşca, M.: Using encyclopedic knowledge for named entity disambiguation. In: Proceedings of the 11th Conference of the EACL (EACL 2006), pp. 9–16 (2006)
13. Cucerzan, S.: Large-scale named entity disambiguation based on Wikipedia data. In: Proceedings of EMNLP-CoNLL Joint Conference (EMNLP-CoNLL 2007), pp. 708–716 (2007)
14. Kulkarni, S., Singh, A., Ramakrishnan, G., Chakrabarti, S.: collective annotation of Wikipedia entities in web text. In: KDD 2009 (2009)
15. Mihalcea, R., Csomai, A.: Wikify!: linking documents to encyclopedic knowledge. In: Proceedings of the 16th ACM CIKM, pp. 233–242 (2007)
16. Bontcheva, K., Dimitrov, M., Maynard, D., Tablan, V., Cunningham, H.: Shallow methods for named entity coreference resolution. In: Proceedings of TALN 2002 Workhop (2002)
17. Li, Y., Wang, C., Han, F., Han, J., Roth, D., Yan, X.: Mining evidences for named entity disambiguation. In: KDD'2013 (2013)
18. Zhang, W., Su, J., Chen, B., Wang, W., Toh, Z., Sim, Y., Tan, C. L.: I2r-nus-msra at tac 2011: entity linking. In: Proceedings of Text Analysis Conference (TAC 2011) (2011)
19. Monahan, S., Lehmann, J., Nyberg, T., Plymale, J., Jung, A.: Cross-lingual cross-document coreference with entity linking. In: Proceedings of Text Analysis Conference (TAC 2011) (2011)
20. Chang, A.X., Spitkovsky, V.I., Agirre, E., Manning, C.D.: Stanford-UBC entity linking at TAC-KBP, again. In: Proceedings of Text Analysis Conference (TAC 2011) (2011)
21. Radford, W., Hachey, B., Honnibal, M., Nothman, J., Curran, J.R.: Naıve but effective NIL clustering baselines–CMCRC at TAC 2011. In: Proceedings of Text Analysis Conference (TAC 2011) (2011)
22. Taylor Cassidy, Z.C., Artiles, J., Ji, H., Deng, H., Ratinov, L.A., Zheng, J., Roth, D.: CUNY-UIUC-SRI TAC-KBP2011 entity linking system description. In: Proceedings Text Analysis Conference (TAC2011) (2011)
23. Nguyen, H.T., Cao, T.H.: Named entity disambiguation: a hybrid approach. Int. J. Comput. Intell. Syst. 5(6), 1052–1067 (2012)

Author Index

Ajmone Marsan, Marco 198
Alagar, Vangalur 35
Alsaig, Alaa 35
Alsaig, Ammar 35

Ba-Vuong, Tru 168
Baber, Christopher 283
Bai, Xiaoyan 271
Bartuskova, Aneta 188
Bayoudh Saadi, Ines 316
Ben Ghezala, Henda 316
Bouhtouch, Anas 57

Cabri, Giacomo 57
Ch'ng, Eugene 283
Choi, Dongjin 349, 359
Cleve, Anthony 304
Cong Vinh, Phan 115, 238

Dien, Tran Anh 125
Dong, Ching-Shen 293
Duong, Thuy Van T. 329

Faruqui, Rokan Uddin 3

Grassi, Daniele 57

Ho, Tuong Vinh 24
Hung-Cuong, Nguyen 168

Inverardi, Paola 304

Jung, Jason J. 339, 349

Khare, Ashish 125, 209, 228
Khare, Manish 125
Kim Quoc, Nguyen 102, 238
Kim, Jeongin 359
Kim, Pankoo 359
Kinshuk 316
Krejcar, Ondrej 188
Kristensen, Bent Bruun 144

Le, Hong Anh 250

M., Bharath 260
Machaka, Pheeha 47

Mancuso, Vincenzo 198
Minh, Nguyen Sy 97
Mohammad, Mubarak 35
Mori, Marco 304

Ngoc-Hung, Pham 133, 157
Nguyen, Manh Hung. 15, 24
Nguyen, Phuong T. 77, 87
Nguyen, Quang-Trung 133
Nguyen, Tri Tuong 349
Nguyen, Hien T. 339, 369
Nigam, Swati 209
Nong, Thi Hoa 219
Novotný, Miroslav 67

Pallapa, Venkataram 260
Peko, Gabrielle 293
Pham, Van-Cuong 157
Pham, Xuan Hau 339

Quyet-Thang, Huynh 168

Rakib, Abdur 3
Rizzo, Gianluca 198
Rossak, Wilhelm R. 77

Schau, Volkmar 77
Shahzad, Ali 198
Souabni, Raoudha 316
Srivastava, Prashant 228
Srivastava, Rajneesh Kumar 125
Sundaram, David 271, 293

Thang, Huynh Quyet 178
Thanh Binh, Nguyen 115, 125, 209, 228
Thanh Tu, Vo 102
Thanh Tung, Nguyen 97
Thuc Hai, Nguyen 102
Tran, Dinh Que 15, 329
Tran, Gong Hung 329
Tran, Dinh Que 15
Trung, Duc Nguyen 339, 349
Truong, Ninh Thuan 250
Tu, Nguyen Thi Thanh 178
Tuyet, Vo Thi Hong 115

Ul Haque, Hafiz Mahfooz   3

Viet Binh, Pham   219
Vu, Duc Thai   219

White, David   271

Xuan Truong, Quach   219

Yong Seung, Lee   339
Yusof, Hafizuddin   283

Zavoral, Filip   67